Cultures of Secrecy

New Directions in Anthropological Writing
History, Poetics, Cultural Criticism

GEORGE E. MARCUS
Rice University

JAMES CLIFFORD
University of California, Santa Cruz

GENERAL EDITORS

Cultures of Secrecy

REINVENTING RACE IN
BUSH KALIAI CARGO CULTS

Andrew Lattas

THE UNIVERSITY OF WISCONSIN PRESS

The University of Wisconsin Press
2537 Daniels Street
Madison, Wisconsin 53718

3 Henrietta Street
London WC2E 8LU, England

Library of Congress Cataloging-in-Publication Data
Lattas, Andrew, 1956–
    Cultures of secrecy : reinventing race in bush Kaliai cargo cults /
Andrew Lattas.
        406 pp.   cm.—(New directions in anthropological writing)
    Includes bibliographical references and index.
    ISBN 0-299-15800-4 (cloth: alk. paper).
    ISBN 0-299-15804-7 (pbk.: alk. paper)
    1. Cargo cults—Papua New Guinea—West New Britain Province.
    2. Acculturation—Papua New Guinea—West New Britain Province.
    3. West New Britain Province (Papua New Guinea)—Religious life and
    customs.   4. West New Britain Province (Papua New Guinea)—Race
    relations.   5. New Tribes Mission.   I. Title.   II. Series.
    GN671.N5L35   1998
    299'.92—dc21   97-44008

Contents

Illustrations and Maps

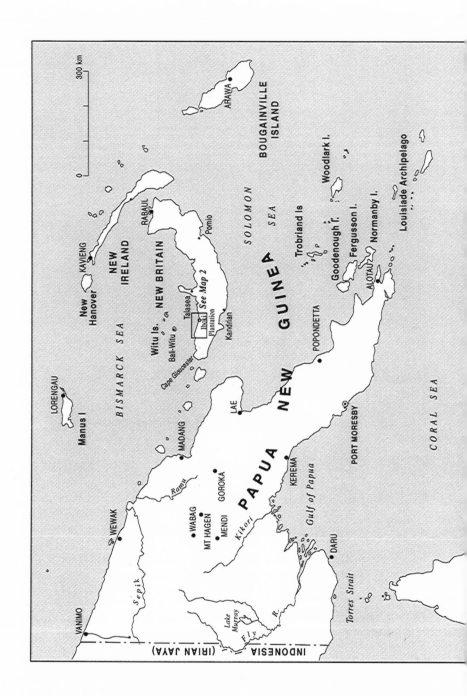

300 km

ARAWA

BOUGAINVILLE
ISLAND

Woodlark I.

Trobriand Is

Louisiade Archipelago

Goodenough I.

Fergusson I.

Normanby I.

ALOTAU

SOLOMON SEA

KAVIENG

New
Hanover

NEW
IRELAND

RABAUL

Pomio

NEW BRITAIN

Talasea

See Map 2

Ibaai
Plantation

Kandrian

Witu Is.

Bali-Witu

Cape Gloucaster

POPONDETTA

NEW GUINEA

BISMARCK SEA

LORENGAU

Manus I

MADANG

LAE

PORT MORESBY

CORAL SEA

Ramu

WEWAK

WABAG

MT HAGEN

GOROKA

MENDI

Kikori

KEREMA

Gulf of Papua

PAPUA

DARU

Sepik

VANIMO

*Lake
Murray*

Fly

R.

Torres Strait

INDONESIA
(IRIAN JAYA)

x

Preface

This book is about cargo cults in Papua New Guinea. Cargo cults are millenarian movements that emerged when Melanesians came in contact with Europeans. These movements sought to realize a new age of equality with white people, with Melanesians sharing the cargo that villagers saw arriving on European ships and planes. Melanesians use the *Pisin* (Melanesian pidgin) word *kago* (cargo)[1] to refer to all sorts of commodities (such as rice, clothing, tinned meats and fish, iron axes and spades, and corrugated iron). Many are convinced that this imported cargo is secretly being produced by their ancestors over whom whites have gained control. In New Britain those beliefs first emerged under the German colonial administration at the beginning of the twentieth century, and they were subsequently modified with the arrival of the Australian colonial administration after World War I, the arrival of Japanese and American soldiers during World War II, and the move toward self-government and independence in the late 1960s and early 1970s. Running through all cargo cult movements is a common desire for commodities, which has become a way of objectifying the realization of a new Melanesian self and a new Melanesian social order.

This book owes a great deal to interviews and conversations with villagers in the Kaliai bush. During a ten-year period (December 1985 to February 1996) I returned to the field six times to collect information on traditional bush Kaliai culture and the history of people's involvement in cargo cults and to check previous information. I have spent about thirty months in the field. In 1986 and 1990 I built houses out of bush materials in the villages of Aikon, Salke, Doko Sagra, and Moluo. People would visit my house in the morning, and I would share food and cups of tea while I questioned people about their beliefs, rituals, and customs. Key informants often stayed at my house until about midday when they would go to their gardens for the rest of the day. I collected much of my material through interviews conducted in this sort of semipublic context in which those providing information were surrounded by family members who would often interject to correct information and add new information.

In the late afternoon, when people started coming back from their gardens, I would again sit down with villagers—not to interview them but to listen to their gossip, jokes, and complaints. Those overheard conversations, mostly among the villagers, would go on late into the night in the men's house, where I would sometimes sleep. From about 1991 onward my fieldwork took the form of my living in the houses of close informants like Laupu at the village of Bolo, Posingen at Meitavale, Paul Samaga at Moluo, and Imokeh at Robos. I was sleeping in the same house and often in the same room as these informants for weeks and months at a time; they became close, trustworthy friends who provided me with detailed intimate information about their thoughts and those of relatives and neighbors. In early 1996 I carried a draft of the manuscript for this book into the field and read to key informants the material that they had provided and the arguments that I had developed around their material. I believe that the ethnographic material in this book is accurate and that those who participated in the cargo cults see its arguments as reflecting their underlying concerns.

When I first arrived in 1986, many villagers were initially too frightened to tell me what they saw as the true traditional stories of their ancestors, for missionaries and government officials had denounced these stories as cargo cult.[2] In the early 1970s Kaliai villagers were jailed for what they refer to as "working" (wokim, performing, seeking to realize) "their stories." On many other occasions they were harangued and intimidated by government patrol officers (kiaps) and missionaries, and this is still the case. Some cargo cult followers initially refused to tell me their secret cult stories, and they did so only after my second fieldwork trip, that is, after they saw that I had not reported informants from my first fieldwork trip to the administration or the missionaries. Even then some people would tell me their stories only at night, when only trusted family and friends were around. When they disclosed their secrets, they often did so with a mixture of urgency and anger at their unfair treatment, not only at the hands of Europeans and Melanesian officials but also at the hands of relatives and neighbors who assumed the overbearing attitudes of government officials and missionaries. Those who gave their stories to me often saw themselves as receiving tacit recognition and legitimacy from an outsider, a sympathetic white man, for beliefs that they now had difficulties stating publicly within their communities. Those who reported neighbors and relatives to government officials and missionaries did so not because they did not have cargo cult beliefs of their own but because they often had a sense of rivalry and outrage at the deceptions of some cult leaders. They also gained a sense of empowerment through becoming aligned with official institutions.

In 1984 the New Tribes Mission arrived from the United States and established a base at Amcor (Gigina) in the Kaliai bush. After an initial period of building houses and an air strip and learning the language, in the 1990s the new mission started Bible classes and appointing "teachers" to morally govern and transform the bush Kaliai. In promotional literature published on the Internet the New Tribes Mission describes itself as "a nondenominational, faith missionary society composed of born-again believers sent out by local churches and dedicated to the evangelization of unreached tribal peoples." Its stated goal is "the translation of Scripture and the planting of indigenous New Testament churches" *(http://www. iaw.on.ca/rifraf/whatsntm.htm)*. From its beginnings in 1942 the New Tribes Mission has grown into a huge worldwide organization that works in Africa, Asia, Australia, Greenland, North and South America, Papua New Guinea, and Russia. In Papua New Guinea alone the New Tribes Mission has about fifty mission stations. In West New Britain it has built a large base in Hoskins (about one hour from Kimbe) that it uses to service mission stations among Aria, Asengseng, Mouk, Lamogai, and Solong villagers. The remote locations it services and their importance to regional and national politicians has made the New Tribes Mission a powerful force in West New Britain politics. My experience of the mission is that it is very well funded. Its missionaries receive regular supplies of cargo by air, they have well-built houses that contain comfortable furnishings, an electric generator, radio transmitters, and computers. Before coming to the field all missionaries participate in a training course that includes not only linguistics but also evaluations of whether they are "sound in the faith and in all fundamental truths," according to the Internet posting. The field goals of the missionaries are to "disciple the believers, help them establish a New Testament church and translate the Scriptures into the tribal language. In time, elders and deacons are selected, and a first generation of tribal missionaries moves out to reach others" *(http:// www.ntm.org/aboutntm.html)*. When the missionaries began these later processes in the bush Kaliai area in the early 1990s, the mission cracked down hard on cargo cult followers, especially those who were speaking to me.

On one occasion a friend of mine was removed from his position as a

"teacher" in the New Tribes Mission because he came secretly to my house
to tell me where heaven and hell might be located and how Noah's ship
might have landed in the nearby Kaliai mountains. On other occasions
American missionaries told villagers to get rid of me because I was encouraging them not to convert to the mission. Converts have informed me
that missionaries instructed them not to talk to me, for I am one of Satan's
followers. My interest in people's stories was said to have "fouled" many
people by pulling their thoughts back to the dark ways of the past. In
practice what this meant was that I encouraged people not to abandon
their traditional culture, and I listened sympathetically to the truths and
dreams of equality articulated by people's stories and cults. I also supported the claims of local "big men" (i.e., elders, leaders) who argued that
the New Tribes Mission's preaching about Satan and hell was simply another white man's trick. I want to thank those villagers at Angal, Meitavale, Moluo, and Robos who resisted the New Tribes Mission's desire to
demonize me and who instead chose to invite me into their homes and
men's houses. In this context of intensified surveillance and repression it
is difficult for me to acknowledge the specific contributions of individuals
without making these people vulnerable to the policing gaze of the New
Tribes Mission and of government officials.

   The New Tribes Mission has now set up an all-embracing system of
surveillance in the Kaliai bush that polices those who attempt to maintain
some sort of autonomous realm of truth outside the Bible and the hegemony of European-inspired institutions. In this book I have revealed only
the names of informants who have died or who, like Posingen, Monongyo,
and Theresa, are already well known for their millenarian beliefs in a Last
Day that will bring racial equality. When I asked Posingen, Monongyo,
and Theresa whether I should reveal their names, they replied that they
wanted me to, for they had already "eaten" (internalized, suffered) the
"cane" (criticisms, humiliations, and imprisonment) that had whipped
their backsides. Writing a book that includes current cargo cult beliefs is
a precarious act that carries the danger of uncertain repercussions for
villagers who provide information. In 1993 I gave a paper at the anthropology department of the University of Papua New Guinea on a clandestine
cargo cult that had developed within the New Tribes Mission. Representatives of the New Tribes Mission came to that seminar and recorded my
talk. The missionaries later told villagers in the Kaliai bush that I was
accusing them of continuing to work cargo cults. The missionaries never
mentioned that I was arguing for a more sympathetic treatment of cargo
cults; instead, the implication was that I was slandering the bush Kaliai to
government officials and other white people.

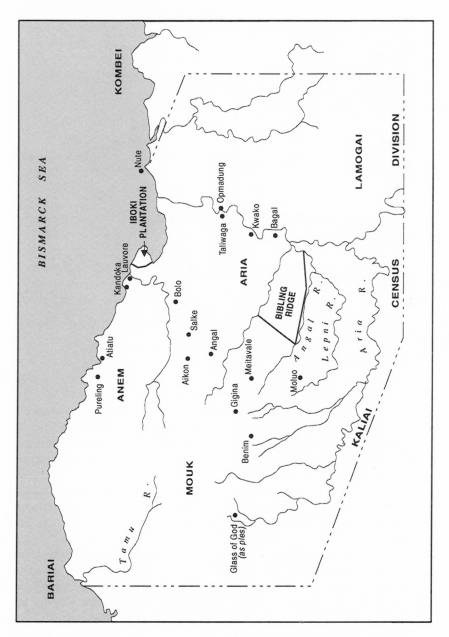

Kaliai census division

Censure's son Posingen, holding a *piksa* (picture) of *moni* **dabol**

Unlike the New Tribes Mission, which cannot stand syncretism and wants to replace it with its own demonic version of a pure Christianity, this book is dedicated to the utopian dimension in syncretism, to the love of recomposition, recombination, conflation, amalgamation, incorporation, embodiment, and montage. Kaliai bush people find pleasure in these activities even if they are directed toward overcoming the pain and anguish of race relations in Melanesia. In part the love of this activity in and of itself represents a form of excess that the mission seeks to contain and domesticate.

All the interviews quoted in this book were carried out in Pisin. I then checked in *tok ples* (i.e., the local languages of Aria and Mouk) the use of particular concepts that arose in these interviews. Most villagers are fluent in Pisin, which they use in everyday conversations, meetings, and cult activities. Instead of translating Pisin into "proper" English, I have sought to maintain the texture and resonances of people's way of talking by translating it in a way that is perhaps closer to transcription because it

Theresa, Censure's daughter-in-law

Monongyo, Censure's son-in-law

exploits the English resonances and metaphors in Pisin. I have done this
in order to transfer into English some of the ontological schemes within
which people operate. To give an example, there is a difference between
the translated English expression "he became angry" and the original
Melanesian expression, "his stomach became hot." The latter captures the
embodied nature of emotions in Melanesia. My occasional use of such
Melanesian colloquialisms instead of more standard English construc-
tions is a conscious choice designed to introduce readers to everyday Melanesian ways of thinking and speaking. Another example is the word *law*.
When villagers use the word law (*lo*), they often posit some overlap in
three forms of routinization—customs, habits, and ritual obligations—
that we tend to distinguish in English. Thus villagers will equate new rituals with the arrival of a new way of living, a new legal system, and new
habits.

I see certain everyday Melanesian Pisin and tok ples expressions, such
as "working stories" and "working ritual," as overlapping with certain
theoretical developments in anthropology that emphasize that stories and

rituals are not simply atemporal structures of meaning but are practices, that is, rule-governed activities. I believe that the everyday phrases that people use to speak about their symbolic activities contain insights and embody forms of knowledge. What took anthropology decades of intellectual endeavor—learning how to think about rituals and stories as practices—can be captured in the taken-for-granted phrases that people use about themselves. That people often assimilate magic, ritual, and stories into their other forms of work, such as gardening, says something about the perceived realm of necessity and labor within which people operate. When people view rituals and stories as forms of work, it says something about how the realms of the symbolic and the real are related in Melanesia. Thus it is important to develop new ways of writing that capture and reproduce the ontological frameworks within which people talk, think, and act. I have tried to do this by incorporating Melanesian colloquialisms in the analytical part of the text as part of a project of developing a theoretical vocabulary that resonates closely with indigenous ontological schemes.

Financial support for this project was provided by Macquarie University, the University of Sydney, and by a grant from the Australian Research Council (ARC). The writing was made possible by a five-year ARC fellowship that allowed me to consolidate and develop arguments with which I was experimenting in book reviews and journal articles. In the field I received valuable assistance from Leon Tribolet, the former manager of Iboki Plantation. He organized my mail, and his hospitality provided me with a cold beer and a welcome change from what was sometimes a monotonous diet of manioc, sweet potatoes, and rice. At an intellectual level this book owes a great deal to discussions and conversations with my friends Jeremy Beckett, Gillian Cowlishaw, Tom Ernst, Steve Feld, Barry Morris, Jadran Mimica, and Kerry Zubrinick. Polly Kummel, Michael Jackson, Nancy Munn, Andrew Strathern, Tigger Wise, and Roy Wagner made helpful comments and provided support. In its later stages the book was influenced by a writing group that included Martin Harrison, Vivienne Kondos, Diane Losche, Lesley Stern, Martin Thomas, and me. The book is also heavily indebted to the intellectual influence and support of my teacher and friend Bruce Kapferer who, at the University of Adelaide, created what was the best anthropology department in Australia and who has ever since been paying the price for it in Australian anthropology. Many chapters in this book were given as seminar and conference papers in anthropology departments at the University of Adelaide, Macquarie University, and the University of Sydney. I want to thank participants in these sessions; their questions often forced me to rethink my assumptions and arguments and to rewrite and clarify my position. Of all the people who have contributed to this project, I want to thank most of all my wife, Judy. Many ideas in this book grew out of conversations with her. She introduced me to deconstructionism and the patience needed for understanding its central concerns. Here I would also like to acknowledge the deconstructive antics of my two daughters, Gina and Dimi. They also taught me the significance of play, displacement, forgetting, repression, and subversion, as well as the meaning of dependence and mirror structures.

Introduction

This book is about people's experiments with meaning and sociability. It analyzes how villagers in Melanesia used mimesis, sexuality, and death in all sorts of imaginative ways that never fully escaped people's reality even though they were organized to displace and reform it.

My focus is the creative work that bush Kaliai villagers put into thinking about and responding to Western processes of social change. I adopt an approach that moves away from privileging public institutions and how they produce subjects; instead, I take up the popular covert beliefs and practices through which people went about both embracing and subverting the disciplinary routines and pastoral regimes of the West. I outline a history of racial conflict in the Kaliai area as a struggle to control the mirroring practices through which reality can be captured, positioned, and defined. For it is always through the detour of mirroring terms, which are continuously contested and reworked, that history is made. This struggle to control the reflexive terms within which reality and personhood are imaginatively constituted was a struggle continuously refought over all sorts of terrain, over all sorts of imaginary geographies. This book uses ethnography to document and analyze people's struggle to move across and occupy the space of the other. It analyzes bush Kaliai people's unhappiness with the forms of specularity that constituted them and how they sought not so much to abolish as to reposition the process of being seen and remade through white eyes. Indeed, the gaze of *waitskin* (white-skins) was often displaced and remade into the familiar gaze of deceased relatives or ancestors who were given white bodies.[1] People gave an autochthonous form to the civilizing processes that were transforming them (cf. Elias 1939). They internalized those processes into their schemes of origin. That is, they transformed Western processes of transformation by mediating and reconstituting them in terms of their autochthonous schemes for figuring the processes of change.

This book is about cargo cults, the incorporation of commodities into a worldview in which the desire and pursuit of commodities provides the imaginary terms for realizing new identities and new forms of sociability. In their cargo cult beliefs people often found forms of autonomy and pleasure from pursuing their own strategies for realizing their desires. However, cargo cult beliefs were also often instrumental in producing new forms of coercion, pain, entrapment, and control that were now mediated by the remade whitened gaze of the dead. Although I believe strongly in the emancipatory and self-determinist qualities of the imagination, it would be a mistake to just romanticize the creative idiosyncratic products of cargo cults. For the human imagination is also always implicated in relations of power that it helps to create as well as to efface. Power itself needs to be imagined; it can exist only through being mediated by certain ontological schemes (Kapferer 1988; Castoriadis 1987). The colonial and postcolonial contexts are interesting, for here different ontologies of power came into contact and conflict, became merged and submerged into each other, and even became dependent on each other. This book does not shy away from taking up the extraordinary and idiosyncratic nature of people's desires and beliefs, for people's fantasies about the real are not removed from but are constitutive of their lives.

People's imaginative practices for reworking their subordination often used unique circumstances, events, and coincidences of meaning in the dominant culture to sustain other subversive worlds of knowledge about the process of becoming white than those that whites gave about themselves. These creative practices were not arbitrary or random in their exploitation of the particularity of circumstances, events, and accidents of meaning, for these creative practices also had a certain systematicness to them that led a community of believers to accept the new formulations as plausible. Indeed, these new formulations had to operate within certain techniques and rules for forming creativity. Yet it was also partly these rules for creating the creative act that came to be reformed in cargo cults. Here traditional ways of authorizing and creating the creative task were merged with what appeared to be European ways of doing the same thing. This allowed people to have a sense of themselves as embracing the Western project of being remade but within their own reworked ritual, magical, and mythological renderings of creative processes.

This book focuses on unofficial, illegitimate forms of popular knowledge; on the covert tactics that creatively reworked the institutional rules, symbols, official discourses, and practices of European culture, not so much to deny their hegemony but to deflect and remake their hegemonic hold. We are dealing here with forms of bricolage, where, as de Certeau puts it, "users make (*bricolent*) innumerable and infinitesimal transformations of and within the dominant cultural economy in order to adopt it to their own interests and their own rules" (1988, xiv). I am interested in the minute tactics of accommodation and assimilation that people developed both to embrace and evade their incorporation into Western institutions. I want to make visible the creative logic of these maneuvers through which people took up and resystematized all those contexts, unique events, and intersections of meaning that they used to develop new worlds of ambiguity. It is a question of focusing not so much on how people denied or rejected European culture, Christianity, and state disciplinary practices but on how these phenomena were reread and reworked in specific ways that rendered them ambiguous, that gave them other meanings (cf. Bhabha 1994). It is necessary to focus on the specific tactics and techniques through which people developed strategic forms of ambiguity that worked to subvert the social order from within. Discussing this process with respect to the Spanish colonization of Indians, de Certeau writes:

> Submissive and even consenting to their subjection, the Indians nevertheless often *made of* the rituals, representations, and laws imposed on them something quite different from what their conquerors had in mind; they subverted them not by rejecting or altering them, but by using them with respect to ends and references foreign to the system they had no choice but to accept. They were *other* within the very colonization that outwardly assimilated them; their use of the dominant social order deflected its power, which they lacked the means to challenge; they escaped it without leaving it. The strength of their difference lay in procedures of "consumption." (1988, xiii)

In the Kaliai bush the new forms of ambiguity that people developed were often an unresolved mixture of pain and pleasure. Those experiences were the result of people seeing themselves as simultaneously inside and outside Western culture as well as inside and outside traditional bush Kaliai culture. These forms of double incorporation and double alienation encoded people's ambivalent attitudes toward both white-skins and their past. This book focuses on these ambivalences and how these tensions were both produced and managed through covert mimetic practices in which people simultaneously embraced and subverted their apparent acceptance of Western culture. There was a logic to these practices of usurpation, to this art of poaching upon and remaking the conditions of one's domination (de Certeau 1988, xi). It is inadequate to gloss these ambiguities, contradictions, and appropriations in cargo cults simply as syncretism or as adjustment movements. They are better seen as part of the parasitical structure of what Sahlins (1981) terms the structure of the conjuncture. By this I take Sahlins to mean that the way Western culture intersects with indigenous cultures has a specificity to it; although the interface of colonial processes of articulation can be formed through coincidences and accidents of meaning, it never has a completely disordered or haphazard character. Like Sahlins, I am interested in the particularity of these intersections and coincidences that allow cultures to interact with and feed off each other. Here it is not simply a question of recognition, that is, of each culture's understanding the other on the other's terms, but also of misrecognitions—both innocent and strategic—that make life bearable and reproducible but also unstable and displaceable. The logic of these practices was partly a parasitical one in which misreadings were formed into coherent systems of ideas that fed off the dominant culture, that created and used accidental seepages of meaning to sustain another way of life (Serres 1982a).

Here we are also dealing with a poetic logic that seized upon metaphors and metonyms, that exploited chance resemblances and associations, to create mimetic channels and magical gateways between bush Kaliai culture and Western culture. Both cultures were poetically combined and reworked in all sorts of fantastic ways that were not haphazard or aimless but whose unusualness or otherness were also part of their truth effect, that is, part of the process of convincing people that they now controlled a secret world of alterity (otherness) that could be used to remake the present. The imaginative nature of these new assemblages of meaning celebrated a creative spirit whose excesses of meaning were often placed in the engendering powers of women, the earth, and death. This book is concerned with the materiality of this poetic imagination, with why certain things are good to think with (Bachelard 1983; Levi-Strauss 1963, 1966, 1979). Why was it that woman, the underground, pools of water, mountains, and the dead were used to mediate the procreative task of redoubling the world? In part we are dealing with how certain things come to figure and mediate creative processes, with how the poetic imagination thinks about and objectifies its fertile powers of reproduction.

Apart from sexuality and death, another significant aspect of the cults was the miming of Western cultural practices. These mimetic activities were never simply a process of passive copying but also active processes of incorporation and transformation of the terms copied. My interest in mimesis is an interest in how people embraced the task of remaking themselves as white but within a framework of copying that used magic, myths, rituals, and poetic resemblances to capture the personhood, practices, and possessions of whites. The meaning of "becoming white" was often displaced into ritual performances and conversations directed toward the dead, who were now made the bearers of the civilizing processes of pacification and Christianization. In addition to being the bearers of these new pedagogic processes, the dead could also become subject to these civilizing processes in cult activities that appropriated and directed toward them the transformational pedagogic objectives of Western institutions.

Colonial authorities opposed cargo cults in part because the authorities were disturbed by cult activities that mimed European symbols, discourses, institutions, and practices but in ways that were oddly out of context. The colonialists saw these strange mimetic activities as the natives falling temporarily into madness (Kaplan 1995; Lattas 1992a; Lindstrom 1993). For here were people miming Europeans but in ways that Europeans did not recognize or accept as their normal selves or even as the normal selves of natives. In his discussion of Plato's critique of mimesis, Lacoue-Labarthe (1989, 129) points out that part of the threat posed by mimesis resides in the way it overly multiplies and fractures the coherence of the self.

> What is threatening in mimesis . . . is exactly this kind of pluralization and fragmentation of the "subject" provoked from the outset by its linguistic or "symbolic" (de)constitution: an effect of discourses, the "self"-styled "subject" always threatens to "consist" of nothing more than a series of heterogeneous and dissociated roles, and to fraction itself endlessly in this multiple borrowing.

What mimesis threatens is partly the ability of a social order to ground itself in stable roles, subjects, and identities. The process of copying whites, of becoming like whites, was promoted by various government departments and missions, but in the cults this pedagogic process came to be mediated and remade by that second life (that second form of birth) offered by death.

The cults embraced the removal of the dead from the living as a way of redoubling the world; the world of the dead created a set of mirroring terms that were removed from the world but were also seen as its essence, as its hidden truth. Here the removal of the dead from the living was embraced as a way of thinking about and of overcoming other forms of removal, particularly other cleavages and divisions in the realm of the living. Many important writers, both in philosophy and anthropology, have argued that fundamental to narrative and human thought is a certain spatialization of sociability (Bachelard 1969; Casey 1993; Heidegger 1971, 145–61; Jackson 1989, 1995; Merleau-Ponty 1968, 258–90; Myers 1984; Smith 1987; Tuan 1974, 1976). For me the topography of cargo cults has to do with situating and repositioning the terrain of the dead. I see the making of new myths and histories concerning fallen origins and utopian endings in cargo cults as always involving the creation of new topographies. Those new terrains often emerged from villagers' merging the places contained in their surrounding landscape and in traditional stories with the places inhabited by whites and contained in the Bible. Given that all social orders involve a certain spatialization of themselves, the reinvention of sociability also requires the reinvention of space and techniques for spatializing differences. Here the reinvention of distance often is mediated by the reinvention of forms of mimesis, for it is mimesis that allows differences to inhabit each other, to reinvent and occupy each other's presence. The issue of space and its politics cannot be removed from the issue of mimesis, for mimesis implies a difference that is crossed or overcome in the act of copying. Moreover, this is done to reinvent and transform both the original and the copy, to make them other than themselves. A certain kind of politics of displacement is created out of mimesis and mirror relationships, and in the Kaliai area this was a certain politics of space and time that involved positing mirror relationships between the living and the dead, the surface world and the underground, Melanesians and Europeans.

It was primarily through the alternative gaze provided by the mirror worlds of the underground and the dead that cult followers sought their new identities as remade subjects. The return to the past and tradition was simultaneously the movement into one's future form as a white subject whose whiteness had been remade by the cults. It was in the underground that people sought their new national identities as Melanesians while preserving the centrality of their localities, ancestors, and spirit children. Cargo cults often involve local processes of nation making. Here official processes of nation making go astray and get deflected into local movements that reimagine the significance of national symbols, discourses, and pedagogic practices. Those local movements involve a certain ritualization of politics that reworks and localizes the semiology of the state. Its official symbols, narratives, rituals, and other practices are reconstituted and repositioned within local movements concerned with what has to be retained, kept in reserve, and disclosed.

These movements are concerned with the space of the unseen, with the invisible. As such they participate in certain universal human tendencies in which a sense of absence is used to create what Schurmann calls "an economy of presence" (1990, 74–75). Here what is present in the world has its character formed by the way absences are figured. To explore this relationship between the seen and the unseen, between what is present and what is absent, is to open up the question of topology, of spacing, and how it is figured and refigured in particular historical economies of presence and through particular historical practices of veiling and unveiling. Cargo cults reinvent this relationship between the seen and the unseen that is at the heart of traditional Melanesian ontologies concerned with masks, trickery, and magic. This creation of processes of disclosure, of rendering present the unseen, mediates relations between the dead and the living, men and women, children and adults, initiates and noninitiates, and—increasingly—between Europeans and Melanesians. Cargo cults have to be understood as involving the intersection and transformation of different economies for rendering the world present through the way its absences, forms of loss, and removal are figured. Cargo cults are attempts to develop new epochal principles, new ontological schemes for organizing human sociability; this is done by developing new practices for disclosing the world, for working secrecy, for understanding those absences that render the world present in a particular way.

REANALYZING CARGO CULTS

Cargo cults in Papua New Guinea are a curious blend of traditional myths, imported folklore, borrowed state practices and ideologies, and reworked Christian stories. For me cargo cults are the political languages that are formed as people come to rewrite the narrative frameworks through which they perceive the moral relationships that tie together the past, present, and future. The work of Burridge (1960) was extremely important in focusing on this ethical dimension of cargo cult myths. Burridge saw cargo cult myths as providing moral explanations for the origins of racial inequalities. Many stories that Burridge analyzes in *Mambu* used an original fault or transgression in the mythic past to provide an ethical explanation of the present as a form of punishment. What is interesting is that this punishment was not so much delivered by Europeans against Melanesians as that the stories held people's ancestors responsible for the subordinate state of their descendants. In this book I use the bush Kaliai area to explore Burridge's point about how people come to live with their past in a cosmology that holds the past ethically responsible for the current state of black people's existence. I am interested in how the past is imagined as one's prison and burden but also in how it provides spaces of freedom and empowerment. This ambiguous and ambivalent relationship that people have to the past worlds of their ancestors has emerged from their being caught between seeing their past through the eyes of colonial whites—namely, as a world of barbarous savagery and ignorance—and their seeing their past as an alternative world of power and knowledge that will allow them to escape the pastoral care and patronage of white people and their institutions. It would be a mistake to see these two visions of one's racial existence as mutually exclusive. My experience of cult followers is that they move readily from a strong moral critique of the past toward practices that embrace the past in order to use it to provide the terms for figuring an alternative form of existence to that which has been prefigured in the moral schemes of whites and their institutions.

This book explores historically some of the moral languages and double binds through which the bush Kaliai have come to relate to their past. I focus on cargo cults that have emerged since the 1960s, as these are the cults about which I have the most detailed information. I explore how in their myths, rituals, and conversations people tried to make sense of how the past was responsible for the present and what relationships to the past would allow them to escape and reconstitute the present. But before I move into bush Kaliai ethnography, I want briefly to use some of the classic ethnographies to review and reanalyze some of the established debates about Melanesian cargo cults. This will allow me to introduce some of my key arguments through ethnography with which readers might already be familiar.

One of the best historical works on cargo cults in Papua New Guinea was written by Peter Lawrence (1964), who collected superb ethnography on cults in the Madang District. Although Lawrence disagreed with Worsley's view (1957) on the inherent political and nationalistic objectives of cargo cults, he was aware of the racial struggles and conflicts that were inscribed in cargo cult narratives and ritual practices. Compared to Worsley, Lawrence wanted to give more weight to indigenous notions of power, that is, to the local ontological schemes that informed Melanesian understandings of existence. Lawrence's approach has been recently developed further by Michele Stephen (1979, 1982), who has explored how the indigenous cultural frameworks within which creativity and innovation were constituted in traditional Melanesian society came to be applied to the arrival of Europeans. Stephen has focused on how dreams, magic, and ritual were instrumental in organizing not only traditional political life and understandings of power but also the new practices and beliefs through which people have engaged Europeans. In this book I want to elaborate on Lawrence's and Stephen's work, which I see as sharing a common focus on how indigenous ontologies give direction and form to people's understandings of colonial power. In particular I want to elaborate on their work by using more contemporary understandings of politics and power as organized around struggles that often have to do with the politics of identity. It is necessary to refigure and broaden the sense of the political that cargo cults are contesting, and in particular we need to move away from a sense of the political as always grounded in the state (cf. Foucault 1977, 1978; Grosz 1989, 1994; I. R. Young 1990). Here it is also necessary to criticize the work of Worsley, for although Worsley's work was explicitly about the political, like most anthropologists of his time he conceived of politics largely as a struggle for control of the state and its resources rather than as a struggle for the control of the narrative terms for figuring people's past, their bodies, and their identities (see Stoller 1995; A. Strathern 1996).

In this book I do not want to deny Worsley's major point, which was made earlier by Guiart (1951), that cargo cults are often embryonic forms of nationalism. However, it is also necessary to ask what nationalism means at the local popular level, where the nation is often understood through local ontologies of power, space, death, and relatedness that are very different from the ontological schemes organizing how Western culture imagines the nation. It is necessary to map out the ontological horizon on which the imaginary space of the nation comes to be conceived. Here I want to advocate joining Anderson's understanding of the nation (1983) as an imaginary community (with its own space and time) to Lawrence's and Stephen's stress on the indigenous ontological schemes through which space, time, and community are formed. We need to develop a historical phenomenology of nationalism in Melanesia that pays attention to the local cultural schemes within which people come to understand the nation as a space of relatedness and coexistence. Here I should also say that I disagree strongly with the way Worsley treated nationalism as a process of secularization, as the displacement of religion by politics. I also disagree strongly with the way Lawrence saw Melanesian nationalism as impeded by the "traditional" focus on the past in cargo cults (1964, 224). For Lawrence this focus was an expression of the inherent conservatism of the cults, which hindered their political development into full-scale nationalist movements. I see the issue as not one about how nationalism was denied but radically reinvented in cargo cults that sought to bring the dead into the brotherhood and community of the nation and that sought to use the dead and the past to give a different perspective to the nation's subjects. In the Kaliai area the cults also used the new ideologies of nationalism to recreate the terrain and perspective of the dead, with the living now seeing their nationalist concerns remirrored in the way the dead saw the living. The gaze of the nation-state, and the way it hails, makes, and recruits subjects through acknowledging them and giving them a place within itself, came to be reworked and shifted into the gaze of the dead (Althusser 1971, 163). New autochthonous forms of interpellation were married to state processes of addressing and constituting subjects.

Despite my admiration for Lawrence's ethnography and my agreement with his theoretical focus on indigenous ontologies, I also believe that his political conservatism prevented him from exploring fully the nature of the political beast he was analyzing. In the second half of *Road Belong Cargo* Lawrence spent a great deal of time denying the existence of the political (as he narrowly defined it) in cargo cults rather than understanding the different forms that politics assumes in these millenarian movements. Perhaps not surprisingly, Lawrence's understanding of the political was similar to that of his opponent, Worsley. Both narrowly conceived of the political as secular and as a struggle to control the state. In the second half of *Road Belong Cargo* Lawrence started to undermine the strength of his focus on alternative indigenous ontologies of power and the way this approach might offer an opportunity to reconceptualize anthropological understandings of the different forms that political action takes in contemporary Melanesia. Lawrence's definition of the political was often just as narrow as Worsley's, in that Lawrence insisted on defining the political in terms of the formation of permanent, secular, centralized, hierarchical, unifying structures. This led Lawrence to take up the absurd project of trying to demonstrate the nonexistence of the political (and even of nationalism) in cargo cults by demonstrating that the cults were unsuccessful in developing permanent, secular, centralized, hierarchical, unifying structures. Lawrence does all this despite acknowledging the existence of an anti-European attitude that wanted whites driven out and their political structures abolished (Lawrence 1964, 259). Although he wrote of the native's feeling of inferiority, Lawrence had difficulty conceiving of alienation as a political arena, even though at the time he was writing, this was the focus of much of the Marxist literature that was coming to be influenced by phenomenology, psychoanalysis, existentialism, and the Frankfurt School (Fanon 1965; Fromm 1961; Horkheimer 1947; Marcuse 1955, 1964; Sartre 1948). Lawrence's implacable hostility to Marxism and anyone not celebrating the Empire drove much of his thinking. Thus, although Lawrence was aware of people's resentment and anger concerning how they were racially positioned, he could not bring himself to understand that identity itself might be a field of struggle and that politics can take the form of a cultural struggle against the mirror structures that make up the terms for thinking and experiencing human existence (Fanon 1968; Lattas 1992b).

It was Burridge (1960), with his focus on moral discourse, who came much closer to understanding the structures of alienation against which cargo cults struggled but which they were also often engaged in reproducing. Burridge was interested in how race came to be encoded mythically as sin. He pointed out that often the original sin of the black man seems trivial and out of all proportion to the racial punishment that follows. Burridge goes on to suggest that perhaps these stories that seek to account in moral terms for the origin of racial inequalities also contain a critique of the injustice of God's punishment and of mythic destiny. Although I agree with Burridge's perceptive comments here, I also believe that Burridge did not fully pursue the powerful existential politics opened up by his approach because of his analytical tendency to reduce politics to morality in a manner that mitigated against his exploring the extent to which the domain of morality might be a domain of domination. This is to say that Burridge never sought to explore how the moral reflections of people upon themselves and their past might be part of the conditions of their domination against which they were partly struggling yet also often reaffirming. In particular Burridge could not bring himself to analyze critically the role of Christianity in forming those structures of self-reflection and self-alienation (Foucault 1982b, 1984). I believe a more Nietzschean view of morality and of Christianity in Melanesia is needed to make sense of the relations of power that operate to form subjects in the pastoral practices and beliefs that belong not only to missions but also to cargo cults.

Throughout this book I will be exploring how cargo cults appropriated not only the empowering emancipatory Christian discourse of moral rebirth but how they also often appropriated certain relations of pastoral power over subjects offered by the moral critiques of Christian discourse. As we shall see later, cargo cults were just as much engaged in processes of cultural hegemony as they were in processes of cultural resistance. At the level of method it is a mistake to treat hegemony and resistance as mutually exclusive opposites. On the one hand, people formulate their resistances using the hegemonic terms that mediate their cultural incorporation into dominant discourses and structures. On the other hand, people also can be further incorporated into dominant discourses and structures by the very strategies of resistance they use to affirm their autonomy and distinctiveness.

TOWARD A BLACK THEOLOGY IN MELANESIA

Now I want to use some of these ideas to reanalyze parts of Lawrence's ethnography on cargo cults around Madang. I want to focus on the politics that can be read into the way people reinterpreted the Bible when they appropriated and made Christ not only into a black man but even into one of their ancestors whom they offended and chased away. We are dealing here with the emergence of local black theologies, and it will be my contention, when we come to Kaliai ethnography, that the Christian story of Jesus's crucifixion comes to provide a powerful moral image of punishment and racial suffering. Lawrence's book documented not only the hegemonic nature of Christian stories but also the malleable and yielding nature of these moral tales. Christian stories were bent and twisted around, such that their moral meanings began to follow certain new contours. This new topography of meaning emerged from the narrative structure of Christian stories as they intersected with the narrative structure of indigenous stories to produce new moral tales that could account for the unequal structure of race relations. I am interested in the specific crossroads and the intricate labyrinths of meaning formed by these intersections. Here multiple coincidences of meanings and various forms of misrecognition operated as essential political tools in the creation of a black theology that indigenized and localized the conceptual terrains of white people and of a new national racialized existence.

When Lawrence first arrived in Garia, people asked him to help them clear an airstrip that was going to bring cargo from God. For many years people had tried to gain access to the cargo in heaven, and they now wanted Lawrence to help them because they suspected they might not have the right techniques. The villagers wanted Lawrence to contact God and convince Him to open the road for the cargo, so that their ancestors could deliver it from Sydney. What is interesting about this piece of ethnography is the way different spaces of otherness, that is, alternative spaces that are removed from the living—such as death, heaven, and Sydney— are collapsed together. Here different images of the outside become extensions of, and equivalent to, each other. They become part of the construction of new imaginary geographies where the outsideness of God, heaven, and the ancestors becomes equivalent to the outsideness of Australia or America (*Amerika*). Different images of distance become more than metaphors for each other; they start becoming each other, where one provides the means for entering the other (see Deleuze and Guattari 1987; Serres and Latour 1995).

Lawrence had an explanation for this collapsing of the distance between heaven and earth. He argued that in traditional Melanesian culture the cosmos was "a finite and almost exclusively physical realm" (Lawrence 1964, 3). People did not have a sense of some transcendental spiritual world that was totally removed from the present. Instead, the dead were seen to be part of the living world—they did not go into an utterly separate supernatural world. The natural and the supernatural were not firmly distinguished. Rather, gods and spirits were often treated as part of the order of nature—they lived within the earth or bush and frequently came in contact with humans. Even though they were more powerful than humans, gods and spirits were still seen as corporeal, as having a body, even if it was not always a human body but an animal, insect, or reptile body. As Lawrence put it:

> We must dismiss at once the concept of the supernatural: a realm of existence not only apart from but also on a higher plane than the physical world. The religions of all peoples studied in the area fully corroborate Bidney's argument that it is often impossible "to distinguish" among non-literate peoples "between the sphere of the natural and that of the supernatural, since gods and spirits are just as much a part of the order of nature as birds and animals." Gods, spirits, and totems were regarded as real, if not always visible, part of the ordinary physical environment. (Lawrence 1964, 12)

In their work on the Kaliai coast the Canadian anthropologists David and Dorothy Counts have quoted this argument from Lawrence and go on to illustrate it with the example of how Kaliai villagers asked them to point out heaven on a world map. The Countses were also asked to send back from America a picture of a deceased wife and to provide her address so others could write to her (Counts and Counts 1976, 300–301). These requests posit and assume certain understandings of space and time. They include no understanding of death as a transcendental space that exists over and above this world. There are just images of distance that have to be crossed or rendered the same. It is this rendering immanent of Christian transcendental spaces that I see as a major characteristic of cargo cults and their politics. Their politics of space is something I want to document and analyze further in later chapters. For the time being I want to point out that these processes of remapping are ways of circumnavigating anew the fields of identification within which subjects locate themselves and that a politics of space is always central to a politics of identification.

In one myth that Lawrence recorded the local god Manup came to Australia, and there he found white kanakas, for whom he built the city of Sydney. When he finished building Sydney, Manup wanted to go back to his true followers in New Guinea to do for them what he had done for whites. To do this Manup turned himself into the Holy Ghost, entered the womb of the Virgin Mary, and was reborn as Christ. When he tried to go back to New Guinea, the Jews turned against him, for they did not want to share what they had with the natives of New Guinea. The Jews crucified Jesus-Manup and kept him imprisoned in heaven, which is above or in Sydney. The missionaries were told to keep all this secret, and they agreed because the missionaries did not want to share their wealth with the natives. In this myth Jesus was killed by whites, and this killing of a black Christ became a form of racial violence that founded and underpinned the current order of the world. In the Kaliai area, and indeed throughout New Britain, many similar stories tell of the killing of a black Christ by Europeans. I see such stories as allegories that use the moral domain of Christian narratives to reobjectify the everyday pain and suffering that whites inflict upon laboring black bodies. The power of these stories comes from the way they condense and feed off people's everyday experiences of race. These stories operate allegorically in that they use an original mythic past to talk about the present. Indeed, they use the distance of the past from the present to reobjectify the experiences of the present. When traditional myths are no longer adequate allegories for talking at a distance about present experiences, people have to invent new myths about the past that can reobjectify the present; this is what cargo cults did in New Britain and in the Madang area. The allegorical power of these new stories comes from the way they reworked space, time, and alterity to create new representations of distance, that is, new allegories through which to resituate the present.

I see Lawrence's story about the crucifixion of Jesus-Manup as an example of how people can seize upon Christ's pain and suffering on the cross and rework it into an explanation that can account for general experiences of racial suffering and physical othering. The original oppression suffered by a black Christ becomes the source of current Melanesian oppression. The crucifixion becomes the origin of the pain suffered in a colonial order. This identification with and blackening of Christ's suffering is also a process through which people render themselves sacred and make their suffering into a sacred truth. This is a process in which people revalue their pain and their racial identities through Christian myths that they appropriate and localize.

In *Road Belong Cargo* Lawrence informed his readers that some cargo cult rituals were designed to free the imprisoned Jesus-Manup. Lawrence never explored how the imprisonment of a Melanesian God operates as a condensed metaphor for the imprisonment of Melanesians in a colonial structure that tried to regulate their ritual practices, body habits, conversations, thoughts, settlements, and movements. The myth about the blocking of Jesus-Manup's return displaces into the realm of narrative the sense that people had that their existence was blocked by white men. People project their oppression onto their god, they think about themselves through thinking about their god. They idealize themselves and their experiences by making their experiences into the experiences of a god that occupies a separate prison and geography. This is a process in which people take their experiences outside themselves, using the alternative time and space posited in narratives to reobjectify their experiences (Bakhtin 1981). Here people use narratives to distance themselves from their experiences only so that they can become more familiar with these experiences (Bloch 1970; Ricoeur 1979).

I want to point out something else about the black Christ in Melanesia and that is the way the son of God, who is the lesser, more human God, often comes to be embraced as the god of the people and as the god of the oppressed.[2] In one set of rituals that Lawrence described, cargo cultists tried to get the original creator—the god Dodo—to bring back this lesser god to New Guinea with his cargo. In their church services people prayed for the return of Jesus-Manup. They also made sacrifices to the dead for his return. In village cemeteries people set up European-style tables that they decorated with cotton cloth, flowers, food, and tobacco. Some villagers destroyed gardens, pigs, and property to impress upon the ancestors and cargo deities the natives' poverty and need for immediate relief. As Lawrence put it: "They would be shamed into honouring their obligations to the living" (1964, 94). Dances were also performed for the ancestors to witness, with the hope that the pleasure of the dance might convince the ancestors to pass on cargo to their descendants. There is here an attempt to keep alive an ongoing relationship with the dead and also to tempt and entrap the ancestors in new relationships of debt. People hoped that by giving their deceased kin a pleasurable ceremony the dead would feel obliged to repay this hospitality with European cargo. The logic of tradi-

xxxviINTRODUCTION

tional exchange comes to be used to get access to European goods. It is not the marketplace and wage labor that will provide access to commodities; instead, the emphasis is on the moral power of gifts to persuade and bind those who receive them. Through the world of ceremonial exchange the world of commodities comes to be not so much negated as familiarized. Its alienating relationships of money and wage labor give way to a world of kinship. Incorporating the European world of commodities into the moral domain of kinship relations shows a desire to bring the world of the European other closer to one's own society and culture. The rituals and stories of cargo cult followers that are directed toward the dead seek to rewrite the world of commodity production in order to domesticate and localize its seemingly all-pervasive alterity. Cargo cults articulate the transformation of commodities into more familiar locally understandable forms, namely, *kago* (cargo), wherein the relationships carried by commodities come to be domesticated and incorporated into narratives of autochthonous origins. Cargo cult followers move commodities out of the sphere of market transactions and wage labor and into the familiarizing domain of a local geography and a kinship system that maintains ongoing ceremonial exchange relationships with one's ancestors and one's origins.

A number of anthropologists, such as Stanner (1958) and Burridge (1960), put forward the idea of cargo cults as articulating an alternative moral order to that brought by Europeans. This concern with the moral dimension of cargo cults can also be found in *Road Belong Cargo,* in which Lawrence showed us people who did not want the dead excluded or hidden from the world of the living but who instead wanted to construct their future by entering into new kinds of ethical relationships with and obligations to the dead. A number of anthropologists, most notably Steven Feld (1982), have documented and analyzed this desire to amplify relations with the dead in Melanesia. They have seen it as expressing certain universal human traits in which a kind of politics of loss is run on a desire for memory (cf. Goodale 1985; Maschio 1994; Schieffelin 1976). I want to develop these anthropological insights further by using some of the recent philosophical work of Derrida (1994) and Wyschogrod (1985), who argue that for all people the meaning of life always has to come from death. Derrida's argument is that the outsideness of the dead always coincides with the search for a justice that is not already here. For Derrida our sense of justice can emerge only from a sense of responsibility to that which is beyond the living present, which is somehow removed from it. Yet this past is also an outsideness within the present, and Derrida speaks of there being no justice "without *this non-contemporaneity with itself of the living present,* without that which secretly unhinges it, without this responsibility and this respect for justice concerning those who *are not there,* of those who are no longer or who are not yet present and living" (1994, xix). The past and the future are removed from and ethically situate the present, and in Melanesia both are often positioned as in the hands of the dead and in the hands of whites. Throughout this book I will explore how cargo cult understandings of white power as coming from the dead had the effect of ethically repositioning Melanesians and Europeans; it resituated their relationships. In effect, people racialized their loss of control over the past and over the outside world of the dead. They used the distance of the past to unhinge the present and to create new forms of responsibility in the domain of race relations. The incorporation of European power into the terrains and myths occupied by the ancestors worked to familiarize white power and its dominating presence. It provided people with a moral template for operating in a new social order that seemed at first sight to be removed from their forms of morality and sociability. The incorporation of European power into the narratives and death spaces occupied by the ancestors also worked to domesticate the new social order; its new relationships were incorporated into and rendered subordinate to local ancestral kinship relationships that people felt they could remanipulate to allow them to cross the new distances imposed by race.

People's struggle to maintain and manipulate relations with the dead was a struggle to use relations of familiarity to manage that which appeared to be outside them; it was a struggle to draw close that which seemed distant. In *Road Belong Cargo* Lawrence gave examples of this, of how people in their dances would shake and shiver; while doing so they would receive messages from the dead who would come to them in the form of Europeans. It was these same sorts of visions and beliefs in the Vailala movement that Williams (1923) saw as signs of madness (Lattas 1992a; Worsley 1957, 88). In fact, this shivering and shaking was the embodied form given to those truths that came to people from their ability to project themselves into the land of the dead, where they could experience themselves as moving beyond the present limitations of their corporeal racialized existence (cf. Clark 1992). I want to use the Kaliai area to explore further this issue of the role of the dead in creating and situating the known boundaries of lived existence and how they, the dead, come to provide a means for traveling beyond the boundaries of existing knowledge but within certain traditional conventions for constituting new knowledge (see Stephen 1979, 1982). Here we are dealing with the tropes used to sustain and organize creativity and the importance of the trope—

of communication with the beyond—in allowing people to insert new determining truths into their realities. These indigenous vehicles and figures of travel are reinvented in cargo cults as part of the repositioning of social relationships, as part of the process of moving on as a person and as a community.

Through the alternative world of the dead, people sought to unhinge and displace the present. When discussing what he called the fourth period of cargo beliefs, Lawrence described how people expected the arrival of guns from the dead. The guns would be brought by Jesus-Manup, and they would be be used to fight Europeans. People claimed their cult was sanctioned by the Bible and that this was the real way of worshipping God. We see here whites losing control of the Bible, whose meanings and stories come to be invested with new racialized understandings of sin, punishment, suffering, and redemption. Given that the Bible is a symbol of white power and knowledge, it is not surprising that people borrow the moral authority invested in it by whites to authorize new truths that often involve a critique of whites. Such borrowings undermine attempts by Europeans to fix and police the meanings of the narratives and practices that they bring into Papua New Guinea. European meanings, narratives, and practices come to be stolen, transformed, and used for purposes not originally envisaged by the Europeans who brought them (see de Certeau 1988; Todorov 1992). People misread the Bible, and that misreading was not arbitrary or haphazard but strategic—politics underpinned the way stories came to be misread. People misread the Bible not because they were ignorant or had forgotten its contents but because they sought stories more meaningful than those given by European missionaries or native catechists. They sought stories more relevant to their lives, stories capable of explaining the origins of racial inequality, while perhaps also suggesting a conclusion to their experienced state of wretchedness and anguish.

Lawrence was aware of how government and church officials were often disturbed by the way villagers hijacked European narratives for civilizing and pacifying the natives. However, Lawrence could not bring himself to analyze the fact that perhaps misread narratives are themselves subversive and they were partly what colonial officials were repressing. This multiplication and twisting of stories was destabilizing. Indeed, state and church officials sought to maintain the narrative boundaries of the reality that they had brought by defining people's newly created narratives as symptoms of colonial stress and mental breakdown (Lattas 1992a; Lindstrom 1993; Worsley 1957). In his own work Lawrence refused to take up the subversive politics of ambiguity in misread Christian stories, although Lawrence's informants did see whites as having an interest in repressing their stories, and they saw the contest as one about competing stories. Garia villagers accused the mission of hiding the truth about God, cargo, and the dead. This perception, that whites were hiding the real story, is still quite widespread in Melanesia, and it sustains a whole set of hermeneutic practices in which people continuously reread Christian myths and search inside European ritual practices for some secret clue that might give away what Europeans are concealing (see Robbins 1997).[3]

In Lawrence's work we often see cult followers copying the rituals and symbolic figures of power belonging to Europeans. One man proclaimed himself king of the Madang area. Another man claimed to be the apostle Saint Paul, and he claimed to have a wireless through which he communicated with heaven about future events. The wireless was also often used in Kaliai cargo cults, for it represented that part of white material culture that clearly embodied the power to communicate with less visible outside worlds (cf. Worsley 1957, 122, 209–10). In their traditional rituals and magical practices Garia villagers (like Kaliai villagers and other Melanesians) often communicated with the less visible world of the dead, and they assumed that this must be the same less visible world from which European electronic messages were coming and going. I see the struggle by villagers to create their own wireless as a power struggle over the control of space, where access to and control over outside spaces allow people to control how they map out the borders of present reality. Every culture situates existence by positioning it spatially in relationship to an invisible outside, and each culture creates its effects of truth by disclosing and crossing into that which it posits to be distant. Yet that outside can also threaten to displace and disarrange the very reality whose borders it maps out. With the coming of missions, traders, and government officials the realm of the outside comes to be occupied by the white man, who claims that everything he brings comes from over the horizon where he lives. In this context people have a sense of having lost control of that hidden presence that they had always seen (in the form of the dead) as determining the boundaries of their existence. One central concern of this book is to use the bush Kaliai area to explore how people seek to displace the white man's seemingly total control over space. I want to explore the imaginary geographies that people develop in order to place themselves in ways that guarantee them control over those secret spaces of alterity that embody a sense of the alterity of another time—not only the past but also the future. The politics of self and identity come to be played out as a spatial politics for controlling that outsideness that reveals and completes the secret of present existence.

Now I want to provide a summary of how the different chapters in this

book realize these concerns. In Chapter 1 I provide an introduction to
the Kaliai bush. I outline its physical geography, the history of European
government and mission influence, and important features of traditional
belief and social organization. In Chapter 2 I present a history of the major cargo cults in the area since World War II. Here I use Kaliai history
to illustrate one major recurring idea of this book: the need to analyze
those local appropriations and seizures of meaning that allowed processes
of cultural hegemony to be deflected and transformed into processes of
cultural resistance. In Chapter 3 I explore the political role of space and
in particular the role of imaginary geographies in bringing together the
different spaces of alterity and power belonging to the Kaliai and Europeans. I explore how cult followers appropriated biblical spaces and the
lands of Europeans, which they married to indigenous images of masalai
places and to local terrains inhabited by the dead in the underground,
pools of water, and mountains. People used their traditional familiar
worlds of alterity to comprehend and gain access to the white man's alternative worlds of heaven, Sydney, Brisbane, Jordan, Nazareth, and
America. In this desire to make known the unknown, make familiar the
distant was also a desire to introduce an otherness into one's being. Cargo
cults are, to borrow a phrase of Ricoeur's, "variations on the theme of
otherness in every domain of communal existence" (1991, 319). Cargo cult
followers searched for other forms of sexuality, for other ways of organizing kinship and gender relationships, for other forms of leadership, for
other songs, dances, and feasts. This desire to reformulate one's communal
existence and to become something other than oneself was spatialized and
often rendered as the creation of a new geography.

All the chapters in this book seek to analyze the underlying formative
schemes through which the Kaliai thought through the task of creating
society anew. In Chapters 4 and 5 I focus on a Kaliai cargo cult during
the 1970s that was informed by traditional narrative schemes that held
women to be the true creators of social existence. This cargo cult was led
by a man called Sen Sio (Saint Sio, also known as Napasisio), which I will
spell as it is pronounced *Censure,* so as to capture the theme of moral
critique that Censure offered (cf. Counts 1971, 1972).[4] In the rituals that
Censure devised, women's bodies provided a means of repeating and recapturing the formative processes of the original world that traditional
Kaliai myths of matriarchy speak of when they tell of how women discovered the masks that became the basis of a new social order. Women's ability to be fruitful and bear children was seen as an everyday instancing of
a procreative power that encompassed more than just the ability to carry

Censure in 1986, with his few remaining female followers, who have just finished working the cult's *lo* (laws)

children (cf. Bamberger 1974; Bettelheim 1955). In effect, women's bodies provided the mythic terms for thinking about other relations of production and appropriation, especially those involving race. Censure also saw himself as creating a new sexual code of conduct, a new ethics of sexuality, that was to be grounded in valuing the mother's blood and in recognizing the emptiness of men's claims to be creators of anything. He argued that it was men's past violence to women that was blocking the coming of a new law of existence. In particular, the traditional custom of men's breaking the necks of widows had alienated and angered the underground female ancestors who were making the cargo. Through his dialogues with the underground murdered mothers of the past, Censure sought to affirm a new form of civilized masculinity that would deliver the social order of the white man through the care and respect it offered native women.

In Chapter 6 I explore how Kaliai cargo cult leaders often used mythic images of bisexuality to try to overcome the fundamental divisions of the social world. There was a desire to return to a precosmogonic world from which current social differences had emerged. In various cults the blurring of the sexual categories of the existing world served to destabilize its as-

sumptions and frameworks of order, and here the androgyne becomes the
mythic figure that prefigures the creation of new forms of order. Here
again I analyze the mythic images that mediate the creative process of
creating creation and how in the Kaliai area the androgyne was an exemplar of processes of beginning. Toward the end of Chapter 6 I switch to
the contemporary context to explore how one current aspiring cargo cult
leader has feminized himself and taken up erotic procreative images to
formulate the process of fulfilling unfulfilled desire and the process of giving birth to a new world

In Chapter 7 I analyze the main cargo cults that bush Kaliai villagers
joined after leaving Censure's cult. Here I focus on the cargo cults of Aria-
speaking villagers in the Moluo-Robos area. I analyze how people's cult
relationships with the dead came to provide a way of negotiating a new
sense of themselves as other, that is, as remade in the image of Europeans.
In their rituals and everyday gestures cult followers started to copy certain
aspects of European culture as a way of reworking their social order by
reworking its embodiment inside their sense of self. The struggle to become something other than oneself was partly a struggle for totalization,
wherein people sought to incorporate and add to themselves all those
other new forms of personhood that seemed to escape or exclude them
and that God had carried away to America when he ran away from the
bush Kaliai. People's struggle to overcome a sense of the world as completed was rendered into a struggle to overcome their uncompleted moral
selves. We are dealing here with processes of self-subjugation, with how
the hegemonic processes of cultural incorporation and colonial pedagogy
were taken up in cargo cults that wanted now to take on the moral task
of freeing the native self from itself so that it could become more like the
white man.

In Chapter 8 I explore these issues in the contemporary context by
examining the recent impact of the New Tribes Mission on Kaliai cargo
cult beliefs and practices. The new mission has brought a much more fundamentalist style of proselytizing, which has sought to eradicate people's
traditional relationships with the dead, masalai, and tambarans. The new
mission has also sought to eradicate all the new cult relationships that
people developed with European culture and the dead. Yet inside the New
Tribes Mission, villagers have developed a clandestine cargo cult that is
sustained because people see the missionaries as having been forced by
their national government and the Australians to conceal the true relationship of white culture to the world of the dead. Local villagers have reread
the projects of the New Tribes Mission in a way that allows them to enter

into an alliance with this new form of Western hegemony, the repressive practices of which have come to be accepted as what is now needed to save the bush Kaliai and bring on the millennium.

Throughout this book I use Foucault to analyze the way modern state power has become dependent upon another form of power that the state has integrated into itself; here I refer to those power relations bound up with the pastoral custody and control of individuals. As Foucault points out:

> Since the sixteenth century, a new political form of power has been continuously developing. This new political structure, as everybody knows, is the state. But most of the time, the state is envisioned as a kind of political power which ignores individuals, looking only at the interests of the totality or, I should say, of a class or a group among the citizens. That's quite true. But I'd like to underline the fact that the state's power (and that's one of the reasons for its strength) is both an individualising and a totalizing form of power. Never, I think, in the history of human societies—even in the old Chinese society—has there been such a tricky combination in the same political structures of individualization techniques and of totalization procedures. This is due to the fact that the modern Western state has integrated in a new political shape an old power technique which originated in Christian institutions. We can call this power technique the pastoral power. (1982b, 782)

It is no accident that the state in contemporary Papua New Guinea often sponsors missionizing by fundamentalist Christians. In West New Britain the national government has allowed evangelical missionaries to set up airstrips in remote locations where they then proceed to try to destroy all those local conceptual terrains and indigenous forms of power that allow subjects to form themselves outside Western structures of individualization. The production of a certain kind of subject through pastoral regimes underpins the modern state (Foucault 1982b, 1984; Stoler 1995). This state requires a certain kind of subjectivity, and the paradox of contemporary processes of pacification and Christianization is that people come to be partly formed into a civilized subject through the very practices they use to resist the state and the church's articulation of these processes.

In this book I move away from an early Foucauldian position that privileged institutions and how they produce subjects. This book is more concerned with Foucault's later work, which analyzes how subjects go about the ethical task of creating themselves into something that they can live with. By focusing on the less visible technologies that people used to create themselves anew, I explore how cargo cult followers embraced but also subverted the disciplinary and pastoral powers that engaged them. I want to make visible the clandestine world of creativity through which Kaliai cargo cults appropriated and reworked the new procedures for becoming a subject that missionaries and state officials were advocating (Eves 1996). Kaliai cargo cults used a set of schemes that did not so much deny the hegemony of the dominant culture but creatively reworked its narratives and practices to deflect and loosen their direct hold on them. By reinterpreting the cultural conditions of their domination, cargo cult followers transformed ambiguity into a weapon. This production of ambiguity used certain schemes of creation; it was not a haphazard and arbitrary process. Instead, it was located within certain ways of doubling the world that used the dead to multiply the vantage points for looking at the world anew. Here mimesis emerged as a project for controlling and remaking the dominant culture by copying it in a way that displaced it and gave it a new external form, one located in the land of the dead.

Cultures of Secrecy

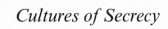

Chapter One

Traditional Bush Kaliai Society and the Arrival of *Ol Waitskin*

The Kaliai Census Division is an administrative unit of about seventeen hundred square miles in the northwest section of the island of New Britain. The 1972 national census listed the area as having 27 official villages containing 3,559 people. The 1990 national census recorded 37 official villages containing 5,054 people living in 927 households. This book discusses villagers who live between the River Banu and the River Aria, in what is referred to locally as the Kaliai bush (see Table 1.1). These villagers still live in houses made of plant materials that they gather from surrounding rain forests. Traditionally, people built their houses on the ground, and they buried their dead close to them inside their houses where they could talk to them and acquire from them magical spells, songs, dances, and other forms of knowledge. Ostensibly for health reasons, the colonial government made people bury their dead in cemeteries on the outskirts of villages. It also encouraged people to build their houses on stilts, away from pigs and dogs but also away from their living memories in the ground.

The bush Kaliai prefer to build their villages on the ridges of hills, away from mosquitoes found in the surroundi..g cool moist valleys where taro gardens are often located. Villagers practice slash-and-burn agriculture, using a garden location for one to two years and a maximum of three years. Traditionally, taro was the major subsistence crop, but today people rely more on sweet potato, manioc, and an imported species of taro known as Singapore taro. People supplement their diet by collecting wild fruits, nuts, ferns, and other edible plants. They also catch wild pigs, cassowaries, wallabies, eels, frogs, and freshwater crayfish.

The part of the Kaliai bush in which people have built their villages is made up of gently undulating hills. The more mountainous areas, which are one to two days' walk away, are used mainly for hunting. Mountains,

Table 1.1
Census Figures for Selected Kaliai Villages

| | 1977–78 Village Census | | | 1990 National Population Census | | |
Village	Total, excluding Absentees	Total, including Absentees		Total Households	Citizens	Noncitizens
Aikon	166	218		35	185	
Angal	136	171		70	408	
Bagai	59	74		10	52	
Bolo	98	148		27	142	
Denga	54	80		20	109	
Gigina	145	145		62	354	3
Gilau (Atiatu)	269	328		31	219	
Gogloa	37	57		19	112	
Kandoka	241	367		88	460	
Ketenge	195	251		43	224	
Lauvore	190	253		39	228	
Moluo	47	66		31	162	
Pureling	126	146		44	229	
Robos	203	216		10	72	
Salke	57	120		18	111	
Iboki Station				8	30	15 Malaysians

Note: The 1990 National Population Census figures are misleading because villages like Aikon, Salke, and Mo-luo existed in name only. Their members had moved to the new villages of Popmu, Sarangtu, and Omuraeneh that had been established closer to the New Tribes Mission at Amcor (Gigina).

like Andewa and Alat, along with waterfalls and cliffs, are where the dead go to reside (Counts 1980). Traditionally, corpses would be buried with their heads pointing toward the mountains so that later their souls could go there to live in invisible villages. Many bush Kaliai have traveled to these surrounding mountains and have come back with stories about having heard the dead talking, singing, and performing ceremonies or about having heard noises made by the chickens and pigs belonging to these invisible villages. I want to explore how colonialism came to operate within a topographical terrain that incorporated this hidden realm of the dead and how these indigenous understandings of space and geography came to mediate and reposition the lived experience of race relationships.

The bush Kaliai have been able to hang onto their close ties with the dead in part because numerous rivers and hills have made it difficult for the government to establish roads. This has resulted in people's isolation from markets and administrative centers like Gloucester, Talasea, and

Kimbe. Government patrol reports often gave poor transportation as the reason that the Kaliai interior had failed to develop economically to the same extent as the Kaliai coast. There are few coconut and cocoa trees or trade stores in the Kaliai bush.[1] Even on the Kaliai coast, poor transportation has always held up development when compared to other parts of West New Britain that adopted cash crops at the same time. What coastal shipping service has operated has always been irregular, and this is still the case. Today it is common for coastal villagers to abandon the cutting of copra and cocoa for months because they have no way of getting their produce to market.

The bush Kaliai say that before European contact they had small gardens and lived a largely nomadic existence. Both the German and Australian administrations saw people's wandering ways as subverting their desire to civilize them, that is, to distance the people from what were seen to be the restless habits of a savage past. The tendency to move regularly to new garden sites and to travel around, following seasonal forest fruits and nuts, was seen as hindering official attempts to establish permanent villages, cash crops, aid posts, schools, and Christianity. It was mainly after World War II that the Australian administration had some major successes, especially with the language groups of Lusi and Anem that moved down to the coast and Banu River. As late as the 1980s kiaps and agricultural officers were still encouraging bush villagers to move closer to the coast where they could be more easily administered. There water transportation has facilitated the taking up of cash crops and people's incorporation into churches, schools, aid posts, and the payment of government taxes. When compared to the residence patterns of bush villages, those villages established along major rivers and on the coast have tended to be more permanent.

Some bush villagers claim that their parents lived only briefly in the official villages established by the administration and that this was mostly during the time of government patrols and census lineups. Historically, bush villages have varied considerably in size, with people coming together for a number of years before splitting up again. Sorcery (**muso**) by outsiders was sometimes given as the reason people fled a large village. My feeling, from watching villages split up in 1986, is that sorcery provides a refracted way of talking about conflicts that develop between rival groups whose close relationships sometimes make it difficult for them to speak openly about experiences of betrayal with respect to the fulfillment of exchange relations and the sharing of food (Evans-Pritchard 1937; V. Turner 1967). Given that agriculture is slash and burn, villagers feel a great deal of pressure to relocate or to split up once they have exhausted their immediate environment with gardening. As soil fertility declines, people find it more difficult to honor their exchange obligations, which leads to gossiping and ill feelings among villagers, who are often close kin. The result is the fragmentation of large villages into smaller residential units, which are often more successful in finding game, for there are not as many people competing for eels, crayfish, frogs, ferns, and fruits in the same environment. Those who live in large villages often complain about how hard it is to find pigs and cassowaries—the noisy presence of many people frightens away game.

My experience of villages that have split up is that this fragmentation is often accompanied by guilt and a longing by divided kin to be reunited. Cargo cult leaders have often tapped into these yearnings for reconciliation, with their cults often holding out the promise of gathering people together again around a common cult site. Indeed, the myths of many bush Kaliai cargo cults speak about an original site where everyone was gathered together with God. It is said that there people lived together in one large primordial house, often referred to as a large men's house. There everyone shared a language, culture, and existence until a wrong was committed against God, who then broke the large building that housed this scene of original unity.[2] This scene of original biblical harmony resonates with traditional bush Kaliai themes of the men's house as a source of shelter, hospitality, gifts, and male comradeship. This story is really a local version of the Tower of Babel story, for when God scatters the original inhabitants of the large men's house to different sites, He also gives them new distinct languages, cultures, and lifestyles that make up the present divided, unequal world. That was when racial differences emerged, and Melanesians lost the Western lifestyle that they had enjoyed when they lived with God. Kaliai cargo cults have often seen themselves as seeking to regather and rebuild this original scene of residential unity. For this reason the cults often took up the administration's desire for larger residential units, only now these were built not so much for development purposes but as part of a millenarian project of reclaiming the past as a means of reclaiming an original blessed existence. We see here the way cargo cults often seem to mime and take on board new administrative requirements that become merged with alternative ways of realizing the white man's existence. Here a millenarian quality is given to the administration's emphasis on unity, good relations, and ordered forms of settlement.

There are five major languages in the Kaliai area: the four Austronesian languages of Aria, Lamogai, Lusi, and Mouk and the Papuan language of Anem. Today many people use local versions of the Tower of Babel story to account for this diversity, with some groups, like the Mouk and Anem, seeing themselves as having a special linguistic relationship to God and His first catechist, Katika, who spoke their language when it was the first language spoken by humanity (Thurston 1994). Recently, Anem cargo cult leaders had their theological centrality confirmed by anthropologists and linguists who came into the Kaliai bush. They informed people about linguistic theories that posited the Papuan language of Anem to have been the first language in West New Britain, with the Austronesian languages arriving later. All the Anem cargo cult leaders to whom I spoke used this information given by whites to support their claims that God had created the Anem first, that He and Katika built the Tower of Babel among the Anem before destroying it and creating the other languages, races, and customs of the globe. Here a curious blend of appropriated reworked science and Christianity sustains an emerging local black theology that tells of how God and His church were first in the Kaliai bush. Indeed, one Anem man, who told me of the "Christian" significance of these linguistic theories, went on to show me the original small bell that

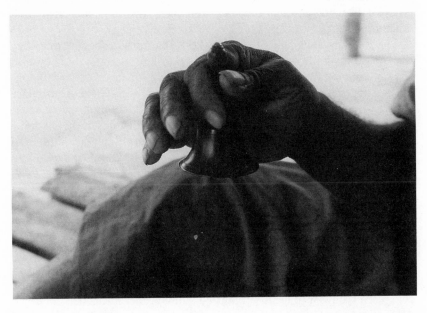

The councillor of Lauvore holding the original bell that Katika used to try to summon the Kaliai to his church services

Katika used to summon people to his church services. He also told me
how some of his Mouk relatives in the bush had a tooth of the Virgin
Mary (*tit bilong Maria*) whom his ancestors had called Galiki.

GENDER RELATIONS AND SOCIAL ORGANIZATION

My major informants in the Kaliai bush were Aria and Mouk speakers
from the villages of Aikon, Angal, Doko Sagra, Meitavale, Moluo, Robos,
and Salke. I also spent two to three months living with a small community
of Anem speakers in the village of Bolo, where Anem is now spoken
mainly by the older generation.[3] Although the Kaliai area has many languages, this cultural diversity has to be seen in a context in which many
villagers speak more than two languages. Intermarriage between language
groups like the Aria and Mouk, and the Mouk and Anem, has been frequent. The different language groups often attend each other's ceremonies,
and they have close exchange relationships. Anem and Mouk villagers
have especially strong close ties; their parents and grandparents often resided together for long periods of time that involved working gardens together, with the men building and sharing a common men's house. Both
groups still work gardens together, and they still frequently visit each
other.

The different language groups in the Kaliai area recognize that they
share customs with respect to marriage, kinship, and ritual. They also
share a common overarching moiety system that organizes their ceremonies, marriages, and exchange relations. Men from the different groups have
a shared secret world of solidarity that involves a common men's house
culture organized around ceremonies and initiation rituals involving dancing masks known as tumbuan (**aolu, nakamutmut**) and other tambaran
(**mahrva**) figures like the bull roarers known as Varku and Vakiqual and
the bamboo wind instruments known as Mukmuk (cf. Chowning 1974;
Counts 1968; Lattas 1989). Another related and shared overarching aspect
of bush Kaliai culture is the strong binary gender logic that informs
people's beliefs, rituals, and everyday practices. Most villages are divided
spatially along gender lines, with the women and children living in small
family houses while the men live in the men's house where they should
ideally spend as much time as possible secluded from the pollution of
women's bodies (cf. Allen 1967; Herdt 1981, 1987; Meigs 1984). A great
deal of everyday labor is also organized along gender lines; men cut down
the forest, build fences, and hunt. The intense effort and danger in these
activities is a source of pride to men, who often taunt women that they do

not have the strength and courage necessary to do what men do. While men privilege their activities, they often also say that women work a lot harder than they do, and they will point to how women do the everyday toilsome work of weeding, planting, cooking, childrearing, breaking firewood, gathering greens, and fetching water. Men recognize that their dominance over women is partly embodied in a division of labor that favors them and is often the source of many domestic disputes.

Part of traditional Kaliai men's power over women was also articulated through a culture of terror and duplicity that involved secret tambaran. These monsters, which were housed in the men's house or behind it, would threaten to eat disobedient women. If the men's house was empty of firewood or water, a tambaran like Varku would come up and cry, warning women of its dangerous presence and of their duties to the men's house. In part men's solidarity with each other came from sharing a secret world of complicity—a communication that they carried the masks and made the noises belonging to the tambaran, and they ate the food given to appease the tambaran's anger. Men's solidarity also emerged from their sharing the secret myth that they had not always been the dominant sex, for the tambaran had not always been under their control. Indeed, secret male mythology has it that tambaran were originally discovered by women, who used them to intimidate men. All the men belonging to the different language groups in the Kaliai bush share the secret myth of how an ancestor called Kowdock reversed this state of affairs. He took the tambaran away from women, and he killed his sister, Kewak, the woman who created the tambaran. Myths detailing this reversal focus on a bull-roarer tambaran that Kewak had named Arku and that Kowdock later renamed Varku when he gave it to men. The creation of a new social order is here equated with the right to confer names upon objects of power. This power to name was something that many bush Kaliai cargo cult leaders took up as they sought to change their standing in the world by discovering, naming, and renaming secret objects of power. In doing so these cargo cult leaders transferred into the realm of racial power some of the traditional mythic paradigms about power that underpinned gender relations; that is, they reenacted traditional mythic schemes that associated changes and transfers of power with acts of renaming. The transformation of names that accompanied the primordial struggle between the sexes over who should rule became the engendering logic or mythic matrix for figuring the overcoming of regimes of racial inequality. Here we should also note that tambaran initiation rituals—in which a boy becomes a man, or a man without importance becomes a big man—involve the learning of secret names. To know the secret names of decorations confers the right to wear them; to know the secret name for *betel nut* allows a man to demand of noninitiates that they fetch it. New names reposition people in relationship to each other, so we should not be surprised to find cargo cults using renaming as a form of empowerment, as a way of repositioning race relations.

THE SYMBOLISM OF GENDER, EXCHANGE, AND MOIETIES

A number of anthropologists have pointed to the importance of gender, sexuality, and reproduction in Melanesian ontologies (Gillison 1993; Mimica 1988; M. Strathern 1988; A. Weiner 1980). In the Kaliai bush, after a village holds a tambaran ceremony, the guests are obligated to repay the food and shell money they received by holding their own tambaran ceremonies. This new ceremony is spoken of as the child (**titno**) of the previous ceremony. A village that holds a tambaran ceremony is said to be pregnant (**somogu**) with that tambaran, and the conclusion of the ceremony is likened to giving birth (**dibirh**). Bowl, a respected Mouk elder, explained this exchange of ceremonies, the way they engender each other, like this:

> Initially Bolo had pregnancy with Mukmuk. They sang out to us. We went down and expelled Mukmuk. Mukmuk then came on top of us. We said that's all right, your debt has come to us, we are pregnant to you. After a short while we "worked" Mukmuk. . . . We expelled Mukmuk. We gave debts to every village. . . . When we fasten the pigs and "bring" [expel] this something [the tambaran], this something will then go on top of another big man. He will work it and "screw" it on to another big man. If Onamanga expels its tumbuan and Aikon gets up its own tumbuan, people will say that the children of Onamanga have come up now. If we expel Varku and later Varku is worked by Bolo then this will be called Varku titno [i.e., Varku's child]; the child of Varku has come up.

What can also be found in bush Kaliai tambaran rituals is the theme of gender rivalry and sexual antagonism, which has also been well documented by other Melanesian anthropologists (Herdt and Poole 1982; Langness 1967, 1974). Indeed, all bush Kaliai initiation rituals conclude with a symbolic battle in which women chase and try to spear the men. In the ritual for Varku the women break down the fence erected by men so that the women do not see the tambaran or the ritual's proceedings. As they break the fence, the tambaran escapes into the bush so that women do not recapture it, and the women then chase the men around the village square, throwing small sticks at them. The men are forbidden to retaliate or make an issue over the women's attacks. These rituals provide women with an opportunity to get some revenge for some of the everyday injustices to which they have been subjected. Publicly, the women are said to be angry over the pain and suffering that men and the tambaran inflicted upon their children. This is also why the men later compensate the women with shell money.

In tambaran initiation rituals the father of the initiate also gives shell money to the maternal uncle (**tumno**) for the ritual work done on the son. This is seen as an exchange between the two moieties, for the mother's brother (like his nephew and the nephew's mother) belongs to the moiety opposite the father's. The two moieties of Big Bird (**Monouk Omba,** *Bikpela Pisin*) and Little Bird (**Monouk Magit,** *Liklik Pisin*) depend upon the other to initiate their children. Along with this ritual interdependence exists a certain amount of rivalry and conflict, which is expressed in the initiation ritual Mukmuk. The initiate squats between his mother's brother's legs, and the initiate's father then whips the boy's uncle across the stomach. In traditional bush Kaliai society the competitive public exchanges between men should ideally occur between men who belong to opposite moieties. The moieties of Big Bird and Little Bird are gendered male and female, respectively, which means that the exchanges between men can take on provocative sexual connotations (Lattas 1990). I see the rivalry between men and women, which was mythically encoded and traced to their struggle over the tambaran, as also being symbolically played out in the competitive ceremonial exchange relations between these two oppositely gendered moieties.

Each moiety in the Kaliai bush is composed of a number of matrilineal clans identified with a particular totem from which they originated. A number of myths tell how particular birds, animals, and plants changed into women who became the first mothers of different matrilineal totemic lines. In one myth about the origin of the moiety Big Bird a male ancestor who is either a cassowary (**alou**) or a sea eagle (**bogi**) travels around and finds the different totemic mothers who founded the matriclans of Big Bird. In the myth of origins of the moiety of Little Bird a female ancestor, a kingfisher (**piraou**), went around and found its different totemic matrilines. These myths posit certain animals, birds, and plants as the first mothers of humanity; individuals acquire their totemic clan identity from their mother's blood. The effect of these beliefs is to make women's bodies

Women with spears chasing the men at the end of an initiation ritual belonging to the tambaran Varku

Traditional decorations worn at the end of an initiation ritual

the source of social order, in much the same way that secret myths of matriarchy posit women to be the original source of that social order established through the tambaran. Another effect of these beliefs is that women's bodies link the identity of individuals to a primitive mythical time when animals and plants were the original kin of humans. Here the matrilineal transmission of an original primordial maternal body creates women's bodies into connectors and mediators with the beginning of time and with other forms of corporeality. Through their blood, women transmit an alternative, previous state of embodiment that disembodies the self, in the sense that it allows the self to become identified with alternative, more primordial ways of figuring corporeal identity. In relating individuals to an alternative primitive corporeal existence, women articulate the continuity of remnants of the corporeal self with mythological time. Woman's corporeal otherness becomes the bearer of the otherness of mythological time. Her corporeality, her blood, is said to be the base (as) of one's being. It is the means for pursuing the truths of the self beyond the phenomenal boundaries of current bodies and the means of recomposing and extending those bodily boundaries into their mythological corporeal otherness. This primordial state of embodiment traced through women provides the allegorical logic of bush Kaliai social organization. It is what allows people to never be fully identical with themselves and what allows them to be coupled in fertile exchanges with each other; the interactions and couplings of Big Bird and Little Bird members are also interactions and couplings of groups gendered male and female.

Chapters 4 and 5 focus on how bush Kaliai cargo cults took up this symbolic positioning of women's sexuality and procreative powers, which they reworked into a millenarian project. In their rituals many cults took up the ceremonial coupling of the differently gendered moieties, for they saw this as embodying the transformative magical power of the ancestors. Followers were separated into their respective moieties, and they sang and danced the cult laws assigned to their moiety. This ceremonial coupling of male and female moieties has to be seen in the context of traditional bush Kaliai marriages, which were expected to occur between individuals who belonged to oppositely gendered moiety groups (Thurston 1994). Custom required a Big Bird man to marry a Little Bird woman and a Little Bird man to marry a Big Bird woman. Marriage here is not just simply a marriage between a man and a woman but also a marriage between the gendered signs of groups. This is to say that the two moieties are part of an engendering binary logic that displaces reproduction into relationships between groups.[4] Positioned as male and female, the two moieties are complementary opposites and represent one means of reproducing relationships between groups within a framework of interdependence that also encodes rivalry. In marrying women of the opposite moiety, men spawn and nurture the offspring of the opposite moiety as a gift and obligation they have to each other's groups. Each moiety is dependent on the other for its reproduction (cf. Levi-Strauss 1972). This reproduction through one's opposite is a major bush Kaliai theme; it is part of a cultural logic in which heterosexual procreation becomes a metaphor for social differences and for the generative potential of all binary points of social conjuncture. In the cargo cult run by Censure we shall find that the white-black racial dichotomy often came to be equated with the Little Bird versus Big Bird dichotomy as well as that between men and women. Many bush Kaliai cargo cults organized their ceremonies around different songs and rituals for Little Bird and Big Bird followers in the hope that by appealing to a traditional ceremonial structure they might be able to entice the dead to reenact these cult rituals so that the cults could use the magical engendering power of the ancestors to displace the present order of things.

Bush Kaliai cargo cults often used the binary logic of the moiety system as a means of figuring and of familiarizing the perceived binary nature of race relations. Thus Censure spoke of two forms of money; he claimed that the present kina currency of Papua New Guinea belonged to Little Bird, but it had been "pocketed" by whites. He predicted that a new currency belonging to Big Bird would come and it would belong to Melanesians. One old cargo cult story I collected from two brothers—Samaga and Septireh—spoke of how Kowdock, who belongs to Little Bird, was responsible for creating the material lifestyle of the bush Kaliai, whereas Moses, who was said to belong to Big Bird, was responsible for creating the lifestyle of Europeans. When the great flood came, Kowdock drifted around West New Britain on coconuts he had strapped together, and he created the bad Melanesian customs of warfare, widow killing, and sorcery. Moses, however, went off to America in a large ship, and he gave white-skins the good customs and knowledge that have allowed them to acquire an affluent existence. This narrative incorporates Europeans into traditional paradigms of difference in order to render those traditional schemes of difference relevant to the structure of present racial differences.

A BRIEF HISTORY OF CONTACT

One reason such cargo cult stories were able to flourish in the Kaliai bush was that poor transportation hindered the development of detailed forms of government surveillance and control. The Kaliai Census Division is about ninety-four kilometers from the administrative post of Cape Gloucester and ninety-six kilometers from Kimbe, which is now the provincial headquarters for West New Britain. Before Kimbe was established in the late 1960s, Talasea administered West New Britain. In 1958 Gloucester was established, and it assumed responsibility for directly administering the northwest section of West New Britain. In 1965 the Cape Gloucester patrol post consisted of a European officer and fifteen native staff members. A Patrol Report in 1970 listed the Kaliai Census Division as "approximately 9 hours sailing by workboat from Talasea and about six hours, by boat, east of Gloucester." The closest the Kaliai area came to having a full-time administrative presence was during the 1980s when a patrol post was set up at Iboki. My experience of that patrol post, in 1986 and 1990, was that it was ineffectual, mainly because kiaps and agricultural officers found rural life boring. Whenever they could, they took off for town or returned to their home villages. Many government officials based at Iboki also resented the one to three days' walk required to reach interior villages. In the late 1980s such patrols were made about two or three times a year and then not at all. By the early 1990s the government had abandoned the Iboki patrol post, partly because of disputes with landowners over who should receive payment for the ground on which the base camp was established.

Like government kiaps and agricultural officers stationed at Iboki, many teachers and medical aid workers also resented being stationed in the Kaliai bush. Indeed, whenever they could, many would go to town or return to their villages. When I first arrived in 1986, I was given a long history of complaints about kiaps, teachers, catechists, and agricultural officers who had not stayed to attend to their duties. Like the residents of many other parts of Papua New Guinea, bush Kaliai villagers are highly critical of a government bureaucracy that promises much but consistently fails to deliver the most basic services from its personnel. When bush Kaliai villagers lash out at government officials, it is for their perceived laziness and lack of discipline. Many people now idealize the time of white colonial rule before 1975 and want to reembrace its world of discipline. This idealization of European rule has led many bush Kaliai to embrace the New Tribes Mission, which arrived at Amcor in 1985 and shortly afterward at Kwako on the River Aria.

Until the arrival of the New Tribes Mission and the appearance in 1990 of a Malaysian timber company, Rimbunan Hijau, the Kaliai had little in the way of a permanent European presence.[5] What there had been consisted of a series of different managers at Iboki Plantation. In the late 1980s the last manager left the Kaliai coast to reside in Kimbe, where he manages the local landowner company that has sponsored logging operations in the Kaliai bush. Before Melanesian independence from Australia in 1975 the bush Kaliai villagers saw only occasional patrols by white government officials and Catholic priests. The Catholic Church's influence in the Kaliai area started at the beginning of the century from the distant stations established at Vunapope, Kilenge, Talasea, and Poi. Father Janssen, who was a trained anthropologist and Catholic priest in the neighboring Bariai area around 1970, wrote, "At least since 1930, the Kaliai were regularly visited by missionaries from Talasea and later on from Poi (Kove)" (1974, 11). However, it was not until 1948, when the Catholic Church established a mission station near Taveliai on the Kaliai coast, that villagers came under more intense pastoral supervision. A 1959–60 Patrol Report listed the European staff at the Kaliai Mission Station as consisting of one priest and three nuns of the Sacred Heart order.

Initially, the Catholic Church focused most of its activities on the Kaliai coast, where it still has a strong following. The church's services were initially conducted in Lusi and later in Anem. According to Janssen, "In the years 1934–1939, most of the Lusi and Kove were baptised in large groups; smaller groups followed after the war. The Anem received baptism in 1948–1954, the Mouk and Aria between 1948 and 1962" (1974, 11). The church's early influence on bush Kaliai villagers was mostly through catechists it appointed to run schools and Sunday services. These early catechists were recruited from the Tolai area of East New Britain where the Catholic Church still has a strong presence. The Catholic Church still uses catechists from East New Britain, although today it also recruits individuals from the Kaliai coast and one person from the Kaliai bush. Catechists were responsible for teaching the word of God, but many were more than passive mediums for official church doctrine. They often supported local villagers who were developing new popular forms of Christianity that fused Bible stories with traditional myths and imported folklore beliefs and practices. My experience of catechists, from the Kaliai area and elsewhere, is that these individuals are very knowledgeable in cargo cult myths concerning a black Christ, Moses, or the catechist (Katika) who ran away from Melanesia. In the late 1960s and early 1970s a number of catechists from the Kaliai coast left their villages to join Censure's movement in the bush.[6] Indeed, Kaliai catechists have often used their authority and familiarity with the Bible to legitimize cargo cult beliefs by claiming that such beliefs are in accordance with the Bible.

The influence of European commerce and administration in the Kaliai area began with the Germans. Around 1910 they established Iboki Plantation, which did not close until 1988. The plantation employed many local villagers as well as contract laborers from other parts of New Guinea. The Germans traded some goods for the land at Iboki, and today people complain of the few goods they received and of how they were tricked into regarding plastic beads as the shell money of Europeans. In its early years Iboki Plantation functioned as a base for German police patrols and for labor recruiters. Many old people, who were then children, remember their relatives running into the bush so that they would not be forcibly taken away to distant plantations. Some who ran away were seeing the white man for the first time and were frightened by his appearance. They suspected he might be a dangerous masalai, *tewel* (ghost), or tambaran.[7] This first perception remains strong and is reproduced in the indigenous word for white man, **pura,** which is also the indigenous word for masalai (Counts and Counts 1976, 294). This perception and naming practice added a certain mystique to colonial power, a mystique that still surrounds *ol masta* (all masters, all whites).

The Germans administered their territories through a system of indirect rule that they established in the Kaliai around 1908 (Janssen 1974, 9–10; see also Murray 1929; Lattas 1996; Rowley 1958; cf. Fields 1985; Kaplan 1995). Patrols would appoint a headman, or *luluai,* who was accountable for his village to subsequent patrols. The luluai had an assistant, known as a *tultul,* who was to take the luluai's place in case of death, accident, or dereliction of duty. The Germans gave the luluai a black cap, and for some Mouk villagers this was significant, for it was like the raised black cap found on the head of a cassowary, a bird that some regarded as their original creator. The cassowary is also referred to as "the father of Varku," which is the tambaran that maintains order in villages by punishing transgressors. We see here the beginning of a certain mythologization of colonial power that trades on accidents or coincidences of meanings in order to use the new culture of Europeans to sustain and transform the world of tradition. Here initial accidents provide analogies that are good to think and act on—until the administration is able to impose its terms or, as was more the case, until new coincidences of meaning emerged to sustain new misreadings about the sources' racial power.

When the Australian government took over the administration of New Guinea from the Germans after World War I, it adopted and further systematized the positions of luluai and tultul. The rule of these "black hats" ended only when local councils were set up in 1967 (Counts 1968, 10–38).

Even then many bush Kaliai did not want to give up that measure of local autonomy and self-government that the system of indirect rule had established. The bush Kaliai have gone through various phases of embracing and rejecting government administration, development, schools, and mission influence. When I arrived in 1986, I found most bush villagers did not send their children to school or pay taxes. They were fed up with development projects and government promises of roads, schools, and aid posts. Aside from the villages of Bolo and Denga, located close to the Kaliai coast, Salke was the only bush village that was interested in the community school, the aid post, Sunday church services, running trade stores, and planting cash crops—cocoa and coconuts for copra.[8] Other bush villagers often criticized Salke villagers' interest in *bisnis* (business). Even in Salke, a significant portion of that village—those belonging to the men's house of Big Bird—regarded the setting aside of workdays for development projects as odious and a waste of time. Toward the end of 1986 the families associated with Big Bird walked away from Salke village to go and live farther inland, closer to the New Tribes Mission and away from the useless projects of bisnis. They were joined later by the families of Little Bird. One reason that many bush people gave for not heeding the government's calls to live closer to the Kaliai coast was that living in the bush allowed them to escape the close surveillance of kiaps, agricultural officers, priests, teachers, magistrates, and councillors (government council leaders). The disciplinary requirement of having to set aside certain days of the week for these officials and institutions was part of what people were resisting. People found this disciplining of time, labor, and bodies to be odious and coercive, especially because they also suspected that this work was a trick that Europeans, government officers, and missionaries were colluding on and foisting upon Melanesians so that they did not discover the true road of cargo.

Bush Kaliai villagers' opposition to development was based partly on their direct experience of its impact in other parts of New Britain, where they had seen development produce more crime, prostitution, a lack of respect for elders, and a general undermining of moral order. Many people have worked on plantations, generally around Rabaul, and they are critical of the hard work, small wages, low prices, and small returns associated with cash crops. People went to plantations to earn money to purchase clothing and cooking utensils. They were also attracted by the chance to enjoy a "European" diet of rice, tinned fish, and biscuits. Some bush Kaliai men who went to work in the wage-labor system of plantations and towns have never returned to their villages. Those who have returned have brought back little in the way of economic investment. Attempts by some to establish trade stores have invariably failed, partly because it is difficult for people to charge their kinsmen what are perceived to be the high exploitative prices of whites. Many bush people still criticize such indigenous enterprises as trade stores and cash crops. Many perceive bisnis to be immoral and associate it closely with the perceived selfishness and ungenerousness of whites. This antibusiness attitude is in direct opposition to the probusiness ideology pushed by patrol officers. Patrol Reports are full of harangues by kiaps against the perceived economic laziness of Kaliai villagers, which the kiaps saw as emerging first from "people's apathetic attitude towards working to help themselves," and second, from people's faith that their cargo cults had a better chance of delivering a European lifestyle (Patrol Report no. 6, 1973–74).

Those Kaliai who have worked on government stations and commercial plantations are familiar with what development means; invariably, these individuals are critical of the official claim that development is the road to a new *sindaun* (sit-down, i.e., existence). One effect of labor migration was that it allowed the bush Kaliai to come into contact with the cargo cult beliefs of other areas, and this often worked to confirm their own cargo cult beliefs. Kaliai villagers are familiar with cargo cults found on the island of Bali, the Pomio area, and the areas around Rabaul. I was given stories of how local villagers living in these areas had successfully used magic to make money multiply and to contact the dead. The mainland of West New Britain also has had many cargo cults with which bush Kaliai villagers are familiar (Chowning and Goodale 1965; Chowning 1990; Pech 1991; Pomponio, Counts, and Harding 1994). From conversations with bush Kaliai cargo cult leaders I know that they have a great deal of knowledge about cargo cults on the north coast—those belonging to the Anem, Lusi, and Lolo. Bush Kaliai villagers also travel frequently to the south coast, and they have told me how their relatives there have cargo cult beliefs similar to theirs. I have also discovered from archival documents in Port Moresby that many beliefs I collected in the Kaliai bush during 1986 also were collected in the Bariai-Kilenge area during the early 1960s by a Catholic priest who was stationed there, Father Rose. I believe that a great deal of overlap and exchange of ideas exists between different cargo cults in New Britain (Janssen 1970, 2). In this book I want to explore how this intertextuality emerges not so much out of the historical diffusion of ideas between regions but from the fact that certain beliefs and practices are good to think with (Levi-Strauss 1963, 1966, 1979). The political and intellectual work accomplished by certain beliefs and practices is what underpins their reuse in different cults at different places and at different times.

Earlier, I pointed out that when whites first arrived many bush villagers suspected that they were either a tambaran (mahrva), tewel, or masalai; that is, monsters who devour humans. In 1991 an old man, Bowl, told me how one of his classificatory fathers had been down on the coast and saw, as a reflection in water, the first white man to come into the Kaliai area. Startled by this image, Bowl's father turned to look behind him, and there he saw a German called Master Paris. Later this German organized local villagers to clear the land that became Iboki Plantation. Seeing the first white man as a reflection in water was significant because tambaran, masalai, and the souls of the dead often reside in water. In the Kaliai area the word for soul, **ano,** is the same word for reflection; this means that from their earliest memories people saw whites as emerging from the reflective space of water, which in traditional culture is inhabited by the dead and masalai. Many bush Kaliai still secretly believe that Europeans are the souls of the dead who have come back as white-skins. Indeed, villagers have been known to cry when seeing a new white man, for they believe they have recognized a lost relative. Australian kiaps patrolling in the Kaliai bush and, more recently, New Tribes Mission missionaries and I have all been seen as either ancestors or as spirit children. For the Kaliai coast Thurston claims that villagers were suspicious at what they saw as Europeans who were not expressing genuine grief at funerals; they also were suspicious of the flowers planted around European houses. Villagers also saw white bodies as similar to corpses: "Their pale, odorous skin, clammy to touch, recollects a corpse and connects Europeans with the spirit world" (Thurston 1994, 201).

As in other parts of New Britain a new genre of stories has emerged in the Kaliai bush that tells of Europeans living at the bottom of local lakes and rivers. These stories are similar to traditional stories about masalai, tambaran, and the dead who live in villages at the bottoms of lakes and rivers. The association of whites with cannibal monsters is so strong that people will sometimes become frightened if they unexpectedly run into a white man. In 1986 a man from Salke village described to me how he was startled by an American missionary who suddenly approached him while the villager was washing. He was afraid that this white man might be a masalai. On two occasions I produced similar fears when I traveled alone in the bush and ran into individuals resting near streams. These momentary fears are informed by popular stories that people tell of how a masalai, tambaran, or tewel can take on the appearance of a white person. Moreover, in much the same way that a masalai, tambaran, or tewel can steal someone's soul and make that person sick, so bush Kaliai villagers today sometimes attribute an illness to a person's having had her or his soul captured by these Europeans who reside at the bottoms of lakes or streams. In his dreams a shaman will travel to these sites, and he will try to rescue the captured soul of a patient by doing battle against the masalai, tambaran, or tewel that has taken the form of a masta (white man) or *misis* (white woman). These monstrous whites steal souls, often the souls of children, and they often do so not to eat them but to raise them as their own. I have argued elsewhere that these new sorts of illnesses are allegories that map the anxieties of parents concerning the capture of their children by a new Western culture brought by missions, schools, and state officials (Lattas 1993). These stories are an attempt to capture the world of the white man, which is now located inside people's bodies, illnesses, and terrains, where the menacing presence can be reobjectified, familiarized, and reworked.

Recent disturbances to the Kaliai environment by logging operations have also given rise to stories about white ogres who surface to menace villagers. One young man named Patrick from the village of Bolo worked for the Malaysian timber company and told me how a bulldozer had unearthed a large masalai stone. Later, in that same spot Patrick ran into a masalai who had taken the form of a white man. Patrick told me that many other workers had experienced similar meetings with these indigenous forms of Europeans. Here the violence that workers inflict upon the landscape comes back to haunt them in the figure of an autochthonous power that has been elevated to the status of the white man but in the process made racially distant to those owning and sharing the same landscape. Here new images of distance are emerging to mediate people's removal from the autochthonous powers of the earth; in particular, there has been a racialization of the distance that now separates people from the dead and from the underground. The white versus black dichotomy has come to be used to think about the surface world versus the underground world and the dichotomy of the living versus the dead. Traditional images of alterity associated with the dead and the underground are used to think about those distances that separate the lifestyles of Europeans from those of Melanesians. There has occurred a certain racialization of the underground and a certain indigenization of racial difference. The al-

terity of the autochthonous powers located in the earth and the alterity of
the white man become ways of thinking about each other's alterity and
each other's potential monstrousness.

The Kaliai's association of whites with masalai was also present in
people's grandparents' view of the clothes that whites wore and shed as
resembling the skins worn and shed by snakes, which are often seen to be
masalai. The perception of whites as cannibal monsters was also encoded
in people's early fears about eating the new sorts of food brought by Europeans. Bush villagers told me how many of their grandparents refused to
eat tinned meats because they feared whites were trying to trick them into
eating human flesh. People were revolted by and suspicious of the smells
given off by tinned meats. I see these emotions as encoding people's ambiguous relationship to commodities and to Europeans, that these objects
of desire might be full of the blood and flesh of people on which whites
have become tall and fat. Such beliefs position whites not only as living
off the flesh of other human beings but as also creating an exchange system
that gets Melanesian people to become unwitting cannibals. These stories
can be seen as allegories that warn people of what they might become if
they unquestioningly pursue the new desires that the white man has created and come to satisfy. Many old Kaliai people still refuse to eat tinned
meats because they are suspicious of the smells. When I offered food to
them, some would eat just the rice and not the accompanying serving of
tinned meat. Although young Kaliai villagers enjoy tinned meats, they
have apocryphal stories about how in towns human flesh is taken from
morgues and packed and recirculated as tinned meat. Inscribed in these
new forms of popular folklore is a critique of the world of commodities
(cf. Lattas 1993).[9] Its relations of production and exchange are rendered as
participating in a gigantic devilish form of greed that works to transform
Melanesians into monsters, into unwitting consumers of human flesh. I
see such beliefs as expressing people's ambivalent attitudes concerning
their desires for commodities and their participation in a new culture of
consumption that produces goods through social relationships that are
unfamiliar and that they cannot control. Foster (1995) has pointed out
that commodities are starting to create new sorts of people, new sorts of
Melanesian identities, and it is these transformations that I see as being
reobjectified into narratives of how commodities make people other than
human, without their being aware of it.

The close association of whites with the monstrous, with masalai, also
appears in early Kaliai cargo cult beliefs. Some people's grandparents
thought that whites were deriving their cargo from the feces of under-

ground masalai snakes. These early cargo cult beliefs resonate with traditional Kaliai myths that tell of how, in the past, people had received shell
money freely from certain holes in cave walls. This shell money was said
to be the feces of underground creatures, with the implication here that it
was the feces of masalai snakes, for they and the dead live in the underground. Early cargo cult beliefs that whites derive cargo from underground masalai snakes resonate with traditional Kaliai myths that hold
snakes responsible for giving humans various songs, paintings, masks, and
certain species of taro and sugarcane. Just as snakes were the source of
indigenous material culture, so people's grandparents assumed that snakes
must be the origin of European material culture.

A number of groups in the Kaliai area still trace their descent to masalai snakes. In 1986 I was told by an old man, who was knowledgeable in
cargo cult beliefs, that one bush Kaliai cargo cult leader had claimed that
whites had also originated from snakes, namely, from a certain species of
snake that had managed to have sexual intercourse with the Virgin Mary.
West New Britain villagers have many stories about masalai snakes having
had sexual intercourse with women. The cargo cult story of a snake that
penetrated the mother of the white man's God uses this local folklore tradition as an act of blasphemy against biblical truths. This story operates
as a revelatory statement about the monstrous nature of white identity
and of the false biblical truths that Europeans spread to disguise their true
serpentine origins. In this cargo cult story traditional Kaliai stories about
women who have been sexually penetrated by snakes have become fused
with Christian stories of the serpent in the Garden of Eden and the sexual
connotations carried by the Christian story of a snake that approached
the first mother of humanity. People have appropriated and reconstituted
biblical theology; they have fused their indigenous themes of serpentine
origins and phallic power with similar explicit and implicit themes in
Christianity.

RECENT CHURCH HISTORY

The absence of ready transportation into the Kaliai bush has allowed villagers to develop their own local black theology; it has allowed them to
keep their distance from direct, detailed forms of ecclesiastical control.
Until the late 1980s Catholic priests made only occasional visits to the
Kaliai interior, about three times a year in 1986. More recently, the new
priest has even stopped visiting the villages of Bolo and Denga, which are
readily accessible by dinghy from the coast. Many government and church

officials, along with villagers who live on the Kaliai coast, regard themselves as more civilized than those living in the bush, of whom they are often frightened. Coastal villagers have been more successful in educating their children, many of whom have gained access to various positions in the government, church, and education system. The coast now supplies many individuals who have become the politicians, teachers, aid post workers, magistrates, and catechists in the Kaliai area. These individuals dislike working in the bush and prefer to live on the coast where fish are plentiful and access to Western goods is better. Coastal villagers tend to regard bush people as ignorant, superstitious, irreligious, wild, and primitive. Bush villagers sometimes like to confirm these demonic images, and they gain pleasure from creating fear in those who try to claim administrative, ecclesiastical, and pedagogic power over them. There is a great deal of tension between coastal and bush villagers that takes the form of sorcery accusations between them. It also takes the form of violent fights, which break out whenever the two groups meet for sports activities or charity events (which often involve the consumption of alcohol).

The need to bring medical services, trade store goods, education, and civilization to remote bush villagers was one reason the New Tribes Mission was allowed to come and build a base at Amcor (Gigina) in 1984. The new mission offered coastal politicians an inexpensive way of being seen to bring development to an undeveloped hinterland. The new mission was from the United States, and it used an uncompromising fundamentalist style of proselytizing that was quite successful in the Kaliai bush. The new mission caused a wave of relocations as bush people moved farther inland to live closer to the new mission. Before 1986 the Mouk villagers of Aikon, Boimangal, Onamanga, and Salke had been living about two to six hours' walk from the coast.[10] When the New Tribes Mission arrived, these Mouk speakers abandoned their villages and pulled their children out of the community school at Bolo.[11] These villagers also gave up their coconut and cocoa plantations, which the administration had been encouraging. They renounced their Catholic Church membership and sought to develop a new church under the pastoral care of American missionaries who promised a new world of salvation. Local villagers who were appointed as "teachers" to spread the word of the new mission claimed that those who joined the New Tribes Mission would not die, sorcery would not be able to injure them, and their gardens would be fruitful and would no longer be attacked by wild pigs. The American missionaries encouraged these views with ambitious claims that prayers to God would be answered if people truly believed.

Since 1986 bush villages that joined the New Tribes Mission have been sufficiently stable for the government to set up community schools at Popmu and Amcor and aid posts at Angal and Amcor. Many see these new large gatherings of villagers around the word of God brought from America as reenacting the original gathering of Mouk villagers under God's guardianship when He, Moses, and Katika lived with the bush Kaliai. Many see the new mission as the Mouks' last chance to hear God's word and thus to redeem themselves for that original rejection that forced God, Moses, and Katika to run away from them to America. The new large villages have, however, made it difficult for people to find wild game. The relocation has also led to the exhaustion of soils and to poor gardens in the immediate environment around these villages. There is now a great deal of ecological pressure for people to establish gardens and villages away from the major New Tribes Mission settlements like those at Angal, Gigina, and Popmu. Some people have already done this, and this has sparked accusations from their "teachers" that they are betraying the last chance the Mouk have to demonstrate a unified commitment to God and that they are reenacting that *bikhet* (pigheadedness) of the past that led God, Moses, and Katika to run away. The teachers have good reasons to be angry and suspicious of people's movements away from the large New Tribes Mission settlements, for part of this is a desire by some to escape the regular church services and the new system of policing that the new mission has instituted to watch over its congregation.

GARDENS, BODIES, AND POLITICS

When they first joined the New Tribes Mission, many converts claimed their gardens now grew better and that this was a sign of God's support for the new mission—He had answered its followers' prayers for help. Opposing these claims were villagers who remained loyal to the Catholic Church. They complained about always giving food to relatives in the New Tribes Mission whose gardens were said to be in a poor state because God was punishing them for having deserted the Church of Rome. Here gardens are a political language; they are part of the competition between missions to woo and hang onto congregants by claiming better access to God's power. This use of gardens to objectify and evaluate the hidden powers that people call upon to situate their lives is not just confined to the modern period. It was also a feature of traditional competitive relations between men. They traditionally used their gardens as a sign of their access to a hidden world of magic that came from the dead. What is distinctive about the modern period is that gardens have come to be used to think about recent social changes. They have been used to think about the power of God tapped by the Catholic Church versus the power of God tapped by the New Tribes Mission.

Previously, gardens had also been used to think about the power of the white man versus the power of one's grandparents' pagan culture. In 1986 many Catholics told me that it was the coming of Europeans, and especially the church, that had led to declines in people's gardens when compared to those before European contact. Many old men blamed the poor quality of gardens, especially the poor state of taro crops, on the giving up of traditional magic. People spoke nostalgically to me about the taro grown by their grandparents: how huge and heavy the tubers were, and how eating a small piece prevented them from feeling hungry again quickly (cf. Kahn 1986).

Taro still has high prestige value; it is the preeminent food to give away at ceremonial feasts. A great deal of skill and magic is needed to grow taro, which makes it a source of pride to men who are able to grow large gardens of big heavy tubers. Today insects and taro blight have forced villagers to become more reliant on imported tubers like Singapore taro, sweet potato, and manioc. This is especially the case for villagers close to the coast who have to contend with hotter temperatures, lower rainfall, and the loss of soil fertility from overgardening around permanent settlements. Given the cooler climate found around inland streams and valleys, bush villagers are more successful in growing traditional species of taro. For bush people taro gardens have become a source of pride that they use to revalue themselves in a context in which coastal villagers dismiss bush people as uneducated, wandering, wild natives. Comparing their gardens to those on the coast, bush villagers negatively characterize coastal gardens as small and containing food that is not as heavy, strong, and satisfying as their bush taro gardens. Indeed, bush people dismiss coastal villagers (especially the men) as lazy individuals who don't have the strength, stamina, and bodies to work successful large gardens. A whole culture of masculinity has been projected onto taro gardens by bush Kaliai men, who now situate themselves within a culture of regional competition that often devalues them.[12]

It is not just the state of their gardens that people internalize into their identities but also the food from their gardens. Part of the power of food as a symbolic domain comes from the fact that as food moves into the stomachs of individuals it is seen as sustaining not just life in general but particular ways of living. The internalization of food is also an imaginary

process of consuming the categories embodied in food in order to internalize and produce certain kinds of corporeal identities and personhood (cf.
Schilder 1935). Thus some bush Kaliai today use differences in diet to
account for what they see as their greater capacity to endure hard physical
labor, particularly that involved in clearing rain forests and hunting wild
pigs. Bush villagers say their bodies have stayed heavy and strong like the
heavy and strong forms of traditional taro they still grow and eat. They
also say that the bodies of coastal villagers have become like the food they
eat—soft and watery. Here differences in diet and lifestyle brought about
by social change are internalized and used to create the identities of people
in different regions. I would argue that the different levels of incorporation
into European administrative structures are also internalized and embodied here. Those who have followed the administration's recommendations
and moved down to the coast come to be seen as having lost the strong
heavy bodies of their ancestors. Such beliefs render the civilizing processes
of colonialism, Christianity, and development as producing new forms of
corporeality, especially for men who experience the softer foods they now
eat as a feminizing process that softens men's bodies.[13] We see here the
ambivalent nature of colonialism and pacification. Although people may
embrace the task of being morally reformed by European institutions,
they also associate it with a sense of loss, particularly of a more robust
masculinity associated with the past.

So far I have analyzed how differences in corporeality are spatialized
and used to objectify the regional differences between the developed coast
and less developed bush. However, corporeal differences are also used to
internalize and objectify other social differences associated with the civilization process, namely, that between the older generation and the younger
generation. Older bush Kaliai men see themselves and are seen by the
younger generation as having stronger bodies and more savage, violent,
emotional dispositions in their stomachs than their sons, who are seen as
less fierce and more domesticated. These perceptions are part of a process
of cultural hegemony that today operates to marginalize the older generation from new institutions while empowering the younger generation,
which is positioned as having the bodies, and especially the cooler stomachs, to handle the new demands, routines, forms of etiquette, and knowledge brought by schools, missions, and government. The initiation rituals
that the older men underwent are seen as having given them a different
corporeal outlook on the world.

Through these painful rituals, with their accompanying strict diets, the
old men are seen as having acquired those emotions of fierce manliness

that underpin their identity as big men. Those emotions are often associated with heat and came from their "eating pain," along with the eating of ginger, lime powder, and various foods such as the "grease" (fat) of snakes. These rituals, along with a largely nomadic existence based on hunting, magic, and the eating of wild foods, gave the old men stronger bodies, with a capacity to endure more pain and work than the new weaker generation of men. The latter do not have the same sense of themselves as located in a hot warrior body; instead, they see their stomachs as having been changed, "turned," and made "cold" by a less nomadic existence, greater reliance on gardens, the church, and the moral training provided by community schools. The processes of pacification, Christianization, and civilization are lived out metaphorically within the body as a process of cooling it, of removing it from all those hot traditional influences that came from ritual regimes and dietary practices bound up with warfare, a nomadic lifestyle, and initiation rituals. The "cooling" influence of civilization has produced new corporeal schemes for the younger generation to inhabit; the level of emotional heat inside their stomachs has been dissipated. This embracing of new corporeal schemes allows young people to internalize the new identities produced through the influence of schools, missions, government patrols, and commerce. Those new institutions are doing more than producing new outlooks on the world, for they do this by also producing new ways of becoming a person; this latter process is what people are internalizing through the imaginary relationships they enter into with their new cooler bodies. The new social order comes to be corporealized or somatized, as young people come to live the projects of civilization and pacification inside the schemes of their bodies. It is here literally a question of being able to stomach the new world of the white man.

The turning cold of people's stomachs and the softening of their bodies and emotions are often spoken of positively, as things to be welcomed. Yet, alongside this position is a sense of loss and apprehension about the present corporeal state of the world. When I first arrived in the Kaliai bush, I was often told that since the arrival of Europeans the Kaliai had been getting smaller (Lattas 1991, 1993; cf. Clark 1989, Jorgensen 1985). Some people attributed the shrinking of their bodies directly to the coming of law, government, and the church. People spoke of their grandparents as "the big people," who were taller and stronger than their current descendants. These ancestors were able to lift huge stones and to throw spears that split stones in half. They had muscular legs and arms; it is said that the doors of today's houses would be too small for them to pass through. I was also told that because people's grandmothers wore grass skirts, children grew quicker. The European cloth now worn by women was said to be stunting children's growth. People also complained to me that their gardens were now not as fertile; they were producing smaller tubers that were not as heavy as the tubers of their grandparents. Some men blamed the coming of the Catholic Church for the new impoverished state of affairs; others blamed the introduction of steel axes for the decline in gardens. Many old men blamed the slow disappearance of a traditional world of magic and saw this as the reason gardens were in such bad shape. These old men mourned the loss of contact with the powers of the dead, whom their grandparents had invoked regularly in magical spells. It is in this context, in which people internalize and objectify their colonial disempowerment in terms of having acquired smaller bodies and less fertile gardens, that we need to situate the attempts by cargo cults to recontact the dead and to reestablish harmonious relations with them.

I see Kaliai cargo cults as a reaction against the threat of an end to the productive dialogue that people had maintained with the dead. In their cargo cults people often sought to hang onto their magical relationships with the dead, but they also started to modify how they contacted the dead. In particular, people started using European rituals, gestures, and technology as magical mimetic vehicles for capturing a European lifestyle that would be delivered by the dead. People started experimenting with what it was possible to believe, with what it was possible to copy and displace into the world of the dead, to magically get back that mimetic image in a realized form. It is this transformative power of the world of the dead, how it takes the simulacrum into itself in order to give it a reality, that I want to explore in the rest of this book. People used their newly mediated relations with the dead (provided by their miming of European culture) not just to acquire cargo but also to experiment with their social relationships and with the boundaries of their bodies and identities. They used the world of the dead to give back new ways for being a person, ways that were partly refractions of European values and forms of personhood but refracted through that world of controlled familiarity and distance provided by one's deceased kin.

Chapter Two

The Early History of Cargo Cults in the Kaliai Area

Before the arrival of the Germans around 1905, and even until the beginning of World War II, a number of cults in the Kaliai bush focused on the dead. In these cults the dead would come up to whistle at night, and people translated these whistles into meaningful words and even into conversations with the dead. People would give shell money and pork to the dead, who in turn would travel to distant areas where they would obtain betel nuts and tobacco for their descendants. I interpret the old men who remember these events of their childhood as having witnessed a culture of trickery similar to that which is today played out with tumbuan masks that children must be tricked into seeing as real. I also believe that people reconstituted this precontact culture of trickery involving the ancestors when Europeans came in order to form cargo cults that, as we shall see, sometimes involved cult leaders who tricked their followers with whistles said to be those of the ancestors.

Some other precontact cult ceremonies involved attempts to acquire gardens that would not require labor—gardens like those the Kaliai had before they wronged Papa (God) and He ran away from them. Two old men who are highly respected for their knowledge of local history, ritual, and myth told me separately about a cult before European contact that involved Censure's grandfather. He built a platform on which he hid and pretended to be Papa. He bored a hole in this platform and inserted his penis. Villagers then had to pass under this platform, and each would hold the penis of Papa so that food would grow by itself. It is said that this man's male relatives, who were aware of the trick, became angry, because they saw Censure's grandfather as inventing an excuse to have sexual contact with their wives, who were in an avoidance relationship with him. These men rose up, speared, and killed Censure's grandfather. Today people say that this man was working a cargo cult, although we might say it was a fertility ritual. The reinterpretation of this fertility ritual as a cargo cult fits in with people's perception that they had knowledge of lost cargo before the arrival of Europeans; it also fits into the strong sexual dimension of some bush Kaliai cargo cults, like that belonging to Censure.

Many people told me that their grandfathers had been secretly working cargo cults inside their men's houses well before the cults came to the government's attention in the late 1960s and early 1970s. The major patrol posts of Gloucester and Talasea were too far away to police people's thoughts in any detail; this was also the case for the Kaliai Catholic Mission Station. Many cargo cult stories that I collected from old men were told to them by their parents and even their grandparents. These are regarded as traditional stories, despite the often heavy presence of Christian imagery. The stories are said to have been transmitted from one Kaliai generation to another since the beginning of time, when Papa lived with the bush Kaliai.

THE JAPANESE AND THE BATARI CULT

Although I collected many early cargo cult stories, I found it more difficult to collect information on cargo cult ceremonies and rituals before World War II. The earliest ceremonies that people remember were those of the Batari cult, which came into the Kaliai area during the Second World War. The Batari cult originated in the Nakanai area. It was adopted by the Bakovi, who passed it on to the Kombei, who then passed it on to coastal Kaliai villagers, who then brought it into the Kaliai bush. The old men, who participated in this cult, remember wearing an arm band that consisted of a white cloth with a red circle on it. They remember how they were drilled continuously so that they would become trained "soldiers" who could later enter the war involving Australia, America, and Japan that they had heard about but that had not yet arrived. These old men remember the specific commands given by their military leaders and the accompanying swift disciplined gestures they executed (cf. Worsley 1957, 130). Yet, despite having good recall of these forms of military dressage, these old men appear to have repressed from their memories certain other details, like the fact that the arm band they wore symbolized the Japanese flag. When I asked them which side they were going to support in the war, the old men became uncertain and hesitant. This might be because Batari initially supported the Japanese, and people now are embarrassed to acknowledge this in the context of the American-Australian war victory and the romantic vision of America and its soldiers that people later came to adopt. Indeed, when I asked one man about his military training, he replied that he and other Batari soldiers were going to support the Australians and Americans: "We were his [Batari's] soldiers. Yes, we were to come up like soldiers so that later we could acquire gold and carry all the rifles and help all the Australians and the Americans with this fighting against Japan. He [Batari] worked it like this, so that we could all go to Australia." Most old men explicitly rejected my suggestion that they were to fight on the side of the Japanese, even though Thurston claims that for the Kaliai coast "older Anem remember that they had initially embraced the Japanese as liberators from the Australians, and since the Japanese ate taro, the Anem were hopeful" (1994, 201). It is difficult to know whether we are dealing with a certain collective form of forgetting that allows bush Kaliai men to live with themselves and their past, for memory is formed partly by the needs, desires, and perceptions that operate in the present (Bergson 1991; Halbwachs 1992).

In his book *This Crowd Beats Us All* Bishop Leo Scharmach documented how Batari initially saw the Japanese as liberators from the world of Australian colonial rule. Batari saw them as the good whites who would correct the injustices of the bad whites—the Australians and Germans.[1] Some Kaliai still regard the Japanese as the good whites, and they tell the story of how the Australians started the war between America and Japan. They say the Australians disguised their planes to resemble Japanese planes, which they then sent to bomb the Americans.[2]

Although they were in the Kaliai area only briefly, the Japanese were quickly incorporated into local understandings about the world of the dead. According to Samaga and Septireh (two old men belonging to Moluo village), many villagers were startled because the Japanese had names that seemed identical to the names of the villagers' deceased parents and grandparents. Edward (an old man of Robos village) claimed that many Mouk saw the Japanese as their returned dead. This perception was reinforced by the claims to immortality made by Japanese soldiers, who believed in reincarnation and in dying for the nation and the emperor. Many bush Kaliai villagers heard Japanese soldiers claim that they were like kunai grass—if they were cut down, they would just reshoot and come back to life. Today many Kaliai say that the Japanese purchased the law of immortality (along with their good existence) from the Americans, who in turn received it from God after He ran away from His Kaliai relatives. Indeed, some Kaliai see death as God's punishment for black people because of their stubborn refusal to listen to Him. Censure's son, Posingen, explained it:

In America if a man dies, they do not worry. If a man on top [an
above-ground, living man], one of those they call an outlaw, works
something [a wrong] then a knife will cut him. If a man steals, they will
just cut his neck, saying: "He is just going to go, but he will come
back." They will cut him through the neck, and this no good body will
be disposed of, but the person who died will come back. It is not
enough for him to die and to go completely. . . . My father said: "It is
different with us, we were pigheaded to Papa [God] and when we die,
we go completely, we do not come back." But you whites, like the Japanese and the Americans, when you die you all come back. For you
heard the talk of Papa. However, we of Papua New Guinea it is like
this: before, we, our ancestors, saw God but they were pigheaded to
Him, and so now when we die we go completely. But you heard the
talk of this Man and so there is nothing to it, when you go, you just
come back.

Many bush Kaliai men who were recruited by the Japanese to carry cargo
came back with stories of how the Japanese must be the dead, for they
had heard the Japanese speaking the local languages of Mouk and Anem.
This perception of the Japanese as the dead was strengthened when the
Japanese built some camps around Mount Andewa, where the dead traditionally went to live. When he was young, one of the major Kaliai cargo
cult leaders—Censure—worked alongside Japanese soldiers; Posingen
gave me this account of his father's experiences:

He storied to us about how the Japanese said: "We are Japanese, we
are not afraid to die, we just keep coming back." My father was with
the Japanese at Alulu, with all the villagers of Pureling. He told us they
were working there night and day, carrying cargo. A large ship [possi-
bly an amphibian tank] would come bring cargo, and it would travel all
the way into the bush. It was not as though its "tail" [stern] would rest
in the saltwater. No, the large ship came all the way. They would then
go and unload this cargo and stack it into huge piles.

Posingen went on to tell me how one day his father boarded a large Japanese ship and was taken below by a Japanese comrade and offered food
to eat.

Inside this large ship were all speakers of Mouk. All these Japanese
were speaking Mouk. Father went down below and wondered: "How is
it that all these men talk Mouk?" The Japanese man replied: "You can-

not start thinking." His *boi* [Japanese companion] spoke to him: "This
here is a war, and now you have come, and you cannot worry about
hearing this language of Mouk. You cannot speak out about it. We,
who have come to fight here, are mixed people. It is not as though one
group has come to fight, we Japanese are mixed. You can hear this, but
it must remain with you and it must remain with us." All right, they ate
this food, and this boi said: "Let us go now." But when he said it, he
said it in Mouk. They then jumped off the ship onto the ground.

When the Japanese spoke of themselves as mixed people, the Kaliai interpreted it to mean that the Japanese were made up of many Kaliai language
groups that had returned for this war. Many old men came back with
similar stories of how the Japanese behaved in ways resembling returned
ancestors. What confirmed this interpretation was that the Japanese
placed taboos on certain streams that people were no longer to fish or
enter. The Kaliai interpreted this to mean that the Japanese were claiming
special sites as their territories, sites that were to be respected in the same
way that people had respected the special rivers and pools belonging to
masalai and the dead, which traditionally people were not allowed to fish
or enter. I was given this account of how, when people went to certain
streams to catch crayfish, they were scolded by the Japanese and ordered
to use other streams: "The Japanese would be talking in the languages of
Mouk and Anem warning people and crossing people: 'Why have you
broken this law? Why did you come into this area? Why didn't you follow
this other river? This river belongs to us!' Everywhere you went you would
be hearing the Japanese speaking Mouk."

The restrictions that the Japanese placed on people entering certain
areas, where they were concealing military hardware, was reinterpreted by
people as the dead seeking to hide the special locations in the mountains
where ships went with their cargo. One woman, Theresa, whose father,
Nausung, had worked with the Japanese, told me, "My thinking is that all
these people were gathered there in this area, because there was a door [to
the underground] there." Other Kaliai villagers, like Monongyo, believed
the war disturbed the ancestors of the Mouk and Anem who now decided
to come out from beneath the ground. Monongyo explained it like this:

> With Andewa, it is an inhabited village [*ples*] and when the fighting
> came to Andewa, close to this [invisible, underground] village of Alulu,
> all this line of Mouk and Anem all came out to fight, for there is a
> door there. Its meaning is this, that if fighting comes up in an area,
> then those [dead people] belonging to the languages of that area will

join this fight. Now I think, with Andewa, all the Mouk and Anem
who have died have gone there. When the fighting started there, this
line of people came up speaking their languages, for they live in
this area.

Along the Kaliai coast some villagers did more than just carry cargo for
the Japanese. They also helped the Japanese fight the Americans. At Pureling and in the Lolo area the Japanese gave some villagers guns, which
they used to shoot down U.S. planes. Later, when the Americans came
and recaptured the Kaliai coast, one individual was executed. People's
perception of the Japanese as their ancestors led some to see West New
Britain villagers' early participation in the war as aligning them with the
underground dead against the Australians and Americans. This was a period in which the dead had decided to break their isolation from the living,
and the war seemed to offer the promise of a new unity with the dead.

   The Japanese were incorporated into other cargo cult understandings.
Edward told me how, after they carried away Japanese cargo, more would
magically appear in the same spot. Another old man, Tigi (of Bolo village), told me how he and other Batari soldiers went and waited for cargo
to magically appear in a cave along the River Banu where some Japanese
had sought to hide when the Allied soldiers retook the Kaliai area. He
spoke of his disappointment that, despite waiting a few nights, they saw
nothing.

   After the Japanese were pushed out of the Kaliai area, some bush Kaliai men were recruited by the Americans to go with them to Buka Island
to fight the Japanese. Today these old men remember fondly the hospitality of U.S. soldiers who shared "freely" European food and clothing,
something still referred to as the law of (*lo bilong*) America. "Law" here
refers to the manners and customs through which people organize a way
of life. These old men came to see the Americans as the good whites, as
opposed to the Australians who had always blocked the good law of
America from coming to Papua New Guinea (Thurston 1994, 201–202;
cf. Worsley 1957, 196–97; Lawrence 1964). Like elsewhere in Papua New
Guinea, in the Kaliai area it was at this historical point that cargo cult
stories changed, with the black god of the Kaliai now running away not
to Australia but to America. World War II entailed a new globalization of
local mythology. The war forced people to refigure the spatial boundaries
of the outside world, and many sought to reconcile the alterity of America
with the alterity of the dead and of the mythic past. The sight of massive
amounts of military hardware that, along with food and clothing, was left

behind by U.S. soldiers led people to focus on an alternative white man whom they could romanticize and juxtapose against the coercive rule of Australian administrators, missionaries, and planters. In the Kaliai area (as in other parts of New Britain) there are stories of how, when their local god wanted to return to his *as ples* (home ground) to do for them what he had done for whites in America, he was prevented and indeed killed by the Australians. The Australians did this because they feared that if everything were free, there would be no need for "boys" (*boi,* laborers) to come to work on Australian-owned plantations in Melanesia. I was told it was not the Australians' continued access to goods (for that would have continued) that led the Australians to kill this local god but more the need to maintain their plantations and a culture of servitude. This murder of the black god of Melanesians becomes that secret mythic founding event that made Australian colonialism possible (cf. Girard 1986; Serres 1991). These stories about a hidden murder construct secret local histories for white rule; these histories confer secrets upon the races as the internal bonds of their solidarity. Here racial conflict is traced in myths of origin to the rule of a law founded in the blood of a black god. His death maintains the cleavages and secrets of a social order built around suffering black bodies.

INTERSECTING FORMS OF MIMESIS

A certain militarization of the dead and of ritual life was one major effect of the war on cargo cults in New Britain. The new law of Batari involved drilling men in the morning and afternoon in various forms of military discipline, like standing at attention, saluting, marching, turning to the left and right, and in carrying "rifles" in all sorts of positions. People referred to these military routines as *lo bilong gavman* (law of government), and through them people expected later to *sindaun* (sit down, live) like whites. Those who followed Batari's law were called his "soldiers," and the long stick they carried was their "rifle." In the Kaliai area these marching rituals were seen as a way of enticing the dead from the underground. Kamonga, an old man from the village of Bolo who participated in this cult, told me how this was a time when people started once again to run frequently into the dead. Indeed, at night people were required to walk around carrying a firestick so that others would know they were living people and not the dead. Kamonga also told me how, while they were marching and being drilled, they would sometimes see the dead marching and being drilled in the distance, in the same way that they were. Here people were performing the ceremonies of power belonging to whites in order to entice and capture the dead inside a new ritual law of government. Through their mimetic practices people sought to bring the dead close not only in terms of proximity but also in terms of behavior. Somehow the joint performance of common military rituals by the dead and the living promised and anticipated a future reunion in a new common culture. Here it is not Europeans who will bring the true "law of government" but a cult that uses the more powerful rituals of Europeans to seduce the dead into coming out to perform these ceremonies.

Kamonga also told me how Batari's soldiers were required to do guard duty and how once when it was his turn he saw a line of *tewel* (dead people) marching. He complained to me that when he yelled "Halt!" to them, they did not respond correctly, by coming to attention and saluting him; instead, they vanished. On another occasion Kamonga tried to catch one of the dead, who managed to escape by transforming himself into a "pussy cat" and then a stick. Kamonga had been on guard duty when something like a cat approached and stared at him. Thinking it might be one of the dead, Kamonga held up his "rifle" and yelled, "Halt!" Startled by his yelling, the creature jumped into the air and landed on the ground, where it turned itself into a stick. Kamonga picked up this stick and carried it to his commander, complaining that it had failed to return his salute when he yelled, "Halt!" Together they went and promptly tied the stick to the central post of their men's house. In another version of Kamonga's story given to me by someone else, Kamonga was on guard duty when he tried to capture a dog, which turned itself into a man and then into a piece of firewood that was later tied to the post. The next day this stick was shown to everyone in the village to confirm people's belief in Kamonga's story and their faith in the cult.

Each of Batari's soldiers was required to carry a stick, known as a rifle. The rifle was carried across the shoulder and brought down to attention at the appropriate command. It was said that when the new law "broke" and a new existence came up, this stick would turn into a real rifle. One of Batari's ex-soldiers told me that they were being trained in how to capture the dead in order to grab them and bring them forcibly into the world of the living. The Batari cult, as it spread from village to village, developed an enormous military apparatus for capturing the dead. An alternative military state or government was being created wherein the disciplinary rituals of European culture were seen as superior techniques for evoking, capturing, and incorporating the lost transformative power of the dead. White power was partly familiarized and indeed indigenized as European

military rituals became magical practices directed toward contacting Kaliai ancestors, who now started to perform them. A space of death came
to inhabit the ritual forms of the European state, and its effect was to
produce a certain indigenization of state power, an attempt at localization.
The ritual framework of the European state acquired a certain magic; it
came to be familiarized and domesticated by being appropriated and directed toward one's deceased kin.

Part of the Batari cult's indigenization of state power lay in the way
neighboring groups exchanged the military rituals of the European state
in a way similar to how people had traditionally exchanged the "laws"
governing new tumbuan masks, tambaran rituals, and other ceremonies.
Ideally, a village had to give a pig and other food so it could "buy" the
new law of Batari, which was also how villages traditionally bought the
rights to new rituals and ceremonies. It was explained to me that if Bolo
had been schooled in Batari's law, Bolo could later pass this law on to
Aikon in return for pork and other food. Aikon could then pass Batari's
law to another village, like Angal, which had yet to acquire it. Some bush
Kaliai villagers who received Batari's law from close kin did not buy it.
The Batari cult spread partly in this rhizomatic way throughout much of
West New Britain, even though the "king" of this cult, Batari, did not
visit many areas that adopted his cult. Despite the focus on King Batari,
and the appointment of local commanders, the cult did not have an effi-
cient centralized military structure that encompassed all its regions. Instead, it exploited local relationships of kinship and exchange. The cult
also expanded by exploiting each local community's longing for reconciliation with its dead and each local community's understanding that its
dead were central to the production of the white man's wealth.

Many of Batari's soldiers believed that by correctly working his strict
laws of military dressage they would be transformed into whites. Here
the process of becoming white was located not so much in adopting and
understanding European disciplinary practices in exclusively Western
terms but more in recognizing these practices to be rituals and thus similar
to indigenous rituals. This reinterpretation of European rituals displaced
them into alternative worlds of representation that lay outside the direct
control of Europeans. The process of copying the white man came to be
mediated through alternative local bodies of knowledge that positioned
differently the mimetic relationship between images and that to which they
referred. Here non-Western magical understandings of mimetic processes
came to take over those official pedagogic understandings of mimesis that
underpinned the use of disciplinary rituals in missions, schools, and gov-

ernment institutions. In the process of making themselves white, people also redefined the ritual terms and performances for becoming white. Other forms of mimesis came to underpin the experience of being colonized; that is, the experience of being disciplined and morally transformed was no longer kept in white hands. Instead, indigenous forms of mimesis came to mediate the process by which people assumed responsibility for the task of making themselves white. In cargo cults the experience of becoming white was mediated by certain traditional processes of becoming (like magic and relations with the dead) that served not only to familiarize but also to deflect and remake colonial disciplinary processes of becoming white.

It was no accident that European marching rituals were associated with a magical transformative power, because whites themselves imbue those same disciplinary rituals with a certain creative, formative power, namely, the goal of producing a more civilized person. The desire to transform people into disciplined moral subjects was the reason that soldiers and police were drilled in marching rituals, and it is also why Melanesian schoolchildren today are marched continuously by their teachers (cf. Elias 1939; Foucault 1977; Morrison 1982). The notions of pedagogic progress and social change contained in European disciplinary rituals were congruent and supportive of people's millenarian understandings of the transformative power of ritual. Cargo cults appropriated and recontextualized the millenarianism of the state and the pedagogic transformative power of state rituals within an alternative millenarian culture that had its own vision of the magical transformative power of ritual. What I am arguing is that the technology of mimesis, which Europeans used to transform people, came to be reinterpreted from a magical standpoint that had its own understanding of how mimetic ritual gestures can transform the world. Much of the conflict between colonial authorities and cult followers can be seen as emerging from the intersection of two competing forms of mimesis that misread each other's processes of copying and each other's processes of transformation through copying.

WOMEN AND THE BATARI CULT'S MILITARIZATION OF
MEN'S CULTS

I want now to look in more detail at the military aspects of the Batari cult, at how it took up European imagery of death and violence, which it reconstituted into a ritual "law" for gaining access to the Kaliai dead. We have here a folding together of different rituals of death and of different cultures of terror. Throughout much of New Britain Batari's soldiers were feared and seen as a law unto themselves. One former Kaliai follower told me how Batari's soldiers had "cooked" a European priest for blocking the law in the Nakanai area. In the adjacent Kombei area Batari's soldiers destroyed Catholic Church buildings. An old Kaliai catechist, Lucas, told me how he and other catechists were attacked and had to hide from Batari soldiers who came from the Kombei area. Yet the violence of Batari's soldiers was only partly directed at whites and their institutions, with the aim of driving them out of New Britain. This was also a form of masculine violence directed at local women; men affirmed their new collective identity as soldiers through their violent intimidation of women. Batari's soldiers were feared and seen as a law unto themselves partly because of numerous stories about their claiming the right to rape women. Indeed, this was part of how people saw the *lo* (law) of being a soldier, and perhaps here they were not entirely mistaken. When Batari's soldiers visited distant villages, women would run off into the bush or lock themselves inside their houses. One of Batari's laws was that no woman was allowed to cross in front of a line of marching soldiers. They could legitimately rape any woman who did. This was referred to as the "bayonet" of the soldiers eating the woman. Likewise, any dog or pig that crossed in front of marching soldiers could be shot without compensation and, in the case of a pig, eaten by the soldiers.

The fear these soldiers produced was used to police village relationships, such as making sure everyone paid their debts. It was also used in domestic relationships to enforce the obedience of wives to husbands. Jakob Laupu (a respected storyteller on the Kaliai coast) told me how he was visiting the village of Taveliai when a group of Batari's soldiers arrived from the Kombei area. At Taveliai a woman had run away from her husband, and her father-in-law, who was angry at her actions, reported her to these visiting soldiers. They punished her by making her carry a heavy sack of dirt on her head while she marched all day inside their ranks. The Batari cult also held out the punishment of gang rape for disobedient women. Although this cult punishment was not practiced or sanctioned in the Kaliai bush, it was reportedly practiced among neighboring Kombei and Bakovi groups and on one occasion on the Kaliai coast. In the Kaliai bush men were more likely to use the fear of gang rape to bond with each other and with neighboring militarized groups of men. Traditionally, in the Kaliai area gang rape was a punishment used along the coast against a woman who violated the taboos and secrets concerning men's tambarans.[3] The Batari can be seen as reconstituting traditional men's house cults, which were now expanded to encompass the new ritual solidarity of men who were using the gestures of a Western military state as the common language of their power over women. Here the governing framework of a European state, which people had been resisting, was internalized and used to provide the symbolic framework for a new codification of men's domination of women. As part of this transformation of European military culture into a huge male cult for terrorizing women there also occurred a certain militarization of gender relations that reconstituted local forms of governmentality between men and women along lines that copied European forms of governmentality (cf. Burchell, Gordon, and Miller 1991). Here those ordering military routines known locally as lo bilong gavman created a new disciplining of women in which men administered the disciplinary regimes of a powerful European state as their new culture of terror.

Today ex-soldiers of the Batari cult in the Kaliai area mention proudly that they did not practice the "law of Batari" concerning the rape of women, as had the neighboring Kombei and Bakovi. Septireh told me he still thought Batari's law was a true law, but because Batari's soldiers had gone and "buggered up" the women, this law had become "blocked" (*pasim*). Kamonga also thought that Batari had been working his law (*wokim lo*) correctly, and he blamed the Kombei for twisting the meaning of Batari's work.[4] Kamonga went on to tell me how Kombei "soldiers" had gang raped a woman from his village of Bolo. She had married into the coastal village of Lauvore and had initially gone there to live, but later she and her husband left and came back to live at Bolo. This woman was referred to as a *hapkas* (half-caste, descended from different groups), and the Kombei soldiers who raped her were partly her own "line," which is in accordance with the traditional custom that calls for a woman to be punished by her relatives. However, as a half-caste this woman also had relatives in the Kaliai bush; when they heard she had been raped, they came down wearing warfare decorations and carrying spears. Afraid, the Kombei responded by grabbing a real rifle and holding it up as a threat to the bush people. The latter, however, somehow knew that the rifle had no bullets, so they responded cheekily by taking out their penises and holding them up to the Kombei. The Batari cult declined in the Kaliai interior soon after this episode. It probably had lasted only a few months.

When I asked Kamonga why this woman was raped, he replied that she and her husband had broken Batari's law by running away from Lauvore village. Kamonga explained that Batari's soldiers required villagers to "sit down good." People were told that if they did not do so, they would miss out on cargo when the new law of existence arrived. Yet this requirement that people settle permanently in a village was also a new requirement that the administration pushed and enforced through regular patrols and annual census lineups. The Batari cult also adopted other administrative requirements, such as Western notions of village cleanliness and hygiene. The cult merged different understandings of order and different regimes of violence to produce a certain militarization of everyday life that encompassed the ordering world of the dead. Here Western forms of order were merged with the *lo* given by the dead, that is, with that framework of order that was made up of the songs, rituals, and customs given by the dead to the living. On the one hand, the state and its symbolic framework were constructed into a male cult. On the other hand, the culture of men's cults was reconstituted into a "law of government" and into an enormous military apparatus for resisting whites. The traditional violent underpinnings of gender relations were recontextualized so that gender solidarity and conflict became a vehicle for racial solidarity and racial conflict. Worsley (1957) was partly right when he argued that cargo cults are embryonic forms of nationalism that unite different groups into new forms of wider solidarity that transcend traditional local loyalties. However, the Batari cult realized this by transforming the bonds of solidarity between men that were part of male tambaran cults into racial-military bonds of solidarity that were grafted onto local domestic concerns and local exchange relations.

THE MADNESS OF MIMESIS

In addition to military rituals, cargo cults have often mimed other aspects of European behavior, such as forms of hygiene, body postures, important roles and identities, and certain gestures of respect and etiquette. One finds handshake movements, the suitcase movement, the submarine movement, cults organized around people having their own offices (also known as "hot houses"), police forces, or around people finding their own banks and maintaining their own forms of bureaucracy and accounting, and in Fiji even cricket clubs with their own governor, chief justice, and chief secretary (Lawrence 1964, 204–13; Steinbauer 1979; Williams 1923; Worsley 1957, 38, 75). These unauthorized forms of impersonation unsettled many colonial authorities, who interpreted this behavior as an example of people unable to cope with the stresses of social change. Williams, one of the first anthropologists to systematize this interpretation, saw these mimetic practices as a form of madness (Williams 1923; Lattas

1992a). Writing about the Vailala movement in the 1920s, Williams referred to cult followers as "automaniacs." The signs of this Vailala madness were villages that received messages from spirits to make a feast, tidy
up the village, be clean in eating, and wash their hands. These actions,
which copied European habits of cleanliness and order, would not have
disturbed colonial officials, except that people did not sanction these new
practices by referring to Europeans as the source. Instead, people referred
to spirits and the dead, with whom they were communicating through
possession and trance. What perhaps most disturbed Europeans was this
paradox—people using their superstitious past to enter the modern world;
here traditional culture was empowered by people's processes of becoming
white. I believe cargo cult followers copied European habits of hygiene
and discipline because they recognized in them images of moral order,
correctness, and propriety; that is, they recognized in them a new and
better law of existence, which is also how Europeans presented these pedagogic forms of dressage. People went further and interpreted European
habits and disciplinary rituals using their understandings of the magical
power of ritual acts, wherein to mime something was often part of the
process of assuming some control over it.

The bishop of Rabaul, Leo Scharmach, applied the European view of
Throughout Melanesia in magical rites copying is a way of coming into
contact, bringing close, and realizing that which is copied. In bush Kaliai
cargo cults people often copied the ordering regimes, rituals, and gestures
of white culture as a way of capturing those secret magical acts that would
deliver the European existence they copied. In the Vailala movement this
copying led followers to be defined as mad. What this definition expressed
was a European concern about losing control of the civilizing process,
that is, those pedagogic forms of dressage that would make villagers like
whites. The transformative power of mimesis in Western disciplinary rituals here starts to go in directions that escape, yet also imitate, the pedagogic projects of whites (cf. Morrison 1982). The mimetic process of becoming white becomes ambiguous and unreliable for colonial, state, and
church authorities, whose pedagogic rituals come to be taken over and
directed toward the world of the dead. Madness as a category of colonial
rule is a way of policing that destabilization of pedagogic activity that is
involved when people appropriate the civilizing project by displacing and
mediating it back to themselves through their dead.

The bishop of Rabaul, Leo Scharmach, applied the European view of
the mad mimesis of cargo cults to the Batari cult. In his book *This Crowd
Beats Us All* Scharmach used satire to describe certain "mad" scenes when
Batari declared himself "king" and his wife "queen."

The Cargo madness was in full swing at Nakanai on the north coast
of New Britain. Batari had proclaimed himself Commander-in-chief
and even King of all Nakanais. His force were 600 men strong, armed
with spears, bows and arrows and sticks for drill. As he had no money
to pay them, he gave each of them a young girl. He selected the most
beautiful one and proclaimed her queen. He dressed her in high-heeled
shoes and ladies' long dresses, looted from the neighbouring plantations. The Ten Commandments of God were abrogated and replaced
by many more of his own devising. Even decent native customs were
abolished and replaced by unrestricted license, rape, murder and terror.
(235)

Later in his book Scharmach showed how Europeans used comedy to
laugh off people's hijacking of European roles and mannerisms. Describing the period after the war, Scharmach wrote:

Batari is no longer king and no longer commander-in-chief of all
contemporary and ancestral Nakanais forever. He is a common villager, tending his garden and going to church as all the others do. . . .
Batari's wife is no longer queen and does not walk about in high-heeled
shoes and ladies' long dresses. To be frank, she says it was a nuisance
anyway. Now she dresses in a scant grass skirt and feels more comfortable, especially about the feet, which no longer ache as they used to do
during her royal days of exaltation. What a pleasure to go barefooted
again! (238)

I believe what most disturbed Europeans were cult activities that did not
so much deny as redirect Western processes of cultural assimilation. What
disturbed missionaries, settlers, and government officials was that ambiguous merging of past and present, tradition and modernity, Melanesian and
Western, inside and outside that cargo cults enacted. I see cargo cults as
producing peculiar forms of outsideness and insideness, unusual forms of
double alienation and double incorporation, that take the form of situating people both inside and outside the realm of Europeans and both inside
and outside the realm of their own tradition. People come to experience
themselves as caught between cultures; their marginality emerges from
their between-ness—not fully this and not fully that (cf. Kapferer 1979; V.
Turner 1969). This structure of double alienation and double incorporation provided a liminal world in which meanings and identities collided,
became resynthesized, and transformed. In cargo cults identities often underwent remarkable metamorphosis, with changes in the structure of iden-

tity becoming a way of working out and realizing the desire for a changed social existence. By focusing on other material about the Batari cult, I now want to explore more fully the politics of people's incorporation and reworking of European selfhood.

SWAPPING SOULS AND BODIES

One major colonial figure who wrote about Batari was Jack McCarthy. Before World War II he was the government officer in charge of Talasea. In his book, *Patrol into Yesterday,* McCarthy describes in detail some other ways that Batari tried to play with the boundaries of his identity as a way of recomposing and unsettling the existing racial structure of the world. McCarthy quotes Batari as telling him that the spirits of the dead came to him at night and informed him that the two of them had swapped souls:

> You and I, Makati . . . died some months ago but we did not know it. We still walk and talk but our spirits are gone from us. At Porapora I am often visited by the tambaran who come to me at night from the volcano at Pago. A month ago three of them came to me while I slept. One of the spirits carried a pressure lamp so that I could see them well. They told me this, "Makati is our friend but he is now dead—and you, Batari, are also dead. The spirit of Makati has now entered your body while Makati's body now contains your spirit. So you must go and tell Makati this, our message!" "In a short time all the whitemen and all the Chinese will leave New Guinea. They will go and not return. The goods that the white spirits have prevented the New Guinea people from having will then be distributed to the New Guinea people. Tell the kiap this for he is Makati, our friend." (189)

Through dying and swapping souls Batari and McCarthy came to live inside each other's bodies. In effect, they took on the role of miming each other's behavior. In death they met and exchanged identities, with this exchange becoming the ultimate act that prefigures and enacts the coming reconciliation of racial differences. Throughout this book I explore how in various cults the Kaliai often sought to refigure the world by pushing the boundaries of their identities into the corporeal schemes occupied by Europeans. What the quoted McCarthy material on Batari shows is how people often located processes of creation in the body, the refiguring of which, as a site of identity and cultural order, provided a means for enacting utopian processes of social transformation wherein people could become other than themselves. The power to create the world anew came to be personified as it came to be embodied in the mimetic task of occupying the space of alterity provided by the body and being of the other. We are dealing here with the embodied nature of images of self-transcendence in a colonial social order in which relationships of power were firmly located in racialized bodies.

Batari's millenarian dream subverted the racial codification of colonial inequalities by blurring the corporeal identities of the existing social order. By moving the white kiap's soul into his black body, while his Melanesian soul went to inhabit the white kiap's body, Batari's dream introduced a certain instability and ambiguity into colonial identities. His dream posited and created a new set of hybrid identities that seem to produce through a different route that same hybrid Melanesian identity that the colonial order sought to produce through missions and development.[5] Chapter 7 explores how Kaliai cargo cults came to appropriate and rework this colonial production of what Burridge (1960) termed the "new man." What often happens in cargo cults is that the pedagogic production of new forms of Melanesian identity by European institutions comes to be reorganized and assimilated to a magical worldview haunted by the doubling metamorphic power of ghosts, spirits, and the dead. The process of becoming white starts to move outside the pedagogic control of state and mission as it comes to be mediated by an alternative worldview that uses dreams, spirits, and the dead to produce new hybrid identities and new ways of becoming white.

It is not through schools, missions, and development but through spirits, dreams, and the dead that the black body can transcend its racial positioning and that knowledge given to Melanesians by Europeans. Through the alternative world of dreams Batari discovered that the spirits of Europeans have colonized and gained control of the space of death. This alienated lost world of power and knowledge must be regained in order to free black men in the present world. The world of the dead is made to underpin and create the lived visible world of existence. Indeed, throughout this book I explore how people construct their liberation as having to be achieved through liberating their world of ghosts. Batari explained it to McCarthy like this:

> The spirits came to me at night. . . . They are the ghosts of men
> long dead who inhabit the volcano of Pago near my village in Nakanai.
> God intended that the black men and the white men who live on earth
> should have equal possessions and so God made all the ships, the mo-
> tor cars, the money and the clothes and the knives, axes and tools, so

that the spirits could distribute them to all who live on earth. These
things reached blackmen as well as white men until the spirits of the
dead who live at Pago quarrelled. Then the white spirits proved too
strong for the black.

The spirits of the black people had no goods to send to their descendants on earth. All the things that God made were held by the white
spirits so that our people in New Guinea are left without these things.
The spirits who come to me at night are the ghosts of my people. They
have told me how to defeat the greediness of the spirits of the white
men. They have told me that to break the power of the white man's
ghosts, the living people in New Guinea must do certain things. If my
people obey me, the goods that God has made will be freed and so they
will reach my people.

The spirits command that all food gardens in the village be destroyed and that all coconuts be cut down. . . . All pigs, dogs and fowls
must be slaughtered and left to rot and no man must eat. Houses must
be broken and the people must sleep in the rain on the ground. Without food and houses the people will suffer, and when this takes place
God will help the spirits of our people so that they will regain power
and give the New Guinea people the goods that the white men have stolen from them. (1964, 180–81)

Here we see clearly the way the world of the dead was figured as determining how life was lived. The material wealth of the living was created by
ancestors who sent it to their descendants, but along the way whites stole
it. The white man's power comes from controlling the place of death. His
otherness is conferred by the otherness of death. He displaces and appropriates the power of the dead to create present inequalities. Moreover, he
actively works to seal off access by Melanesians to the space of their dead.
Many cargo cults are organized around undoing this closure; they seek
to unravel the tricks and secrets that sustain the white man's privileged
relationship to the dead.

NAMES, COINCIDENCES, AND TRUTH

Cargo cult stories are often about how certain individuals through persis-
tence, ingenuity, and unique circumstances are able to circumnavigate the
publicly given knowledge of whites. One such story tells how Batari went
to Talasea and there he saw some cargo with the word "Battery" on it.
Batari tried unsuccessfully to claim the cargo from government officials,

arguing that his name was on the cargo because it had been sent to him by deceased relatives (Mair 1948). In the Kaliai bush I collected many similar stories that also rely on unique circumstances and coincidences of meanings to confirm people's suspicions that the existing world is a huge deception perpetrated by whites. Throughout New Britain many people believe that whites are changing the labels on shipments of cargo, that they remove the names of Melanesian people and substitute their own. Philip, a catechist from the Pomio area who has been living in the Kaliai area since 1980, told me about similar beliefs among Koriam followers in the Pomio area. He told me how, after a big man named Sale died, some of Koriam's followers went to Rabaul and saw a car with a "For Sale" sign on it. When Koriam's followers returned home, they told people that Sale must have sent this car for his children.

> This big man died, his name was Sale. He belonged to my village of Mile. Before, when this cargo cult of Koriam came up strong, there was a car which had been shipped and on top of it they had written "For Sale." Everyone stood up and said it belonged to this big man Sale. They all stood up and said: "Hey, this something he works at [in the land of the dead], the name of the big man stops on it. He wrote it, his name is on top of it, and he sent this car to come to his children. It is now waiting in Rabaul." They all came speaking like that. They lost this "sale," and they made it like Sale. This thinking of theirs, they received it from Koriam, all this thinking belonging to cargo, and they say that "this big man [Koriam] talks true. All our cargo, cars, planes, all our line that has died has worked it all and sent it, but all the masters work at fouling all this."

One big man on the Kaliai coast who was convinced that the Australians were fouling the cargo asked me why Australian harbormasters kept turning back ships coming into Rabaul. He did not believe their claim that these ships had illnesses (*i gat sik*). He was also suspicious of the rule that required harbormasters to check the cargo of overseas ships. He saw the Australians as checking that no cargo from the dead slipped past their control to reach Melanesians. This big man then went on to use this narrative scheme to explain the current inequalities that have emerged between different Melanesian groups that have uneven access to Western goods. He explained that for some reason the names of the Tolai were not removed or rubbed out as thoroughly as the names of other Melanesian groups. This meant that when the Tolai boarded overseas ships their names were still partly visible, and they could recognize and claim the cargo sent by their dead relatives.

These stories are partly about the lost power to assign names and to control the world of naming, which passes through the world of the dead. As such these stories resonate with traditional magical spells that require the names of the dead or secret names from the dead. The traditional power of names to create something new and to reorder the world has been elaborated and sustains a popular folklore cargo cult culture that speaks of Melanesian heroes who stumble across and undo that controlled world of naming and labeling that sustains European power and those of certain elite Melanesian ethnic groups. Many Kaliai told me what they believe to be the "true" story of a Tolai man who boarded an overseas ship and recognized his father's name on a car. He took its keys and drove the car into the hills. It is said that the Australians searched frantically for him for two days; then they heard that the car was seen in a certain area, so they went there and arrested him. The Tolai man was taken to court for theft by the Australians, who claimed that the car was not his. However, in the courtroom the Tolai man responded with this awkward question: "Whose name is it that sleeps on top of this car?" Embarrassed and silenced by this disclosure, it is said that the Tolai man won the court case but that the Australians paid him a large sum of money to keep quiet about what had happened. What such stories illustrate is the way cargo cult beliefs are no longer concerned only with explaining black-white racial inequalities; they have become concerned with explaining the regional inequalities that now exist between different Melanesian groups. Here the new forms of participation in white culture by certain Melanesian groups are sustained by hidden payments, secret forms of sharing, that transform those Melanesian groups into accomplices, people who are expected to be complicit in hiding the role of the dead in the production of commodities. These stories posit a new structure of secrecy as having emerged to underpin the new structure of regional inequalities that now exist, giving some Melanesians, with the secret consent of whites, access to the wealth of their ancestors.

Laupu told me another Kaliai cargo cult story that seeks to explain the new regional inequalities between Melanesian groups. He claims that when God ran away to America He ran westward and not eastward, as is claimed by most other Kaliai cargo cult stories. Before God arrived in America, He stopped off briefly among the Tolai and gave them some of His knowledge and secrets. As Laupu put it, "The good God went to you, made a school come up, made your existence all right. He went to the

Tolai and made all the Tolai come up all right. But not us because we were *bikhet* [pigheaded]." Laupu went on to say that this was why the Tolai now had shops, cars, corrugated iron-roofed houses, and why some had even been able to marry white women.

TIGI: POLICING THE POLICE

Running through many cargo cult stories is the theme of transgression and knowledge, of a black man who stumbles across the white man's secrets and who is then persecuted for his disclosures. One Kaliai villager seen in this light is Tigi. He was a police constable who was dismissed after he returned home for a two-and-a-half-month leave in 1963. While in the Kaliai area Tigi used his position and travels as a police officer to give credibility to his claims to have uncovered the white man's secrets. A report at the time stated: "He was one month overdue when he was caught spreading false reports in his home area" (Patrol Report 1963). Tigi had been part of a police guard assembled in 1957, when Prince Philip, husband of Queen Elizabeth, arrived in Port Moresby. At the coastal Kaliai village of Kandoka Tigi organized a large meeting that included villagers from Bolo, Biliku, Lauvore, Taveliai, Ketenge, Gilau, Dauli, and Kariai. Wearing full uniform and standing in front of the kiap's rest house, Tigi delivered an address in which he claimed the queen's husband had said: "All of the 'Cargo' that is in Australia does not belong to the Europeans. Your ancestors produced all these goods. . . . I sent a man to check and see if you people of Papua and New Guinea were getting your 'Cargo' but this man did not find out for me as he was killed on route [*sic*]" (Patrol Report 1963). We see here the theme of a good white man who tries to find out and rectify what has happened to the cargo sent by the dead. There is also an accusation here—that certain people (by implication Australians in Melanesia) have a strong interest in maintaining the existing state of affairs and so they kill the king's messenger.

In his recorded confession Tigi claimed that the district commissioner—Mr. Foldi—knew that what he had said was true and so did Sergeant Penge of Kandoka village, who reported Tigi's claims to the authorities. In fact, Sergeant Penge had been with Tigi as part of the police guard assembled around the queen's husband. The administration's response was to dismiss Tigi, but it first sent him to Rabaul to be examined by a doctor for a mental ailment—ostensibly a mild form of epilepsy. The suggestion here was that his stories were a product of mental disorder. The following confession was extracted from Constable Tigi on September 6, 1963:

I am Constable Tigi. I am a policeman in the Royal Papua and New Guinea Constabulary. When I was only new in the police force I went to Port Moresby to meet the "King." The "King" said, "You people hear this story." I heard it—he said, "If you go back to your villages you can tell this to your people. When Queen Elizabeth comes she will show you the place ("banis") and speak to the man that looks after this place. The Queen would go and ask him, "What about this place? Why has it stayed idle for so long?" The man said, "if you want to come inside this place you will have to pay tax. You cannot combine ("bung") the tax, you have to halve it. Half will go to the Government, the other half will go to God." The man told the Queen, "If you like, you can go to Port Moresby and talk it over with the 'King.'" The "King" told us this in Port Moresby and said, "Where ever you go you can tell this story to others at your place." The "King" continued, saying, "The Queen had found the place and told me to pass this message on to you." He told us this in front of his big house in Port Moresby. The "King" also said, "All the cargo that comes from this place is for all of us, native and European. But at the moment there is a man sitting between this cargo and ourselves and that is why you have not received any." The "King" through his interpreter said, "You should all clean your graves good. When we all die they will bury us there. You know the European graves are all clean ones and they decorate them well." This Morobe who was at this meeting took a photo of a grave of his forefathers and had it developed. The people who developed the film asked him (Morobe man), "Where did you get this picture?" He answered them, "It is a photo of the grave of my forefathers." The people who developed this film told him that they had better check with the government about this picture. The Government called for him and asked him where he took the picture and he answered them, "I took this picture only because the flowers appeared beautiful." The Government told him that this grave is strictly forbidden to be photographed. The Morobe went to gaol for this. The government continued saying, "When you fulfil your gaol sentence you cannot take more photos" and the Morobe said that he would not. I returned to the village and told the people this story. Aipau told me that he would call a meeting of all people and I could tell them the story. I told them the story on Friday. (Patrol Report 1963, Gloucester)

We see in Tigi's story that the queen emerges as the potential liberator of Melanesians. She finds out that the cargo has been blocked by "a man"

Tigi in 1995 when I interviewed him. He died soon afterwards.

and sets about having it freed. Although the queen spoke of a man who was blocking the road, in 1995 I interviewed Tigi about this, and he informed me that this man was "talk-box" (speaking in a concealed way, allegorically) for the mission: "The mission blocked this road, for it worked talk to go to the government, and then the two of them together went and blocked it." Given that the colonial administration was staffed largely by men, we see here a hint of the way gender can provide a way of thinking about an alternative form of power that transcends or exists outside the ruling order. When I focus on Censure's cult in Chapter 4, I analyze the way a certain destabilization and inversion of the gender dichotomy provided the mythological and ritual terms for destabilization and inverting other dichotomies of power like the white-black racial dichotomy. There I will further document how the queen could be seen as offering an alternative regime of existence in which what is subordinated—namely, the feminine—comes to be acknowledged as the true ultimate form of power, capable of undoing those immediate forms of male power

that engage people. In Tigi's case the queen comes to be associated with the revaluing of the importance of the earth, graves, and traditional Melanesian beliefs about the dead. The revaluing of the feminine and its elevation to a position of exemplary state power are associated with the revaluing and freeing of all that the white man subordinates and conceals.

Cargo cult discourse often creates its effect of truth by positioning itself as revealing the concealed. Truth figures as the hidden coming into the world of light (Derrida 1979; Heidegger 1977; Nietzsche 1886). There is here the pervasive idea of revelation, that surface meanings and appearances are not the complete story, that truths are secret and emergent rather than immediate. One repressed truth that surfaced in the case of Tigi involved why whites kept their cemeteries in such good order. In his confession Tigi mentioned how a Morobe man had photographed the graves of his ancestors and was jailed by white officials who wanted to hide the truth about graves.

> Formerly all the people in Papua and New Guinea were all right. One day a Morobe man took some pictures of the graves of his ancestors. This New Guinea man took the pictures and then sent them to be developed by Europeans. The Europeans saw these pictures. When they saw these pictures they asked the New Guinea man, "Where did you get these pictures?" The New Guinea man replied he took the pictures at the graveyard. The Europeans asked, "Who informed you to take pictures at the cemetery?" The New Guinea man replied, "It was my idea." The Europeans then said, "You cannot do this, we are keeping this a secret. Now you have discovered this secret." (Patrol Report 1963, Gloucester)

Kaliai villagers who heard Tigi's account claimed that when the Morobe man had his photographs "washed" (developed), the colorful plants next to the graves were no longer visible as plants but as the faces of people who lived long ago.[6] When I asked Tigi about these photographs in 1995, he told me that these ancestors took the form of Europeans; they had white skins. Here the camera becomes a magical tool of revelation, providing an alternative vision of the world, namely, that provided through the eyes of Europeans. The camera is associated both with Europeans and with vision, and these two associations are fused such that the camera becomes that alternative way of visualizing the world possessed by whites. In another Kaliai cargo cult run by a woman called Melo in the late 1970s, the camera was again used to reveal the world as different from the way it appears to the naked eye. She would photograph her followers and tell them that later they would see themselves with white skins. We need to note that through their pictures cameras relocate the world by creating a double of it. In Pisin this representational double is referred to as tewel and in Mouk as **ano,** both of which also mean *soul.* In traditional culture the alternative world of the dead was also a double of this world and so were the souls of people that were spoken of as tewel or ano. In traditional Kaliai cosmology the picture of something was also its soul, the spiritual essence, or double, of an object or person. Most magical spells in the Kaliai area work by operating on a "picture," on the soul (ano, tewel) of the object to be manipulated or captured. Cameras participate in this magical relationship between representations and the reality to which they refer. Images capture the hidden reality of objects, their secret form—such that the colorful plants at a grave are revealed in photos to be the living dead, who now have white skins. In providing an alternative positioning of objects within the world of representation the camera becomes associated with the alternative hidden reality of objects, which in traditional culture is their souls. The camera relocates and displaces the very world of objects it reproduces, and this is why the camera can become a magical instrument in cargo cults and a vehicle for alternative visions of other worlds. In other words, cameras displace the world into another medium of existence offered by the space of representation and in doing so seem to promise that relocation and displacement of existence that the cults are interested in magically producing. Cameras are good to think with in cargo cults because they offer the promise of an alternative second existence, which they partly realize in the way they materially reproduce the world outside the world.

As a technology of mimesis, cameras are also a device of memory. They hold out the promise of more powerful mnemonic techniques that reside in the hands of Europeans, who seem to have better ways of accessing the dead. The traditional rituals in memory of the dead, to honor and summon their presence, become merged with the memorializing techniques of whites (their photographs, cemeteries, and flowers). Participating in the common work of memory and mourning, cameras acquire the characteristics of traditional rituals that focus on summoning, disclosing, and tapping into the world of the dead.

Villagers who were present when Tigi was arrested told me that his fellow police officers turned around and chastised him. They did so not for making up stories but for acting so naively in revealing these secrets when he knew that the government wanted them kept concealed. Many villagers still believe that Tigi was not punished for spreading false stories but for breaching certain requirements of complicity that his role as police officer required. In particular, he breached certain taboos about revealing what he had heard at the meeting and what he knew about the photographing of graves. One man likened what happened to Tigi to the withholding of information by the church "when it [the church] comes inside Papua New Guinea, it does not reveal [*autim*] the true law but holds back the law." Another man, Thomas, told me that Tigi was punished because Tigi reported the queen's prediction of a coming new law. The queen predicted a day when the sun and moon would appear on opposites sides of the sky, and then the sun would change. This was said to be *tok bokis* (talk-box, an allegory or metaphor) for a new time. A new way of lighting up the world is the image for talking about an end to those dark secrets that sustain racial inequality. The queen's message was that the Last Day (as referred to in the Bible) would come soon, and then another kind of man would appear, which was taken to mean the dead.

I heard a number of other stories about Tigi. Bowl, an old man who joined the New Tribes Mission, gave me the following story of how Tigi had long ago discovered the power of God's written word, which they— New Tribes Mission converts—were now trying to find. This story was about Tigi's time as a police officer on the mainland of New Guinea:

> There was a man from New Guinea. He was of the Catholic Church. He stood up and said [to his congregation]: "Youse are always being pigheaded [bikhet], youse are bikhet for what reason? Do you want me to work something in front of you, so that you see it with your own eyes, so that you believe?" Another man rose and said: "And you will work what? Are you God?" Then another man from New Guinea also stood up and said: "Is it true or are you are talking humbug?" This man here—the catechist, he then stood up. . . . All the men were sitting down, and he stood up and talked. . . . The catechist picked up four leaves of paper, he hung them up like this, and he said: "All right, all of you see this. I will preach first." Then he started preaching. When he was finished, he said: "All right, you see this paper." Now one leaf of paper rose and started preaching, copying his sermon. When it finished, another rose and preached again. When it finished, another stood up and preached. When it finished, yet another rose and preached again. When all this was finished, he said: "Now you have seen this, now you must all believe. All of you must sit down, sit down good. Do not be bikhet and roam around in the bush." That's all. Tigi saw all this in New Guinea. He came to us and storied about this.

I said: "This something is like this. We are of the islands. This belongs to our big island; later this something will find us. If there is a strong man here, he will acquire that belonging to us, and we will then be able to see it as well."

This account calls upon people to give up their nomadic ways, to become settled domesticated subjects under the pastoral care of a Melanesian church. Tigi's story here calls upon the Kaliai to discover someone of strength among them who might release the power that lies sleeping around them. There is here the empowerment of a new sort of Melanesian man whose power comes not simply from tradition but from discovering the world of magic that is hidden in the cultural texts of Europeans now in Melanesian hands.

All these different stories about Tigi gained credibility partly because he had been a police officer. It was no accident that Tigi wore his police uniform to address his large audience and that he was standing outside the *haus kiap,* that is, outside the house that all villages had to build as a rest house for visiting government patrol officers. In the 1960s another bush Kaliai man, Aikele, retired from the police force and returned to the Kaliai bush, where he started a cargo cult at Bibling Ridge. Aikele used his close ties with certain European kiaps to legitimize his claims that he had access to the secrets of European wealth and power. Both Tigi and Aikele are examples of how the colonial state never fully captured the indigenous population it incorporated in its administrative structures; indeed, it often lost control of them. In different parts of Melanesia, police officers—like the cargo cult leader Yali described by Lawrence—have figured prominently in cargo cults (Lawrence 1964, 121; Worsley 1957, 57, 79–80, 185). Indeed, Lawrence (1964, 59, 98–99, 118–19) saw cargo cults in the Madang area as having been influenced by the 1929 Rabaul strike that native police had joined, along with plantation laborers. In addition to Tigi and Aikele, I know of three other police officers in groups adjacent to the Kaliai who came back to their home villages with cargo cult stories. I believe that a strong cargo cult subculture developed within the colonial police force and that it amounted to an alternative ideology of state power. Those recruited as native police became caught between the contradictions of two ways of codifying power—those of traditional myths and of Europeans—which they set about resolving by reworking and blending local folklore traditions with the iconography and rituals of state power. When these individuals returned to their villages, they often became powerful local leaders who used their access to the state to create an alternative, unorthodox semiology of state power. Here we should note that Tigi's fellow police officer, Sergeant Penge, who reported Tigi to the authorities, was, according to the administration's report, "also not sure if Tigi's story was true or false—a fact that indicates how gullible these people still are."

KORIAM: POLITICS, MONEY, AND TRICKERY

The other interstitial group that often figures prominently in Melanesian cargo cults is politicians (Bettison, Hughes, and van de Veur 1965; Chowning and Goodale 1965; Trompf 1991). They often became caught up in the millenarian dreams of their followers and within the millenarian dreams of the state, which had its own ambitions to reshape the world. It was not just the "natives" who had ideals about a radical new, better world, for the institutions into which politicians were incorporated also had a utopian agenda. The institutional millenarianism of the state sought to realize its utopian ideals through a pedagogic culture that used disciplinary rituals, council government, development, schools, missions, and educational talks by kiaps.[7] In the Kaliai area speculation that the world would soon change radically was especially pronounced around the time that elections were held to mediate the transition from colonial rule to self-government and independence. A certain millenarianism of self-autonomy existed within the political discourse of the state; its political education campaigns promised reform, a better world that elected representatives close to the people would deliver through good administration. Throughout West New Britain, cargo cults have often fed off the expectations of change created by state elections, the arrival of new missions, new forms of currency, and new development projects. Here official processes of change, transition, and reform were hijacked by other utopian projects that did not trust whites to deliver real change but that instead placed their faith in a reworked world of black magic, with which people felt some identification and control over. The state's promise of change and progress was appropriated and integrated with local perceptions that saw a familiar world of death as the true source of all changes in wealth and power. We are dealing here with the transformation of images of transformation— the language of change that accompanied new Western institutions was assimilated into those forms of change that people sought to realize through ritual practices directed toward the dead. I want to explore such issues by focusing on the next major cargo cult: that of the politician Koriam, whose cult arrived in the Kaliai area in the early 1960s.[8]

Like Batari, Koriam never came to the Kaliai bush. Instead, his cult was carried up from the south coast of West New Britain, where Koriam was born. Today Koriam's movement survives in the Pomio area. Koriam's movement did have some early success on the northwest coast of West New Britain. Although there were no official councils in the Cape Gloucester area in 1965, unofficial councils were linked to the Koriam movement. These councils provided an alternative structure of administration to the European colonial state. According to a 1965 Patrol Report, the Koriam movement had appointed its committee members to a number of villages in the Kilenge-Lolo Census Division:

> It is the duty of these committee men to ensure that . . . children go to school. Other fields covered by these committee men include health and agriculture. Basically the idea is sound but unfortunately the majority of the committee men are very young . . . often with a history of cargo cult activities. The Village Officials of the area, with very few exceptions, do not have the drive and initiative which marks a leader and reflect the generally apathetic attitude of the people as a whole. They confine their activities to catering for various patrols' needs and do an excellent job of concealing any minor problems that the village may have. (Patrol Report 1965, Gloucester)

In his notes on cargo cults among the nearby Lolo, Father Rose (n.d.) documents the deification of Koriam, which was occurring as the 1964 elections approached. Koriam was reported as saying that the dead would soon come back from their graves. Even those who died from now on would come up to Koriam, and he would tell them that they could not die, for the dead now wanted to come back to the living. Koriam was said to be like God; when he spoke, things would appear out of nothing. If a man ignored Koriam's talk, Koriam would take this man down a road, and the man would vanish. Other Koriam cult beliefs include the claim that the areas that people had cleared to plant coconuts were not really for coconuts; this was simply the *tok piksa* (cryptic, allegorical talk) of the government. Instead, these areas were to wait for the dead, who were going to return and work their villages there. Another belief involved the story of how Koriam met his deceased father and mother, who told him to take a cloth and put it down on a grave. After a while money came raining down on this cloth. When it was full, Koriam carried it back to the village. Father Rose also records his informant as saying:

> Yet another talk, they all say God originated from here in New Britain. However all the big men of long ago, they killed him. All right he

ran away from us and he broke a piece of the ground which went with him to America. At that time, there was man called Kaikmata who stayed with him in America. Now, at this time, at the time of the *Eleksen* [election], he wants to come back to us and it is for this reason: all the time, all our grandparents, fathers, mothers and maternal relatives have been sending all the cargo belonging to us but all the masters have been removing all our labels [*ol is rausim namba bilong mipela*] and they have been putting all their labels on the cargo. All right, God was sorry for us and he sent Eleksen to come up to us so that later everything belonging to us would come straight to us. All right now in 1964 they all say that God and Kaikmata will both come. When they come we will see the sea crowded with ships and the sky crowded with planes.

Here we see the theme of a black god wronged by his people, indeed killed by them. He becomes resurrected and goes to the land of whites, who benefit from his knowledge. In 1994 a group of Kaliai villagers who visited the Lolo area told me how the Lolo had informed them that "they killed Jesus and he sleeps in their bush; they say that they themselves, their ancestors, killed him." The bush Kaliai believe that this god who was killed by Lolo villagers was their trickster god Titikolo, who is known for changing his name as he visits different areas. Each group in the Kaliai area has stories about the different tricks that Titikolo performed and that led their ancestors to chase him away. We have here the formation of a black theology that has a regional basis that ties people together in interdependent schemes of complicity and guilt. Each group is partly responsible for helping to chase away this god, and each now shares the punishment for having done so.

In Father Rose's information we can see that this black theology also posits that God comes to forgive the kinsmen who chased Him away. The election is God's attempt to reempower those He had punished. Here the election campaign language of the state, with its token promises of black power in a legislative chamber, becomes transformed into other "truer" images of black empowerment—namely, the return of a black Christ and of the dead. A frequent feature of cargo cults in West New Britain is that they have been often inspired by, and felt validated by, the political transformations and education campaigns that colonial officials put in place to mediate and "clarify" the transition to self-government and independence. Chapter 3 describes how Censure's movement in the 1970s claimed that its cult rituals brought about independence and a new national flag for Papua New Guinea. When the no. 2 patrol for 1974–75

came up to Angal village, scared villagers told the patrol that their councillor, Posingen, the son of the cargo cult leader Censure, had said that "if
the day of independence comes, that two bombs will be dropped in our
village." Many bush Kaliai equated the coming of independence with the
coming of the Last Day, which Censure's cult sought to bring about
through rituals directed at the dead.

Today in the Kaliai bush Independence Day celebrations (held September 16) are occasions that still generate millenarian expectations. These
are major spectacles that draw together villagers, politicians, government
officials, missionaries, and visiting and resident Europeans. Different language groups come together to perform various *singsing* (festivals involving songs and dance), often as part of a competition. These ceremonies
are more tightly choreographed than some traditional singsing pretend to
be; the decorations and paintings are more uniform and the dances are
more disciplined and regimented. These official spectacles in honor of the
nation and its roots in people's customs are a stimulus to all those cult
followers who likewise seek a new ritual formula for solving the nation's
problems. These celebrations are officially justified as helping the nation
by producing solidarity, peace, and goodwill between the diverse groups
and races that attend and that make up Papua New Guinea. These celebrations are a giganticizing of the state and of ritual and, accordingly, they
feed the cargo cult focus on the nation as requiring spectacles, ceremonies,
and rituals.

One man, Imokeh, told me how on Independence Day in 1985 the provincial member for Bariai spoke to people at the mouth of the Banu River.
He informed everyone that the first prime minister of Papua New Guinea,
Michael Somare, held something in his hand and that after forty years of
independence this something would be uncovered. Imokeh told me that
everyone's interpretation was that the new law of equality and cargo would
then be finally revealed. Imokeh went on to tell me how he had also associated Independence Day celebrations with the coming of a new law of existence. A few years ago he gave a letter to the New Tribes Mission to pass
on to the government. The letter requested government funds to hold an
Independence Day celebration that Imokeh believed would release the law.
According to Imokeh, the law was a big stone and the celebrations would
lead to its shattering into small pieces that would unblock and free the
new law of existence to come to Melanesia.

On the Kaliai coast the introduction of decimal currency in 1966 also
had the effect of reviving millenarian expectations that the world would
be remade according to a new system of value. A patrol from Gloucester

in 1966 recorded the following beliefs of Mopi and Moro, two cargo cult leaders from the Kombei area who spread their message along the northwest coast of West New Britain:

> Mopi and Moro held Kivungs [meetings] at Taveliai, Pureling and Tumunai. The main theme of these "kivungs" seems to be—When the Germans came they came with their gold, there was no law, they gave us knives and axes and we worked for them. Then the Australians came, there was no law, they gave us knives and axes and we worked for them. Then the Japanese came but they did not stay long, they came only to fight. Then the Americans came and gave us money and everything was all right. Now when February comes a law will be broken and we will sit down on our land and everybody will have money the same as Europeans. I understand the reference to a law being broken means that when Decimal Currency arrives everyone will be given a handsome share of the money and that all the people will have as much money as the Europeans. The money will be just given to the people for nothing.

For Mopi and Moro the introduction of decimal currency promised a new world of value, which would be a more moral world similar to that more equitable and generous treatment of Melanesians practiced by the good whites, the Americans. This would be a new world in which Europeans would no longer be able to block or misappropriate the cargo sent by people's ancestors. Mopi and Moro's influence was confined mainly to the coastal areas and did not penetrate the Kaliai bush. Yet their millenarian expectations about decimal currency were reenacted in the Kaliai bush in the 1970s, when Papua New Guinea adopted a new national currency, kina, that many bush Kaliai also expected to inaugurate a new world of value for Melanesians. When this did not happen, people complained to me that whites had been able to "pocket" (steal) the money that should have gone to the bush Kaliai.

In all these movements we see cargo cults seizing upon moments of social change for that moment of otherworldliness embodied in the new state of affairs that they foretell and promise. This officially authorized and administered new state of affairs comes to resonate with the cult's sense of the otherworldliness of a future that incorporates the other world of the dead. As part of this mythologizing of social change, certain politicians like Koriam (and Michael Somare), who were centrally involved in mediating these institutional changes, came to acquire an aura of magic, if not divinity.

Most bush Kaliai found out about the Koriam movement through their contacts with relatives on the south coast. In the 1960s, when bush Kaliai villagers visited the south coast village of Soren, they noticed that Koriam's followers had cut down many coconut trees. When I asked Samaga, who had seen this, why the trees had been cut down, he answered, "They cut them down so the law would break [come]," and he quoted Koriam's followers as saying: "These coconuts came up with all the masters, and they are blocking the law." On the south coast Koriam's followers also exposed the secret cult items of the men's house to women (cf. Worsley 1957, 128). The masks of tumbuan were exposed and so were the tambarans Varku and Mukmuk. Samaga and his son Paul gave me this description of how two of their relatives went down to Soren, where they participated in these activities:

> Paul: Now my two grandparents, the father of my wife and my uncle Kulo, they all went there, and they joined all the as ples [home villagers], and they had this something [the tambaran] come up [that is, into the open]. This was the work of Koriam. This was its head [toward the end of the work]. They revealed all this something—Varku, tumbuan, and Mukmuk and all the women saw it.
>
> Samaga [*INTERJECTING*]: They all said that this something [men's house secrets] was blocking [pasim] the law, so they were going to make them all come up so that the women could see them, and then the law could then come up. . . . This something is sin, it is something we hide, it is *pekato* [sin]. The talk of Koriam was like this: this was sin, it should come up so that all women could see them, and the law would then come up.

The Koriam cult's exposing of men's secrets to women started on the south coast and came up as far as the bush Kaliai village of Benim, which is about two days' walk from the Kaliai coast and about one day's walk from many other bush Kaliai villages. At Benim the men decorated themselves like women: they put on the grass skirts of women, and they cut coconut shells in half and fastened these to their chests to symbolize female breasts. The men then came out singing, "We are all women now, we are all women now." Bush Kaliai men who heard this story recognized and agreed with the gender symbolism of the Benim men's actions. As Septireh put it: "Yes, yes, its meaning goes like that. When something like this comes up, like this here [exposure of men's secrets], then we men are just women." Septireh then told me what he heard had happened at Benim:

I didn't see it, but they storied about it. They held a meeting, and they sang during the night. When dawn came, they brought tumbuan [masks] out from the **silasila** [fenced enclosure]. This man whose name is called Mokeh, he has now died, he carried a tumbuan. He stood in the middle, and all the men and women were around him. The big men then spoke: "Do youse know the person who is standing up here?" Now all the women were *longlong* [ignorant]. After a while Kisa went and removed the tumbuan mask. He took it off, and there was Mokeh, he was there standing up. All right, they tied Varku [a bull-roarer tambaran] to a stick and brought it in front of the eyes of women. Now with Mukmuk [bamboo wind tambaran] they dug a hole and put it inside [to blow it]. They then worked a huge fire and put everything onto the fire. Now all the women who saw this something, they are all finished, they have all died. There are now all new women.

These Koriam cult activities were not taken up in the rest of the Kaliai bush, where men also resisted joining activities along the north coast that exposed men's house secrets to women (Counts 1968). In the Kaliai bush, people focused on Koriam as embodying an alternative form of government to Europeans'. A patrol from Gloucester in 1962–63 reported that inland Kaliai villagers were claiming that Koriam had been holding meetings on the south coast, "telling the people that he has the permission of the government to hold these meetings, and that his job is to make new laws for the natives." Kaliai villagers were waiting for Koriam and his meetings to arrive in their area. People were quoted as saying: "He [Koriam] is going to rouse [purge, expel] all the poison [sorcery] out of us [natives]." Koriam here takes on the cleansing mission of using the new law and powers of the state to rid Melanesians of their use of sorcery to kill each other. Most Kaliai cargo cults with which I am familiar have operated as antisorcery movements—that is, as part of a desire to rid black people of the sin of sorcery, which God gave to Melanesians as a punishment for their bikhet (Lattas 1992c; cf. Marwick 1975).[9] Kaliai villagers see sorcery not only as a murderous impulse but also as a monstrous way of maintaining order to which black people have to resort to punish transgressors. Europeans were exempted from this murderous regime because they treated God better.

Koriam's popularity in the Kaliai bush was partly the result of a folklore tradition that developed around him. Many stories exist about white colonial officials trying to murder and torture Koriam, but he always manages miraculously to escape from them (cf. Worsley 1957, 34–35). These stories are humorous, and they celebrate Koriam's heroic escapes from his white captors and his transcendence of their devilish and cruel schemes. I see the feelings of empathy for Koriam created by these stories as partly resonating with the pain that people have felt at the hands of Europeans. The stories that I collected about Koriam in 1986 and 1990 were similar to those outlined in a 1962–63 Patrol Report. The report claimed that the stories had been carried into the Kaliai bush from the south coast by Lamogai villagers. The 1962–63 patrol recorded these stories about Koriam as

a) Put in jail several times, accumulation of which extends to 7 years
b) Boiled in a 44 gallon drum of water by government officials
c) Rolled down a mountain in a 44 gallon drum by government officials
d) Been sent to Australia
e) Hung by his hands and legs over a fire
f) Been to Rome to see the Pope (Patrol Report 1962–63)

In the versions of these stories that I collected, Koriam was equated with the cheeky mannerisms of the trickster hero known as Titikolo, who in traditional mythology was chased away by the Kaliai. When people's ancestors tried to kill Titikolo, they would inevitably find that he had escaped, and he would taunt them: "Who are you trying to kill? It is me over here!" When telling the stories of Koriam's escapes from white kiaps, people use the same teasing taunt: "Who are you trying to kill? It is me over here!" In one story that I heard, the kiaps tried to throw Koriam out to sea in a forty-four-gallon drum, but by the time they returned to the wharf, Koriam was there waiting for them, saying: "Who are you trying to kill? It is me over here!" People get a great deal of pleasure from repeating this cheeky retort, which resonates with the pleasure they get from repeating the retort of their trickster hero Titikolo. As we shall see shortly, for many Kaliai Titikolo is a black Christ or Moses figure, who in some stories is reported as having been killed by whites. Koriam's stories resonate with the themes of this black theology that surrounds Titikolo. Indeed, Posingen speculated to me that whites had killed Koriam because of his success in politics and because Koriam was striving to become the "boss of all the whites."

AIKELE: DEVELOPMENT AND NARRATIVES OF TRANSGRESSION

I have so far analyzed the way political changes, election campaigns, Independence Day celebrations, and the arrival of new forms of money were incorporated and used to sustain people's millenarian expectations. The development projects of the state, which state officials often saw as a way of counteracting cargo cults, could also have the opposite effect, fueling cargo cult desires. I want to illustrate this point by analyzing the next major bush Kaliai cargo cult, the one started by Aikele in the early 1960s. Aikele had been a respected police officer, and he used the high regard in which government officials held him to organize the Bibling Ridge Community Development scheme, in a place that could be reached by a thirty-mile boat trip up the Aria River. The scheme was started at the request of bush people, and it involved the mass planting of coconuts that would later be processed into copra at Iboki Plantation. As we saw earlier, throughout New Britain coconuts were often the focus of cargo cult activities, and in the case of Aikele his cult was partly organized around the story that coconuts had originated in the Kaliai bush when God lived there (Janssen 1970, 2). The 1965 annual report points to Bibling Ridge as an example of a commitment to development that was generally lacking elsewhere in Gloucester Division. By 1965 the bush villagers of Aikon, Angal, Benim, Gigina, Moluo, and Robos had joined this scheme and had planted fifteen hundred coconuts. An agricultural officer's report, dated October 28, 1966, estimated that six hundred villagers were living at Bibling Ridge. There different villages established separate settlements, while the government went about trying to subdivide this ridge into separate blocks. Individuals were to receive individual titles to land under the Lands Tenure Conversion Ordinance. The government referred to this form of land privatization as *rationalization:* "Work is now in progress to rationalize a community development project at Bibling Ridge in the inland Kaliai area. The rationalisation is to take the form of settling this community on individual blocks of land to which the individuals will be later granted title" (Patrol Report 1964–65). The government's rationale for sponsoring this form of land tenure, which cut across traditional communal forms of land ownership, was that it led to greater productivity. Government officials chose this form of economic individuation because they were not happy with the earlier communal coconut "plantations" from prewar and postwar schemes. The government claimed: "Most of these community owned groves are only occasionally worked. Our current policy is to dissuade further communal plantings and encourage individual or family efforts. In the more progressive areas of the sub District the people are requesting rationalisation and conversion to individual lease or title and it appears that this tendency will continue. The majority, however, retain customary practices" (Patrol Report 1964–65).

Patrol Reports at the time mention that many people were unhappy with the government's plan to divide up their land into individual land titles, and by 1967 most villages had deserted the project. Kaliai villagers are still suspicious of suggestions that they settle and work separate blocks of land. They see the privatization of their land as the first step toward government sponsorship of outside groups for settling in the Kaliai bush. At Bibling Ridge people's attitude toward the government scheme changed, and they started destroying the coconuts they were supposed to be planting. The government then started listening to reports it had been receiving earlier, namely, that Aikele was running a cargo cult. Indeed, Aikele started to organize opposition to the development project.[10] A Patrol Report dated June 27, 1966, contained the following information, received at Benim village from someone who had come to join Aikele's cult:[11]

> Aikele is definitely against any development on Bibling Ridge. When
> coconuts were sent to be planted in the area before, he apparently
> burnt many of them and told the people they were not to support any
> administration scheme for development.[12] He is alleged to have said
> that if the people did participate in development of the area that, when
> the cargo arrived, they would not receive any share of it.

Aikele's and other people's opposition to development came to be tied up with a more general rejection of anything to do with the government and its services. In October 1967 an aid post orderly reported that Aikele [who was then a *luluai,* or headman] and another luluai from Bibling Ridge had refused to send even their sick people to the aid post at Bagai and that a man had died as a result. According to official correspondences on the matter: "If these two luluais would have let him come to the aid post for help, he may have lived. . . . The two luluais have stated they don't want nothing to do with Government or the Councils. A speedboat with a policeman was immediately dispatched to look into the matter." Like other villagers in West New Britain, Aikele also opposed joining the new system of local councils. Many people told me that they ran away from Bibling Ridge in part to avoid having local councils imposed upon them, for these were associated with more work and higher taxes. A Gloucester Patrol Report, dated June 27, 1966, claims: "Aikele has apparently said that if the people remain on the Kandrian side they will be forced to join the Council. He says that if they join the Council they will not have enough money to pay Council tax and their women will have to work as prostitutes to get money enough to pay the tax."[13]

We see here the way new state structures are seen to promote the law of money and of towns and how these are positioned as subversive of traditional morality and order. Aikele's prophecy, that councils and their taxes would produce prostitution, was meant to frighten followers away from the new forms of economic incorporation that people associated with the arrival of more detailed forms of government control. Yet, despite his critique of council taxes, Aikele was collecting his own taxes. To the administration he claimed he was simply collecting money for the development project, but to his followers Aikele claimed that the money was to be used to purchase the new law of existence. Earlier we saw how Tigi had informed people that the queen had spoken of a new law requiring taxes: "Half will go to the government, the other half will go to God." A perception widespread in the Kaliai area is that the new law of existence has to be bought. Many believe that the Japanese, Chinese, and the bishops of the Catholic Church have bought their law from America. Indeed, when the New Tribes Mission arrived, villagers from Benim and Gigina collected money, which they gave to buy the law of America. Today people say these villagers were unsuccessful because they collected only a small amount of money—one hundred kina (about U.S. $150). They also say that Aikele was more successful in collecting these special taxes. Aikele claimed those who paid his tax would acquire the new law, whereas those who didn't pay would remain "natives." One informant, who gave Father Rose (n.d.) the names of seventy-six people who had paid Aikele's taxes, claimed: "There is some more talk, they all say that a man who pays Aikele's tax will no longer be taxed by the government, or have to go to jail. Supposing he makes a wrong, they all say that the Government and all the master know about Aikele. Another talk, they will ship [*kapsaitim*] all white men back to their places and Aikele will boss everyone."

When the government tried to stop Aikele's taxes, many people believed that the government was trying to stop someone who was getting too close to creating a new existence. This is how one person explained it to me:

> Aikele taxed all the men. He combined this money with his own money from his checks to make it come up so many hundred, so many thousand. This large lot of money has been lost. The government came and took this money and spent it all. Now there is nothing. The government blocked the road of Aikele, and everything stopped. This is the way of government—you know what the government is like. Now Papua New Guinea is boss, and things are easier. But before things were hard. Colonial government was boss. If things had gone right then, Kimbe [the new provincial capital] would have come up at Bibling.

Aikele spoke *em yet* [he was boss], so the government worked it so nothing came up. It was a government no good, that of the Australians.[14]

Aikele saw his work as having been blocked not only by the government
but also by the Catholic Church. As with Koriam, many believed that
Aikele traveled to Rome to free up the cargo that whites were blocking.
According to Father Rose's informant,

> Aikele spoke to everyone to put forward money that was to come to
> him and he would bring it to the kiap. However the kiap gave it back
> and Aikele along with his *hatman* [tax collectors] they all went to Ra-
> baul. They stayed there whilst Aikele went on to Rome, so that he
> could open the door and the cargo could come up and so that the Last
> Day could also come up.
>
> They all say that the mission is blocking the cargo. They all say that
> the people who have died are in Rabaul in one house. They all say that
> the Komunio [Holy Communion] is the blood of the priest.
>
> Another something they say about Aikele is that he tried all sorts of
> work but didn't like them. Later he found this work and he bought it,
> this work is the road of Jesus.

We see here the way Aikele's work assumed biblical proportions, becoming a vehicle for Jesus's work. Part of the aura that developed around
Aikele came from the numerous stories that people told about Aikele's
special relationships with Europeans. These stories were often about
Aikele's heroic patrols on the "mainland" (New Guinea), where he is said
to have brought "law and order" to wild people who had never seen
whites. I was told how Aikele was a very good shot with a rifle and how
he used magic to put these wild natives to sleep or to "foul" their thinking
so they no longer thought about fighting. Bush Kaliai villagers speak
proudly of Aikele's role in helping to tame the wild natives of New Guinea.
They also proudly tell similar stories about another relative who joined
the police force and who was rewarded with ceremonial honors for his
fighting capacities. These stories are about Melanesians' becoming an extension of state processes of pacification. Here the state uses the "native"
skills of Melanesians—their good eyes, acute sense of hearing, and hunting skills—but also their world of magic, to conquer and domesticate the
savage remnants of a Melanesian past (cf. Taussig 1987). Here the civilizing projects of the state become dependent upon an alternative form of
knowledge, a world of magic and sorcery belonging to a Melanesian past,
which is redeployed and redeemed as a form of black power to which

people must resort to bring the world of light to those living in the dark world of their ancestors. Inside the state a world of sorcery and magic comes to be domesticated and used as part of the state's processes of domestication.

Many bush Kaliai know the story of how Aikele acquired the trust of his European kiap by rescuing him during fierce fighting. It is said that the kiap crouched between Aikele's legs, while Aikele used his rifle to fight off the wild natives of New Guinea.[15] As a reward for saving his life, this master told Aikele: "You go and get up this work of yours, and I will help you with this work of yours." This was said to be the start of people gathering at Bibling Ridge and of Aikele's checkbook. The latter was a pension that Aikele received for his work in the police force but that people interpreted as Aikele's having special access to the white man's cargo and money. Aikele told villagers that his kiap had said that cargo would come for them but that they first had to listen to him; if they were pigheaded, he would tell his kiap, and people's cargo would not arrive. Aikele instructed villagers to move to Bibling Ridge so that, when the law broke, the cargo would have to travel along only one hill. Aikele also claimed that the ground would magically open up so that rivers would become wider and deeper, and ships could then carry cargo into the Kaliai interior.

Many people supported Aikele because they believed that his relationships of personal debt with his kiap allowed him to cut across those taboos and secrets that prevented other Melanesians from gaining access to the white man's secrets. Some say Aikele's kiap took him to Australia; others say his kiap took him in a submarine under the ground and into the mountains of the Kaliai area. There Aikele and his kiap loaded their submarine with cargo made by the Kaliai dead. Samaga remembered Aikele's accounts of these events like this:

> He [Aikele] fought with his gun, and he protected his kiap, so his kiap gave him this talk when the two of them went inside [a Kaliai mountain]. He said to him: "Aikele, you think this is a mountain? Now where do you think cargo comes from? Cargo comes up from the area belonging to you and it leaves." . . . This is the talk of Aikele. He would say [to bush Kaliai relatives]: "What do you think? All these mountains standing up here like Alat and Gilimeh, and others, all cargo is in these areas." He would say: "A ship goes inside. We would not know about this ship when it comes, goes down, picks up cargo from here, and then leaves. It will leave, go out, and then come back to us." He used to speak like that. . . . He used to say that they, he and his kiap, would go

inside and pick up cargo. He would come and say: "All these mountains, they are enough for the cargo." He used to say that all the people
who had died, that they all had it [the cargo]. The *as* [origin] of the
cargo is here [in the Kaliai area], and the ship would come pick it up
and go out at Port Moresby. From there cargo would come back to us,
and there would be enough for all the plantations. It is not as though
he worked all this from his own thinking. No, all of this came up from
his kiap. For the two of them went to battle, and he fought on top of
his kiap, and his kiap then worked this. This [talk, knowledge] did not
come up from Aikele himself.

Many cargo cult stories are narratives that seek to breach and alter the
space that seals off people's everyday vision. Thus they often involve
planes, submarines, ships, holes in the ground, wirelesses (radio transmitters), telephones, and dreams. They are stories about breaking out of contained spaces and of transgressing a boundary. The hero avoids becoming
contained in a location, and his journey becomes the culture's search for
a larger space to inhabit that includes the space of the other. The narrative
form that the struggle for freedom takes in cargo cult stories consists of a
geographical search for alternative spaces, which exist beyond the boundaries of what is currently known. It is a struggle to occupy the secret space
of the other and often to become the other. In these narratives people
search for a topography whose differences can encompass and account for
the structure of the racial inequalities that make up their existence. The
spatial distances crossed in these narrative journeys come to stand for the
overcoming of the cultural, social, and political distances of race. In crossing over and violating the normal spaces they are supposed to inhabit, the
heroes of such stories breach that chasm that divides, contains, immobi-
lizes, and maps out people's subordinate racial identity and status. The
following story about Aikele, which was given to me by Septireh, illustrates these themes. Here Aikele crosses a boundary and ends up in another country, which is inhabited by Europeans but also by the Kaliai
dead, who have turned white and are living a Western lifestyle:

> When he was a policeman, they all went and broke through the
> bush at this big river Manimu [he may mean Vanimo]. This river Man-
> imu is the border of Papua New Guinea and another country. There is
> this big blackboard [sign] at Manimu; it marks the separate sea belong-
> ing to Papua New Guinea and the separate sea belonging to this other
> country. He went and broke through this area, this bush. He traveled
> into the bush, coming up to some people who had never seen the white

man. He and his police-master traveled farther and farther into the
bush until they broke the boundary with this other country. The police-
master took out his compass, and they came up to a certain place.
They came up to an automobile road. They did not come up to a road
like ours, they came up to a main road made of bitumen. The Australian police-master told them: "The compass has brought you to another country, you must not say anything. I do not know whether they
of this country will fight us? Load your cartridges."

They walked a bit farther, looking at the marks on the various
roads. They came up to one road, and the police-master told them to
wait. The police-master telephoned his camp, and then he turned and
told them that separate cars would come to collect them to take them
to different destinations. Aikele's car came. It was the car belonging to
his mother and father [who had died]. He climbed into the car and was
taken to his mother and father, they "kissed" and they all cried. He saw
his grandfather. He also saw that they had built him a house, which was
waiting for him to come and live in when he died. Aikele wanted to go
into the house, but his mother and father said: "You cannot go into
this house, you are still two skins, we have made it ready for when you
die, when you have only one skin left."

The master had arranged for them to all meet in the morning. The
women worked quickly to make a feast. This food was not the food of
the white-skins, it was our food. They gave Aikele four baskets, and
then the car came. His mother and father cried as Aikele left. The car
traveled slowly away, with the mother and father holding onto Aikele's
hands and crying as he moved away. All the cars gathered together. Everyone lined up, and the police-master gave a strong law [rule] to all of
them: "When we go back to the station, you cannot mention this place.
I am a police-master, I am a good man, I brought you here to see your
fathers. I acquired cars to come pick youse up and take youse to your
separate places of sleep. When we go back to the station, you cannot
talk, otherwise a big court will come up. The food you have received
you will finish it along the road so there are no questions asked by your
wives or children. This is a strong taboo, a strong law. If you break this
law and talk, you will be jailed, no other chances given." They broke
the bush, used the compass, and came up to the sea. They came back.
Aikele had spoken with his mother and father, who had told him they
would meet him again later in Rabaul.

When his time as a policeman finished, Aikele went first to Kavieng,
then he went to Rabaul. There he met his mother and father again.

They gave him money. They told him to go back to his village and to
get up work there [development work]. The *as* [beginning] of the work
[at Bibling Ridge] is like that.

In this story we see the theme of people having two skins, with the soul
seen as a second body. The dead inhabit a second white skin, which they
use to live in the land of whites.[16] There the dead enjoy a European lifestyle, and they prepare European-style houses for their children to live in
when they die. Through the concept that each individual has two skins or
bodies, people come to internalize and embody the dual worlds created
and associated with worlds of racial secrecy. The secret world of Europeans now becomes a hidden possibility that they will inhabit in the second
body conferred by death.

This theme of the world as organized around a giant secret serves to
collapse together images of separation: the separate existence of Europeans and Melanesians becomes merged with the separate existence of the
dead and the living. These two forms of separation are folded onto each
other; they become implicated in each other, for they emerge from a common understanding of social distance as underpinned and created by secrecy. In its very nature secrecy creates unequal worlds of meanings, divisions between those who know and do not know the secret (Simmel 1950).
Traditional culture used this figurative dualizing potential of secrecy to
create the power relationships between men and women, initiated men and
uninitiated men, and old men and young men (Allen 1967; Barth 1975).
With the coming of Europeans the differentiating capacity of secrecy was
used to understand the unequal power relationships of race. Secrecy then
became a way of understanding the cultural differences between Europeans and Melanesians. In 1986, at the village of Doko Sagra, some close
relatives of Aikele repeated what another bush Kaliai village had told me,
namely, that whites had erected a huge silasila to conceal the truth about
their wealth and power. Traditionally, a silasila refers to the fence that men
build around tumbuan masks to keep secret from women and children
that it is men who put on these masks and that it is they who eat the
tambaran's food at the expense of sharing it with women and children. In
using this allegory, Aikele's relatives were positioning whites as men of
trickery and themselves as occupying the role of uninformed women and
children. Whites here are rendered as running their own men's house cult,
the secrets of which serve to masculinize them while feminizing Melanesian men.

This allegory, in which the cultural differences in knowledge embodied

in a racial order are understood through the gender inequalities in knowledge instituted by tambaran cults, can be pushed further. Most Kaliai
women have more than an inkling that men's tambarans are not real;
moreover, Kaliai men also know that the women know. It is more the case
that the women must pretend that they do not know that tambarans are
men's tricks. I would argue that the racial feminization of Kaliai men is of
a similar order of complexity, for it too involves a public secret, that is, a
secret that is known but cannot be acknowledged publicly. Kaliai men see
themselves as knowing the truth—that there is a European secret about
the dead—only they must pretend to Europeans that they do not know
or believe this secret.

Aikele's story is partly a way of talking indirectly about this general
world of feigned ignorance in which the rewards, taboos, and threats of
Europeans are meant to co-opt Melanesians into forms of complicit silence. The shared secret that Aikele and his fellow police officers must
keep is partly a way of talking about how an elite group of Melanesians is
made to participate in sustaining the secrets of European power. Yet we
also need to remember that Aikele tells his secret story to fellow villagers;
he thus breaches the taboos of complicity imposed by his kiap. By secretly
telling his story, Aikele creates a hidden world of noncomplicity outside
the complicity required by his kiap—or, more accurately, Aikele's story
creates among villagers a new form of complicity about being non-
complicit. Here the kiap's warning to his police officers operates as a re-
minder to listeners of their need to also pretend to be complicit in sustaining European secrets. Here whites come to be secretly out-tricked by
those whom they secretly try to deceive. Melanesians come to create new
forms of complicity among themselves that have to do with their covert
noncompliance with the complicity required by all *waitskin.* Here secrets
come to be caught within secrets, with people entering into a secret relationship with secrets. The meaning of Aikele's story was not purely internal to the story but to its context in which the secret *telling* of the secrets
posited by the story subverted them in order to create other secret bonds
outside the story, bonds that had to do with people's covert relationship
with themselves and the white man's secrets.

Today many bush Kaliai remain supportive of Aikele's work. I was often told that if Aikele's work had been allowed to succeed, the provincial
capital would have been established at Bibling Ridge instead of Kimbe.
Many villagers in the Moluo-Robos area see Aikele's work as the government's first attempts to build Kimbe. Today these villagers blame the sexual transgressions of their young women for starting disputes that led to
fighting among different villages and their departure from Bibling Ridge

in late 1967. Women are blamed for the bush Kaliai's losing Aikele's attempt to give them a world of plenty, which would have been their own version of Kimbe. This memory resonates with the biblical story of Eve's role in humanity's expulsion from Paradise. When the Kaliai tell the Garden of Eden story, they emphasize that it was really sex between Adam and Eve that brought not so much humanity's downfall as the downfall of black people—they lost an original Paradise that took the form of the white man's lifestyle. At Bibling Ridge the Kaliai had another chance to have this paradise, but the moral looseness of their women lost it. Today the moral hegemony of Kaliai men over women is constituted partly through the way historical events, like those at Bibling Ridge, have been used to reenact and localize the Christian narrative of woman's role in the Fall. Here men use the desire for cargo and its loss to reconstitute the moral hegemonic framework of gender power relations transmitted by Christian myths that blame women for the loss of paradise.

GOD GOES TO AMERICA

The Kaliai have localized Christian narrative schemes in other ways that continue this process of their morally owning their racial subordination. One major story around which Aikele's cult was organized was about a trickster god whom the Kaliai wronged and chased away to America, where he befriended a "rubbishman." This rubbishman lived alone. He is described as having no father and mother and as having been chased away by all the other white men. We have here the theme of the lost black god who becomes a stranger to his people, who deserts his relatives and race to help another ostracized stranger, who shows greater hospitality and acceptance of him. In some versions of this story the god of the Kaliai initially appeared as a crocodile to the American rubbishman, who was not frightened by his appearance. The god then left and came back as a snake that coiled around the body of the American, who still remained unafraid. In the Censure cult's version of this story the American lifts the snake's body onto his shoulders and has difficulty doing this because the snake's body is heavy and swollen with cargo. This snake then puts its tongue into the American's ears, but the man does not squirm. It puts its tongue around the eyes and into the nostrils of the American, who still remains without fear. The snake then puts its tongue into the American's mouth, and the two are said to kiss. The snake-trickster-god of the Kaliai then knows that the American is his true friend and so gives his knowledge to the American.

Similar stories abound. They are often about a serpent god who runs away because of the immorality and disobedience of his kin. One of the best analyses of how a traditional resentful hero is assimilated to Christ and the cargo lost is provided in Michael Young's on Goodenough Island (1982, 1983). On the Kaliai coast this serpent god is called Moro, whereas in the Kaliai bush he is associated with the trickster figure Titikolo. The serpent body of these local gods embodies strangeness and otherness, which come to be positioned as the source of plenitude and creation. In the story of Moro the top half of his body is human, whereas the bottom half is snake. Moro is said to have concealed his body inside his house, and he made up a taboo to keep people from entering. While Moro resided with people, they did not have to work; instead, food came up by itself in people's gardens. All of this, however, was ended by Moro's wife. She began to wonder why her husband never slept with her. One day she decided to spy on her husband. But he saw her spying on the secrets of his serpentine body, and he became angry and fled from the Kaliai area. This is a story about people losing control of God and a heavenly paradise to whites because of a local woman's disobedience. These stories work to indigenize the Christian story of the Fall while also making it historically relevant to people's lives. All the bush Kaliai cargo cult stories that I know accuse people's ancestors of chasing God into the hands of whites. The loss of His creative presence deprived the bush Kaliai of a life without work and gave Europeans their comfortable material lifestyle. For their disobedience the Kaliai received the punishment of a false culture made up of pigheadedness, ignorance, masks, sorcery, and warfare. Here people internalize and transform the social, economic, and political inequalities of race into a moral fault that has soiled their identities and culture. People's sense of moral inferiority, which is partly a product of the civilizing and pedagogic projects of whites, comes to be objectified and measured by the loss of those forms of value embodied in commodities. Alongside traditional forms of relatedness through kinship and moiety, stories about lost cargo create a new sense of racial belonging that is mediated by the moral world of commodities, that is, through internalizing and sharing the new forms of racial value that commodities imply and objectify.

In terms of contemporary nationalism in Papua New Guinea, Robert Foster (1992, 1995) has analyzed how people rework items of mass consumption to create new national Melanesian identities in which people's imaginary relationship to the nation and themselves is mediated by their imaginary relationship to commodities. Foster is interested in nationalism and consumer goods in mass culture; I am more interested in the local forms of nationalism that emerge when people imaginatively make com-

The central post of a Catholic church at Lauvore, which has been carved to represent the half-serpent and half-human ancestor Moro, who is also known as Titikolo, Jesus, and Moses

modities embody local myths that depict today's Melanesian existence as racially grounded in ancestors' transgressions. My interest lies in the local forms of nationalism that emerge from the reworked traditional and Christian narratives that people use to make moral sense of commodities and their circulation within the nation. For me cargo cult stories are partly evidence of the way mythic thought posits no distinction between the private and public aspects of actions, between personhood and sociogenesis. The world is not abstractly ordained by blind fate but is given form through chance and individual actions in a primordial time. Here sociogenesis is grounded in the transformations of a narrative plot revolving around the unique junctures and accidents of biographical time. What the Creator does as a private person has public consequences that are passed down to his family and race. Our notion of ethical responsibility as an exclusively individual concern is played down in a mythological tradition, which partakes of the moral deliberations of a kinship society in which relatives are mutually responsible and share in compensating for each other's crimes. This sense of inherited sin is also a feature of Christianity, with its understanding that humanity shares in the collective sin and punishment of Adam and Eve. Cargo cults rework the theme of an original inherited sin to make it into a racial fall. Many such stories are told in the Kaliai area. In some stories Adam and Eve are brother and sister and have local Kaliai names. The church's claim that they ate a forbidden fruit is said to be either a lie or talk-box (concealing talk). Instead, villagers believe that Adam and Eve had sex, and because of this God expelled them from an original world of plentiful cargo, which Melanesians could have continued enjoying along with whites. Here the fate of Kaliai ancestors determines the fate of all Melanesians, and Christian images of the Fall are appropriated to place the Kaliai mythically at the center of a new national existence. Unlike Worsley, I would argue that locality is not effaced by cargo cults' taking up a new national consciousness; instead, locality gains its significance through its cosmic centrality to the nation. Repositioned as the source of a black national existence, the Kaliai are also the center that can redeem the world for other Melanesians.

To explore cargo cults is to undertake what Bersani (1990) called a "genealogy of the culture of redemption." The economy that whites bring is not simply a monetary economy but also a moral economy in which people think about their poverty and subordination as a punishment, or as a collective debt that they are paying. Cargo cults often involve people who are starting to own and reproduce this Christian language of humanity as constituted in sin, but they do so not because they enjoy producing a sense of racial inferiority and self-alienation but because to acknowledge the ground of one's racial fall is also to find the ground on which villagers can reempower themselves as historical actors. It was Burridge (1960) who first pointed out that the process of owning one's Fall in cargo cult stories was also, strangely enough, a process by which Melanesians empowered themselves by positioning themselves as actors in charge of their destiny. I want to expand Burridge's point in order to argue that from a position of self-depreciation people can relaunch the project of making themselves anew, namely, as redeemed racial subjects. Through appropriating a Christian sense of sin, cargo cults also appropriate from the church the project of redemption and the control over people that is conferred by managing the quest for salvation. The appropriated discourses of sin and self-condemnation used by cargo cult followers often operate as a prerequisite for authorizing new practices and techniques of social control that appropriate from Christianity its technology of pastoral care, that is, its redemptive techniques for controlling and producing the moral grounds of racial subjectivity. In Chapters 3, 4, and 6 I focus on how people came to produce and manage this appropriated culture of guilt, whose ownership allowed cargo cults to establish their pastoral practices of self-formation. I am not saying that no traditional practices of self-formation existed, for these clearly did exist throughout Melanesia (Battaglia 1995; Herdt 1981, 1987; M. Young 1983). Instead, I am saying that the Kaliai bush people borrowed a certain culture of sin, redemption, and salvation to create new ways of ethically caring for and constituting the self.

Nearly all the cargo cult leaders I know use the story of the Kaliai's original bikhet (disobedience, pigheadedness) to God to reinforce cult loyalty. These leaders position themselves as reenacting the pedagogic role of the original teacher-God; they present themselves as bringing back God's moral school, His original church (*lotu*). They often warn their followers that before, God did try to school the Kaliai, but they rejected his school and were punished with ignorance and poverty. Followers are positioned as having a second chance to correct the Kaliai's original rejection of God's school. This understanding of the cargo cult as reenacting its myths about the past was often given special prominence when followers started deserting a cult. The disobedient relationship of people's ancestors to God then became a mythic template for figuring the disobedient relationship of cult followers to their leader. Cargo cult myths that deal with the punishment of the Kaliai were used to police the loyalty of cult followers. The myths operated as moral lessons, warning followers against neglecting their cult obligations or deserting the cult, for the historical consequences of this are all too evident.

The policing effect of these stories about the Kaliai's original bikhet should not be seen as confined to bush cargo cults, for these stories also underpin the moral incorporation of coastal villagers into schools, the church, business, council government, and provincial and national politics. Cargo cult stories about God's running away from his disobedient kin are not stories belonging only to backward rural folks; these stories are well known by the educated elite of teachers, catechists, magistrates, councillors, and politicians who live near and on the Kaliai coast.[17] Indeed, these stories underpin coastal villagers' greater participation and acceptance of the general need to be civilized by outside structures. Along the coast these stories are one means through which a small educated elite legitimizes its rule by drawing upon a surrounding folklore culture concerning the need to be morally improved.[18] Here the power of state-church representatives comes not simply from their pedagogic role of transmitting white culture but also from the cargo cult narratives that operate as moral lessons—pointing out that the failure of the Kaliai to listen to their teachers in the past is responsible for their unsatisfactory lives today. Paradoxically, cargo cult stories can make possible the hegemony of state-church representatives, for they can underpin people's acceptance of the need for external moral guidance and authority. Here the local power of state and church is founded on those subversive local narratives that they often seek to squash. This is a theme I explore further in Chapter 8, in which I analyze how the moral hegemony of the New Tribes Mission was made possible by the very cargo cult culture it often sought to eradicate.

TITIKOLO: THE KALIAI TRICKSTER GOD

Although people derive their authority in cargo cults from using biblical stories, they also rewrite Christian stories as part of their struggle to map out some sort of intellectual autonomy. In men's and women's houses I often heard people debate and question their stories and those belonging to Europeans. People struggle with Europeans at the level of ideas. By rewriting Christian stories people use the authority of white culture to escape full subordination to the terms of white culture. One reworked biblical story that I heard told was of how the Virgin Mary carried two children: one was Jesus, who created the present existence of whites; the other child, or "king," was the god of the Kaliai people. He is the lost god and creative power belonging to black Papua New Guineans. Some refer to this lost god as Titikolo, a trickster figure known for continuously changing his name. Most cargo cult myths held by the Anem and Mouk are centered on Titikolo. In traditional folklore stories he is a seducer of other

men's wives, a man who continuously devises tricks to have sex with unsus-
pecting women. Yet many people regard Titikolo as a misunderstood
teacher, for his English name is sometimes said to be Moses. Titikolo is
also the origin of the alphabet. In 1986 I was taken to a cave at the headwaters of the Banu River and shown where Titikolo first painted the alphabet before he was chased away. In two separate villages I was informed
that Titikolo had also painted the alphabet around the vagina of his maternal uncle's wife, which was why people's ancestors tried to kill him. Some
people see Titikolo's tricks as the origin of all those deceptive practices
and customs that belong to *mipela blakskin* (us black-skins). Some villagers say that their ancestors misunderstood Titikolo's tricks—he was really
"testing" their willingness to forgive him, but they wronged him, and he
ran away to friendly America, where he gave white people his knowledge
and power. In some stories Titikolo was killed by the Kaliai, and when he
came back to life, he went to America. This story is equated explicitly with
Jesus's crucifixion, indeed to the point where Titikolo comes back to life
after three days. The story of Titikolo is an old one; many Kaliai villagers
heard the cargo cult version of this story from their grandparents.[19] The
story was revived when the American New Tribes Mission started its literacy classes; to many people this was the return of their lost knowledge,
their lost alphabet, from America. Here is how Posingen described the
views of the Mouk cargo cult leaders who joined the New Tribes Mission:
"They say that this man they put on the cross was Titikolo. The number
one man was Titikolo. This man, when he first came up to our area, was
called Titikolo; when he went to you white-skins, he became Jesus."

    What happens in Kaliai cargo cult stories is that biblical figures tend
to be sometimes collapsed together, so Titikolo, who will be called Jesus,
will be also spoken of as Moses, because the two are regarded as teachers.
This ambiguity in identities is also sustained by the fact that Titikolo is
known as a wandering hero who changes his name when he arrives in
different areas—among the Mouk he is known as Yange; among the
Anem as Titikolo; among the Kombei, Kaliai, and Bariai as Moro; and
farther west as Namor. In the version of the Titikolo story that I collected
from Bowl, whites were said to have become angry over Titikolo's continuous name changes, so they killed him. Titikolo was killed because he had
too many identities, encompassed too many personas. The trickster hero
comes to embody a form of ambiguity and instability of meaning that
whites cannot tolerate. We need to remember that in traditional culture,
people have multiple names, whereas for the census forms of Europeans
they and their families have to assume one name—one surname to be

transmitted patrilineally. In some stories Titikolo changes into a crocodile and then a snake when he comes up to America: half-animal, half-serpent, and half-human, his body is full of those ambiguities that never allow black identity to be fully identical with itself. The utopian promise of such figures emerges from that instability and transformation of meanings that is articulated by their tricks, bodies, and identities.

After Bowl finished telling me his version of Titikolo, his younger brother interjected: "Bowl has lost a little bit of the story. When Titikolo came up to your territory, all the Russians became cross as to why he had come to their place and with him changing his name. All the Russians held him and tied him up. The Russians took vines with thorns on them and put them on his head. They put a large rope around his waist, and they started killing him with axes and hammers." Later, when his brother departed, Bowl repudiated his brother's version of the story as not the one they heard from their father. Yet what his brother's unorthodox version shows is the way stories are continuously reworked as the global frameworks of meaning in which people are embedded change. The story that Titikolo was killed by the Russians is an attempt to participate in the culture of world politics that is relayed continuously to people when they visit towns, plantations, and the coast—where more radios are operating because people have greater access to cash and batteries.[20] From the mass media a few people have picked up the negative connotations projected onto Russians and that they are the enemy of the Americans—the good whites. The mass media's narratives of evil can be merged by cargo cult followers with their reinterpretations of biblical and traditional myths about the origins of evil. Cargo cult narratives reform the space of people's thoughts as people come to tap into Western narratives of global power to provide the mythic terrain within which the cosmological process of creating the world can unfold. Space and power are closely linked, and the struggle to appropriate the power of the white man is partly the narrative desire to incorporate the distant spaces that the white man inhabits and claims to know most about. The globe now becomes the mythic terrain for mapping out and situating the new local nationalisms of race that take the form of cargo cults.

When people were telling me the story of Titikolo, I noticed a certain textualization of human existence that came from villagers' seeing their life to be a story. Indeed, all bush Kaliai cargo cults refer to themselves by the Pisin word *stori* (story, a narrative about secret and lost forms of power).[21] For cult followers the space of colonialism is a narrative space, more specifically, the space of an uncompleted narrative. Many bush Kaliai view themselves as living in a space of darkness brought about by the failure of their creator to complete the stori of human existence. Because of the bikhet of the Kaliai, Titikolo went and worked the land of America first, leaving his place of origin unworked. People talk about this as the "head of the story" having been worked first, but the as (beginning) of the story remains unfinished. Here life is figured as an uncompleted story or, more accurately, a story gone wrong—the second half is said to have been worked and completed while its first half remains unworked. For many cult followers the story that has produced racial inequalities can come to an end only by bringing the creator back to the beginning of the story, that is, by enacting a narrative that reengages those mythic determinations that are at the very origins of otherness. The death and loss of the creator are what many bush Kaliai mourn. People's sense of lack is embodied in the myth of a lost or murdered god. People have a sense that things are waiting to be completed and that this will happen with the return of their god. In 1986 people told me that he had already come back but that he was hiding. Many Kaliai cargo cult leaders have taken on the millenarian task of finding a lost original presence that has become removed from the Kaliai; they try to bring back their black God. The recent arrival of the American New Tribes missionaries has seemed to many people to be a way of completing the circularity of the story: the head of the story comes back to complete the beginning. This also fits into the narrative structure of some Kaliai stories, which takes a circular form, with people able to predict the end of a narrative by the gradual movement of the hero back to where he started. Many people were waiting for Titikolo, their teacher, to come back, and they saw his alphabet and school as coming back to them in the adult literacy classes of the American missionaries. Many people also saw the American missionaries as their returned ancestors, which is also another form of a lost beginning returning to its origins.

I want to go back to the story of Titikolo and explore why the trickster is a figure of travel and why it is so apt to portray God as an uprooted wanderer. I want to argue that this trickster god is not simply traveling across space but also across social norms, names, and conventions (Pelton 1989; Radin 1972). He is in Victor Turner's sense a liminal figure full of ambiguity, in that he condenses multiple meanings within his persona. He is an outlaw who is not subordinate to the laws that govern others. His serpentine body marks the fact that his is a liminal being made up of multiple forms of existence. His serpentine body also contains multiple skins that resonate with the double-skinned bodies of individuals, of life and death, body and soul, but also of the black and white existences he produces. We need to remember that in shedding their skins, snakes also renew themselves, acquiring a new shiny skin to take the place of an old dirty skin. It is not accidental that tricksters are snakes and figures of redemption.

People have a strong sense of identification with Titikolo; they see him as embodying all those human faults and desires that people recognize as the basis of their racial identity. People often spoke to me with a mixture of guilt and pride about the petty deceptions and tricks that their interactions with whites often involved: how they would lie about how much petrol they needed, or how rough the sea was, or how much something cost, so that they could be slightly overcompensated by white employers. People had a generalized sense of all this as the customs of mipela blakskin (us black-skins). Titikolo is an idealized version of people's sense of themselves as tricksters, as deceivers. It seems to me that the following material by Taylor, although about the West, captures well this mirroring specular relationship between a people and their god:

> Within the Western theological tradition, the "original" scene of nomination involves God and man. The relation between God and self is thoroughly specular; each mirrors the other. In different terms, man is made in the image of God. This imago is an imitation, copy, likeness, representation, similitude, appearance, or shadow of divinity. The imago dei confers upon man an identity; this establishes a vocation that can be fulfilled only through the process of imitation. The specularity of the God-self relation forges an inseparable bond between the name of God and the name of man. (Taylor 1984, 35)

In the bush Kaliai area the god of trickery who errs is often positioned as the god of creation. There is here a recognition of erring as the power to create. We are dealing with why a figure of creativity is portrayed as an outlaw, an adulterer, a seducer of other men's wives, an adventurous wanderer. Is there not in this figure of transgression a sense of the act of creation as lying outside the norms that inaugurate and bind the world (Bataille 1985, 1987; Derrida 1992, 312; Weiss 1989)? In a sense the creator cannot be captured by the norms that he creates, for he is also something outside them, more than them. In this book I explore how the Kaliai go about figuring this creative outsideness and the creative role assigned to transgression. In the case of Titikolo the image of the wanderer is the image of a trickster who cannot be fully named—that is, fully mastered and subsumed under one name. The creativity he represents is embodied in that movement and destabilizing of identity that he represents. He is a figure of individuality, and this individuality comes, paradoxically, from his multiplicity. He originally belonged to the Kaliai, and he tested their acceptance of him. He did this through his tricks and through his frightening serpentine body.

Given this emphasis on God as a trickster, on meanings never being fully identical, we should not be surprised to find forms of trickery inside cargo cults. In the case of Censure's cult, this involved the secret eating of food put aside for the dead. Many of Censure's ceremonies involved sacrificing pigs and setting some pork aside for the underground. The rest of the pork had to be shared by all the men, women, and children; all the followers had to receive a piece. Many ex-followers claim that the food set aside for the dead was in reality eaten secretly by Censure's family. I see Censure as creating new structures of secrecy in which the clandestine consumption of food by men in tambaran cults became the model for organizing hierarchical relationships inside his cult. Other tricks performed by Censure included having his daughters hide inside mats and then whistling so that followers would think it was the dead talking through whistles. Yet these tricks did not diminish or undermine Censure's family's faith in their cult, which they continued working long after everyone else had left (Evans-Pritchard 1937; Levi-Strauss 1972, 167–85). I believe that Censure's understanding of himself as the god of Papua New Guinea also led him to assume that uncompromising form of individuality embodied in Kaliai notions of a trickster god who stands beyond the reach of others, partly through that excess of meaning embodied in his secrets and tricks. Trickery is a technique of individuation, a way of marking and defining forms of outsideness, which in their outsideness can approach Christian understandings of the sacred, of God, of a Creator who resides and is something more than the rules that bind others.

AKONO: THE RUBBISHMAN AND THE POWER OF A DIRTY SKIN

The stories about the outcast god Titikolo resonate with a genre of local stories that speak of another outcast trickster hero called Akono, also known as Akrit (Counts 1982). In traditional Kaliai stories Akono is a figure of knowledge and power who has two skins (LeRoy 1985, 181–97; Panoff 1968). Akono tests people's acceptance of him by tricking them and putting on a putrid decaying skin. Many old people say that Akono was the traditional god of their grandfathers. Some say he is the same person as Titikolo, which is not surprising given that both are tricksters

(Lattas 1992b). Akono is described as wearing a filthy skin of smelly rotten sores that he uses to conceal another more beautiful, shiny skin. He is often spat on by other villagers, from whom he hides not only his skin but also other knowledgeable secrets, like how to make sago. Those secrets are later incorporated into society when Akono's secret skin is discovered by a woman he married. Today people say that Akono's hidden, beautiful, shiny skin is like the white man's skin. Akono hides his secret racial identity and power inside the smell of his decaying black skin. Through his two skins Akono comes to encompass and transcend the binary divisions of a racial order. In part, his stories speak about divisions among Melanesians, for Akono is ostracized and spat upon by his kin, from whom he hides the hidden alternative racial identity that lurks inside a black skin. These stories are partly moral critiques of the ungenerous attitudes of people's ancestors, who could not see beyond a world of surface appearances in order to recognize the god hidden among them.

Throughout the Kaliai bush, people refer to God as a rubbishman. I know of two cargo cult leaders whose godlike status has partly come from their incorporating the defiling aspects of Akono's persona into their own persona. They have immersed themselves in this powerful mythic image of a despised, ostracized outcast. When I asked Posingen why people referred to God as a rubbishman and why Akrit was seen like this, he replied that this dirty skin "is the magic [*papait*] of Akrit" (cf. Douglas 1966). I responded that people pointed out that the cargo cult leader Mapilu washed only occasionally and that his followers would speak in hushed, meaningful ways about how his clothes were old and torn. I told Posingen that I thought Mapilu was copying Akrit, and I asked him whether this was right. He answered that he was not sure about Mapilu but that his father, Censure, had refused to wash his skin for the following reasons:

> With Father, its meaning is like this—if he washes and gets rid of the dirt, he also gets rid of the *kaikai* [food, a euphemism for cargo] from his skin. . . . With these other men [cargo cult leaders], I am not too sure of their meaning. But with Father, when he worked it as he did, and dirt was on him, he said kaikai was on his skin, it would not be good if he removed it. It is like this: if this dirt stays, and he wins this work [ritual law], and it [a new existence] comes up, then he will wash. All the kaikai will then come up on his skin, all something that wants to come up [cargo] will come up from his skin. It is of this kind, his power is like this.[22]

Many people believe that Censure received his dirty skin from sexual intercourse with a masalai who took the form of a *misis,* a white woman. She rubbed her vagina all over his body so that the polluting mixture of vaginal secretions and semen would adhere to his skin. According to an informant quoted by Janssen (1970, 4, 9), she wanted her smell to remain on Censure so that he would continue to think of her, and so she instructed him not to wash. She also told Censure that from the smell and dirt on his skin would come the knowledge that he would give to others. Censure was instructed to gather other villages together, and they were to give five young girls to him. Today Censure's family denies this story, and his relatives point out that they were "courted" (brought before the kiap) over this story. Yet many ex-followers told me that they had personally heard this story directly from Censure. In a Patrol Report dated May 21, 1970, P. N. Sisley records Censure's cult as having two stories:

> The first I heard from Napasisio [Censure] and the second [was] told to me by the Councillor Sela of Aikon who claims he heard it from Napasisio himself. The first story is that Napasisio claims that one night in a dream he was visited by God who came in the form of three men and he was told that he had been selected to lead his people to a better life. Then and now God speaks to him with the wind and tells him what and how to do the things he does. Councillor Sela also told me this story but said that Napasisio also claims that while walking in the bush one day he met a "Devil Woman" on the path. She invited him to have intercourse with her, which he did. When he did this she covered him completely with her organ and during the course of the act instructed him on the process he was to follow to improve the lot of the people and nominated him the leader. When they were finished she turned into a snake and slid away into the bush.

As in some other bush Kaliai cargo cults, snakes were important in Censure's cult. People said that when Censure traveled into the underground, he saw that the lower half of God's body was like a snake (Janssen 1970, 9). Some snakes were seen to be Censure's underground nephews, Sen Kilok and Sen Seuve; other snakes were spoken of as "bosses" of the underground, which was also known as Papua New Guinea Down. These subterranean bosses would turn into snakes when they came to the surface world to what was called Papua New Guinea on Top. These snakes mediated between two versions of the nation; they mediated the identity of the nation with its double. Censure would speak to these snakes in a special language he called "English" (cf. Worsley 1957, 80, 90). He would show these snakes signs of respect by standing at attention and saluting them in gestures people likened to those of police. The snakes were said to respond by moving their heads, by making similar gestures of respect. Censure's followers often fondled and kissed snakes, holding them and putting them onto their bodies, for they believed them to be people from the underground. Monongyo (Censure's son-in-law) described to me the physical intimacy that developed between cult followers and these underground snake people:

> I want to talk about these two men [bosses, underground spirit children]. We belong to Papua New Guinea on Top, we cannot see them all, but when these men of the underground want to come on top to us, then they will change into snakes. . . . They will come, and they will not be like the snakes that belong to us on top, which are cross and bite us with their teeth. No, if our hand goes out to them, they will just lie down, or their tongue will come and lick our hand. We can hold their bodies. We can hold them and they will not become cross. [Monongyo mimes patting the snake.] We would work at patting their bodies like this and their heads like that.

I see the symbolic importance of snakes in Censure's cult as emerging partly because their ability to shed their skins renders snakes similar to the two-skinned god Akono, who was a model for bush cargo cult leaders like Censure and Mapilu. Snakes embodied that shedding of skins that people associated with the transformative time of death and with the coming of the Last Day (M. Young 1983, 61–91, 253–55). Many bush Kaliai villagers expect that when the new law of existence arrives, they will shed their black skins to reveal the new shiny body of the white man beneath (cf. Worsley 1957, 113, 210, 224). The Kaliai have a great deal of evidence to support their view of humans as made up of two bodies. Recently, when an old man died at Lauvore, people came back with stories of how his skin peeled off, revealing a lighter skin underneath. One bush Kaliai shaman told me that in his dreams he had traveled to the land of whites, and there he had seen deceased Kaliai villagers who now had lighter skins, straight hair, a Western lifestyle, and occupations like harbormaster that normally were reserved for Europeans.

CENSURE'S CULT

In the next three chapters I focus on certain themes in Censure's cult that have to do with how people thought about the underground in relationship to the dead and a European existence. But before I go into these more specialized chapters, I want to give a general introduction to Censure's movement as a way of completing the general history of Kaliai cargo cults.

Censure's movement started toward the end of 1969, and its number of adherents grew rapidly. Many who left Aikele's cult at Bibling Ridge, including Aikele, came and joined Censure's new cult. Censure had also been at Bibling Ridge, but the new cult he started was not organized around a development project; instead, it focused on stories, especially those directed at getting the story of human existence right. Censure claimed that his stori cult started at Bibling Ridge when he storied to a European kiap about the true maternal origins of humanity. He believes that his story bested the stories of those who called out their totemic origins in a pig, dog, wallaby, plant, or bird and those who called out simply the names of the mothers who carried them.[23] Censure instead called out the names of two women who were the first mothers of the moieties of Little Bird and Big Bird.

After leaving Bibling Ridge, Censure went with the villages of Angal, Benim, and Gigina to Palupalu, where they stayed for a number of years. There Councillor Sela urged (hatim) everyone to plant coconuts and concentrate on business. However, in 1969 the spirit children Sen Kilok and Sen Seuve came up and instructed Censure to go find the special pools— "Nazareth" and the Glas bilong God (Glass of God, that is, the mirror and binoculars belonging to God)—that became the initial center of his cult. It was then that villagers moved to Meitavale and away from Sela and the promised utopia of council government and development.[24] Censure claimed that the Glas bilong God originated the first coconuts from which the human race was created. There the Kaliai were carried by coconuts that have green shells, whereas whites were carried by coconuts with orange-yellow shells. When his cult was new, Censure adopted the term kulau, which refers to a young coconut fruit that is sweet and refreshing to drink. According to Gloucester Patrol no. 1 of 1971: "Napasisio has not travelled much in his life and has only worked on plantations in the Talasea area and thus regards coconuts as being the major item in prosperity." Before the Germans arrived, the Kaliai area had few coconuts, and these were said to be found only in those few places where Titikolo had put them before he left for America. In particular, Titikolo is said to have removed the coconuts from around Angal, where he was then working church services, and to have carried them down close to the Kaliai Catholic Mission Station. In many cargo cult stories the transfer of coconuts coincides with the fall of the bush Kaliai into ignorance and whites' acquisition of the secret knowledge of how to make cargo. This is very much a plantation-economy view of wealth, which coincides with the fact that up until the late 1980s most bush Kaliai men went and worked on coconut plantations and are most directly familiar with European wealth in that form. Coconuts were also the road to prosperity that government officers were pushing. We should not be surprised therefore that the bush Kaliai associate the loss of God with His moving coconuts away from the Kaliai bush and down to the coast, where the white man's power, wealth, missions, and schools have had their greatest impact.

Initially, Censure's cult was confined to the bush Kaliai villages of Angal, Aikon, Bagai, Benim, Gigina, Moluo and Robos; many of these villagers came to live at Palupalu. It was estimated that eight hundred people were first involved in the cult, which mixed Christianity with a desire to go back to the past but to a past cleansed of its sins. According to a Patrol Report by D. N. Dalgleisah:

> They believe that by following the better aspects of their ancestors [sic] way of life such as returning to live in their old village sites in the mountains and wearing traditional dress, by rejecting the bad aspects of their forefather's mode of living such as tribal fighting or even domestic squabbles, and also by following Christianity, then they will be protected from sickness and end up living in the manner of Europeans. In fact, they believe that had their ancestors lived in this way from the beginning that they would now be on a par with Europeans. This has meant that they have left their present villages and have returned to their old traditional village sites in the mountains and are living in rough bush shelters, have little food and refuse to attend the aid posts or send their children back to school. (1970, 2)

Censure's cult was partly organized around Christian stories of the Last Day. When in early 1970 a patrol visited some coastal Kaliai villages, it found that Censure had "spread the story that after he left the coast there would be a tremendous earthquake followed by a tidal wave and if the people did not leave their villages and come up into the mountains where he was they would all perish" (Sisley 1970, 1). Many coastal villages did temporarily abandon their beliefs and commitment to development as the road to the white man's lifestyle. The coastal villages of Gilau, Kariai, Pureling, Ketenge, Taveliai, and Tumunai came and joined Censure in the bush. They, like others, believed that the more people who came into the stori to be schooled by Censure, the faster the new law would come. Sisley (1970) claims that when his patrol arrived, the cult had 1,358 active followers living at its campsite. Followers also went with Censure into the mountains to visit special ponds. People said that those who didn't go would later have to buy their cargo with hard-earned dollars instead of receiving it free. People's strenuous journeys into the mountains often took on the qualities of a pilgrimage, with followers expected to help each other out and to freely share their food, tobacco, and betel nuts (Janssen 1970, 20–21). Before leaving their home villages, followers would hit the ground with a stick and then speak to those in the underground, informing them that they were going to see the place that was the *as bilong* [origin of] coconuts, humanity, and the stori. Before arriving at these pools, where it was believed God and the dead resided, followers also had to confess their sins. At public meetings followers would hold a long stick and hit the ground while reciting their sins. This sound and the confession would travel underground and come to the special cult site of Mount Sinai, which was near the Glass of God. These confessions were also said to come up to Censure wherever he might be (Janssen 1970, 23). Sorcerers also had to confess, and they did so privately to Censure. People said that those who didn't confess would throw up when they drank from Nazareth later. These pools were also referred to as "doors," and to secure their right to a share of the cargo, villagers sacrificed pigs there to straighten wrongs and "clean the road." People ate the pork, but its soul went down below to be eaten by the dead. As Monongyo put it: "The blood will go down, and they [the underground dead] will see it, and it will buy this something, it will buy cargo. They will see it and then start distributing cargo, following this pig." Sisley described one cult site as containing the following important stones (traditionally, stones with names were associated with masalai and the dead, with figures of change):

> five prominent stones which are the symbols of the Cult. One is known as the Gold stone. This is where all the money will come from on the last day. Another is called the Power stone and this will assist the people achieve the new society. An example of what it will do is that on the last day this stone's Power will make the country level and a lot easier to work.
>
> The three remaining stones are symbols of the history of the people's attempts to break through into the white mans [sic] life. One is a very old weather beaten stone which signifies the attempt of the early ancestors to achieve the position of the white man. Unfortunately they failed. Another weather beaten stone commemorates the attempts of the recent ancestors but they also failed. Finally the third stone is the symbol of the present Cult but this attempt, according to its leader, will not fail. The only other feature of importance in the valley is the pond. This waterhole holds the spirits of the ancestors and when in the area

the people chant their songs so that the ancestors' spirits can hear
them. The cries of frogs from this pond is [sic] interpreted by Napasisio
as the ancestors speaking back to them, using the English language.
This idea lost a little importance during the time I was in the Kaliai
and the replies of the ancestors are now conveyed to the people by
means of a whistle.

   Another important aspect of the cult is a hole in the ground near
there [sic] camp. This is where the cargo will come from on the last day.
Only selected people are taken to this site and only at night. There the
chosen ones stand in line, three men then three women etc., and chant
throughout the night, and Napasisio explains the meaning of the Cult
to them. (1970, 3)

   In addition to discovering special lakes and holes in the ground—
known as telephones—through which to communicate with the dead,
Censure's followers discovered a piece of iron (*reil* or *rel*) that some saw as
part of a railway and others as part of a bridge to cities in Australia where
the dead resided. Like everything else of significance in Censure's cult, this
piece of iron was found by women. At the right time it would be fully
unearthed to reveal a ladder that would let the dead return from their
underground hiding place, and they would come carrying cargo for their
descendants.

   The administration was concerned not just with the rapid growth of
Censure's cult but also with its antichurch, antigovernment, and antidevel-
opment sentiments. Indeed, Censure was jailed twice. He was first jailed
in 1971 for two months at Gloucester, while his followers were punished
with the arduous task of building a road along Avelalu Ridge from the
coast into the bush. During that time many coastal villages (Pureling, Taveliai, Ketenge, and Atiatu) remained loyal to Censure's cult; as Posingen
put it, "All the time they worked at coming; it was not as though father
went to jail, and they became frightened and moved. No, they still worked
at coming" to Meitavale. One large bush village that did leave early on
was Moluo. It abandoned the special ground that Censure had assigned
to Moluo villagers to live and receive their cargo. They went back to their
own area, and in the late 1970s many there joined the new cargo cults
started by Malour and Mapilu that I will analyze in Chapter 7. In the
meantime a few villagers from Moluo continued to visit Meitavale.

   In terms of people's commitment to Censure's cult, Patrol Report no.
2 for 1971–72 claimed: "The cult which only last year controlled 60% of
the people in this area is currently dormant . . . however the songs and
dances of the cult are still occasionally performed." Many people were

also reported as still wearing the cult's dress and facial decorations. The district commissioner, *Masta* (Mr.) Ellem, regarded by Censure as his underground brother, informed Censure that he could continue working his law but that he was not to attract other people to his village.[25] In his report of September 3, 1971, Ellem claimed that after Censure's release from Gloucester Corrective Institution on May 5, 1971, the cult was revived: "The same villages are involved in the cult but there has been an estimated decline of 5% in the actual number of persons following the cult." Censure and four of his followers (Monongyo, Kulo, Amulmul, and Warenga) were jailed for recruiting women for Censure's "harem." While they were in jail at Gloucester, government officials burned down the village of Meitavale, then made up of *haus-skru,* or what a report called "highlands type long houses" (Patrol Report 1971–72). Earlier, the villagers of Angal, Benim, and Gigina were told that they could go live at Meitavale, but "they would have to build houses suitable for a 'nuclear family' and not the unsanitary 'long houses'" (Patrol Report no. 1, 1972–73). Before Censure's cult, the Kaliai bush had not known these sorts of communal family dwellings, which were now built to express people's desire for new larger forms of social unity (cf. Worsley 1957, 161). After their houses were burned down, Censure's followers moved back to Palupalu, but they later returned to Meitavale where they again built new longhouses. The villages of Aikon, Angal, Gigina, and Benim were still in Censure's cult. During this period Posingen and Sela ran for the position of councillor, and the administration was disappointed when Posingen won, for he used his new position to move everybody away from Palupalu and back to the cult village of Meitavale.

Although many coastal villages came into Censure's movement when it started, they did not stay long in the bush, only two or three weeks; they soon went back to the coast, where many of them remained sympathetic to Censure's cause. Indeed, Censure and his bush followers often visited the coastal villages of Atiatu, Gilau, Ketenge, and Pureling; at each village they would spend a couple of weeks schooling people in the new cult ceremonies, dances, and songs that Censure was still acquiring. Censure was arrested at Meitavale a second time in 1973, and he was sentenced to three months in Hoskins Corrective Institution for illegal activities said to consist mainly of "the attempted procurement of underage girls" (Patrol Report no. 6, 1973–74). Three other cult leaders were also sentenced at Talasea, for two months. During his father's absence Posingen took over the running of the cult, but this did not stop its rapid decline in numbers. By 1975 patrols were reporting that the movement no longer had any major influence and that cargo cult beliefs had lost the support of the young men.

Government officials were concerned by Censure's attempt to undermine the influence of the administration and the Catholic mission. In his report of his interview with Censure, Sisley gave an account of how Censure's movement involved people's rejection of all the new structures that were then seeking to incorporate Kaliai villagers:

> When asked by myself what were the Cult's attitudes to the Administration Napasisio told me that the Cultists would no longer recognise the authority of the Council, the Administration nor the House of Assembly. By following the Cult the people have elected Napasisio their representative in all spheres. Also the cultists will not, according to their leaders, pay tax to the Council nor send their children to Administration or Mission aid posts or schools. The reason for this attitude being that if the people involve themselves in things outside of the cult they risk confusing the ideals of the cult and hence jeopardizing the arrival of the last day. Involvement in economic activities are also out for the same reason but the people are still planting gardens and collecting food.[26]

What I find interesting is that even as cult followers rejected official European institutions, they were engaged in practices that closely resembled those of Europeans. They marched, saluted each other, and raised the flag; when a 1975 patrol came upon Censure's movement, it noticed that

> There are some strange things like the House Kiap, House Cell and Office. The house Kiap is used for hearing civil cases like: family troubles, speaking obscene language to other persons, arguments, or not turning up for their meetings. The magistrate is the Councillor Mr Posinga [Posingen], son of the cult leader Mr Napasisio. The cell house is used when the magistrate finds them guilty. The regulation of the cell house is: the punishment from six to six being locked up. This does not happen most of the time because the kiap or magistrate imposes a fine of not exceeding one dollar or imposes on native money tambu. The money that the Magistrate collects is being kept by the magistrate Mr. Posinga and his father Napasisio for their own good. I think the action [sic] will be taken against them regarding this matter. I've found this out from having conversations with them. The house that Mr Napasisio and his son Posinga live in is called the House Kiap. The office is used by Mr Napasisio for any personal matters that the members face. (Patrol Report 1975)

We see here that people are embracing the empowering symbols of order in white culture, which they used paradoxically to mediate and authorize partial autonomy from the hegemony of Europeans. Another example of this was the singing and dancing of cult followers around a flag made of bark cloth and painted with two birds, representing the two moieties. Here a symbol of white administrative power comes to empower traditional symbols of social order and of autochthony. Likewise, when cult followers danced and sang around the flagpole, their ceremonies often mimed the marching and saluting gestures of the military and police, yet followers were divided into the female moiety of Little Bird and the male moiety of Big Bird. The cargo cult drew on the engendering logic of the moiety system, which it married to the logic of traditional magical practices in which people operate ritually upon a symbolic image of what they desire to produce or realize. As we shall see later, we are dealing here with the engendering logic of mimesis; people inserted certain principles of exchange and procreation into their copies of Western culture.

DOMESTICATING THE LANDSCAPE

In addition to imitating state structures of power, Censure copied certain aspects of Christianity, like the Catholic Mission's attempt to get rid of dangerous masalai sites. Today New Tribes Mission followers claim their mission did this. But before both Censure and the New Tribes Mission, throughout West New Britain the Catholic Church went around blessing masalai sites with holy water that turned them to inert stone. Censure copied this pastoral strategy of domesticating the landscape. Following in the footsteps of the Catholic Church, Censure sought to remove the danger that the dead and masalai posed to the living at certain sites, mainly certain rivers and pools. He did this by schooling people in the secret names of the "boss" of these areas and by also calling "the names of the power of the mountains." I was told that before, if you went into certain areas and spoke disparagingly to an animal like a pig, it would turn around and eat you. Censure revealed the name of the boss of all pigs, Amulmul, and he put this name on one of his lieutenants. Censure created a school for each of the two moieties that consisted of teaching the secret names of those residing in the earth and in the mountains in order to familiarize followers with them. Naming is here a process of socializing the underground, which ends its unfamiliarity and danger. I was informed that the calling of the secret names of those in the underground changed them such that they were no longer evil but benevolent. By calling their

names Censure changed their stomachs—that, is their emotional tempera-
ment—so that masalai sites now became accessible to gardening and
hunting. They also became "doors" (*dua*) of information.[27]

This domestication of the landscape was not the same as the Catholic
Church's petrification of masalai sites that rendered them inert stone. Censure never wanted to seal off the landscape but to exploit its transformative potential. In his cult another way of naming the world seemed to offer
the possibility of bringing the plenitude of the underground space of death
into the social. Naming the secret gateways and sites would once again
render knowable and visible the hidden creative forces in the earth from
which people had become removed. Through possessing the lost names of
the earth, people would regain control over this lost world.

For cult leaders like Censure the meaning of human existence had been
obscured and covered up by the language of *skul* (school) and *bisnis* (business). Censure wanted to go back to the knowledge of the ancestors, which
used to come from the dead and the beings residing at masalai sites. The
relationship between Melanesians and Europeans, the past and the present, the living and the dead came to be condensed around certain pools
and holes in the ground where the sealed-off space of one region opened
out onto another. Here different physical spaces provide the conceptual
terrain for mapping out the different categories that organize social life
into separate spheres of existence. The opening up of the underground to
the above-ground space of human knowledge became an image for dis-
solving the clearly separated categories of an existing social order and even
the distinction between self and other. Cargo cults performed their rituals
at sites where they had artfully connected the spaces of the living and
the dead, the past with the present, the lifestyle of Europeans with that
of Melanesians.

There has been valuable work done by anthropologists like Basso
(1984, 1988), Feld (1982), Myers (1984), Munn (1971, 1986) and James
Weiner (1984, 1991) on traditional indigenous notions of space and time.
However, what is also needed is an interpretation of that politics of space
and time created by contact with Western culture. In the next chapter
I analyze people's resistances to the processes that involve Christianity's
colonizing and displacing their imaginary geographies. People's resistances took the form not so much of an outright rejection of biblical car-
tography but more one of reworking it in order to map it onto their spatial
terrains. People reworked their indigenous imaginary geographies, which
they blended with their reworkings of European imaginary geographies.
In the next chapter I focus on cargo cults as part of a politics of space.

Chapter Three

Punishment and Utopia

Death, Cargo Cult Narratives, and the Politics of the Underground

In this chapter I map out some of the imaginary geographies concerning the dead that bush Kaliai cargo cult leaders developed as part of their struggle to uncover and resituate the spaces of power belonging to Europeans and Melanesians. In the 1970s and 1980s many cargo cult leaders, like Censure, Kail, and Mapilu, took up the traditional underground world of the dead as that utopian realm of otherness that would allow people to remake themselves in ways that both mimed and were different from those mimetic processes officially authorized by Europeans. These leaders saw their struggle to reclaim control of the world of the dead as a means of regaining control of the changing terms of their existence. People's heavy investment of time and resources in cargo cults was often an investment in regaining control of their boundaries by reclaiming the empowering imaginary spaces that could return alternative forms of reality and value to them.

Many bush Kaliai villagers still regard the underground as their space of power, and many increasingly have come to see it as their alternative form of heaven. The new images of the underground that people developed drew upon traditional narratives about masalai and the souls of the dead, as well as images and narratives drawn from the white man's lifestyle and his heavenly kingdom of God. The unearthing of new geographies for the dead often involved fusing aspects of European culture with the formative role that the space of the dead played in traditional Kaliai society. Throughout traditional Melanesia dialogues with the dead often mediated the production of knowledge, authority, and power (Herdt 1977; Herdt and Stephen 1989; Stephen 1979, 1982). Through dialogues with the dead people acquired advice, magic, and a sense of control over their lives. With the coming of Europeans the Kaliai incorporated Europeans, Western technology, state rituals, and Christianity into their narratives, understandings, dreams, visions, and ongoing conversations with the dead (Lattas 1992b, 1993). In doing so, the Kaliai have modified their traditional understandings of space by using their dialogues with the dead as part of a process of displacing and mapping out differently the pedagogic arena occupied by white-black relationships. In particular, through new dialogues with the dead, people have sought to impose new local meanings upon the civilizing processes of pacification and Christianization. These foreign processes came to be localized, internalized, and transformed as people struggled to give an indigenous content and context to the moral process of breaking and remaking the self. These processes were transferred and transformed into new forms of emplacement. A new geography of places emerged to resituate individuals, their communities, and their race but also the pedagogic processes that were reforming them. Owning the processes of forming a new moral self involved internalizing those processes into a new geography of places where they could be controlled and owned by the cult community.

In the second half of this chapter I focus on how the Censure cult positioned the underground as that alternative world of the past in which the sinful actions of the living had accumulated to block a new and better existence. Many bush Kaliai came to see the underground ancestors who were going to deliver a new law of existence as also blocking its arrival. In the process of seeking to move the utopia of the dead away from a celestial Christian kingdom and back into local subterranean terrains, the bush Kaliai also developed a concern with why the new world of existence was not yet surfacing. Many suspected that this might be because their relationship with the dead somehow had become problematized or damaged through some moral fault. Indeed, Censure's followers tried to straighten and repay this moral debt by offering pigs and shell money to the dead. People's transferral of God's kingdom and the utopia of a white existence into the underground also coincided with the displacement of forms of moral accountability from a celestial father God and toward subterranean local ancestors whom the living had somehow offended. The underground came to relocate those forms of moral accountability that orthodox Christianity associated with the mirror space of heaven and the moral bookkeeping practices of God. A new structure of mirroring and moral accountability was developed in the underground to mediate and reconstitute the existing moral terrain of black existence.

In Censure's cult people came to see their precolonial pagan selves as having damaged their relationships with the underground dead. The underground ancestors were believed to have become alienated from the living because of the violent behavior of people toward each other while they were ignorant heathens. Through the space of the underground the Kaliai began to reobjectify that moral problematization of their identities and sociability that was being enacted above ground through processes that involved internalizing the white man's culture. The underground became a way of reenacting but also of displacing the moral problematizing forces of pacification and Christianization that were resituating and remolding people's identities. Through the alternative world of the underground, people could map out differently the new moral boundaries of identity that had emerged because people saw themselves and their past through European cultural eyes. The struggle to create new geographies in Kaliai cargo cults was often a struggle to create new hybrid vantage points for seeing the world and oneself from terrains that escaped, but also incorporated, the positions of Europeans and the ancestors.

TOWARD A HISTORY OF HEAVEN IN MELANESIA

Before I turn to more detailed Kaliai ethnography, I want to explore the theoretical significance of death in forming the ontological horizon of human existence. Theorists like Derrida (1994) and Wyschogrod (1985) have pointed out that how death comes to be situated in a culture also shapes and determines how human existence is situated and experienced. I want to argue that the politics of colonialism is often a politics concerning the desire to control the conceptual placing power of death. Colonialism in Melanesia was not entirely a process of people having their physical space taken over by Europeans who demanded less nomadism and permanent villages. Christianity and the state also brought and imposed new geographical understandings that were meant to provide the terms for installing and fixing present existence. In particular, people's understandings of space changed as their indigenous imaginary geographies came to be colonized by the imaginary geographies of Europeans. Christian images of heaven and hell, the Garden of Eden, and the biblical lands of Israel, Jerusalem, Egypt, and Rome have increasingly taken over the horizon of people's thoughts. These places and terrains belonging to Western culture were often not received passively and without question. Instead, throughout Melanesia these Western spaces have often been creatively interrogated and repositioned in movements called cargo cults, which have often sought to imbue these Western spaces of alterity with local meanings capable of making sense of the origin of racial inequalities.

I want to use bush Kaliai ethnography to write a local history of heaven (and to a much lesser extent of hell) in Melanesia. Here I will draw on some insights produced by the historical work done on the imaginary geographies in Europe by writers like Le Goff (1984, 1988) and McDannell and Lang (1990). These historians have explored the social production and transformation of imaginary geographies like heaven, hell, and purgatory. They have explored how changes in those spaces mediated the changing nature of social relationships. In particular, with respect to medieval Europe, Le Goff has shown how the birth of purgatory as a separate space mediated the intrusion of a money economy into feudal social relationships that were organized around Christian notions of moral duty. His point is that imaginary geographies do not just emerge arbitrarily; these fictitious spaces have a historical context that they work to articulate and create. Imaginary geographies cannot be dismissed as fictions removed from the real world, for these other worlds also often come to be immersed in social relationships that they are instrumental in producing and policing. Indeed, imaginary geographies can take on the ambiguous role of operating as vehicles for both the domination and liberation of people.

On the one hand, imaginary geographies can be used to control behavior in the present world by giving it a moral relevance for a future world (Weber 1930). On the other hand, imaginary geographies can have the utopian effect of providing people with a site from which to be able to stand critically outside their world to experience occupying an alternative, better form of existence (Bloch 1995; Ricoeur 1979, 1991, 308–24; R. Williams 1990). Kaliai cargo cults have often articulated both properties in the way they have developed new understandings of space in order to resituate the dead and the living. The new spaces of alterity that cargo cults created came to embody people's desire to be liberated from existing forms of control, but they also harnessed and incorporated these desires into developing new forms of social control, namely, new disciplinary practices, taboos, rituals, and social relationships; adherence to these would lead the underground dead to return with cargo. These new liberating spaces of alterity, with their new forms of social control, were developed around accepting the desirability of what Europeans had—cargo. The desire for cargo was reworked to provide a new moral framework for conferring value and acceptance upon new cult practices, understandings, and forms of control that often mimed those of Europeans. Just as capitalism is based on a certain fetishization of commodities to create its social relations, so the cults' fetishization of cargo created new ways of objectifying and mediating sociability. Here commodities were embraced and reworked to provide the idealizing terms and values within which sociability must be recast. The cults took up and reworked the fetishization of commodities, the way their objectifying power can be used to mediate and create social relationships, but they did this also by relaying the world of commodities through the world of the dead, through a certain fetishization of death that came to inhabit the commodity form.

IDENTITY AND GEOGRAPHY

For all human beings identity is never an original fundamental given that exists independent of space (Bachelard 1969; Casey 1993; Heidegger 1977, 319–39). Instead, part of the culturally shared nature of all identity comes from the way identity is formed from the way people imaginatively place themselves and all that from which they differentiate themselves. For centuries Europeans have used the imaginary geographies of heaven, hell, the Garden of Eden, and the ancient lands of the Bible to form the boundaries of their being by situating themselves as Christians in the world. Europeans have also used their imaginary relations to the terrains of Asia, the Pacific, Africa, and America to objectify all those forms of humanity and sociability that they have imagined as their opposites (Clifford 1988; Fabian 1983; Todorov 1992; Whitney 1973). Along these lines Said (1978) has explored how the West's understanding of itself as Christian, rational, and ordered came from its construction of the space of the Orient as a space of heathen irrationality and disorder. Said's point is that politics and territory enter the imaginary structures of identity, and this is partly because all cultures rely on space as a model for organizing the boundaries of concepts of order and of desire. However, it is not just Europeans who project all that they imagine themselves not to be onto the alternative terrains occupied by others, for indigenous cultures do the same in terms of how they imagine the alternative worlds of the West and of the dead. Here I want to take on board one of the major criticisms of Said's work, namely, that it ignores how those on the other side of the colonial encounter imagine the West and the project of colonization. Said focuses on the politics of the West's imaginary geographies; I want to focus on the politics of indigenous imaginary geographies. The part of Said's book *Orientalism* that I want to use is his point that territory is always part of the politics of identity and that a certain politics of space intrudes into and becomes a major organizing aspect of self-other relationships.

People often are capable of rethinking themselves and their forms of sociability only by rethinking the spaces that they inhabit; people often do this by rethinking and mapping out differently the spaces of alterity that define and mark off the boundaries of their world. In other words, people rethink themselves and their forms of sociability by rethinking the space inhabited by the outside. People seek to transcend the current structure of self-other relationships by reterritorializing the boundaries of their being, and often this involves reterritorializing the space occupied or claimed by the other (Deleuze and Guattari 1987; Foucault 1967; Said 1978).

In this chapter I map out the politics inscribed in that reterritorialization of identity that indigenous groups enact when they come to appropriate and indigenize the imaginary geographies of Europeans. Kaliai cargo cults often reworked the boundaries of people's identities by reworking the horizon of the world that Europeans used for placing themselves and others. Moreover, Kaliai cargo cults often set about exploring the limits of both indigenous and European imaginary geographies. They searched for common points of transition. In doing so they often uncovered the space of death as a terrain shared by the two cultures (cf. Taussig 1987). This should not surprise us, for in all cultures death is a crucial realm of meaning. Death forms the ultimate temporal horizon toward which all life moves, and as such it gives a teleological form to life. Moreover, death's removal from the living provides a space of otherness through which one can define the present terms for living life. I see cargo cults as a struggle to control the conceptual placing power of the space of death, where the struggle to control the conceptual terms of one's existence is dependent upon controlling those borderlands of otherness used to define the boundaries of lived existence.

DEATH AND CARGO CULTS

Traditional Kaliai stories often speak of people meeting the dead and acquiring from them various species of taro, sugarcane, and other food crops (Counts 1980, 1982). Today people keep up this contact with the dead in their dreams. Through dreams villagers acquire from deceased relatives new magical spells, songs, rituals, and masks. In dreams a dead relative will come to guide a shaman, so that he can find the masalai, or sorcerer, who has stolen a sick person's soul. The dead were traditionally part of the ongoing life of Kaliai society. They were accessed continuously, and the gateways to them had to be kept open if life was to remain productive and healthy. To keep the dead close to the living, the dead traditionally were buried beneath men's and women's houses. Through travels to the dead and back Kaliai society created its narratives of transformation. This was the way it figured the task of going past the fixed visible nature of existing things to acquire something new. Through contact with the invis-

ible dead there emerged in stories and dreams the potential for a new
state of affairs. This transformative potential was what Kaliai cargo cult
followers sought when they visited graves, holes, lakes, and waterfalls leading to the dead. At the lakes they visited in the mountains Censure's followers came to see their *namba* (number), that is, the mark or sign that
would later open up a door in their village. There they made speeches to
the dead requesting cargo. It was explained to me: "With the namba [the
signs visited by cult followers], it was so that the door [of cargo] could
come up to them all. So that later, when we started working this something
[the *stori,* their cult] and it came up good, then everything like cargo would
come up to the door at their village, and they would sit down on top of
it. . . . The namba is like this, it goes to their door."

After leaving these cult sites in the Kaliai bush, followers returned to
their home territories where they built new villages on sites that Censure
had found and that consisted of certain holes leading to the underground
that were known as telephones and doors.[1] These gateways to the dead, to
the alterity of the past, would later open up to reveal another time that
was to come.

Like many other Melanesian groups, the Kaliai often render life and
death as the visible and invisible sides of the existing world. Kaliai cults
often posit European ascendancy as coming from whites who placed
themselves between these two worlds in order to control the movement of
goods and people between them. The travels of the Kaliai to towns and
plantations have not undermined their belief in the hidden powers of the
underground. Indeed, Posingen told me how, when he was at Rabaul in the
late 1960s, he saw a hole in a hill that was guarded continuously by government officers. He claimed that at night European and Chinese men would
drive their trucks into this hole and come out in the morning trying to cover
up their cargo with canvases: "All these trucks filled with cargo, which run
early in the morning, they come from where? Some come from ships, but
others come from, I think you know where. We do not know, but you know."

The Kaliai see whites as having an interest in keeping separate the two
worlds of the living and the dead. In this context the realization of a new
law of existence becomes identified with crossing this divide. Kaliai cargo
cult practices have been mostly directed at trying to reunite relatives separated by death, for only when the living and the dead coexist will Europeans and Melanesians have a common utopian existence. Ending one system of alienation (the living from the dead) is here made to promise the
end of another system of alienation (Melanesians from Europeans).

Kaliai cargo cults have focused on what are seen to be doorways between the visible and invisible worlds. Posingen saw the volcano at Rabaul

as a doorway to where the dead were making cargo. Other Kaliai villagers told me the same about other volcanoes scattered throughout New Britain. One young man referred to the volcano at Gloucester as a factory for cargo. One shaman, who has been heavily involved in Kaliai cargo cults, told other villagers that it was no accident that whites had built all their major administrative centers at volcanoes. He claimed whites had done this to prevent people from discovering the secret that volcanoes were workshops. This shaman was quoted approvingly by a fellow shaman as having said, "All the government stations are at these volcanoes, at Rabaul, Talasea, and at Gloucester. All the huge government stations are where these fires are at. . . . Now look, the government has come, and it has blocked the door belonging to us [volcano at Gloucester], then it went over there and blocked that door [volcano at Talasea], and at Rabaul it also blocked the door." In the Kaliai area there are stories about people entering volcanoes and discovering another world. Some stories involve the seismological surveys that European scientists carry out around volcanoes. The native assistants, who are occasionally lowered by a rope from a helicopter into the volcano's mouth, are reported to have seen something like a masalai, a man, a road, or another place. Many people are suspicious of why Europeans have made it taboo for Melanesians to travel up the sides of volcanoes. Volcanoes are often thought of as masalai sites, which in turn are seen as doorways to other secret worlds (cf. McCarthy 1964, 189; Worsley 1957, 115). Like mineral deposits and holes in the ground, volcanoes are places of mystery and power that others come to respect in the same way as Melanesians. Here whites and Melanesians share a secret respect for these places, a respect they hide from each other—which divides them but also secretly unites them.

PRAYERS AT GRAVES AND THE RESURRECTION OF MONEY

Other stories confirm to people that whites know something valuable is under the ground. In all the area of New Britain where I have done some fieldwork—Bali Island, Kaliai, and Pomio—I have collected stories about people's suspicions concerning the practice of Catholic priests who would visit a village and then go pray at its local cemetery. This was an attempt by the Catholic Church to gain legitimacy and followers by fusing Christianity with local forms of respect for the dead. However, what this religious ceremony did was to generate rumors that European priests were secretly receiving money from these prayers at graves. Posingen told me how European priests would visit a grave three days after someone had died, and money would magically appear there. He also told me that this followed Christ's rising from the grave after three days. As proof of his claims Posingen gave me a story about a man from the nearby Bariai area who knew this secret. On the third day after someone's death the Bariai man went to the village cemetery and spied a visiting priest praying. Soon a mailbag full of money appeared in the priest's hand. The Bariai man leaped out, kicked and beat up the priest, and took the bag of money. The priest stood up and scolded the Bariai man, saying that he did not have to beat him, he could have simply asked for the money. The Bariai man replied: "If I spoke to you about this, you would have been frightened, and you would have blocked the money from me. For I know, all the time you have been receiving money when people die. I knew that this time you would again go to the grave to get money, so I went and hid there. When you received the money, I jumped out. I knew you wouldn't give me the money if I asked for it, so I kicked you and grabbed the money." The priest offered the Bariai man money to keep quiet about what he had seen. This prompted the Bariai man to offer to give back some of the captured money, but the priest refused, telling the Bariai man that he could keep it all. Insulted by this rejection of his hospitality, the Bariai man angrily informed the priest that because he had refused the money, the Bariai man would reveal the secret, which is why we now know this story.

In this story the Catholic Church's attempts to poach upon traditional forms of respect for the dead are poached back to sustain cargo cult narratives of respect for the dead. Appropriations are in turn reappropriated: they are taken back to confirm understandings of the secret magic that underpins race relations. Here traditional Melanesian understandings of magic associated with graves and the dead come to blend with a Christian vision of the magic surrounding Christ's death. The transformative power of death in Kaliai culture comes to be joined and indeed reinforced by the transformative power of death in Christianity. Inscribed in these synthesizing practices is a sense of racial inequality as founded in Europeans' possession of a more powerful system of magic for engaging the dead. Implicit in such stories is also the theme that the bodies of the dead rematerialize at graves as money. Christ's resurrection is here democratized and becomes a potential redeeming gift in the death of all people. Such stories use Christ's resurrection to resuscitate not the powers of one man—Christ—but the local powers of all the dead. Here the material world of money is resituated, placed within other circuits of meaning that use the transformative moment of death in Christ's resurrection to reobjectify the creative transformative powers of local graves and the dead.

When I asked a shaman at Bolo, whom I will call Laupu, whether he had heard the story about the Bariai man and the priest, he replied he had not but what he had heard in his village were warnings to be careful about priests who wear black robes and go to graves at night. He quoted other villagers as saying, "When the priests come to us, and it is becoming night, then we must look out good, for it would not be good if they went to the graves and received a large amount of money." The previous day Laupu had told me how after three days he went to his father's grave. There he heard noises coming from inside the grave, which then opened up; a light came from it that was Laupu's father coming to the surface. I asked Laupu if he was dreaming, and he replied:

> No, I wasn't. I saw it straight, he was walking, and he came on top. He came on top, and it was like light coming up. He was holding a huge bag of money, and he came on top. It was not a good time because there were then plenty of men in the men's house. If it had been somewhere more distant, it would have been all right. But all the men in the men's house made a noise. My hand wanted to go down to grab it [the money], but because all the men made a noise, he moved back. The light moved back, and he moved back. A cat then came on top. A cat came on top, and it went and sat down in front of the grave. I was standing up and I could hear it. I was watching the light, it was becoming dimmer and dimmer. I said: "I have buggered up my journey. Why did these men make a noise?" My stomach was no good [angry]. The time when this something moved, when this light moved and went back down, then my father he also started going back with this something. When the light was very dim, then the cat came on top. It came on top, and I don't know—was it him [his father]? I think it was him, and he came and sat on top of the hole [grave] like that.

What is interesting about this story is how a dead person who has gained access to European wealth turns into a domestic animal that belongs to Europeans. The Kaliai do have traditional understandings of the dead as sometimes coming back as a wild pig or cassowary that will seek revenge upon the living for some past crime, or for not having been around to care for a person when she or he died or to show respect and sorrow at the death. In Laupu's story not only do the dead possess European wealth but they also assume the form of European animals. A domesticated European presence comes to inhabit the transformative space of death. A new form of animality associated with settled domesticity and the civilization process now comes to mediate the transformative world of the dead. People's world of transformations and metamorphosis has itself come to be transformed, remediated through new images of death, animality, alterity, and becoming.

MAILING LETTERS TO THE DEAD

Kaliai cargo cult followers have often sought out the secret magic used by Europeans to contact the dead, and this has often underpinned people's cargo cult use of European culture. In particular, the power of Western technology to tap into mysterious hidden forces like electricity, chemical reactions, and the laws of mechanics and thermodynamics gives technology the magical aura of tapping into an invisible hidden realm of power that for many people is analogous, if not the same, as the invisible hidden realm of power belonging to their dead. As we shall see later on, cargo cult leaders like Censure had a number of holes in the ground that were called telephones and that he used to ring and talk to the underground dead. On other occasions Censure used a stick that he claimed was his "wireless" to talk to planes overhead that were reportedly being flown by some of his underground children. Telephones, wirelesses, and planes carried a certain magic that was also sometimes attached to letters and foreign newspapers, for these also cross large distances and come from unseen spaces. Many people gave me the story of how Censure had competed with another cargo cult leader, Mapilu, to mail a letter to the dead. Each wrote a letter that he then put inside a mat. Villagers at Moluo, who were sympathetic to Mapilu, told me: "Mapilu worked something like a miracle," for when the mat was opened, the letter was gone. When telling me his version of this story, Namore of Moluo village complained bitterly about how Mapilu had been "courted" (taken to the administration) by people and that his work had almost come to an end.

Namore went on to tell me of another success the Moluo villagers had in contacting the dead. This involved newspapers that belonged to the dead coming into the Kaliai area in 1974. In the Aikon-Angal area (where Censure was working his cult) these newspapers came up to Aepo, whereas in the Robos-Moluo area they came up to Namore and Mapilu, who were later to start their own cargo cults (discussed in Chapter 7).[2] It is said that these newspapers contained the names of deceased Kaliai villagers who were also asking their descendants to write back if they wanted more "good news." This was taken to mean more knowledge about how to transform bush Kaliai existence so it was like the European existence lived by the dead. Namore described these events like this:

> One newspaper came, and it contained the name of one of my ancestors who had died a long time ago, before the government and the Germans had come up to us. . . . This newspaper came, but we do not know what true road it came along. When it came, we were sur-

prised. . . . It contained the following talk, my ancestors worked this
talk: "Yes, Wading [name of a living man], you are one color, I am another color [a dead person who has turned white]. You do not know
about me, I do not know about you. Are you a good man or a rubbishman?". . . It also said: "If you would like more knowledge, then
write and we will send you more knowledge." This newspaper came,
and it contained all this good talk. We looked at this and we thought:
"All these people who have died, where are they living?" All right, the
[Catholic] mission stood up and said: "Ah, Jehovah's Witnesses!" . . .
But we said, "No, how do they know about our ancestors so they can
write about them in their newspapers?" . . . Well, these newspapers are
still something we think about.

Later, when a second batch of newspapers arrived, they were intercepted
at Kaliai Catholic Mission Station by the priest who was a Tolai. He reportedly became angry, for "they were full of the names of people [dead
people] so he burned them all on a fire." This simply confirmed people's
understanding of the Catholic Church as seeking to block their dialogue
with the dead and of its now being helped by a Melanesian elite that had
allied with Europeans.

Bush Kaliai cargo cult myths treat the current racially organized divisions of the world as having emerged from the separation of the dead
and the living. Indeed, people expect the inequalities between whites and
Melanesians to end when death loses its separate existence. Kaliai cargo
cult leaders struggle to enter the death worlds that the white man keeps
close to him, with this becoming the means through which people seek to
regain possession of themselves in the present. The struggle to control the
world of the dead is a political struggle over space and especially over
those spaces of alterity that map out the boundaries of knowledge, power,
and identity in the present. The struggle to control the world of the dead
is also a struggle over time, for the underground world of the dead is that
world of the past that needs to be reclaimed by the living, if the living are
to have a future, if they are to situate themselves differently in a time other
than the present.

I see the creative magical role assigned by Kaliai cargo cults to the
space of death as congruent with the phenomenological fact that all existence involves a dialogue with death, which forms the horizon of all human action. Traditional and cargo cult images of death as plentiful, as
magically creative of material wealth, are the language of desire that embodies and objectifies the phenomenological power of death to mediate

and create people's worlds, their understandings of reality. But more than this, the emancipatory, liberating connotations projected onto the dead emerge from the fact that the underground space of death allows people to travel beyond authorized narratives, especially those of Christianity and the state. The underground is a space where resistance narratives can voyage beyond that policing of identities and truths that European institutions seek to enact through their policing of geographies of death. The creative labor that people put into cults is part of a desire to keep the alternative terrain of the underground talking, for this hidden world of magic is coextensive with those narrative displacements of themselves that take people beyond the limits of their world as it is revealed and authorized by whites and their representatives. The weapons of the weak lie in their stories about death, in the underground narratives that hold out the promise of being able to circumnavigate the world differently, in being able to move beyond its visible forms, fixed conventions, and familiar boundaries. This is what cargo as a form of plenitude and pleasure partly objectifies, namely, those underground forms of plenitude and pleasure opened up by the activity of storytelling.

In his analysis of the history of how Westerners think about cargo cults Lindstrom (1993) makes the good point that Western anthropologists have often not been able to accept the desire for material goods in others and have thus often constituted cargo cults in purely moral terms in order to render them more acceptable to the West.[3] Although this is true for some recent anthropologists, one deficiency of Lindstrom's work is that it never seriously pursues this good point to its conclusion in order to treat seriously the desires of cult followers. For Lindstrom the only desiring subject is a Western subject who desires the mirror space of the other to reflect his desires in their desires. This analytical position is concerned only with mirroring as a Western practice and not with the practices of mirroring through which indigenous people objectify their desires for themselves via the white man and via their dead. Kaliai society merges the desires and pleasures offered by commodities with the desires and pleasures offered by certain moral narratives. The coupling of material wealth to the avenues of narrative displacement opened up by the underground dead is not a perversion of moral goals; instead, the desire for material goods becomes part of the production of the desire for certain kinds of underground worlds that are metaphors for certain kinds of subversive, clandestine, above-ground existences. The desire for a comfortable European lifestyle is fused with the pleasure opened up by resistance stories when they construct other secret existences not controlled directly by surface whites but by one's underground ancestors elevated to the status of whites. These are ancestors over whom one can imagine having more influence, for, unlike the white man, they are close kin. The displacement of a Western existence into the underground gives a sensual and commodified form to those other desires and pleasures that are opened up by narratives of displacement and the experience of emancipation carried by those narratives. Commodities are condensed metaphors of desire and pleasure within which all sorts of other desires and pleasures can be implicated and objectified.

LOSING CONTROL OF THE SPACE OF DEATH

I want now to explore in more detail the sorts of death worlds that people developed in response to Europeans and the imaginary geographies of death (and also of origins) brought by Europeans. My analytical starting point is the idea that the arrival of Christianity alters the way the world is experienced by altering the way death is understood. By giving new meanings to the ultimate human future, Christianity uses death to redefine the temporal projects and parameters of human existence. The Kaliai have come to perceive their loss of control over present reality as emerging from their having lost control over the space of death. Many bush Kaliai villagers told me that their parents and grandparents regularly used to run into the dead in the bush. They told me that the loss of contact with the dead was a recent phenomenon that people attributed to the coming of Europeans and especially to the coming of the Catholic Church. When I arrived in 1986, many bush Kaliai blamed their recent loss of contact with the dead for illnesses, gardens that were less fertile, and game that was less plentiful (Lattas 1991, 1993). A few old men attributed the decline in gardens and game to government officers who stopped people from burying their dead inside houses. People's parents had done this to keep the dead close, so they could acquire from them magical spells for gardening and catching game. When using a magical spell, someone will quietly call out the names of ancestors who were good hunters or gardeners. Those ancestors came and helped people's parents grow huge taro tubers that weighed as much as heavy stones, and they helped people find game and the souls of the sick captured by sorcerers and masalai.

There is an element of truth in people's sense that their external world changed and that their dead disappeared, for Christianity's vision of heaven has worked to undermine people's ongoing dialogues with their dead. That the dead no longer come up to chat and meet with people is a way of objectifying the problematization and withdrawal of certain traditional imaginary spaces that had been used dialogically to establish people's reality. People's experience of themselves as having lost control of the present world occurs alongside that rewriting of the meaning of death that Christianity enacts as it rewrites the space of the future that forms the horizon of present actions. Rewriting the meaning of death is a rewriting of the meaning of life, and for this reason cargo cult followers struggle for control over the terms of present existence by struggling to rewrite and regain control over knowledge of the world of the dead.

Rather than opposing Christianity outright, many bush Kaliai villagers are struggling to reconcile their traditional beliefs with Christianity in order to use Christianity to lend support to those other spaces that lie outside and often subvert the "public talk" of the church. In their struggle to find a clandestine middle ground some people claim that God Himself created underground places and filled them with masalai and the dead. Many New Tribes Mission followers have found it hard to give up completely the topography of their grandparents. While I was in the field, a few risked the condemnation of their teachers and the European missionaries to sneak up to my house at night to reveal their thoughts about the underground dead. On one such night Namore told me: "There are men underneath and men above. All the men who die go down underneath. All the men who do not die are above. All right, all these men underneath, like underwater or under other things—like mountains, before they would gather [above-ground] people together, saying: 'Come let us go sing.'"

Namore went on to give me a traditional story of how the dead had invited the living to a ceremony by a waterfall, on the River Lepni. Waterfalls are traditionally the places where the dead and tambarans reside. Namore has been involved in three recent cargo cults in the Kaliai bush— those led by Censure, Malour, and Mapilu. He is still involved covertly in the Mapilu cult, which has a significant cult site on the River Lepni where Namore's story took place. There long ago two brothers were beating bark when the people of the waterfall came up to them. The dead sister of these two brothers was with these other dead people, and she invited her brothers to a *singsing* (festival with songs and dances). She instructed them to rub fragrant leaves on their bodies to conceal the smell of their humanity from the underground dead. The brothers were then told to close their eyes, and when they opened them they were standing in an underground village. At the underground singsing many dead people kept asking: "What is it that smells nice here?" but they were told, "Oh no, there is only us here, there is nothing else that smells around here, there is only us, the people belonging to this singsing." The two brothers sang with the dead until it was dawn and time to distribute the pork that traditionally concludes all ceremonies. Their sister then came and gave them a leg of pork to carry back to their mother and father. They informed her they had no way of getting back, but she simply instructed them to close their eyes; when they opened them, they were standing where they had originally been beating bark. The leg of pig that they had been given had multiplied into a huge quantity of pork. Without any prompting on my part, Namore gave me the following observations about the significance of this story:

> Now, Andrew, I say this proof of things used to come up to people, like us, especially to the previous generation. These kinds of places, our ancestors knew about them, so did their descendants. . . . They would tell us that this area is a village and that we should not think it is an empty place: "There are people at this waterfall, for we went singing there." They would show everybody the door: "We went down here, our sister told us to close our eyes, and we went down here. . . . When we finished singing, we closed our eyes and came back to this area." . . . Well, Andrew, these kinds of occurrences were around, and all the big men knew of them; up until the time of the Germans, they were still happening. Then the Catholics came, the church came, and now this something, when people try to work it, nothing happens, it is blocked. There are now no longer "people" who talk there, it is totally blocked. Before all our fathers when they buried people, we saw that, like our grandparents, they buried people with their heads and legs in a certain direction [toward the mountains] so the dead later could stand up and travel in the right direction. We know about this, but I want to know . . . why, when we now try to work the same things, everything is blocked? The road is now blocked. We no longer hear people sing or yell out in all these places. These places are totally blocked.

This narrative of the Kaliai's disempowerment singles out for criticism not the Germans or the state system of indirect rule, which had little day-to-day policing consequences for the Kaliai, but Christianity. The Catholic Church is associated with the loss of ancient wisdom and with the landscape's coming to be sealed off to deny the living access to those spaces of plenitude that the dead traditionally provided. Today Namore is part of an influential group of New Tribes Mission followers who secretly work cargo cult rituals, songs, and feasts to reactivate connections with the underground. They believe that without the reopening of a dialogue with the dead the Kaliai are doomed to white subordination and the futile law of *bisnis* (i.e., trade stores and cash crops). No doubt Namore's observations reflect some of the recent rivalry between the Catholic Church and the New Tribes Mission. This rivalry is expressed as an accusation that the Catholic Church has introduced a rift between the dead and the living, alienating people from their relatives and the powers of the underground. These views, which are highly critical of Rome, the pope, and the Catholic Church, were behind the mass conversion of Catholics to the New Tribes Mission. Yet Namore's accusations are not totally new or specific to the New Tribes Mission, for in 1986 I heard the same views from many Catholics, including Namore, who was then a Catholic. Like villagers throughout New Britain, Censure's followers also believed that the pope was blocking the new law of existence, and, as we saw in the last chapter, such views can also be found in the 1960s' cargo cults of Koriam and Aikele.

Although some bush Kaliai villagers are thankful that the Catholic Church has blessed masalai sites with holy water that turned them into inert stone, others, like Censure, Namore, and Mapilu, believe that the cost has been to deprive the Kaliai of beneficial access to the underground. Namore also blamed the loss of access to the underground on increased surveillance and policing by those aligned with Christianity and the government. He criticized the persecution suffered by cargo cult leaders who sought to find a stori that would reveal why the underground has become blocked: "It is like this, if a man tries to find a stori [a cargo cult], so he can look at something true, and other people find out about this, then these other people 'court' [condemn, persecute, jail] him. But our grandparents saw something, and it is still there. Help came up to our grandparents, this kind of help came up to them all." Namore and his brother-in-law, Mapilu, have been "courted" a number of times for working a stori. Both are critical of "the road belonging to business," and they believe their stori is more likely to deliver a European existence than development projects. In his observations to me Namore also criticized those whites who blamed Melanesians for their poverty, and he criticized the policing strategies of the New Tribes Mission, which uses the fear of Satan to silence stories about the underground:

> What story of our ancestors will help us? We work at finding it. But
> some now look to the government. . . . Yet, all the big men told us:
> "This underground is something important; the mountains have all
> kinds of marks; and they have people inside." Now the Bible informs us
> [preaching of the New Tribes Mission] that this sort of talk is *tudak*
> [very dark], that it is a lie of Satan. This sort of information [from the

Bible] now blocks our eyes. Our ancestors knew something, but they
did not pass it correctly on to us. You [whites] all talk that the cause
lies with us, but I feel that you are hiding things, that you are stealing
things. The king and queen worked the law, and this law has covered us
up, it has covered up the law of everything being free. I work at finding
the road, this road [to the dead and everything being free]. They
[whites] gave us the road of business, we worked this road, but we still
exist like our grandfathers. All these black-skins who support whites
[poroman yupela] work at faulim mipela [tricking, deceiving us].

Namore here accuses educated Melanesians of helping whites to distribute
misinformation about the true sources of wealth. He blames Christianity
for a loss of interest in stories that in turn has resulted in people's depower-
ment. There is an element of truth here, for people's beliefs in the underground did underpin local indigenous forms of power. With the recent
coming of the New Tribes Mission the older generation, people like Namore who were knowledgeable about the landscape, have lost their authority and power in relation to the young men who read the Bible and
who claim to know the true geographies that situate the stories of God's
actions.

Earlier we saw how Namore's story associated the alternative terrain of
the dead with images of plentiful pork, whereas the loss of knowledge
about the places of the dead was associated with the hard road of business,
which the Kaliai were coming to be tricked into adopting. People's powerlessness is here associated not simply with the loss of tradition but more
specifically with the loss of alternative geographies in which to place themselves. What I see as also being mourned was the loss of those alternative
perspectives offered by the ability to place oneself upon an alternative
geography in order to see the world through the eyes of the dead. Namore
complained that the talk of Satan was covering up people's ability to see
the marks in the landscape and the stories about it. It is perhaps the rich
plenitude of stories that Namore also mourns, for he equates losing access
to the plenitude of death with having lost the power to tell one's stories.

Cargo cult followers like Namore struggle against Christianity's policing of indigenous narratives and assert the need to rediscover underground
images of power and creativity. The underground here becomes a space
for developing resistance narratives. Its concealedness allows for the development of a secret counterculture based on traditional images of the underground as a space of origins. Inscribed in traditional stories about
people traveling into the underground was a movement back into both

the space occupied by ancestors who created one's body and the terrain
occupied by those primordial masalai beings who in myths are the origin
of clans, songs, paintings, masks, and landscape features. The magical creative power ascribed to the underground by Kaliai cargo cults comes from
its housing the primordial generative sources of one's self, one's culture,
and one's physical environment. We are dealing with a genealogical model
of the creative process in which the first beings and spatial terrain of the
past are reinvoked, for they embody powers of change. There is also an
element of revitalization in this attempt to recreate the present by recapturing contact with primordial spaces and beings of the underground.
There is an empowerment of the past going on here that seeks to use it
to provide the cultural autonomy and power to go beyond one's present
situation and that future that Europeans and their *poroman* (i.e., Melanesian allies, friends) in the church and government want to map out for the
bush Kaliai.

Namore complained that in these dangerous underground places where
everyone once spoke of tambarans and masalai, the young "new line" of
men now spoke only of Satan's presence. Like Censure, Namore wants to
reempower these masalai sites and have them seen positively. He suggested
to me that God had put monsters at these sites to guard their secret
treasures:

> These places have something, like when we spoke about this place
> which has gas, they call it "masalai" but something is there under-
> neath. . . . I think there is something there that looks after this hole.
> The Big Man put them there to look after the gold, he put them there
> to look after something? . . . We find people calling them dangerous
> places, but, no, there is something there; this something that gets up all
> kinds of work [cargo] is there.

Namore went on to discuss geological explorations in the Kaliai area,
which he made sense of in terms of indigenous notions of underground
power and wealth.

> The scientists [geologists] came and had a look at this site [masalai
> site] and said: "This site truly contains something which is covered up,
> but it is there." We say a masalai is covering up this something which is
> there, all this work is there, all these things which the white man works
> are there. We are afraid of this something, but it is there. They [the
> scientists] came and found this something out and said work would
> come up.

Like other cargo cult leaders, Namore sees the problem of racial domination as one of trying to rediscover that lost knowledge of the ancestors
that will allow people to escape the narrow spatial terrain and vision of
the world into which the white man seeks to confine the Kaliai. He, like
others, sees the role of stories as the need to develop new geographical
understandings of the world, and part of this involves the need to reconcile
the imaginary topographies of Christianity with those of tradition. Currently, many Kaliai villagers who have joined the New Tribes Mission do
not know what to make of a space like hell and the figure of Satan, which
the New Tribes Mission has projected onto the world of the villagers'
grandparents. Many people are also unsure of where heaven is and find it
hard to imagine a world that can hang up in the sky all by itself. Namore
gave this description of how people were unhappy and confused over the
way the spaces of their ancestors had been suppressed and taken over by
Christian geographies:

> I want to know what it was that came up and made this something
> leave us [contact with the dead] and that now blocks our thoughts.
> What has done this! . . . All right, the church came up, it spoke: "If you
> do not hear our talk, when you die you will go to Hell." All right, we
> work at weighing up these things: "This place where people [the dead]
> used to live, this time when everyone went to sing, where is it?" We
> now have many thoughts: one about hell, and the other about what all
> our ancestors knew . . . these two different thoughts are in our heads.
> Now there is a third, heaven, that makes three. With hell we talk: "All
> our ancestors went and saw this place where did it go, have the souls
> [*tewel*] of everyone [the dead] gone to this place? Or what has hap-
> pened? Will these people come and eat us humans or what?" Our
> thoughts work at weighing up all this.
>   The church [New Tribes Mission] came and . . . talks like this about
> this place which our ancestors knew: "This is the place where Satan
> stops and tricks you, you must come this way." All right, now we work
> at following Jesus . . . and these thoughts about the past which should
> school us we no longer follow them. We look toward your customs,
> and our customs, we have laid them down. All right, now plenty of us
> people are mixed up, we are all mixed up [*Na plenti man i faul, mipela
> olgeta i faul*]. If a man wants to stori, he cannot. The custom of busi-
> ness has come up to all villages. . . . It is true God made us, but where
> is this something which was true and belonged to our ancestors? There
> are a few of us who believe that our ancestors gave us something true.

Namore complained to me, with a mixture of bitterness and puzzlement, about the way Christianity has transformed the traditional danger and otherness of the dead and of masalai into the demonic otherness of Satan. He rightly sees the emergence of Satan and hell as part of the incorporation of the bush Kaliai into business and European customs. The alienation of people from the geography of their grandparents is used to ground people's loss of autonomy and to map out the spatial conditions within which European hegemony is realized. Christianity is here experienced as dispossessing people of their indigenous spaces and in particular of those spaces of alterity within which an alternative, more utopian placement of the self could be enacted.

By reducing the ancestral topography of the Kaliai to Satan's tricks and lies, Christianity creates a new topography that internalizes masalai sites and the world of the dead. These regions are transformed from being sites outside a person's body to being subjective fictions played inside people's minds. The space that masalai sites and the dead had occupied previously is now radically changed as these spaces come to be located inside the tricky minds of subjects. Here all those alternative placements of the self and of existence that were provided by tradition come to be rendered as emerging from estranged forms of subjectivity. The outside space of the dead and masalai come to be transformed into alienating fictions that are used to posit a divided self where conscience must struggle against the fictions imposed upon it from the outside by Satan and the culture of one's grandparents. The world of the underground now becomes a demonic subjective reality that is partly demonic because it takes people's thoughts away from God. Cargo cult leaders, like Namore, struggle against these dividing practices of Christianity that are predicated on alienating people from their past, which they do by transforming the geography of people's traditional world into a subjective fiction. Kaliai cargo cults have been resisting this subjectification or interiorizing of the geography of their dead. People struggle to empower themselves by maintaining their ongoing dialogue with the traditional exteriority of the world of the dead. In this, there is a recognition that one's domination and hegemony come from the subjectification or interiorizing of one's culture and its landscape. Its objectivity is what has to be preserved, for its exteriority provides the alternative terrain of authorization through which one can ground other voices and other meanings outside church and European control.

For older men like Namore there is genuine anguish as they try to put together their new-found belief in the Bible with their firm belief in the reality of their grandparents' world:

The Bible talks this something of your grandparents', it is not true. However, a few of us know [otherwise], and it remains with us. At the mountains we have heard plenty of different sounds and yelling [made by the dead]. . . . The Bible speaks of heaven, but this place where all the [dead] people talk, what is this place? Are these [voices] the souls of all people or what? This place where we think that only water falls down is not like that, before people went down below at this place and then came on top. What sort of place is there? All right, we work at thinking about all this.

Namore told me he had not been able to work through this disparity in geographies, that he was still trying hard to find the true place where the dead went to live. He complained how his children now spoke only of heaven. Although he belongs to the New Tribes Mission, Namore has been secretly using his knowledge of the Bible to try to reempower bush Kaliai mountains, waterfalls, and masalai sites. He even suggested to me that one local mountain might have been where Moses' ship landed (cf. Kolig 1980):

This tide came up, and this ship landed at a mountain which the Bible calls "Arat." My thinking is like this: "Where is this mountain— in America or Judaea or Israel or in Australia?" Now with Arat, there is a mountain that our grandfathers called "Alat," which is in our area, and I think: "Is it also in America or Judaea?" Our thinking is like this, we have two thoughts. When the ship drifted, the Bible talks it came to rest at Arat, but our ancestors called this mountain Alat, and we work at thinking about this.

Today the New Tribes Mission works hard at policing this appropriation of biblical spaces that is going on in cargo cult thinking. Recently, around the Aria River the new missionaries showed people a map of the world and pointed out where Galilee and other biblical sites were compared to the United States. Some people were shocked that America was so far from the lands of the Bible. Many saw the New Tribes Mission as attempting to hide the true geography of the world from them. Other people could not accept that Galilee and Jerusalem were not in the Kaliai area. One New Tribes Mission follower gave me this account of how people saw the missionaries as tricking them: "They [cargo cult followers inside the New Tribes Mission] all think that this map is nothing and that you white-skins are really the dead, and youse have gone and come back. . . . They think that these places reside only in our own area." In searching for a middle ground, for those crossroads where the lands of the Bible intersect with their landscape, the Kaliai are seeking to merge a number of different understandings of the creative process. There is a certain empowerment of the Kaliai that comes from transferring the sacred creative biblical spaces of whites to the Kaliai area. Here the creative cosmography underpinning traditional myths of origins merges with the creative cosmography belonging to Europeans. This process is also reinforced by stories of how whites, either through airplanes or submarines, travel into Kaliai mountains where they secretly acquire cargo at the Kaliais' expense.

THE MEITAVALE CULT: WOMEN AND THE CREATION OF NEW GEOGRAPHIES

I have sought to sketch thus far some general ways in which space, politics, and identity have been closely intertwined in recent bush Kaliai cargo cults. Now I want to use these ideas to focus on Censure's cult and the way it transferred the sacred geography of the Bible to the Kaliai bush. In his 1970 Patrol Report on Censure's movement Sisley gave this description of the major cult site—the Glass of God—at the headwaters of the Aria River (see map on page xv):

> At this waterhole are numerous examples of the influence of the Old
> Testament on the Cult. Two mountain peaks behind the pond are
> known by the names of Mt. Sinai and Galilee, a small waterhole come
> [sic] marsh known as Jordan and a large stone, which on the last day
> will convert to a large city, called Nazareth.[4]

In renaming the Kaliai landscape after these ancient biblical sites, Censure sought an alternative placement for Kaliai existence. He was creating a new space around the Kaliai to resituate their perspective on the world, the horizon of their existence. One other place that Censure discovered was a lake called the Red Sea, which Posingen informed me was "the *kamap* [come-up, origin] of you whites; it is not our come-up. Our come-up is from the round water, the *Glas bilong God* [the mirror, binoculars, and looking-glass of God]. The Red Sea is the come-up of all of you [whites]." After telling me proudly how his father found the two mountains Galilee and Sinai, Posingen went on to criticize the New Tribes Mission for telling people that these mountains were to be found only in the lands belonging to white-skins. "Sign [an American missionary] came and turned it all and covered them [the mountains] up," Posingen explained. "Sign wants to call these mountains to go toward the white man only and not toward us. If we call these mountains toward us, he complains about it. If it comes toward West New Britain, he covers it up. He does not like it and covers it up."

European hegemony is here experienced as a struggle to possess people by controlling the spatial boundaries that underpin their new reformed sense of self and belonging. The domination of people here is experienced as a struggle to police all those hybrid geographies, all those new synthetic forms of knowledge, that people use to reinvent their sense of belonging to the past and to the world. People come to repossess their sense of the past by refiguring it through their appropriation of the sacred spaces of European culture. When the Catholic priest and anthropologist Father Janssen arrived in the Kaliai area, he found it was full of biblical spaces, and in his 1970 report to the administration he produced a map showing the mountains Sinai and Galilee, along with the *raunwara* (pools) Nazareth and Jordan.

One important omission from Janssen's report was that Censure often directed women to go and map out the cult's new sense of space. Women were sent into the mountains to explore and find the lands of the dead, the secret sites where whites were receiving cargo. Censure's daughter-in-law, Theresa, described their journeys like this: "No man went with us, he [Censure] put us women, us young women ahead. The older women came behind with all their boss, their husbands." During these exploratory journeys the women discovered the mountains Sinai and Galilee. They also found heaven; it was a huge cliff beneath which was a giant abyss; the cliff was heaven because anyone who fell from it would die. At night the young women often chose to sleep at raunwara, hoping that they might run into the dead there. Theresa told me of one occasion when they had some success, for she heard a dead person yell out. She woke up the other women, saying, "You two, get up, and let us put on our *purpur* [ceremonial grass skirts], let us *bilas* [decorate ourselves], and go now; I think this is a sing-out [call] belonging to us, let us go and hear it." The women rose, decorated themselves, and started singing the cult songs known as Atwaneh and Seaneh. They then went back to the village and reported their successful close encounter with the dead. One reason women were chosen for this task of exploration was that, in traditional Kaliai myths, women discovered the secret objects of power—the masks or tambarans—that formed the basis of a new social order. Censure was convinced that women would again discover a secret that would institute a new social order, a new society in which Melanesians would live like whites. Women's arduous journeys into the mountains were to explore not simply a physical horizon but also the limits of an indigenous mythological horizon that located the creative powers of primordial time in the procreative powers of women's bodies. These wanderings were exploring the mythological boundaries of the concept of woman and were trying to reinvoke her primordial procreative powers to disclose the creative powers of the dead and of whites. Traditional myths of matriarchy, which involved women who were discovering and creating the instruments of a new social order, were used to try to discover and create that alternative social order of the dead that Europeans were using to sustain their livelihood.

In the mountains women performed rituals and songs belonging to the dead to entice them from their hiding places. Theresa described to me one expedition during which they came up to a hill called *Ros Ples,* which was "where all the big men say that Jesus was born." From there the women traveled to the base of Mount Sinai where they heard someone blowing a trumpet shell (*taur*). Censure had earlier instructed the women: "You cannot follow the road which all the big men used before; you must go and cut a new road that is yours." The discovery of a new road is a euphemism for a new road of knowledge created by women that is going to be different from the road of the past that belonged to men. Whereas the big men used to journey around the base of the mountain, the women, following Censure's advice, climbed upward. They climbed past a cave and onto stones where they worked the cult songs of Atwaneh and Seaneh. They then journeyed to another mountain where they heard the dead blowing another trumpet shell and beating drums. Theresa claimed that there they came close to discovering a secret site of cargo, for they heard a mysterious plane land in the mountains: "The plane's engine was crying; it landed and the noise stopped. They made the engine die, and it landed there at Sinai. It was not as though we heard it go past Sinai, onto this place and then that place. No, it landed at Sinai, cried there, and then they made the noise die. When it went down on Sinai, the fog cleared and all the mountains were totally visible." While his wife was speaking, Posingen interrupted to tell me how suspicious it was that this fog came up just as the plane was landing and lifted after the plane had landed. He saw the fog as concealing where in the mountains planes came to take away cargo.

Kaliai cargo cults have often focused on mountains, not just because they were traditionally associated with the dead, for this also begs the question of why this traditional association was good to think with. Like water and the underground, I see mountains as objectifying and articulating that sense of the concealed and of the hidden, which Heidegger (1977), like Nietzsche (1886), saw as indispensable to all human thought (cf. Derrida 1979). The sense of a hidden order lurking behind the real was used in cargo cult attempts to unearth and create new domains of knowledge and to displace existing forms of knowledge. The mountains objectified the cult's struggle to reveal another space of existence; the alternative terrain of the mountains became the alternative terrain of whites and of the dead. The mountains, with their high rocks, crevices, and passages, suggested hidden spaces cut off from the rest of the world. Here spatial images of alterity and outsideness become ways of conceiving alternative worlds full of hidden unknown powers belonging to Europeans. There is an attempt here to refold the world so that the distant can be made close, so that the world of Europeans can be localized into the world of the dead and into the folded terrain of the past and the present, which mountains embody.

SPIRIT BEINGS AND THE NEW LAWS OF EXISTENCE

Censure organized women's journeys into the mountains on the basis of information he received from underground "spirits." Under Censure's guidance the women found the pool of water called the Glass of God and a nearby smaller pool called Nazareth, which was noted for its magical healing qualities. Posingen boasted of how many villagers along the coast (Atiatu, Pureling, and Kaliai) came to Nazareth and were cured of all kinds of ailments: "Some whose nose had been cooked by engines [asthma] and others who had been really sick, this raunwara [pond] straightened them, and they are now all right." Initially, the major underground beings with whom Censure communicated were Sen Les (Saint Laziness), Sen Seuve, and Sen Kilok (Saint Clock). Sen Les was a child of Censure's who had died at birth. He belonged to Big Bird, the moiety of Censure's wife, and it was from Sen Les that Censure received the law of Atwaneh, that is, the cult rituals, songs, and names belonging to Big Bird. Sen Seuve and Sen Kilok were the spirit children of two of Censure's sisters who had died and later carried children in the underground (cf. Janssen 1970, 30). Censure, as the mother's brother (**tumno**), was in a special kinship relationship to these two children. He belonged to the same moiety as they and received from them the *skul,* or law, of Seaneh belonging to Little Bird. Posingen explained to me how his father received much of his knowledge in the form of visions: "He [Censure] did not receive talk in the form of a person coming up and speaking to him. It was not like that. It was him alone, who would go stand up, and talk would be worked in his own thoughts." To his followers Censure claimed: "These singsing have come up alone from my thoughts. It is not as though I received them from a grave or from a businessman or something like that. No, I acquired them from my own thoughts."

The ritual knowledge that Censure received was often said to be a "picture" (**ano**) of something real that was to be found in the underground and that was later to come to the surface world. The correct working of this ritual picture would lead to its realization. Rituals were also sometimes described as "drawing" or as "painting" a picture. Often this ritual picture was made up of symbols, practices, and items of material culture drawn from a European existence that the cult wanted to recreate in the Kaliai area.[5] People borrowed from the dominant European culture in order to get a foothold in its existence and to get some way of manipulating its hold over them. Copying was not a passive process of miming the dominant hegemonic culture. Involved was a politics of insertion and appropriation in which people resisted, not by situating themselves completely outside the dominant culture but by taking on and reworking its symbolic terms to gain power and their own frameworks of meaning. An example of this was the way the dead, before independence, gave Censure a "picture of a flag" around which cult followers marched, sang, and danced. Followers also sang special songs as they sacrificed pigs by hoisting them up the flagpole in an attempt to strangle them. To this day people believe that their successful ritual working of this "picture flag" led to the emergence of the national flag of Papua New Guinea. Censure told his followers that the underground had informed him: "You go hoist this [cult] flag, and try flying this flag so we can see it. If you do this, the flag of Papua New Guinea will come and change this picture flag of yours. The flag of Australia will go back and that of Papua New Guinea will come."

Censure also claimed that the success of his rituals led to the departure of Australian currency and to the emergence of a new national currency, *moni kina*. In 1986 he complained to me that whites had been able to "pocket" (steal) moni kina and for that reason he was working on *autim* (outing, revealing, creating) another new issue of money called *moni* **dabol** that would belong to Melanesians.[6] Before he died, in his rituals Censure worked the picture of moni dabol, which was also referred to in *tok piksa* (cryptic, allegorical talk) as *famili moni* (family money). Censure was convinced the arrival of this new currency from the underground would deliver a new and better form of value to Melanesians. If someone went to a store holding a note of moni dabol, that person would be able to purchase everything in the store. The word dabol also crosses a number of languages, and it is pronounced like the English word *double* and the *Pisin*

Censure's daughters holding a picture of the flag given to the surface world by the underground

word *dabol* and carries the same connotations of doubling and multiplication. In the Kaliai bush dabol is also the *tok ples* (local language) word for a black clamshell found in inland rivers. Censure chose this black clamshell because it stood in sharp contrast to moni kina, whose name *kina* comes from the Pisin word for a white clamshell found on the coast. The blackness of this new icon of monetary wealth—moni dabol—resonated with that revaluing of black existence it was to bring about. This black clamshell also symbolized regional differences in the Kaliai area, for dabol, in coming to be found in inland Kaliai rivers, was the alternative form of wealth belonging to the undeveloped bush. As such it represented a road of knowledge and progress that rivaled that of the developed Kaliai coast where business and social change were expected to be delivered through using moni kina. Moni dabol represented the bush's assertion of itself as an alternative site of value and as a truer form of social change to that instituted along the coast by government officers and Europeans.

These two clamshells, these two forms of money, embodied the differences of a racial order and the regional differences produced by uneven development. Here the dichotomies of white versus black, European versus Melanesian, and coast versus bush were assimilated to the autochtho-

A symbol of never-ending money, a *piksa* (picture) of moni dabol. The new leaf is enclosed in a casing that resembles a *kina* (oyster) shell, which is the name and symbol of PNG's currency. This casing has been cut away to reveal another *kina* shell casing which in turn, if it had been cut away, would have revealed yet another *kina* shell.

nous binary schemes of Little Bird and Big Bird. Posingen also informed me that before Censure died, he made his followers work the picture of moni dabol in their rituals. This picture of moni dabol was the leaves of a certain tree, whose new leaves were enclosed in a casing that resembled a kina shell (see photo above). When this casing was opened, it revealed not only a new leaf but also a smaller kina casing containing yet another smaller leaf that would later grow past the previous one. Inside this smaller casing was yet a still smaller casing with an even smaller new leaf. This kina-shell case contained a reduplication of itself within itself; it doubled itself, reproducing the icon of new monetary wealth inside itself. We have here something that is good to think with, in the sense that this leaf's reduplication of itself was a good image for the utopia of never-ending money, of money reproducing itself. Many cargo cults in the Kaliai area, like other cults throughout West New Britain, have often had rituals for magically increasing money. In this picture of moni dabol we have a kina shell, which is the state's icon for money, coming to enclose and reproduce other versions of kina within itself.

I asked Posingen to describe some ceremonies performed at Meitavale around the picture of moni dabol. He described a ritual in which they built a fence around the telephone door of a small mound known as Mountain Truk. This fence was circular, but it was not allowed to form a sealed enclosure, for this would block the hole/road leading to and coming from the dead. Instead, the fence had to be open at opposite ends to allow a clear passage from the underground to those above ground. Like many other rituals in Censure's cult, the law of moni dabol involved Censure's schooling of women in a new language that he called English. Posingen saw this school as miming Western classroom lessons with the women as Censure's pupils: "We stopped down below and worked its drawing and its law [law for moni dabol]. It was like when teachers school children. My father schooled all the mothers, and they followed him in this tok ples [Censure's English]. They followed him and he schooled them like children." The last part of this ritual for "drawing" moni dabol involved moving *pipia* (rubbish), which was the cult's euphemism for cargo.[7] At the visible level the pipia to which Posingen referred was the stomach of two pigs that had been killed. Their stomachs had been set aside close to the telephone door, and Censure sang out to the men: "Tell you mothers and sisters to gather this pipia and put it here, to heap it up, and to put some ground on top and plant the stomach of your pigs there." According to Posingen, the real meaning of this picture talk was that

> They [the women] had to place and carefully look after something
> of theirs. They had to heap up their cargo, they were heaping up their
> *kaikai* [food]. It was not cargo, it was good kaikai they were heaping
> up. Later, when the machine comes up, it would work their kaikai. Its
> meaning goes like that.

During this ritual Censure also ordered his followers to dig up a stone that was sleeping close to the telephone door. He told them: "You dig this up, for we are working the picture of money, you turn this stone which sleeps close to the door and which is blocking the door, you must turn it." Undergrowth had covered up this stone, which was also thought to be a "picture" of Stone Sakail, the original ground of creation on which God stood when he created the world. *Stone Sakail* is also the traditional name for the island of West New Britain, the starting place of all creation.[8] It was a primordial stone beneath West New Britain that was being symbolically turned in this ritual, and this was done to reveal the money and cargo beneath. Posingen quoted his father as saying: "You turning this stone is like turning stone Sakail, the picture goes to stone Sakail, it is like turning the island Sakail which is underneath like stone. If you turn stone Sakail then moni dabol must come up." Posingen then went on to explain his father's thoughts like this: "Father asked us to turn it, so that which was down below could come on top, and that which was on top would go down below." The turning of this stone was symbolically turning the primordial ground underpinning people's existence. By setting this stone in an upright position this ritual sought to invert the world in order to bring what was concealed in the underground to the surface where it could displace the existing order of things, which would then be driven underground.

In some of his other rituals Censure also tried to recreate the ground on which people stood. During one ceremony at Meitavale people danced in the village square, and their legs shuffled dirt together to form a mound that came to be called Mountain Klam. It was said that as more and more people joined the cult, this small mound grew larger and larger and of its own accord. Later, when followers deserted the cult, this mound became smaller and smaller, until it disappeared when Censure died. I was told that if people had stayed in the cult, this mound would have kept growing to provide a new terrain that would have linked the Kaliai area to other parts of Papua New Guinea. When the cult was at its peak, this mound had started to acquire offshoots, or ridges, that were referred to as its "hands." One hand was said to go toward Rabaul, another toward Talasea, and the third toward the top of a Kaliai mountain known as Alat, which is where cargo and the dead were to be found. Monongyo told me that whites had "pocketed" everything from Andewa, so Alat was now left as the mountain containing the cargo belonging to Melanesians. This mound known as Mountain Klam was also used as a telephone by Censure. He would climb on top of it to address his followers, to tell them what new talk he had received from the underground. Monongyo claimed that inside Mountain Klam was an underground Christ with whom Censure communicated:

> This mountain, we call it a mountain, but it is like a house, it is the house of all the talk. This mountain here, it is like this, it is the mountain of Jesus. The mountain of Jesus is standing up. Some telephone talk used to come up from this mountain belonging to Jesus. This mountain was huge. If everybody sat down good, then it would have kept growing and become large. If everyone remained straight, then this mountain would have kept growing, for it is the wind of God.

In effect, what Censure was doing was recreating the spatial boundaries that positioned people's sense of themselves. One of the other ways that

Censure sought to relocate his followers' sense of identity and their existence was through bringing on the Last Day. Its earthquakes would come and flatten the Kaliai landscape to make it more accessible to cars, ships, and cargo. Censure and his followers would hit sticks together to make noises that anticipated and sought to bring on the earthquakes of the Last Day. But they were also concerned that these earthquakes not come on too strong and destroy them. As Theresa put it, "We wanted it to come up, but it was not to come up too big; it should come up small." For this reason special rituals for the Last Day were performed at the River Sul. There cult followers gathered together small stones. Men, women, and children held these small stones, some words were spoken, and then they threw the stones into the air so they would splash into the river. Theresa described the significance of this picture of the Last Day like this: "We threw them like that, in this kind of picture, so that later when the earthquake came up, and the bush was damaged, well, the bush, because of the earthquake, would not be thrown down into the sea." During this ritual women danced with cordyline leaves, throwing them this way and that to make the stones that would be hurled on the Last Day travel far from the bush. Posingen claimed that this ritual law of the Last Day also was worked for "getting rid of all the dirt belonging to darkness. It [the dirt] would go down into the Glass of God, all this something—all the customs of fighting, sorcery and killing other people; all the magic for buggering up something [sorcery for destroying people and gardens]."

Theresa went on to tell me how Censure sought to protect his followers from the Last Day by ordering them not to cut any plants unnecessarily as they walked in the bush. If people were building a house, they had to cut just enough timber for it; they were not to waste timber and destroy trees unnecessarily. Censure informed his followers: "Everything is a person. Later, when the Last Day comes up, then this meaning will come out. When the Last Day comes up, then all the leaves, trunks of trees, and the stones as well—everything will then talk." When I asked Posingen to clarify what this meant, he answered that later, when God came back to Papua New Guinea, the small trees would become human and talk. Their talk would strengthen the ground, so that the earthquakes of the Last Day would not move the ground around too much—it would remain strong and intact despite all the shaking. Censure warned his followers: "Now supposing you cut all the small trees and bugger them all up, then when the earthquakes come up, all these small trees will bugger you up; for you have made it so that the sea will come and cover us up."[9] Posingen quoted his father as saying: "We say they are just simply trees, but later when the

Big Man comes up, then they will all become human, and they will talk. They will talk, and they will help us, and they will strengthen this ground so that when the Last Day comes up, the ground will not move around too much; it will remain strong while the earthquake is going on." The attempt here is to refigure people's relationship to the environment such that they come to respect it and see it as concealing their future within itself. Though Censure wanted to change the boundaries of people's identities and the horizon of the world within which they situated themselves, he did so by embracing the terrain and environment of the bush Kaliai in a way that made it speak and reveal other hidden forms of residence and occupancy. Now I want to document in more detail the relationships that Censure developed with the underground.

SCHOOLING THE UNDERGROUND

Censure's ritual laws for creating a new existence involved teaching his followers different schools of knowledge belonging to the different moieties. These two schools were equated with the secret magical laws of Rome (i.e., the Catholic Church). Little Bird followers learned the school of Sen-law-Roma, while Big Bird followers learned the school of Sen-for-Roma. These two schools involved learning long genealogies and the new names for plants, for different parts of a house, and for domestic and other everyday items.[10] This renaming of the world created a new sense of reality; it changed the terms within which people comprehended their existence.

The first law that Censure schooled his followers in was called the Wind of God, and it entailed learning and performing the songs and dances known as Atwaneh and Seaneh.[11] When traveling long distances, followers would sing these songs so that they were magically transported to their destination faster. One old man told Janssen: "The songs are our medicine for the road" (1970, 34). The singsings were also used as punishments for transgressions, with an offender or his group made to sing the cult's songs all night and even for a couple of days. Yet these singsings were also popular; many ex-followers told me of the moving incorporative power of the cult's songs and the beauty of the dances and decorations that accompanied them. The aesthetic attraction of cult ceremonies was used to gain converts. Posingen told me that followers worked the Wind of God to attract new followers. He claimed: "It did not matter who you were, you would worry and come inside." The aim was to make people cry, to move them so that they came to be captured by these songs of sorrow and felt compelled to enter the cult.

These moving songs and dances were also directed at the dead. They too were meant to be touched emotionally by these songs so that they would join Censure's cult. At the same time, as Censure sought to convert the living, he was seeking to convert the underground dead. He wanted the ancestors to be affected to the point that they would perform the cult's ceremonies in the underground. I believe that Censure sometimes sought to capture and incorporate the living into his cult by first claiming to have captured and incorporated their underground dead. I say this because Censure's conversion of the underground to his cult often outstripped his conversion of those villagers who resided above those underground terrains. For example, on the south coast of West New Britain above-ground villagers did not join Censure's stori, but I was told by Posingen that their underground dead did join. Censure often visited the south coast and talked to the underground dead there in ways that I think were designed to entice his local relatives to convert to his cult like those on the north coast had. My sense is that Censure tried to capture certain villagers for his cult by first capturing the underground terrains that underpinned people's understandings of power and their sense of control and ownership of the hidden terms of their existence.

Censure spent a great deal of time schooling the underground in his new laws. Initially, he schooled his underground children—Sen Kilok, Sen Les, and Sen Seuve—and they then schooled the underground ancestors. Posingen explained it like this: "We worked it and then *tumbuna* [ancestors] would work it. We worked it on top so that sorrow [*sori*] would go to them all and then tumbuna would get ready and work it back to us. They too would work it. Father would learn us to work it, and Sen Kilok would school them down below." Cult followers hoped that the incorporative power of their moving songs would call up feelings of pity in underground ancestors for the state of their descendants and lead their ancestors to want to come outside and join the living. As Posingen put it: "Its meaning was like this: tumbuna was close, tumbuna wanted to come up now, and we worked this meaning [the songs] so as to move tumbuna, so as give worry to tumbuna." Many people saw the killing of pigs in cult ceremonies, their lack of attention to gardens, their hard labor, hunger, and lack of sleep through working cult rituals for the ancestors as meant to arouse in their ancestors feelings of pity. These self-imposed forms of suffering were an attempt to trap the ancestors into relationships of guilt, so that the dead would feel sorry for their living kin who were putting so much effort into honoring them. This was an attempt to trap the ancestors into a debt that could be repaid adequately only if the dead brought their underground European lifestyle to the surface.

Censure's cult reflected a desire to make the underground and above-ground worlds perform the same ceremonies, share a common culture.[12] To some extent this mirror relationship was not totally new but also derived from Kaliai tradition in which the dead and the living copy each other's ceremonies. Namore, who had been part of Censure's cult, told me that when his grandparents worked a singsing for taro, they saw themselves as copying the songs, dances, and customs of the dead. The customs of the living were authorized because they reproduced those of the dead from whom they were derived. In reenacting the customs of the dead one sought to please them and to encourage them to look favorably on one's taro gardens. Namore also told me how his grandparents used to say, "Look, suppose we singsing over taro and pig, then all these men who died will be happy, and they will singsing as well." The world of the dead here mimes the world of the living, and this miming is not of the order of a picture miming a reality but of the order of two realities miming each other's representations and, indeed, miming each other's miming of each other. In jointly performing the same rituals the underground and the above-ground start to become doubles of each other. They start to mirror each other's representational practices and to become each other.

Censure, perhaps more than any other cult leader, took up and developed this theme of mirroring and doubling (cf. Bercovitch 1989; Feld 1982; Panoff 1968; Rank 1971). After coming back from visiting the Glass of God, followers received from Censure a new name that belonged to an underground person. In tok ples this underground namesake was known as **ilaten,** or **lem abirh** but more frequently in Pisin as poroman, or *wannem.* Ex-cult followers told me that they believed that their poroman lived with God in the raunwara known as the Glass of God. Posingen explained people's new names as a form of baptism into Censure's new law: "With the [new] names of all men, it is like this—with the mission, it washed [baptized] them with Catholic names, but my father worked this now, so their names would come up with this [new cult] law." Traditional Kaliai initiation rituals also involved initiates' acquiring new names that they were to be called after they had learned the new tambaran's law (its secret songs, dances, and names). When Censure gave a person a new name, he also explained what position the namesake held in the underground. For example, Censure's son Posingen was given the name Silong, which was the name of the man who bossed all the other men in the underground. One of Censure's lieutenants received the name Amulmul, who was the boss of all wild pigs and masalai. Monongyo, who was in charge of raising and lowering the cult flag at Meitavale, was given the name of a man, Senabom, who was in charge of the cult's flag in the underground. A daughter of Censure's received the name Salubeh, which was the name of a woman who bossed all the other women in the underground. The effect of these names was to make the internal hierarchy and structure of the cult mirror the hierarchy and structure of the underground. Cult followers were informed that it was from their underground poroman that they would receive their specific cargo, and this was also dependent on how hard they worked the cult's laws. Censure did more than import the identities of the underground into the world of the living. The dead and the living did more than share similar names. They also became doubles of each other's mannerisms, behavior, and attitudes. If an above-ground individual was lazy in accepting Censure's school, it was said that her underground poroman would also be lazy in working cargo for her above-ground namesake. Here the underground person functions as the alter ego, or as the mirror half, of the above-ground person. I was also told that if a cult follower insulted another follower, he also insulted the poroman of the other person; he injured the underground double of his opponent and in so doing buggered up the road to cargo. Compensation in the form of pork might have to be paid; the soul (ano) of the pork would go down below and be consumed by the injured poroman and the other dead. Posingen explained that the ritual laws of his father were hard, and this was partly because Censure required those involved in arguments to give pigs to compensate each other's offended underground poroman.

> Now supposing you and me argued. . . . Well we would have broken a law. It is like this, we would have buggered ourselves up. . . . We would have buggered up our cargo with this argument. It is like this, if the two of us argue, I am crossing your poroman in the underground and you would be crossing my poroman in the underground. It is for this reason that its meaning is that we bugger up our cargoes. If I started the cross first, you would not have to do anything, but I would have to fasten a pig. I would work two *pram* [strings of shell money] and this *tambu* [shell money] would go to Otit [Censure], but the pig would go down below [to the telephone, door], and we would show it there. We would fasten it at the door and kill and let die this wrong of ours. The pig will be killed. [Theresa interjects, saying: "It will straighten you so as to straighten your poroman down below."] The other person would do the same as yourself.

Here the moral order of the community comes to be policed through those new structures of value embodied in cargo and through locating the realization of people's desires for cargo in an alternative terrain that displaces subjects and reobjectifies the consequences of their actions. Censure's power over his followers came from his controlling their imaginary relationships to their underground doubles. Censure used his control over the imaginary geography of the underground to create new moral boundaries for positioning people's sense of themselves. He baptized people into new names, which immersed them in an alternative sense of themselves.

The underground repositions subjects in another moral terrain; it becomes a way of objectifying the characteristics of subjects, a way of talking about them but at a distance and via the detour of their alter ego, or mirror self. This was no doubt partly a mechanism of social control whereby cult followers were controlled by depicting the consequences of their laziness and bad habits in an underground world that mirrored and embodied their future. In many ways the underground provided Censure with what heaven had provided the Christian clergy, namely, an imaginary terrain for positioning in the present world the consequences of transgression. Both heaven and the underground work to give a geography to the future; they police subjects through giving them another presence in a world that promises to fulfill all their desires. This process of doubling subjects, of making them occupy more than one space, had other aspects. The underground world of the past also served to condense and objectify those moments of traditional culture that people were struggling with as moments of themselves.

STRAIGHTENING THE DEAD

Cult followers saw their underground namesakes as already living the white man's lifestyle, and many saw them as living inside a white skin. Individuals were told to expect their specific cargo to come from their wannem, or poroman. Along with these claims Censure would also say that the arrival of cargo had been held up by grievances that the dead had against the living. Censure spent a great deal of time visiting different telephone doors, trying to discover what was preventing the dead from coming to the surface. In trying to solve the grievances Censure often ended up exploring the different moral norms that separated the dark world of the past from the more morally enlightened state of existence that the Kaliai now claimed as the basis of their identity.

Although Censure's cult saw itself as dependent upon the underground dead, the cult was also built around a moral critique of Kaliai ancestors. They were accused of embodying all those old bad habits and ways of thinking that were preventing Papua New Guinea from sharing in a new law. For this reason Censure started schooling those in the underground in the Wind of God and later in a second set of rituals he called *lo bilong tumbuna* (law of the ancestors). Censure saw his telephone conversations and the discipline of his new rituals as a way of reeducating the dead, for they had not participated in the moral transformations that had occurred in the above-ground world that had discovered God, stopped fighting, and had sought to civilize itself. I see Censure's battle to eradicate the pigheadedness, anger, and immorality belonging to the dead as a way of speaking allegorically about the pigheadedness, anger, and immorality of the living. The dead, which were spoken to through the telephone, represent those voices of the past that reside in the memory and habits of the living. The dead represent an underground displaced fragment of oneself with which the cult enters into a dialogue in order to reform and reconstruct that part of the identity of the living seen to come from a flawed cultural heritage.

Censure told his followers that the wrongs and sins of the past were blocking the law. Most ancestors were ready to come, but they had been stopped by a few underground individuals who had old grievances that they wanted to straighten out. As Posingen put it, "Tumbuna wanted to come, but if there was one man in a small place who was stuck, then nothing would happen. Father would have to find him, work this man [compensate, appease him], work it, and work it, so that this wrong was finished." At his telephone doors the dead queried Censure about some of the violent crimes that had been committed against them. The dead wanted to know why they had died so violently at the hands of the living. Those who had been murdered would hold those now residing above ground responsible for *stretim* (straightening, compensating for) the sins of their grandparents, and they would not allow the cargo to come until their grievances had been addressed. Sometimes Censure would arrange for the living to "buy" these sins of their grandparents by bringing shell money and pigs to the sites inhabited by those angry individuals whom their grandparents had murdered. This compensation was said to clear the thoughts of these ancestors so that they would now want to join the other dead and come to the surface.

Through conversations using his telephones, Censure worked hard at trying to negotiate away the anger of the dead. He would talk in a conciliatory way with them until their thoughts started to become clear and angry thoughts no longer blocked the coming of the new law. The anger of a few vexed individuals was said to be responsible for their rejection of the new school through which Censure was trying to reform the dead. The violence of the past was blocking the transmission of that moral knowledge—the

Wind of God and the law of Tumbuna—that would clear away the ancestor's angry thoughts. Posingen explained how his father would try to find the underground sites where someone was "stuck," and there he would try to help this person to come up with the others whom Censure had already "straightened" (compensated) and clarified: "If there was a man who was stuck and not clear, that is, he was not clear for he could not hear the talk and the law of Tumbuna, which was being worked, he would say, 'I am not clear about this law, you all go, I will stay.' Now it would be like this, the Wind of God would talk to my father to go find this man."

Posingen gave me the example of one such man whom his father went to find. He was Apolu, who had been killed at Spool, close to the south coast village of Molo. When Censure visited this area, Molo villagers took him to where Apolu had died. There Censure was queried by Apolu, who demanded to know why people had told lies that he was a sorcerer and had then killed him. He was angry about the way he had died, for while he slept, people locked him inside his house and then set it on fire. Apolu spoke to Censure: "I rose up confused, and while the burning house ate me, you all worked at spearing me. What am I, for you to do this?" Apolu wanted to die honorably, saying, "If you came, sang out to me, and we fought and you killed me, that would be all right. But this time, what happened? Why did you come and give me this sort of pain? I slept well, you locked the door and put fire all around." In taking up the aggrieved underground dead of the south coast Censure was perhaps trying to extend his cult into this area by creating and feeding off a sense of moral crisis that people had regarding their relationships to their past and the dead. Censure authorized his cult practices of reconciliation with the dead by taking up and further developing that moral problematization of people's relationship to their past, which had been created by the civilizing processes of Christianization and pacification.

Apolu strengthened his demands for compensation from the living by saying that without it he would not allow the "law of Papua New Guinea" that Censure was working to be successful. It was a new national law of existence that Censure was negotiating with the dead. The space of the nation here emerged from a requirement that it incorporate and deal with its underground history, that it address its dead. Posingen went on to give me the following conversation between his father and Apolu.

> He [Apolu] spoke: "Do you think this custom [of setting him on
> fire] is good? Now you want to work the law of Papua New Guinea,
> but what was this something you worked toward me? What sort of

thing did you work to me? Now I am telling you, you are not enough
to win anything, until I win you." Apolu talked like that to my father,
his stomach was cross. Father said: "Forget it, you cannot worry about
this, we will finish it." My father worked at holding some shell money,
he worked about ten *pram* [stringed shell money], and he said: "I will
buy your previous body, I will buy it." But Apolu spoke: "No, if you
want to buy it, you do so also with a pig; it is not enough for you to
play with me like this [with small compensation]. What do you think,
what do you think this time now is? For moni kina and moni dabol are
now at this time inside [the underground]; moni dabol is in my hand,
don't you know? If you like to come good [with good intentions and adequate compensation], that is all right, if you want to work this something [compensation] to come to me, then work it good. Fasten a pig
and I will go, but if you do not, then no way—it is not enough for me
to go. What is it that Papua New Guinea now wants to work, so that it
goes ahead and comes up clear? But before you all worked what to me
and you buggered me up like that? What did you then think? I am not
rat whom you can set alight in the kunai grass."

Posingen went on to tell me that Censure offered to straighten this wrong
of Papua New Guinea's, saying: "I will buy this wrong of mine, of Papua
New Guinea. It is true, with this wrong it is not as though anybody worked
it, it comes to us of Papua New Guinea who worked it." Even though the
men who committed this wrong against Apolu were now residing in the
underground, it was their living descendants in Papua New Guinea who
had to compensate Apolu, for it was the above-ground world that committed these offenses. As Apolu put it, "This wrong belongs to Papua New
Guinea—all the children who remain must buy me." After talking with
him for a while, Censure was able to get Apolu's stomach to become
slightly colder, and he was able to get Apolu to accept some shell money
as compensation. Apolu took the soul of this money, but that did not stop
him that afternoon from chasing and throwing stones at those going back
to the village with Censure: "It was afternoon time, and Apolu had gathered stones. He was throwing them into open areas and was running this
big line which was coming back. For they had killed him, like they had,
and his *tewel* was residing in this area. He chased all the men, and they all
came back and slept at Molo."

Through his dialogues with the dead Censure engaged in giving back
to the living a means of reclaiming their monstrous history and atoning
for it. As national citizens, people took on the task of seeking to atone for

all their inherited crimes and murders so that they as national citizens could be relieved of the consequences. Through acknowledging the faults of the past and offering compensation for them, the living asserted themselves as different from a heritage that had become the burden of Papua New Guinea. We see here not only the way the hegemonic discourses of civilization, pacification, and Christianization have problematized people's relationship to their past but also how that problematization comes to be internalized and refigured in ways not anticipated by Europeans, the church, and the state. The pedagogic processes of civilization, pacification, and Christianization come to be reimagined; that moral problematization of the past that they establish comes to be internalized and renegotiated within an ontological structure that cannot conceive of a nation that is totally removed and alienated from its dead. In Censure's cult the colonial moral problematization of the past was internalized in a way that kept alive the positioning power of underground sites, which now became sites for mapping out and exploring the moral boundaries of a new existence as national citizens.

Whereas the ancestors wanted to know from Censure why they had been killed, he would try to learn what crime they might have committed that led others to want them dead. Posingen gave me the following account of that maneuvering around responsibility for the past that took place at the telephone holes:

> Well, the poor man who had died would talk out to my father. He would say: "I worked this kind of practice [some sort of wrong], and this man sorcerized me and I died." Father would say: "But it is your fault, you must not work these things." [*The deceased man replying:*] "This that I worked was not a true wrong, I worked it like this, and this man killed me for no reason." These men would work at turning my father over these issues.

These confessions of the dead to Censure were referred to as washing their *pipia* (dirt). Once their skins had been cleaned, the dead could acquire Censure's new school. Censure was here rebaptizing the past, cleansing the ancestors of their dirt so that they could become morally reborn and come to live with the living. Censure sought to overcome the blocking of the law through a dialogue that established with the underground a consensus about who was responsible for the misdemeanors of the past. There was an attempt to come to some sort of agreement with the dead that would divide up and allocate responsibility for those past crimes that had alienated what Censure referred to as Papua New Guinea Down and Pa-

pua New Guinea on Top. The nation here was being spatialized and dichotomized into an underground and an above-ground version of itself. A
new national identity was being remirrored and renegotiated between
these two halves of Papua New Guinea. Perhaps the mirroring constitutive
role of the imaginary space of the nation in relation to Melanesian villagers was also being remirrored here in the mirror constitutive relationship
between the underground and surface worlds. The underground was a way
of reflecting on national processes of self-reflection and self-constitution
that could now be remirrored in a subterranean world that deformed and
deflected those national projects of pacification and Christianization. The
mirror problematizing effects of nation making in the surface world could
now be displaced and caught within a unique mixture of underground
mirroring effects in which all sorts of dispersions, forms of interference,
scatterings, and polarizations could be achieved; their effect was to explore
people's unique rendering and ownership of their problematization as national subjects.

To his followers Censure would acknowledge that he was not always
successful in convincing the dead to give up their grievances. Some, who
were stubborn and remained angry, would prefer to stay sleeping on their
beds rather than come out of their good houses to dance and sing the
new law of existence that Censure was bringing to them. These pigheaded
ancestors were seen as rejecting the purifying rituals through which Censure sought to wash away the dirt of the past. In the case of an ancestor
who was like this, Posingen told me that Censure would rely on his underground spirit children to find this ancestor whom they would then pull
from his house to join in the underground ceremonies that copied those
worked by cult followers above the ground:

> Its meaning is like this, he has to be pulled and made to go outside
> so that his dirt can be cleaned. He has to be thrown outside, so he can
> go now [with the other dead to the surface]. They [Censure's spirit chil-
> dren] must pull all these men who don't listen to the [Censure's] talk,
> and they must come outside [of their houses]. Before when [my] father
> worked the Wind of God on top, and it went down to them all in the
> underground, some listened to the talk, but some others did not listen
> to the talk but worked at sleeping. They did not go outside to work
> and learn the law that Otit [Censure] gave from Papua New Guinea on
> Top to them all down below.

Otit was a name given to Censure by the Wind of God, and it was also
the cult's name for the God of Papua New Guinea who was to bring the

underground on top to live in the surface world. Many cult stories involved miracles that Censure had worked that proved his divine status. What I find interesting is the way Censure fused the biblical figure of God with the imagery of an emerging new nation that would be a Christian nation. Censure took on the role of grounding God, of moving Him from the transcendental sphere of heaven to a more immanent plane of existence in the surface world where He would assume a disciplinary custodial role over the living and the underground dead.

Censure's relationship to the underground was not just one of appeasement, conciliation, and compensation. He was also engaged in a moral critique of the dead. Indeed, Censure told his followers that the anger of some of the dead was feigned. They were not really cross about being killed with spears and sorcery—they just wanted to block the law "by being *bikhet* [pigheaded] and sleeping inside the house, so they could continue just sleeping and eating." In their underground utopia the dead were already receiving good food without working for it, and some would complain that Papua New Guinea on Top did not have much food, so why should they come to the surface? Posingen accused these ancestors of selfishness: "They did not want to hear the Wind of God and think of another man." He reported their thinking and conversations this way: "You cannot hear this talk and go outside, ignore them [those above ground] and this rubbish talk. We will stay inside our houses and eat this good food. Why should we go outside? If we go outside, will we eat good food or will we see just rubbish?"

Censure's nephew in the underground, Sen Kilok, was in charge of schooling the underground, and he would discipline those dead who were pigheaded. Sen Kilok would hit them and physically toss them out of their houses. As Posingen put it, "Kilok would work down below, and Father [Censure] would work on top. Kilok would go beat all these rubbishmen who were inside [their houses]; he would put a cane to their backside so that they would come close [to the surface]." Sen Kilok was even reported as burning down the underground houses of some who had stubbornly refused to perform Censure's new ceremonies. Posingen went on to inform me that it was the ancestors of the Lusi and Anem that Sen Kilok often had to discipline like this. Censure claimed he had straightened out all the grievances of Mouk ancestors but that the ancestors of the Lusi and Anem were making it difficult for his cult to succeed. No doubt, Censure was here developing excuses for why the cargo had yet to arrive, but what he was also doing was constructing regional identities by capturing different groups' specific sense of their moral history. Indeed, I believe that Censure

initially succeeded in attracting the more educated and economically developed Lusi and Anem groups into his cult because he was able to feed
off that problematization of their identities that came from their looking
at themselves through the gaze of the new institutions that had to a greater
extent captured their lives. Censure enticed these more "developed"
groups into his cult by telling them that their ancestors had committed
bigger crimes that required more compensation and commitment on their
part. In the end, however, Censure was not able to hang onto these groups
for the same long periods of time as other nearby bush villages, like Aikon,
Angal, Gigina, and Benim. Today many bush people blame Censure's
death on the coastal villagers whom he lured into killing pigs and giving
shell money that was meant to compensate their dead.

Censure took up and refigured that colonial problematization of identity that came from Lusi and Anem villagers' self-hatred for having been
people who fought frequently with spears and who had killed many people
with sorcery. In his telephone conversations with the underground Censure
started to unearth their murderous past, and what he uncovered fitted into
people's specific knowledge of how in the past, when the rains failed, their
grandparents had fought because food was short. In particular, Lusi and
Anem villagers had often fought each other over cycad nuts (*baibai*),
which people still rely on in times of drought. Here Censure was trying to
straighten out a history of regional conflicts so that the memory of these
injuries no longer continued to divide Anem from Lusi villagers, as well
as the living from the dead. Through the space of the dead the Kaliai
sought to resolve the memory of those monstrous murders they had committed upon each other. This memory was not given purely by the past
but was formed partly by the Kaliai's seeing the past through the civilizing
eyes of the new law of Papua New Guinea that Censure was developing.
It was perhaps no accident that Censure's movement emerged in the early
1970s around the time of independence, for what is independence if not
this process of Melanesians' assuming responsibility for their pacification
and Christianization? Censure took the logic of independence with its
Melanesian pastoral powers and applied it not only to those living on the
surface but also to those living underground. They too had to be morally
cleansed, disciplined, civilized, and reeducated through the ritual work of
his cult. Here Censure took the transformative logic of Kaliai magic and
initiation rituals (which operated through songs, dances, and secret
names) and merged this with Western disciplinary rituals and pedagogic
projects that sought to deliver the new, self-disciplined, independent citi-
zen of Papua New Guinea.

One new cleansing ritual that Censure devised was called *Kamtrengen.*

It involved followers who danced with sticks that represented the spears the ancestors had used to kill each other. The underground was also required to perform this ritual "so as to cut [away] all these sorts of wrongs." The school of Kamtrengen would finish all the "laws," that is, habits and customs, of fighting that had belonged to the ancestors. Theresa and Posingen explained it like this:

> THERESA: This story [of Censure's] stood them [the underground dead] up. They would now work this law of theirs [Kamtrengen] so as to cut these wrongs belonging to them all. Censure spoke to us, and we worked it [Kamtrengen] like that, so that it would also cut this law of theirs, where they had buggered up others by spearing them. It would cut all this away altogether, so that it would be gone.
>
> POSINGEN [INTERJECTING]: He [Censure] spoke like this: "This is their law, now you all must school in it. Papua New Guinea must school on top, but they [dead] too must school. All our ancestors have to come and be schooled in this *lotu* [Censure's church]. All the people down below have to be schooled in this church. They will watch you all, and they will be schooled by this [watching and then reperforming cult dances and songs]."

Censure was inventing a new imaginary relationship to the nation. His cult's decorations, songs, and rituals were designed for an imaginary community that incorporated the dead as spectators, participants, and as future citizens. Censure's pastoral role was to produce the new model citizens for this nation through a dual process that transformed local rituals into disciplinary techniques and Western disciplinary techniques into local rituals.

Censure's pastoral role was also one of trying to produce the new nation by reconciling people with their dead, their past, themselves. Now I want to look at another of Censure's conversations with the dead in order to further document and analyze the issues that people were negotiating through Censure's dialogues. This particular conversation involved a man, Katu, who had been killed while he was on top of a stone. Katu came up to the telephone door belonging to the Lusi at Dekodeko. Posingen described to me how his father went to hear this "court": "He worked court, in that he [Katu] came and crossed my father: 'How is it that you are Otit? And how is it that before when I was on top of a stone, plenty of man came and shot me with their spears? Why did they not wait for me to go down below, and then they could shoot me?'" Censure informed Katu that he had not been born at the time of this fight and did not know about it.

But Katu replied, "No, you know! You at this time are Otit, and you know about all things." Censure asked Katu to tell his story; he tried to calm him by allowing him to air his anger. After Katu had spoken for a while, Censure tried to turn the tables on Katu and on the grievances of the dead in general. Censure started to question the right of the dead to always hold the living accountable for these above-ground murders. He pointed an accusing finger at the dead, saying that they had in fact committed the crimes for which they now wanted the living to compensate them. Posingen gave me this account of his father's dialogue with Katu:

> Father spoke: "Ask yourselves, not me. We, this new line, do not know about this kind of thing [killing people]. This line [that killed] belonged to you. You alone buggered up people and went around killing yourselves, you alone. The reason for this is that you did not have enough food." [*Katu asks:*] "What, why did we not have food?" [*Censure replies:*] "You did not have food because of you, yourselves. For youse alone chased away the Big Man [God]. He ran away and punished you all. This punishment of yours is not having enough food and eating all sorts of bitter fruits and yams. This [wrong and punishment] did not occur with us. We of this time are not pigheaded, we stop good, plant our food, and eat it. But before when you all did not have food, it was to do with youse, it was your punishment." He [Censure] worked this, and Katu then said, "I think it is our fault."

Here Censure tries to convince the dead of their participation in sin. Censure's conversations at his telephone doors were witnessed by his cult followers, and through him they were conversing out loud with the very tradition that helped form their thoughts and identity. I see these dramatic telephone conversations as objectified reenactments of an interior process of revaluation, wherein people play out on a stage (through Censure) an interior drama going on within themselves (cf. Hess 1991). In this scenario, in which Censure convinces the dead of their guilt and their need to reform themselves, the Christianized, pacified Kaliai self speaks back to its origins. It tries to convince those voices of the past inside itself about the right ways to place themselves and their relationships to their living offspring. All human beings have multiple identities and multiple voices inside themselves through which they carry on a dialogue that establishes who they are. The psychological condition of multiple identities and voices that underlies what some psychologists pathologize as schizophrenia is simply an extension of the normal condition for living as a human being (Laing 1960, 1961). The underground that was morally reworked by Censure involved a dialogue of self-alienation that expressed how people struggled to live with underground voices that had rejected them, an underground past that they also had difficulty living with. These subterranean voices tormented people with a memory of immorality that had to be appeased. People struggled to renegotiate the voices of their heritage, and utopia came to be identified with that moment when people would be able to live untormented with those underground voices that their cult had brought to the surface.

A psychoanalyst would see here a therapy session in which the unconscious has its tensions resolved through a process that brings those tensions to the surface of consciousness (cf. Wilson 1975). There is an element of truth in this psychological perspective as long as we remain aware of the historical and social context within which the unconscious gains its formative content. In the case of Censure's cult the underground and the dead operated as figurative structures for objectifying and working out the submerged, repressed renegotiations of community identity and selfhood that occurred as Melanesians assumed responsibility for civilizing themselves. We need to keep in mind that the anticipated, longed-for moment of catharsis was objectified and given value as the surfacing of a new world of commodities. The pleasurable moment of disclosure contained its own world of racial desire. We also need to keep in mind that it was through the medium of Western technology, the telephone, that Censure struggled to form both a new consciousness of the past and a new consciousness for the past. It was not simply that the Kaliai wanted to see the past differently; they also wanted the past to see itself and the living differently. This new reflexive moment was captured and objectified in the medium of a Western technological artifact that brought people back to themselves and their origins anew.

The space of the underground has always operated for the Kaliai as a reflective space, which both belongs to them (in that it is inhabited by their grandparents) but is outside them. In their cargo cult reworkings of the underground the Kaliai were developing new reflective mediums for repositioning themselves, but to do this they first had to change the way their dead saw themselves and their descendants. In reality this reflective space was not really outside the living; it was fictitiously placed outside as a way of granting independent status and objectivity to certain ways of positioning subjectivity, of forming knowledge, of creating the process of creation. What Censure was cleaning in the underground was the terrain of the past upon which people could continue to speak in a familiar way with themselves and yet with the semblance of objectivity. These structures for objectifying and viewing one's community through a familiar outside position had to be rehabilitated. Despite all his critiques of the ancestors, Censure never rejected their existence or the need to exist in a relationship with them. Indeed, Censure's battle to reshape the sentiments and morality of the ancestors was also a way of holding onto these objectifying voices. It was a way of hanging onto those circuits of meaning that emerged through the living projecting and making their concerns those of the dead. Here it is a question of the detours and distances that a culture produces inside itself and how it comes to manage those detours and distances. To some extent all identity emerges from the process of overcoming an original cleavage or division that is posited to exist in the world (Derrida 1987; Lacan 1977). Through the creation and overcoming of distances people map out and reclaim the grounds of their existence. In the context of cargo cults those detours and distances come to mediate all those structures of alienation that fragment people and prevent them from living together with their dead and in racial and ethnic harmony.

We are dealing here with how the divisions of race and ethnicity come to be informed by a reworked Western discourse that thinks about difference in a temporal way as bound up with the burden of a primitive past. I have suggested that the problem of how to live with one's murderous ancestors was partly a refracted rendering of the internal psychological problem of how to live with the murderous heritage that had given rise to one's being. The framework of self-alienation within which people searched to uncover their underground was one of how they, as pacified Christian natives, could live with themselves as the children of heathen murderers. The imaginary geography of the underground provided the terrain through which people could objectify and rework the cultural conditions of the past that were said to be holding up their movement into the white man's lifestyle. Guiart (1951) was right to argue that the discourses of missionaries and state officials often associated material progress with moral enlightenment and that this reinforced and gave rise to cargo cults. I would argue that people applied this association not only to themselves but also to their dead. Censure's cult was also a new church (lotu) whose new ritual laws and disciplines were directed at pacifying, civilizing, and indeed baptizing Kaliai ancestors. Here followers were reenacting and renegotiating with the processes of their pacification, civilization, and Christianization, only now they were not just subject to those pedagogic processes but also vehicles for them.

The underground world of the dead can be seen as the objectified form given to those psychological components of the self that were perceived as coming from a monstrous past. The underground provided a site of condensation within which could be placed all those violent emotions, murders, and misdemeanors that the white man, the state, and the church demanded be left out of everyday life. The darker side of humanity was projected onto the ancestors and, through negotiating away their anger, people sought to negotiate away a shadowy voice that ought not to speak inside themselves. Yet despite this moral critique of the underground, it also embodied those past selves and those primordial autochthonous beings seen as indispensable to Melanesians. Ultimately, the underground would bring the cargo, not whites. The underground, although it is the source of one's continuing present punishment, was also people's space of freedom for going beyond business and the truths of the European Bible. The underground was the burden of the past, but it was also that realm of autonomous secret truths that allowed the past to open up and offer a different future. Kaliai cults privileged the light of the white man's knowledge, but their counterdiscourse also privileged that which was hidden, that which remained in the shadowy underground, for this was ultimately the source of Censure's knowledge and the source of the cargo.

THE POLITICS OF SPACE

In this chapter I have explored the way multiple spaces are used to make sense of the colonial encounter. The creation of different spaces disconnected from each other is a way of figuring structures of alienation, both within and between human beings. People think about racial differences through those images of difference and separation provided by their separation from the world of the dead. The struggle to engage, communicate with, and reform the voices of the underground was set up as the necessary precondition for entering the lifestyle and personhood of the white man. The underground was people's concrete image of a layered existence built on hidden truths. This image of different layers of knowledge between the living and the dead provided a way of figuring colonial differences—of what it means to occupy and speak from different cultural positions in the world. We are dealing with space as a tool of thought, where the multiplication of spatial varieties provides images for different vantage points in knowledge and thus for the problem of cultural difference. Another way of saying this is to say we are dealing with indigenous images of multiculturalism in which whites are positioned as seeing the world from the standpoint of the dead. With their airplanes, ships, and submarines whites are secretly visiting the dead and taking away not only the cargo but also a secret position of knowledge. Utopia for the Kaliai will come when they too can enter that hidden space of death that the white man secretly colonizes and uses as his vantage point.

In Kaliai cargo cults racial divisions are displaced into geographical divisions. The white-black dichotomy comes to be explored through the familiar terrain of the living-dead dichotomy. The cult's mapping out of racial subordination renders it as emerging from having lost control over the familiar terrain of death. Racial subordination takes the form of a lost underground and a belief that only through a ceremonial alliance that breaches the underground's closure and isolation can the separate racial existences of the living be overcome. Here it is a question of how people think about the otherness of the future and the otherness of a European lifestyle through using that image of familiar distance provided by the dead. It is a question of what indigenous images of otherness can come to mediate the unfamiliarity of the future and of Europeans. It is a question of familiarizing the unfamiliar, of what are the available familiar conceptual schemes through which the unfamiliar can be thought about and brought close. I see the underground as one of the bush Kaliai's most powerful metaphors for a removed realm that is still close. For here was a space of invisibility that contained people's kin; here was a form of concealment that potentially could be opened up, that could be related to and negotiated with. We are dealing with the operations and mechanisms that an indigenous culture uses for rendering the distant close; what are its techniques that mediate the distances it posits?[13]

INTERSECTING SPACES, INTERSECTING NARRATIVES

In bush Kaliai cargo cults racial politics often took the form of a struggle for control over imaginary geographies that people did not see as imaginary but more as alternative spaces, as spaces of alterity. For many indigenous groups this struggle to maintain access to outside spaces has often been part of a struggle to maintain control of the narrative spaces that locate and mark the boundaries of existence. We need to note that the time of a narrative always involves the crossing of space, a journey, a circulation of subjects and also of meanings between spaces, that can come about only if there is distance, that is, multiple spaces that can be related together and crossed. In traditional Kaliai culture the production of the distance that makes narrative possible often comes from positing and journeying to those terrains of otherness provided by the lands of the dead. With the coming of whites those spaces of otherness belonging to the dead have become the image for thinking about other terrains of otherness belonging to the West—like heaven, America, Australia, or the Bible's ancient sites. Here a certain mediating logic, for familiarizing otherness, places the Kaliai dead in European geographies and Europeans in the geography of the Kaliai dead.

Kaliai cargo cult leaders and shamans struggle to find places of intersection: where heaven, Australia, America, Japan, and the lands of the Bible meet with the various terrains of their grandparents. These individuals outrage state and church authorities with the unauthorized links and bridges they create between these multiple spaces. In collapsing and folding together different spaces, in implicating them in each other, these individuals are searching across different terrains for ways of connecting local mythology and practices to present historical circumstances and the global world in which the Kaliai now find themselves. This searching for an opening in the landscape, for a middle ground, was the form taken by people's attempts to gain control over their destiny and history. Serres wrote perceptively about how history, as a narrative structure, is often this unique bringing together of multiple spaces. He argued that history is, ultimately, like all narratives, a journey between spaces, a linking together of spatial varieties:

> The fact is that in general a culture constructs in and by its history an original intersection between such spatial varieties, a node of very precise and particular connections. This construction, I believe, is that culture's very sense of history. Cultures are differentiated by the form of the set of junctions, its appearance, its place, as well as by its changes of state, its fluctuations. But what they have in common and what constitutes them as such is the operation itself of joining, of connecting.[14]

Cargo cult narratives often unfolded the promise of a new history by unfolding a new map of the world. In their cargo cults people explored and made sense of the existing world as one made up of multiple unconnected spaces that needed to be rejoined. In the Kaliai bush, history was the stori or narrative that accounted for the creation of these spatial differences while also promising and offering the means of overcoming them. Cargo cult leaders and the heroes of cargo cult stories were often empowered by their discovering, creating, and passing through particular points of intersection in these fundamental spatial disjunctures that made up the present world. I am interested in the narrative schemes that people used when they posited these alternative geographies that did not so much supplant the real as add new territory to it, territory that ultimately repositioned the real. The liberating potential and the euphoria of freedom experienced by followers emerged from the experience of transcendence that came from adding another layer of meaning that recontextualized and rendered ambiguous existing visible terrains of meaning.

More than this, I would suggest that in these alternative geographies the human imagination was allegorically adding itself and its operations to human existence, with the constitutive powers of the human imagination now objectified and rendered as the creative power of the world of the dead. It is perhaps the hidden creative powers of the imagination that are allegorically figured in people's sense of their hidden underground spaces as the true creative spaces underpinning the world. In narratives that mourned the lost magical power of the underground and that attributed its loss to the arrival of Europeans, people were giving embodied narrative form to their lost power to create a displaceable world, to occupy other established vantage points for seeing the world anew. The world of transformation traditionally mapped out by these underground geographies was now fast disappearing: they had become blocked and petrified by the blessings of the Catholic Church and more recently by the intrusion of more coercive forms of proselytizing by the New Tribes Mission. I see the alternative forms of emplacement offered by the underground as objectifying those alternative forms of emplacement offered by stories. Through the constitutive worlds of their dead, people developed alternative narrative terrains that allowed them the illusion of viewing human existence from outside itself. We need to explore the indigenous techniques that people use to produce the new distances that make new narratives possible, that allow them to displace the positions they hold in the world in order to create a new history—that is, a new narrative journey that rejoins differently the spaces and ruptures making up the world.

Narratives and the work of the human imagination are a structured practice; in this chapter I focused on the role of spatial images of distance in opening up narrative domains dealing with other distances in the realm of social relationships. The itineraries for the journey, the concrete sites chosen for speaking the truth about the world, are conceptual tools; they are part of what Serres referred to as "the technology of this discourse and its special morphologies":

> They are no longer simply elements; they are like the tables of the
> law. They are operators expressing the operation of mythical discourse
> itself, which, from its origins, has as its function the linking of spaces
> among themselves, the linking, for example, of separate ecological

niches, each one defended tooth and nail. No one leaves here and no
one enters—except those who speak geometry, the discourse that has
communication as its goal. Myth attempts to transform a chaos of separate spatial varieties into a space of communication, to re-link ecological clefts or to link them for the first time: from the mute animal to the
proto-speaker. (Serres 1982b, 50)

Ecology here is the multiple terrain of different distances occupied and
formed by categories. What I take Serres to be arguing is that the creative
work of the imagination is underpinned by classification trees that parti-
tion and segment the world into separate conceptual divisions or realms
whose crossing and rejoining becomes the narrative time of myth and history. There is here a close interlocking of space and time; indeed, the crossing of space always takes time; it creates and gives form to time, to history.

The Kaliai try to control their future by trying to maintain control of
the geography that contains and embodies their past. Moreover, they resist
incorporation into the future posited by schools and development by both
adopting and reworking the primitivist images of their past that are
brought by whites. People fight to maintain control over their future by
striving to maintain control over the multiple spaces that they can inhabit;
that multiplicity is what confers the experience of freedom, movement,
and indeed the power to create history. The struggle to preserve both traditional and newly invented extraterritorial spaces was a struggle to control
those exterior domains through which people could become something
other than themselves. Recently, the New Tribes Mission has sought to
control people's processes of becoming by controlling these lines of flight,
that is, those imaginative domains that allow people to reposition themselves. The New Tribes Mission sees heaven as the only proper extraterritorial space for viewing the world, and it has used the policing images of
hell to control people's use of other geographies, which are denounced as
Satan's tricks. This attempt to abolish people's extraterritorial spaces is an
attempt to centralize the projects of human history into that horizon of
the future provided by heaven and hell.

THE SPACE OF DEATH AND THE SPACE OF CREATIVITY

To explore the Kaliai space of death is to explore one of the major cultural
schemes through which creativity was culturally enacted. Traditionally, it
was through the world of the dead that the Kaliai created and authorized
new magical spells, songs, dances, and perspectives on the world. People

used the alternative world of the dead to produce new narratives and new states of affairs for the living. The privileging of another hidden position outside existing visible surroundings was the means through which people either confirmed or destabilized existing circumstances. From a phenomenological perspective people's understanding about a secret underground that is the origin of all things can be seen to emerge partly from a conscious awareness of the implicit techniques and hidden rules that make possible the creative putting together of knowledge. This awareness by consciousness of the tacit knowledge that underpins its operations is itself a form of tacit knowledge. Heidegger and Nietzsche pointed out that a great deal of culture is explicitly concerned with mediating the gulf between the seen and the hidden, the visible and the concealed. In part this concern, which is often a focus in the arts and in stories of all cultures, is a way of objectifying an awareness by consciousness of its own dependence upon hidden conceptual processes and implicit cultural schemes. The underground here is a metaphor, a way of talking allegorically about this hidden dependence of thought on implicit rules and techniques of composition that make up what can be called, to borrow a Jungian phrase, the collective unconscious of any culture, or from Bourdieu's perspective, its habitus (Bourdieu 1977). In Kaliai cargo cults this cultural unconscious, objectified as the underground, came to be reworked in order to become a way of reflecting upon the hidden rules of composition underpinning colonial racial power. Here that which was concealed in the earth stood for the hidden techniques and practices for creating creation that the white man concealed from the black man.

We are dealing here with the cultural techniques and practices used to figure and create creativity. For most human subjects these techniques for knowing how to know are implicit, and I would suggest that the Kaliais' concern with discovering the true underground state of things emerges partly from a recognition that this implicit order of knowledge, which forms how one knows how to know, has become problematized. I want to argue that people's sense of the constitutive power of other hidden worlds was not misplaced, for people's identities do emerge through a hidden set of concepts and processes that form their cultural unconscious. The Kaliais' imaginary terrain of the underground was a way of objectifying this tacit awareness that reality was underpinned by something that was hidden, that was unconscious. It was not accidental that the other was often located in this imaginary hidden terrain, for it is always through hidden rules for situating the other that social reality and identity emerge. People renegotiated their identities not only among themselves but also through boundary structures provided by those images of alterity embodied in underground others.

In the next two chapters I want to explore how in Censure's cult women came to occupy the underground and how racial subordination was experienced through a dialogue with the imaginary space(s) of otherness occupied by women. Women often became the underground voices that men conversed with in order to renegotiate themselves. Through recognizing the repressed power of women and men's crimes against them the terms of a new social order could be negotiated with the dead. Here it is a question of how subjects both realize and seek to go beyond their racial-moral identities through reworking the symbolic space assigned to women.

Chapter Four

Race, Gender, and Geographies of Guilt

Christianity and Kaliai Myths of Matriarchy

In this chapter I explore how, in Censure's cult, racial power relationships came to be framed and constituted by the same myths that underpinned traditional gender power relations. Women's subordination to men provided the terms for thinking about racial subordination. It is a question of how people realized their racial-moral identities through the symbolic space assigned to women and of how people sought to rework their racial-moral identities through reworking their symbolic positioning of women.

In particular, I want to focus on the cultural forms through which the Kaliai came to resurrect an empowering notion of femaleness that did not so much abolish the male god but instead established alongside him an alternative, unacknowledged, repressed form of creation that people seized upon as an empowering metaphor of their own situation. People's desire to control the same powers of creation as Europeans was worked out as the rediscovery of the lost primordial procreative powers of woman. The Kaliai projected their domination onto the domination of women, and they sought a means for working out their liberation through practices and myths that revalued and rediscovered woman as the underlying creator of the world.

THE FEMALENESS OF THE EARTH AND OF CREATION

Censure's cult did contain the concept of a male god, and this often had strong, patriarchal Christian overtones. Indeed, Censure saw himself as Papua New Guinea's version of the male god of the white man. He was often called Otit, which was the cult's name for the god of Papua New

Censure's female followers dancing the cult's *lo* (laws, i.e., rituals)

Guinea. Yet Censure also often sought to downplay the power of a male god to create something new; in his myths and rituals Censure often assigned to woman the role of creator. Censure saw himself as drawing on traditional Kaliai myths of matriarchy, which tell of how, in the beginning of time, a woman discovered the masks and other tambarans (Varku and Mukmuk) that became the basis of traditional Kaliai social order.[1] A woman created the new instruments of power that inaugurated a new social reality (cf. Bamberger 1974). While discussing Kaliai myths of matriarchy in 1986, Censure explained this cultural logic to me like this: "There is not one thing which comes out of nothing; woman only works something to come out of nothing. Your good living and good food comes from a woman. You and me, men, came up from one mother. If there was just men, then it would not be enough for us to come up plenty. With everything else it is the same."

In Censure's cult, women were the main people schooled in the new rituals, songs, and dances that Censure acquired from the dead. This was also in accordance with Censure's claim that in America a woman had created the new law of their good existence. As he put it, "Everything has its origins with a mother, everything comes from one woman, **Piraou** [kingfisher, the totem of Little Bird moiety]. She is the hand of God. She

Censure's wife, Lalamae, proudly demonstrating some of the cult's dances

154

is the true God. Everything, whites, me, animals, trees came from her. . . . Everyone talks 'God! God!' but in America woman made the law [a new existence] come up." Although Censure kept the idea of a male god, we can see from what he said that he also made creation reside in a hidden repressed truth concerning the feminine. His cult was concerned with revealing and managing this secret truth, which it used as a double-edged weapon against the patriarchal values of both Christianity and traditional Kaliai culture. The public celebration of woman's reproductive powers was used on the one hand to challenge the Christian view of a transcendental male god who was radically removed from the earth; on the other hand, it was also used to challenge the patriarchal principles of traditional Kaliai culture and especially Kaliai men's claims to be the prime movers and architects of all that existed. Censure was highly critical of the *longlong* (ignorant) customs of tradition that he, like many other Kaliai, saw as God's punishment to black people for their *bikhet* toward Him. Yet Censure did not completely break with the past. Through his visions, meetings, and conversations with the dead Censure often returned to the past to rediscover those alternative forms of value and existence that might have belonged to the Kaliai had they been more obedient to God.

Specifically through taking up and developing traditional myths concerning women's power to create, Censure produced a way to escape the imprisoning world of his grandfathers while maintaining a sense of returning to secret bygone truths. Censure's struggle to create a new social order drew heavily upon traditional Kaliai myths of matriarchy that tell of a time long ago when women created a new social order that privileged them. It was then that women discovered the secret of how to create terrifying masks and other tambaran that take the form of unusual, loud sounds made from bull roarers and bamboo flutes. According to Kaliai mythology, in the primordial past, when these tambaran had yet to emerge, the sexual differences were more blurred. At that time women and not men had beards, whereas men had breasts, which women did not possess. Women gave birth to children, but they then passed their children on to be wet-nursed by their husbands. This period of androgyny, in which men are feminized and women are masculinized, was a period of relative equality between men and women. There was, as yet, no culture of terror, no secret monstrous tricks through which to create the violence and fear that later became the basis of traditional Kaliai society.

All men of the different language groups in the Kaliai bush share the secret story of how one day one of the first mothers of humanity, Kewak, was breaking firewood when a piece of wood flew off, making a loud whirring noise. From this Kewak gained the idea of making a bull roarer. She informed men that its unusual loud sounds were the cries of a tambaran called Arku that she and other women controlled. Kewak discovered the trick of how to create the illusion of a monster, which she then used to terrify men by threatening that it would eat them. When men heard Arku's cry, they would run into the forest, hide, and there nurse their children, while women danced, sang, and secretly feasted with the tambaran in the village square. On one such occasion Kewak's brother, Kowdock, was running away, holding his child awkwardly to his breast, when he tripped and broke his lime powder container, which is shaped like a phallus.[2] He angrily stood up and asked, "Ah! How is it that all the women work and give food to the tambaran and we run away? I have broken my lime powder container. You all stay here while I go see these women. They are what, these women? They are not men, so that they work it so that we men run away." Kowdock returned to the village and started chasing the women. He captured the tambaran Arku, which he renamed Varku. Since that time men have ruled women through these monstrous tambarans that they hide in their men's houses.

Some men say that Kowdock chased Kewak into the sea where he broke her neck. The ripples created by her drowning body became the origin of waves; before this the sea was flat. In some accounts Kewak crawled out of the sea and turned into a stone that can be found at the coastal village of Pureling. After killing his sister, Kowdock took the tambarans away from women and gave them to men. He also took the breasts from men's chests and gave them to women, while men in turn received the beards that women then wore. Here the creation of a new social order coincides with the creation of new forms of embodiment, a coincidence that cargo cults often explored and sought to recapture in all sorts of ways. Kowdock's killing of his sister is said to be the origin of traditional widow-killing ceremonies in which, after her husband's death, a woman would be taken to the men's house and shown the bull roarers and other men's house secrets. The woman would then have to be killed to preserve men's control of the tambaran and their control over women. The deceased husband's brothers would give shell money to the widow's brothers for them to come and break their sister's neck. These widow-killing ceremonies were said to reenact Kowdock's killing of his sister. Here men's social order is ritually reconstituted and commemorated through repeating an original murder and scene of usurpation. Men repeat the original murder of a mother as a way of reproducing a memory and a secret pact with each other, the source of their solidarity and power.

Traditionally, a widow was expected to taunt and provoke her *tambu* (husband's brothers) into killing her by accusing them of wanting to keep her alive so that they could marry her (Chowning 1974; Chinnery 1925, 21–23). These taunts were meant to alleviate men's sense of guilt about these murders, a guilt that was never fully alleviated and that culturally manifested itself in people's fears that the ghosts of these women (**dongen**) would come back and seek revenge upon the men who killed them. Many traditional bush Kaliai stories are about angry murdered widows confronting, chasing, and seeking to eat the men, especially the husband's brothers who paid for them to be killed. As we shall see later, an important part of Censure's cult involved his attempts to straighten out men's relationships with these murdered mothers, who were seen to be blocking the coming of cargo because of men's violence toward them.

The site where Kewak was killed by Kowdock is full of regional significance. Traditionally, it was taboo for a canoe to journey close to this site. Any that did risked being pulled under water. This site has also been incorporated into cargo cult narratives. People believe that European ships journey secretly to this area, and there they go underwater and then underground to receive the cargo made by the dead inside Kaliai mountains. Theresa gave me the following story of how, when she was a girl, she went to Pureling village, and there she and others saw a mysterious European ship that was covered in the vines, flowers, and ferns of the Kaliai bush. People did not see the ship gradually arrive from over the horizon; instead, they suddenly heard its engines cry. When they looked up, they were puzzled about what direction it had come from. One elder ordered two men to go up to the ship, but each time their canoe came close, the ship pulled away. It went on like this until their canoe was far out to sea; they then decided to come back. At that point the elder stood up and pointed out that this ship had emerged from nowhere, and he asked people to think about why it had appeared at that spot where Kewak had died. Theresa quoted this big man as saying, "All big men, you cannot talk about this ship, I think it has come up from where all our grandfathers used to story about that woman whose name is Kewak and who turned into stone. I think this ship has come up from this area, so you cannot think plenty [other thoughts]." Theresa went on to tell me that everyone's thinking was that this ship had come to get cargo from inside Mount Andewa. At that time a man at Pureling had been employed on ships that traveled overseas, and he told local villagers how these ships would go secretly inside Mount Andewa to load up with cargo. Referring to this man's disclosures, Posingen commented, "When this ship came up, everyone's thinking was like this: 'This ship is drifting like this, and later it will go down, into the hole, and get cargo at Andewa and then go out.' When it [the ship] goes out, it goes to you whites alone. We know about this, but the road of this something [cargo] we do not stop along it or know about it [how to access the road].'

In this reworked story of Kewak an original mother becomes part of the earth—waves and a stone—and the site of her death becomes a secret site of power for whites. Through the site of this woman's murder whites take cargo from the Kaliai area. Whites here appropriate what the deceased relatives of the Kaliai are producing, and they are able to do so through a crime that the Kaliai committed against one of their first mothers. Woman here is rendered not only as creating traditional Kaliai social order but as a vehicle for the social order of Europeans, who secretly use the site of her death to create new inequalities of a racial kind. Kewak, who created the inequalities between Kaliai men and women, also becomes a mythic figure for figuring the creation of racial inequalities. Kaliai myths of matriarchy are here reworked to encompass Europeans, to draw black-white existence into the secret structures of gender inequality. Here the secret of the white men's power over Melanesians comes from the same fertile source that produced the secret of Kaliai men's power over women. There is in all this a doubling over of secrets; they come to be married together because of a common assumption that all power is underpinned by a secret that has its source in women. Here the generative potential of secrecy is made to reside in the generative potential of women. The creative power of secrets, that is, their ability to create social relationships out of the inequalities of knowledge that they institute, comes to be assimilated to the procreative power of women's bodies. Indeed, as I mentioned earlier, some bush Kaliai claim that the trickster god Titikolo secretly wrote the alphabet around a woman's vagina and for this reason was chased away to America. There he gave Americans his alphabet when they gave him a woman to marry.

One of the most original reinterpretations of traditional Kaliai myths of matriarchy was made by Censure, who blended these traditional myths with Christianity to produce the radical claim that Jesus was a woman (Lattas 1991; cf. Bynum 1982, 1992). Here the preeminent mythic figure of power for Europeans, Jesus, was merged with the preeminent mythic figure of power for the Kaliai, woman. The bearer of a new social order in Christian mythology became equated with the bearer of a new social order in Kaliai mythology. Censure accused Europeans, and especially the Catholic Church, of hiding from Melanesians the truth that Jesus was a woman. Posingen explained to me that Christ had two forms—his public European form as a man, which was a trick, and a more secret form in which Jesus was really certain underground women whom Censure's cult referred to as Tamasina: "These people whom we call Tamasina, when we go to public talk, we call them Jesus. But when we go to the knowledge of my father, they are Tamasina."

This rewriting of the mythic figure of Christ did not come from the Kaliai's not knowing the details of church scripture. Instead, people were deliberately misreading the Bible in strategic ways that allowed them to indigenize Christ's identity while maintaining a sense of the distance and otherness of this mythic figure. The effect of these reading strategies was that the transcendental God of the church became more grounded, more localized, and indeed familiarized as Christ's identity came to be displaced into the bodies of deceased ancestral mothers who resided in the earth. Christ's removal from the living was still preserved—there was still a sense of distance—but God was now less transcendental, less otherworldly, and his white male identity was denied. Censure explained the significance of women like this:

> Mary Tamasina for us is Jesus. The church's claim of Jesus being a man is a lie. They are working *tok piksa* [talk-picture, i.e., imaginative or deceptive talk]. In tok piksa they say Jesus is a man, but Jesus is a woman. Everything belongs to mother, to mother only. We men are be-ings who sing out for things to come, for this to come, for that to come. We sing out like that. But food comes from woman, food came up from woman, all cargo, everything came up only from woman. In tok piksa Jesus is a man but no way. Jesus is Tamasina—a woman who works food.

The creative power of a feminine Christ and of women in general is here established in opposition to men, who simply sing out for things. Here women are positioned as the true producers of sustenance and cargo, whereas men are simply consumers and appropriators of what women pro-duce. This also is the major theme in traditional Kaliai myths of matriar-chy, namely, that women created the instruments of power—tambarans—that men later stole. Censure used this traditional narrative scheme to jus-tify the central creative role that he assigned to women in his cult; he also used it to depower white men, who were now positioned as living off what a woman created, for it was a woman in America who created their good existence. This narrative had the effect of undermining the patriarchal structure of a colonial order made up of white men in the powerful roles of administrators, kiaps, priests, doctors, plantation owners, and business-men. These powerful white men were now rendered as concealing the truth that they were not sufficient to create anything.

Censure used the word Jesus in three ways: to refer to a special group of underground women who were going to create the Kaliai's new existence; to refer to the woman in America who created the white man's good exis-tence; and to refer to the person whom the Bible reports as having been crucified. In terms of the latter, Posingen told me how that part of the original Bible known as the Judea Bible refers to Jesus as a woman. This was said to be in the Old Testament, which spoke of a time when the two kings, Caesar and Herod, were both in charge of Rome, and "they did not want this woman to surpass them [*i go pas long ol*]." Posingen claimed their thoughts were that "this woman has gone in front, and too many people are following her and working her law, and why should this be so? It should be that we win her, that we men go first and woman comes behind." Because this female Jesus threatened men's claims to be the pre-eminent gender, the two male kings, Caesar and Herod, ordered her to be killed. This is similar to the way Kowdock kills his sister, when he angrily asks, "What are they, these women? They are not men, so that they work it so that we men run away." In terms of the killing of the female Jesus by Caesar and Herod, Posingen pointed to men's pride, disrespect, and out-rage at a woman's changing the male terms within which power ought to be coded:

> I believe Jesus is a woman. If Jesus was a man, I do not believe that Caesar and Herod would have spoken to have him killed; he would still be alive. But because she was a woman, they spoke: "Why should this fucking kind of woman go in front of us? Why? Kill her and get rid of her. If she remains, she will just pull too many people into following her, and we kings will not have work, we will not have people. This woman pulls too many people into following her." They followed her because of food, because all this bread would come up by itself, and Je-sus would give this bread to all the five thousand disciples. She would give the bread to this five thousand, they would fill up on food, cover the rest, and carry it away.

Here the power of the European state is coded as the power of men, and it comes to be challenged by a more popular, equitable, and caring system of norms and practices that are brought by a woman who freely shared bread. Posingen saw men's desire to be in charge as having had the general effect of repressing the alternative economy of care and generosity offered by women:

> Supposing a woman goes in front of something, then all something will be free. Now supposing a man goes in front, then all something is not enough to be free. No, a man will go and turn it, and this something is not enough to go out and be free. However, if a woman goes in front, then something has to be free. But no, it wasn't like that. Woman wanted to go in front and work this something to be free, and all the men rose up and killed her.

This is what the state is repressing, the alternative economy and system of distribution that belongs to woman. She comes to be idealized as the bearer of an alternative form of rule in which prestige is derived from caring for the disadvantaged. The Kaliai often accuse Europeans of selfishness, and in this story I see the Kaliai as projecting the idealized norms of their social order into a feminine figure crucified by the state. The crucified world of the feminine here plays out as female-male conflict, the white man's current repression of an alternative order of value that people associate with themselves, and their gifts to each other. A certain idealization of themselves (as Melanesian subjects) is crucified by the white man's kings. Here the feminine economy of gifts gives way to a more coercive male economy that is predicated on competition and status rivalry.

This killing of a female Jesus by men also has an element of internalized guilt, for the story was seen to resonate with, if not reenact (*bihainim*), Kaliai men's murder of Kewak. In the Bible Jesus was killed for trying to empower the poor in relationship to their rulers; likewise, in Kaliai myths of matriarchy Kewak is killed for trying to empower and move women into a position of dominance over men. Those who empower the weak come to be murdered. They are killed for trying to create the rules of a new social order. Censure merged European understandings of Christ as the bearer of a new law of existence with Kaliai understandings of woman as the bearer of a new law of existence. In Kaliai mythology Kewak created the tambarans that enforce the norms of traditional Kaliai society. If people are disobedient, the tambaran comes up and demands compensation. It threatens to eat the gardens and pigs of transgressors and even the transgressors themselves. Censure's cult focused on the murder of law givers, Kewak and Christ, who were merged to create new biblical narratives about the violent coercive nature of male power in the past. Yet we also need to remember that Kowdock's killing of Kewak was replayed by the Kaliai in rituals in which widows were killed by men. The Roman kings' killing of the female Jesus, who distributed food, resonates with the Kaliai practice of men murdering the mothers who nurtured them. Indeed, as we have already seen and as we shall see again later, the story of the crucified female Jesus is a story that resonates with all men's injustices against women and against the alternative moral economy she embodies.

CATHOLIC CHURCH REPRESENTATIONS OF CHRIST

Posingen claimed that many early catechists who came into the Kaliai bush confirmed Censure's interpretation of Christ as being a woman. The catechists brought with them drawings of Christ that depicted him naked and without a penis. Only pubic hair covered his genitals, which some people saw as a representation of female genitalia. While telling me this, Posingen also voiced his suspicions about the new representations of Christ that, like the current statues in Catholic churches, include a cloth that conceals Christ's genitalia:

> In the early days, when the church first came up to us, some of these catechists talked to us about this [i.e., Christ's being female]. . . . Now the new ones have changed it, and they have worked the picture of Jesus being like a statue which is covered up in cloth. But the first time he was naked, he had no cloth, his body was visible, and there was just hair around his genitalia. He had no penis, he was a woman. . . . In the true past, when the church was new, they drew Jesus without clothes. He was a woman, he had breasts. The first time he was a woman. Now they have thought again, and they changed things and covered him up. All the catechists before, like old Lucas, they spoke about this. . . . All these people who are now teachers, when they came into the work of my father, they believed. When my father said that Jesus is a woman, they said, "Father, this is true." Lucas spoke like this, and so did all the paper-men [educated men] along the coast. Then the mission came and changed it so that Jesus went to being a man, and that is what we now follow.

Christianity's representations of Christ have never portrayed a strong male body but always a softer, more frail-looking feminine body, sometimes with a slightly sagging male chest that Censure and his close supporters interpreted to be a young woman's developing breasts. The Catholic Church's attempts to deny and repress any explicit representation of

Christ's sexuality served only to deny him a penis and thus constituted him as feminine. Posingen accused the present Catholic Church of changing its mind about depicting Christ's true sexual identity, which it now preferred to cover up. When I queried him about why the church would do this, he told me: "It is like this: this something is the origin of you and me, and it cannot stop clear, so we can see it; they must hide it." Posingen claimed that preachers today always used the name Jesus to avoid specifying Christ's sexuality and that "it was us people who pulled [elaborated] this talk so that Jesus became a man." When I asked Posingen how many people still shared his father's belief that Jesus was a woman, he replied, "Most of them have given it up. They all now say: 'Papa is Jesus, Papa is Jesus, and he holds you and me, and we pray to him.' Most of the New Tribes followers have given up Censure's talk. Some along the coast think that much of what Censure did was true but that he made a mistake with one small part of it. Many of the national kiaps [who came on patrols into the Kaliai area] told Censure that his work was true."

THE QUEEN AND KALIAI MYTHS OF MATRIARCHY

In addition to the representational practices of the Catholic Church, Censure's cult found confirmation that its interpretation of a feminine Christ was correct in the representational practices of state officials, especially Australian colonial officials' swearing of allegiance to a queen.[3] Her picture held a prominent place in government offices, and she seemed to be the center of many official rituals, speeches, and claims to sovereignty. As Posingen put it, "My father and those [catechists] belonging to the Old Testament which was here before, they would say that 'Jesus is a woman. . . . If Jesus was a man, then there would not be a woman as queen; instead, a man would stand up in this position. But it is not like this, for Jesus is a woman, so a woman now stands up as queen.' . . . She is the boss of you whites and of us in Papua New Guinea." Here one part of Western culture comes to be used against another part: the feminization of state power at its highest level is used against the patriarchal aspects of Christianity. Here we are also dealing with intersecting images of feminine power from different cultures and more especially with the way the European monarchical figure of the queen came to reinforce cargo cult reinterpretations of traditional Kaliai myths of matriarchy. The West's fetishization of state power came to be rendered as participating in the Kaliai's fetishization of women's reproductive powers. Here two different ways of fetishizing the feminine intersected, creating a shared structure of ambiguity that destabilized the established patriarchal conventions of both Christianity and Kaliai tradition. The fact that all cultures have to engage the feminine allowed the figure of woman to emerge as a common mediating term that could bring together the different symbolic resources of European and Kaliai cultures to create new processes of becoming not totally subordinated to tradition or to the white man.

Posingen noted that although Papua New Guinea had a queen as its head, it had failed to benefit from the norms of generosity belonging to women because Australian men had inserted themselves into her government. There they subverted the alternative order of generosity that she offered:

> With youse Australians, supposing the queen alone looked after everything here [in Papua New Guinea], then all something would be free. There is the queen, however only youse men are in the government, and so with the government all something is not free when it comes to us of Papua New Guinea. It has been totally blocked. The reason is like this: if there was just the queen alone who was boss, then it would go straight. The queen is the boss, but all of youse men go and want to stand up for government [positions], and so with all the laws of the queen, youse have downed them.

GENTILITY, CIVILIZATION, AND THE FEMININE

Another aspect of European culture that supported the cult's claim that woman was more powerful than had ordinarily been thought was what people saw as the greater respect that European men showed their wives. The culture of gentility that white men played out publicly toward white women was taken to mean that women have a secret value that whites were tacitly acknowledging. Gestures of common courtesy came to be seen as acts of deference and humility toward the true source of creation. Posingen gave me this account of an experience with white culture that for him confirmed his father's interpretation that woman had to be revalued and transformed into Christ:

> I want to talk again. I think Jesus is a woman, for *misis* goes to the side of *meri* [woman]. If you look at white men, you white men do not cross women, you do not hit your wives. . . . I saw this all in town and at Talasea. When the wife and master [*masta*] travel in the car, then the masta will sit down, and his wife will go talk with another master in a

house. They will stay together in the house, but her husband will be waiting and waiting. He will then blow the horn, and the misis will reply, "Shut up" [*laughter*]. She will say, "Shut up!" The master will just bend his neck down, sit down, and wait on the driver's side. The misis will continue talking and talking, but the master will wait. . . . My thinking is that it is because Jesus is a woman that this is why I see this. But us natives, we do not respect women [*ruru long ol meri*]. We beat them, put spears on top of them, kill them, but you masters do not do this. You know about the origin of things, and you respect women [*ruru long meri*]. You respect woman because woman is the origin of food, which does not come up from us men. This is why you masters respect women a great deal. It does not matter what the woman does, you will stay and wait, and you are not enough to talk, "Come on, let us go." Not with us natives, it is not allowed for our wives to go talk with another man. From this a cross will come up. Her husband will angrily ask her, "Why did you go talk to him, for what reason? Is he your husband so you can go talk to him?" Well, the village will be wrong [disordered] now. But with youse, this is not so. She will go talk and talk, but you will stay in the car and wait. I saw this in Rabaul. I was there waiting, my stomach was hot. I wanted to tell him: "Ah, master, I think your wife has gone to have sex."

This narrative ignores some European men's private violence toward their wives. Instead, it focuses on that public male culture of good manners toward women, which is still part of the social order of Western society. For Europeans public gestures of polite regard, courtesy, and graciousness toward women were forms of civility that differentiated them from the coarse manners of natives. These good manners were signs and evidence of good breeding and of a superior moral culture. It was also in these hegemonic terms that the Kaliai reinterpreted these ceremonial rules of respect, which they saw as containing an alternative ethics for governing the relationship between the sexes that was superior to that of the Kaliai's. For this reason Censure forbade his male followers to beat their wives or children. European good manners were interpreted as embodying an alternative secret truth about women that the Kaliai had lost sight of and was somehow linked to their fall. The West's romantic articulation of itself as civilized was accepted (and taken on board) but in a way that allowed the Kaliai to empower certain traditional myths about woman as creator, which Censure's cult used to criticize the traditional masculine culture of their grandfathers. Via the mediation of Western culture, the past came to be used against itself. The West was incorporated mythically to provide a form of distance and to create new moments of reflection in which people could own the moral primitivist critique of themselves made by the civilized West. In particular, the moral inadequacy of the Kaliai became condensed into their immoral treatment of women, the sources of creation. The West came to be romantically imagined as an alternative space of trust between men and women, and people suspected that whites were deriving their lifestyle from their better relationship with women. It was in the following terms that Posingen contrasted gender relations among Europeans with those among natives: "True, there are few misis who think no-good about their master and what he is doing, a few misis only, I saw them in town. But with most of the misis this is not so. It is the same with masters. The masters respect their misis too much, they will not bugger them up, or work all kinds of things, but not with us natives."

We see here people internalizing the negative characterizations of themselves that the civilizing process brought. In particular, men's identity became morally problematized with the development of a culture of guilt in which the traditional power relationships between men and women came to be criticized from the standpoint of Western culture. European cultural hegemony was made possible in Melanesia because it promoted and was constituted from such inferiority complexes (Fanon 1968). Here people's struggle against the white man was transformed into a struggle against themselves and especially against that imprisoning culture from the past that their grandfathers had bestowed.[4]

Censure's cult took up the European critique of native tradition but in a way that did not involve a complete rejection of the past. Instead, his cult used the white man's culture to rediscover and reempower lost ancestral truths—specifically, myths of matriarchy that posited an original age of power and creativity by women. These myths' apparent valuing of women's power to create over men's power was reinterrogated, for it seemed to locate an alternative structure of value in Kaliai culture that could make sense of those alternative structures of value belonging to whites. The alternative time of female power posited by Kaliai myths became the alternative existence occupied by Europeans as well as the alternative existence promised by a new future. Here different forms of alterity became substitutable for each other, that is, the alterity embodied in the mythic past allowed people to approach and reclaim the alterity of the white man's culture as a version of their understanding of the alterity of the future.

THE MOTHERS IN THE EARTH WHO NEED TO BE
STRAIGHTENED

Toward the end of the last chapter we saw how Censure claimed that some underground male ancestors were unhappy with the living and were refusing to work Censure's laws. I want to turn now to explore the special grievances that underground female ancestors had against the living and how Censure tried to create the new world of white existence by straightening out men's relationships with them.

At his telephone doors Censure would listen to dead women's grievances, and he would report these to his followers. One major matter that the female ancestors wanted clarified was why above-ground men had broken the women's necks in widow-killing ceremonies. A great deal of Censure's time was directed toward understanding and appeasing the anger of these murdered widows. At the telephone doors Censure and all the men of the Kaliai area were made to hold court before these underground women, who used their control over the destiny of the living to force men to reflect on the male values that had required their deaths. These occasions became a court of conscience, a tribunal that forced men to denounce and distance themselves from the violent claims of their sexuality. The separation of the living from the dead, which was holding the Kaliai back from the white man's world, was figured to have its origins in a culture of violence that separated men from women. Through his dialogues and negotiations with people's underground grandmothers Censure explored the moral terrain of traditional Kaliai gender relations, which he criticized and sought to renegotiate as the basis for establishing for Kaliai men a new moral identity that came closer to that of European men. Through acknowledging the sins of the past and through negotiating a new ethical relationship with women in general, Censure sought to move Kaliai men beyond the coercive masculine world of their grandfathers and, in effect, to develop for them a new form of masculinity (cf. Irigaray 1993). Like all social orders, traditional Kaliai society was built around gender, so it is not surprising to find people seeing all order, including a new racial order, as being an alternative gender order.

Posingen described to me how on one occasion his father was visited by about fifty dongen, that is, the ghosts of widows whose necks men had broken. Censure was seated in the men's house when he heard them coming; he looked up and saw them. He was said to be unafraid, although he was reported as firmly holding on to his tomahawk. As they approached, one underground mother urged another: "Ask him! Ask him, about what was the meaning behind us dying! Why did all the men kill us so that we followed our husbands? What was the reason for this? Ask him good about this!" Initially, Censure did not reply. He recognized some women who had died recently, but many who had lived long ago he did not recognize. One he did recognize was Monongyo's mother, who was secretly killed after the Second World War. She was the last Mouk woman to be killed, and she came up to Censure and asked, "*Pikinini* [child], I want to know why we of the underground were killed by all of youse. We of the underground were killed for what reason?" Censure's response was to pretend not to know the answer. He told the women that he was sorry but he did not know: "If I was a big man and knew about this law, you could ask me, but I do not know about these times." The women were unhappy with this response, with his feigned modesty, and Posingen gave me this long account of his father's heated dialogue with these murdered mothers:

But some other woman spoke: "You ask this man strong! Ignore him working this sort of talk towards us." . . . His [Monongyo's] mother kept asking: "We are asking, why was it that all the men worked at killing us? You must talk about its meaning, what was the reason?" Father thought, his thinking went all right, and he said, "True, I do not know. All the big men who killed you, I think this was their way." The woman said, "That is all right, you can reveal it, it is not enough for you to block this talk." Father spoke, "Its meaning is like this: before you walked around with the big men, shared the same food, slept together, walked together in the bush and other places where you slept overnight, the man found something like a betel nut or smoke which you shared. This here, they killed you for this."

The woman [Monongyo's mother] then rose and said, "No, this kind of thing where we have sex, do we kill people so as to follow another person, over this?" The woman turned the talk like this: "This kind of thing, where with our husbands we walked and had sex, did you kill us over this, ah? Now you talk about this meaning." Father was there, and this woman worked this talk to him: "This where we have sex and water [semen] comes to us, and you men work this water to come to us, this is not something true, it is something nothing. Now how is it that you wanted to kill us over this?"

Father said her talk was true, and that "now at this time, we of the new line, do not know about this [custom], but before with our grandfathers they killed you for this reason that I spoke about, there are not plenty of reasons. It was for this reason, a man thinks no good about you with another man [a future husband], all right because of this, all your brothers think no good about you, so your very own brothers spoke [agreed], and they killed you. It was not someone else who spoke and killed you. It was because of this alone. Your husband gave food to your hand, and you held it, you received good food, and the two of you ate it together. Well, all the man's line thought about this food belonging to youse two, so when your husband died, they killed you so as to follow him."

The woman responded back: "You talk about food and that is all right, it is true about food. But there is this other something, when you spoke that we with our husbands walked and slept together, well, this something [semen] is water nothing, so for what reason did you kill us over this?" The woman worked this, but some other woman said: "Ask him strong, so he can work this talk and reveal its true meaning, so that we know and can then go. For he is working this work of his, and he must know all the meaning of this, and he can tell us."

Well, now my father worked some thoughts that went to the knowledge that belonged to him, that is, it went to his work and he spoke: "Well now, before with *tumbuna* [ancestors], all tumbuna were longlong [ignorant, confused]. They were slightly longlong, and they worked all these sort of things, but now when it comes to this time of ours, we now do not work this, for we are all clear. For we are not enough to go bugger up all you women. You women are all people for cooking food, whatever food is about, you work it and we men eat. Your talk is true, it is true, we men are something nothing, but you women are something true. Food comes up from you, and it is all right. But before tumbuna was longlong, and they buggered up you women, and it is not straight. But we now, we do not have these kinds of thoughts about buggering up woman. From you women good food comes up, you work all food and whatever else, and it comes up good and we eat. However, tumbuna was longlong."

The woman spoke back: "Pikinini, your talk is true, it is straight. We heard it and you gave good talk to us, we will go and you can stop. This talk of yours is true.

Posingen went on to tell me that before leaving his father, the murdered mothers who had been transformed into tambaran (dongen) asked Censure to give them a certain child to eat, which would be their going-away feast. This was also spoken of as the revenge of these women on the living and as their demand for compensation. Censure refused to give the child, telling the women that the child was a close relative and that if they wanted to kill and eat someone, it should not be there, close to Meitavale, but much farther away. The women left, thanking Censure for having straightened them on the true reason that they were buried with their husbands.

This dialogue is partly a critique of men for having made monsters out of their mothers; it is a critique of the violence of the past, which is seen to be still lurking in the underground women's revenge upon the living. In this dialogue Censure affirms a new culture of male respect for women that breaks with the past customs of his grandfathers whom he denounces as longlong. Censure proclaims himself to be part of a new wiser line of men that recognizes and respects the reproductive powers and caring role of mothers. Here the underground that the Kaliai live with is an underground world of male guilt over the murders that men committed in the name of jealous acts of sexual possession and in the name of their memories, when men proclaimed themselves important enough to solicit someone else's death to mark theirs. In the dialogue with underground women that Posingen related to me, women accept the point about having been killed because they shared food with their husbands. Their sense of outrage is directed at the possessive claims of a phallic male sexuality, at its pretense to be something important that could require their deaths. They refuse the subordination of their lives to the exclusive claims of this sexuality and instead seek to counteract its assigned self-importance by asserting that it has no substance, that it is simply empty water.

This denial of male reproductive power by underground women can be seen as part of a new dialogue among the Kaliai concerning whether men or women truly embody the power to create life and sociality. The coming of a white patriarchal god and European patrilineal understandings of kinship have often worked to privilege Western structures of patrilineal descent, such as children's assuming the name of their father in village census line-ups and at school. Although Kaliai villagers traditionally traced their descent through men, this was not seen as an alternative social order that was mutually exclusive of those matrilineal totemic-moiety groupings that people in Pisin call *famili* (family). Yet in conversations with me in 1986 some men criticized the fact that they had no famili and that only women had famili. By this these men meant that women transmitted the totemic blood ties with which people identified. These same men told me that in reality woman played no part in procreation, that she was simply an empty *bilum* (basket), and that it was men's semen that created life. At Salke village another elder told me that people's understanding that women create life was false, for in reality God creates and places the child in women's wombs. Many men told me that whites had the proper kinship, one that classified a son as belonging to his father's family. Since 1987 many of those who have joined the New Tribes Mission have been trying to adopt a European kinship system. The transmission through women's blood of different totemic lines is experienced as a fragmenting evil that alienates fathers from their children and white culture from black culture. Some see it as the punishment of a false culture given by God when he ran away. Affirming male predominance in reproduction has now become the language for invoking the superior powers of production that whites are seen to control, whereas the traditional privileging of the maternal is held responsible for the bush Kaliai's backwardness.

The subordinate position of indigenous culture has led many to internalize a depreciated sense of its value, which takes the form of seeking to reject its means of reproduction. I see Censure's cult as opposing this process. When followers from the coast came into Censure's cult, some did not know to which moiety they belonged. By looking at the lines on their hands and the size of their chests, Censure assigned a moiety membership to them. Other followers had willfully married their own *pisin* (bird); they along with everyone else were instructed that from now on they were to follow the line of their mother and were to organize themselves in terms of *Bikpela Pisin* and *Liklik Pisin*. Some of Censure's rituals were directed at preserving the incorrect marriages of his followers, marriages that otherwise would have been torn asunder when the Last Day came. Censure used his cult and his dialogues with underground mothers to reaffirm the social organizing centrality of women that came from their role in procreation. His cult emerged in a context in which there was some discussion over whether men's semen or women's blood was the more important substance in procreation. Censure used the authority of underground women's voices to dismiss men's semen as empty water. Instead, he held men's privileging of their sexuality as responsible for the past murders and crimes against women that were now holding back the Kaliai.

In the figure of Censure, men conversed with their representations of women's voices on male sexuality. Men stared back at themselves through the eyes of women or, more accurately, through the mirror function of female voices that Censure internalized and revealed. The underground is a complicated mirror, and if it represents the unconscious and gives voice to its feelings of guilt, it does so through a complicated system of voices capturing and speaking as others. This is partly a process in which men appropriate women's voices, which they simultaneously internalize and objectify into a conscience that shames them. Through a dialogue with their objectifications of women's voices, men struggle to give voice to their new civilized identities, which they contrast with the primitive violent acts of men's past for which they now want to compensate dead women.

It was no accident that Censure connected men's sense of being morally reborn as pacified, with the forcing of men to hold court before angry female voices that demand an apology and a new relationship of respect. To some extent it is also the internalized, reworked voice of colonial pacification that men speak through these angry female voices of the past. Here men map out a new form of civilized masculinity that offers its apologies and a new relationship of respect to women for their caring labor. Relevant here is that, in official discourse, primitivism and barbarism were often equated with the subjugation of women. The colonial process of moral enlightenment was often rendered as one of producing a new-found respect for women in those who had not known it. Evidence of this attitude in colonial policy is provided in the following letter, dated July 5, 1971, from the Department of the Administrator at Konedobu (Papua) to all the district commissioners. It was entitled "Political Education: Participation of Women in Public Affairs":

> An extract from the Minutes of the Child Welfare Council (which was considered by the Political Education Committee recently) drew attention to the need for greater participation of women in public affairs and in the political education programme. Nations which, by custom, relegate their women to the home are depriving themselves of considerable potential talent in addition to condemning their children to unsophisticated early tutelage. Women should be given every encouragement to complete their education and partake in local affairs such as committees, Councils, and educational courses and seminars such as those for economic development and political education. This should help break down the considerable psychological barriers erected by traditional society in Papua and New Guinea. Close liaison should be maintained by all field staff with Social Development Officers, schools and Mission organisations concerned with female welfare.

In the 1979 "Gloucester Local Government Council Fifth General Election Report," the following comments were made about the fact that no woman had been nominated in any ward in the Kilenge Lolo Census Division: "[This] is not surprising considering that is [sic] in the minds of most PNG people that the women must not go beyond men that the womens [sic] role within the community could not be respected by the males. The society is still primitive that there was not looked to be any woman who

are eligable [sic] or had some qualifications to anable [sic] them to challenge men on such issues as this." I see Censure as partly appropriating
and reworking this colonial discourse that revalues women. He internalized and reobjectified this discourse as the voices of underground women.
The voices of dead female ancestors that Censure speaks, though ostensibly from the past, were also European-empowered voices that involved the
internalization of discourses of pacification and civilization and their being echoed back via an underground terrain of otherness belonging to the
bush Kaliai. In these dialogues, in which Censure asserted that men today
had a new respect for women, he was partly celebrating the pedagogic
moral influences brought by schools and missions but also by his own
cargo cult, which was also seeking morally to produce a new kind of Melanesian subject and for that reason referred to itself as a *lotu* (church).
What underground voices are actually speaking in these conversations
with the dead is quite complicated because it is overlaid. I am suggesting
that Censure extended the pacification and civilization project into the
terrain of the underground past, which became the terrain of moral accountability for developing a new form of masculinity in which men used
their desire for cargo to mediate and validate their desire for new relationships with women and new forms of identification for themselves.

Relevant here is the work of Donzelot (1980) in which he has shown
how European women and children became the bearers of a humanitarian
civilizing project. Donzelot explored how in Europe institutions like
schools, philanthropy, and social welfare work sustained their interven-
tions into the family, whose domestic relationships they restructured,
through the alliances and moral support they gave women and children in
opposition to men. I believe this process was and is still at work in Melanesia but that its practices and discourses of intervention get perverted
along the way as they are recontextualized by being internalized into other
imaginary schemes for figuring social relationships that often privilege the
dead. In Melanesia empowering the repressed voices of women has been
one discourse that the European state and church have made part of their
techniques of social control. Censure took on a European-inspired moral
critique of Melanesian society that used the figure of woman to sustain its
humanitarian agenda and the movement away from a primitive state of
existence (cf. Hamilton 1989). In taking over this discourse Censure also
took over its problematization of male identity and its accompanying technology of pastoral power. Censure recontextualized these Western pastoral techniques by mediating their transformational objectives through the
indigenous world of the dead, which was people's traditional world of

transformation. New forms of self-discipline would be authorized for the male self through a world of guilt that was internalized and managed by being located in underground women, in the mothers of the past; they had given birth to those on the surface, and they would again mediate the birth of a new male self.

Censure's cult was directed toward managing a new hybrid culture of guilt. Here the traditional forms of guilt that men had, and that took the form of vengeful female ghosts, came to be married to a colonial-inspired moral critique of tradition. It is necessary to be aware that Censure's cult also had an interest in helping to create this new culture of guilt, which his cult fed off, by offering the means of resolving it. Censure's cult, like many other cults in Papua New Guinea, exploited a culture of guilt that originally had been created, sustained, and managed by European institutions, for this guilt formed a crucial part of European moral authority and hegemony. Throughout Papua New Guinea colonial intervention often took place in the name of protecting Melanesian women and their children; it took place within a humanitarian framework that sought alliances among Melanesian women by offering them and their children protection from men's violent customs. Here it should also be noted that many men welcomed the abolition of warfare, widow killing, and the more violent aspects of their tambaran culture. Men came to denounce their resort to violence and took up the invitation to seek forgiveness inside European pastoral institutions and inside a new relationship of respect for women. We are dealing here with the emergence of a new national ideology centered on the family as a moral space of self-identity and self-transformation. I see Censure's cult as localizing this ideology. Like other cargo cult leaders, Censure appropriated European pastoral techniques that produce structures of self-alienation while claiming to be healing these alienating wounds. European moral hegemony fed off a world of traditional guilt that was recontextualized and transformed into a redemptive project, but the cargo cults also reappropriated that colonially reconstituted world of traditional guilt. Censure's cult indigenized Western pastoral techniques, Western caring practices for producing and healing self-alienated subjects, which it now used to produce a new sort of guilty Melanesian subject who wanted to own and atone for his history.

I see the official backlash against cargo cults as not so much directed toward their superstitious content, which Europeans, state officials, and missions have often been able to accept and dismiss as evidence of the simplicity and backwardness of natives. Rather, what perhaps most disturbed these powerful groups was that appropriation of pastoral tutelage that came when a cargo cult took over the role of mirroring subjects to themselves in self-alienating ways that required those subjects to become reunified through the redemptive labor of cult activities. Europeans found threatening this indigenization of colonial guilt and the appropriation of the moral authority and power that its production conferred on Melanesians. In the Kaliai bush colonialism's policing of cargo cults became, in effect, a struggle to control the imaginary geographies through which people appropriated and internalized the mirror function of a European moral critique that came now to reside in the eyes and mouths of the underground dead and of women.

The moral domain of cargo became part of the reevaluation of sexual identity and of the ethics of gender relationships. The new forms of value brought by commodities provided new ways of objectifying the domain of sociability to create and institute other voices, values, and codes of conduct between the sexes. The desire for cargo brought to the surface other desires in the realm of human relationships. Cargo merged with these to become a way of materializing and grounding a new moral domain. In this search for new ways to become other than oneself we find all sorts of experiments in identity and various ways of superimposing meanings; these new overlaid meanings become passages leading to more commingled states of affairs in which the project of a man who is speaking the voices of women was the project of Melanesians who were speaking the white man's discourse and seeking to become white. Crossing into the terrain of women's voices mediated the process of rejecting the longlong customs of one's grandfathers to create a new form of masculinity whose rebirth as more like the white man would come from being reborn through a dialogue with the mothers in the earth who had carried people. This murdered form of procreation in the earth has to be appeased so that the creative processes in the earth can emerge and be used to resituate black men's relationship to white men by resituating black men's relationship to women. In all this lies the paradox of going back to beginnings and autochthonous origins in order to move toward the future and the foreign; this movement is what is feminized, its creative interface sexualized.

Chapter Five

Sexuality, Reproduction, and the Utopia of Mirror Worlds

In Censure's cult the struggle to approach and reclaim the redemptive alterity of another world took many forms. In Chapter 2 I mentioned how Censure renamed his followers, giving each the name of an underground person who was that person's *poroman* (ally) and who was making her or his cargo. From the underground Censure also acquired a new language that he used to rename significant features of the visible and invisible worlds. This new language was said to be "English"; it was spoken of as a new *tok ples* (local language) that Censure acquired from certain underground women, whom he called the Wind of God. Using this underground language, Censure sought to create the world anew through a language that seemed to approximate the mystery and power of that used by whites. Cult followers, who were schooled in this new language, learned new names for everyday items such as a bed, different parts of a house, and different plants. Censure schooled mostly women in this new language, which Censure continued to acquire throughout his fifteen years as cult leader.

Women told me how in the morning they would gather to recite long lists of names that they would finish at midday. Each moiety had its own names to memorize. Censure's renaming of the everyday world gave it not only a new phonetic form but also a new organizational form, with the binary logic of the moiety system structuring the categories through which the world was now to be apprehended. The fact that this new language came from underground women, and women were its main students, served to marry their procreative bodies to this new language's creative powers, which lay in its magical promise of a new future world but also in its phenomenological power to organize a new perception of reality. Women's procreative bodies became vehicles for the powers of language to shape the world; these world-formative powers reside partly in the ability of words to summon a sense of reality through how they categorize and relate aspects of the world.

In its rituals, songs, dances, and schools the Meitavale cult assigned a special mediating role to women in terms of accessing and embodying the creative powers of the underground dead. Monongyo explained to me that the cargo would come from a new law of existence, which resided partly in the dancing hands and legs of women: "They [the women] must throw their legs here and there, as well as their hands here and there. This is because the law is in our legs and in our hands. Our legs work it and our hands work it. This is its meaning, its meaning is as we spoke yesterday, that a woman will stand up and open the law out. That is why women sing." It was, I believe, no accident that new songs and dances were equated with the "law" of another existence, for ritual itself also creates a short-lived alternative world of existence. Indeed, I see ritual's reconstitution of the everyday body's experiences through new songs and dances as anticipating and prefiguring that reconstitution of experience to be embodied in the coming of another world. I am suggesting that the reason cult songs and dances were experienced as magical practices for realizing another world was the experience of alterity generated by their rhythms, where song and dance were used to remanipulate the body's experiences of time and space (Dufrenne 1973; Langer 1942, 1953: Kapferer 1983). New dances and songs created new imaginary structures for the body to immerse itself within. Here new regimes of time were marked out through cult songs and dances, which also provided new ways of moving through space. I see ritual's refiguring of experience at a corporeal level as foreshadowing that refiguring of identity and the body that was to take place in the future when people were to become white and were to experience through their new bodies the pleasures of a Western lifestyle.

Within the poetic logic of Censure's cult the fertile body of woman was joined to the creative power of cult songs and dances that would realize utopia through managing and directing women's creative labor. Ex-cult followers told me that on one occasion when the ceremonies failed to deliver cargo, Censure took female followers down to a nearby river for them to wash. There he made them undress, and he inspected their vaginas, claiming that the road belonging to cargo had become blocked.[1] The road that was to be opened up by Censure's rituals led straight into the bodies of women; their concealed interiors, their ability to move something from a dark unseen space into a visible world, was precisely that birthing moment of disclosure that Censure sought. Women's bodies are apt vehicles for thinking about the effects of truth, for thinking about moments of revelation in which that which is hidden or absent moves into the world of light and public possession. It was no accident that the ritual disclosing work of women became the new labor of their bodies.

One interesting aspect of Censure's rituals was that these powers of production located in the rhythms of women's bodies were sometimes likened to the rhythms and powers of production embodied in machines. This information came up while Posingen and Theresa were explaining to me how women who danced were heaping up cargo in their individual underground rooms. Those who were lazy and refused to dance would find out that they had no cargo when their underground rooms came to the surface. Posingen went on to describe how the rhythms of dancing women's bodies mimed the rhythms of machines:

> With respect to our legs and hands, when we throw our legs and hands [dance the law], it is like a machine, we are working the picture of working [making] something. Now when you toss your hands and legs, then you are working something of yours to go and heap itself in your room. Now with another person, who does not throw her hands and legs, she will not have something in her room. For she wants to sleep, and she does not want to come and work the picture by throwing her legs and hands. To throw your legs and hands is to work the picture of operating [*traim*] a machine.

When describing the complicated new dances that Censure taught his female followers, Posingen told me how initially no one could follow them because they were as fast as a machine: "Father was working this kind of law of his, we call it 'law,' but it was these dances of his. He would toss his legs like a machine. He would turn them like this and turn them like that. There was not one person who could follow these steps." After performing these dances, Censure invited women to come and copy his movements, telling them they were to be schooled in how to work the machines that would later work food for them ("food" was Censure's euphemism for cargo). Censure also spoke of himself as schooling the women in the "law of tomorrow," and he explained to them: "If you all learn this, then its meaning is like this, that later when you women want to stand next to a machine or some other thing, whatever machine you want to run, there will be no problem, for you have already acquired your knowledge. You are now working the picture, but later, when something true comes up, you already will be clear about it." Here internalizing dance meant internalizing the knowledge for operating machinery. The regular rhythms of both allowed them to be magically assimilated to each other. People's attempts to control the same powers of production as Europeans were mimetically transformed into an attempt to control the powers of reproduction operating in the rhythmic gestures of women's bodies. In women miming and becoming the "picture" of a machine we have both the technologizing of women's bodies and the feminizing of the reproductive powers of technology. Women's powers to reduplicate, to create something new through childbirth, was now displaced into the labor of ritual so that this disciplined ritual act of reduplication could assume a fertile form that was its magical reenactment of the mechanical reproductive powers of Europeans. The procreative power of women's bodies, which informed the ritual labor of copying, gave rise to a procreative form of mimesis in which the repetitive gestures of ritual would capture the repetitive reproductive powers of European technology. Posingen told me how his father informed women that in their rituals they were miming machinery that was being operated by their namesakes in the underground:

> All right, he [Censure] would give this [ritual knowledge from the
> dead] to all the women, saying, "All women, you work it good like this,
> for you are working a picture, but down below there is a true engine
> that belongs to all those who will work at getting the food [cargo]
> ready. Later when we [dead and the living] are gathered together, your
> poroman will give all your food to your hands. You will see it, and you
> will be happy."

The successful working of cult rituals would allow the underground engines that were to manufacture "food" to come to the surface. Posingen described how in one cult ritual the women worked the "picture" of an underground engine:

> We did not work an engine [a real engine], we simply spoke about
> it. . . . There was only an empty picture, in us gathering together leaves,
> talking about them, and in working it [the engine] by tossing our legs
> in all sorts of ways. It was only in terms of dancing. This [ritual] school
> came from Censure. After he had worked it, they [women] would then
> copy it. Later they would see things eventuate. In *tok bokis* [talk-box,
> an allegory or metaphor] we say, "when the ground will move," that is,
> when we [the dead and the living] gather together. They [women] would
> then receive this school, that is, they would receive this engine so that
> those on top could work food. This here on the ground [the rituals, the
> pictures] they would forget about it, for the engine would come on top
> and work all kinds of food [cargo].

We are dealing here with how one system of production interprets another system of production and with how one system of reduplication organized around the reproductive powers of female bodies interprets the reduplicative powers of a technological system of reproduction. Here a society with an organic maternal image of reproduction finds it hard to conceive of mechanical reproduction except by assimilating it to the labors of women's bodies. Through the ritual control of women's bodies Censure unearthed a new creative form of mimesis in which the disciplined repetitive labor of women would provide the new order of existence and its future mechanical forms of reproduction.

THE SCHOOLING OF WOMEN

Censure's genius lay in marrying two traditional forces of production in Kaliai culture—those of woman and those of the dead. Censure claimed that the ritual labor of above-ground women would be mimed and transformed by underground women into the making of cargo. More specifically, the poroman of an above-ground woman, her underground namesake, would work cargo for her above-ground representative in proportion to how hard the above-ground woman worked the cult's laws. Those laws involved women performing cult songs and dances each Thursday, which was the day Jesus was expected to arrive. Those laws also involved women cleaning the wide roads that led from Meitavale village to surrounding streams.[2] Each woman was assigned to sweep a certain part of a road. Theresa explained that in cleaning her section a woman was marking out an underground room that belonged to her and was building up cargo in her underground room:

> Now it is as I said before: women would have to clean these areas
> all the time. Now supposing a woman left her room to stop nothing [ne-
> glected it]. Then she would not have cargo. Something of a woman's
> [her future cargo] would go according to her room. This, that she had
> worked before, would still be there, but there would be no new cargo
> added to it. I am talking about all this line [of people] down below that
> works the cargo.
>
> Now supposing a woman did not work her room [clean her portion
> of the road] and it became overgrown, then another woman could
> come and work the room of this woman, and this something belonging
> to it [the cargo in the room] would come to her and the other one
> would have nothing.

I was told that the rubbish the women swept from the road went down into the underground where it became cargo. We have here women coming to be policed through the mirror space of the underground, which reflected and realized all their desires and labors. The underground and the above-ground are made to exist in a strange kind of a mirror relationship, wherein those above-ground are referred to as the pictures of an alternative underground reality. Although we might be tempted to see the underground as an imaginary space, it was not experienced as such by the Kaliai, who in their rituals constructed themselves as embodying the imaginary space of the mirror that must reflect and capture an alternative reality located beneath it. In this imaginary figuring of the imaginary, the imaginary world of the underground is rendered real, whereas the real world of rituals is experienced as a world of artifice. We have here the difficult situation of talking about imaginary geographies that are not experienced as imaginary but as real and where instead the ritual work of the cult was referred to as "drawings" and "paintings" (**sapringen**) of an underground reality.

TELEPHONING CHRIST

Censure's representations of the fertile powers of the underground focused on certain women in the earth, to whom he referred variously as Tamasina, Jesus, and the "boss of the ground." By revealing the individual names of these underground women Censure gained them as allies. They, along with his children and nephews in the underground (Sen Kilok, Sen Les, and Sen Seuve), helped him convert the rest of the underground to the work of his cult. One account says that Censure had twelve underground female followers who were known as his disciples. Posingen explained that "they were not enough to hear the Wind of God; only Censure could hear the Wind of God." These bosses of the ground helped Censure by relaying his school to other underground women. The first two women who helped Censure with the laws Atwaneh and Seine were called Legineh and Seine. They belonged to *Liklik Pisin* and *Bikpela Pisin,* respectively, and they schooled their sister moiety members in the underground. These two women were said to have been "lifted up" by Censure and "they held the *as* [origin] of the ground belonging to us." The next two women who replaced Legineh and Seine were Arogo and Liliah; they in turn were followed by Bilah and Yamo. Censure was in charge of changing these women; he would rest them and appoint new ones to relay his school (known as the Wind of God) to other underground women.

Censure mediated the relationship of the underground back to itself. He derived knowledge from underground female Christs known as the Wind of God whom he then used to reeducate the rest of the underground in ways mirroring that reeducation that he was working above ground. In effect, Censure believed the cargo would come by bridging the distance between these two worlds and that this distance could be bridged by the two worlds copying a common world of ritual knowledge. Posingen gave me this description of how his father visited telephone holes and used his "English" to school the underground women in the same knowledge that he gave to above-ground women:

> He would turn talk [i.e., speak his English] and first school all the underground. He would work at talking to them. It is not as though he schooled all of them. He would first talk to all their female bosses, who would then school them all. He would give the rules of the school to all their teachers. Later when this was finished, their teachers would learn all their pupils. Father would then turn to us and would work at schooling us on top, that is, us now of Papua New Guinea. He would turn to us, saying "All women, you all line up now."

In this reference to Papua New Guinea we see the way a new national existence and identity are being forged as emerging through controlling the bodies of women, through controlling their reproductive labors via the mediation of the underground. As mentioned earlier, the surface world was often referred to as "Papua New Guinea on Top," and its boundaries were mapped out through a subterranean version of itself that was often called Papua New Guinea Down. The imaginary community of the nation was an above-ground world focused on a certain ritual disciplining of women, who had to be made to capture mimetically the labors of an underground version of themselves and of the nation.

In Chapter 2 I mentioned briefly how women found the cult's significant geographical sites, Mount Sinai, Galilee, and heaven. Women also found the telephone holes leading to the underground. These holes were also called wirelesses and doors. They were often located above underground streams, and the noises coming from them were interpreted as the cries of underground engines and workshops. At the cult's different telephone doors, Censure appointed female followers to poroman (be paired with and mime) the underground female Christs who resided at each door. I was told of one occasion when Censure named four young girls to be the Christs of four telephone doors close to the Kaliai coast. The girls were decorated and made to stand up at their different "doors."

Censure then made a speech proclaiming each girl the boss of her separate door. He also instructed the girls that they were to come regularly to Meitavale so that the underground women who resided there at its telephone—Mountain Silo—could also come to know them. Every Thursday the young girls came to Meitavale, and with other people they went down to Mountain Silo where people worked the law belonging to these female Christs. When I asked Posingen why these rituals were performed only on Thursday, he replied, "The reason why Thursday was the day of the telephone is like this—Mother will come down, Jesus will come down on Thursday. So for this reason we gathered then to talk. Jesus will not come down on just any day—no, it will be Thursday; this was why we all gathered together on Thursday."

Censure told the above-ground Tamasinas that if they worked hard, their underground namesakes would also work hard: "Your [individual] poroman [namesake, spiritual double] are at your door watching you. If youse work good, then they will be happy with you and they too will work good, but if you work lazily, then your poroman will not work good, for if you are lazy, they too will be lazy." Monongyo explained the ritual work of the women like this:

> They would work talk and all these things belonging to the law, like dancing with their legs and other similar things. It is like this, if they worked this according to the law, and threw their legs and other things which Father [Censure] worked at learning them, then if they followed this, those down below would also do the same, they would copy them. Now if they were lazy and just stood up, then those down below would just stand up and look, and there would be no person to work the law.

Women here are made to enter into an imaginary relationship with their assigned doubles and indeed with themselves. Living women come to mime, reproduce, and partly embody the powers of underground female Christs who will be the source of free food and cargo. Censure's cult was popular among women, and I suspect this had to do with Censure's celebration of women's procreative powers, which were made to embody the powers of the dead.[3] However, we should not overlook the fact that it was a man who mediated women's relationships with their imaginary identity (ies). Censure used his telephones and doors to the underground to create and control women's imaginary relationships with themselves via the detour of their underground namesakes whom he uncovered and revealed.

Censure received the Wind of God from special underground women, and he translated this information for his female followers so he could control and police their participation in his cult. I was told of one occasion when Censure asked the underground women whether, if those above ground were to receive food from them, his followers would be able to "stand up and win" through it. The underground women replied that they were many and were not able to give their food, for there were not enough above-ground women in Papua New Guinea to hold all this food: "Food is ready and waiting, but if we were to give it, who would hold it? If you women of Papua New Guinea are strong [committed to the cult's ritual work], then you could hold this food and pull it [to yourselves]. Along with Otit [Censure] you have to be strong. Otit is enough to pull us so that we can come out and we can then be together, but it's up to you all." The underground here is a space of excess fertility that demands and calls upon above-ground women to gather together at Meitavale behind Censure—if there were enough above-ground women in the cult, the cargo would come. The number of women in the cult must duplicate the number of women down below; only then would utopia surface.

Censure's status as Otit, as the god of Papua New Guinea, comes from his mediation between above-ground women and underground women. He mediates between two spaces of procreation, trying to get women to be doubles of themselves, to copy each other's work of mimesis. Censure must get the women above ground to correctly perform the ritual songs and dances of the underground that come from the Wind of God. The underground women in turn have to copy the efforts of the ritual labor of above-ground women, especially their poroman. Through the ritual labor of women Censure creates a magical correspondence between the world of the living and the world of the dead, a correspondence that might allow the two to become reunited. A certain productive, procreative relationship was made to exist in the mirror relationship between these two worlds. It was no accident that women were tied closely to the representational practices of cults and that they, more than men, were bound closely to enacting the mirror function. The mirror function is what becomes procreative as it comes to be displaced and mediated by women. The redoubling mirroring powers of the human imagination become merged with the redoubling fertile powers of woman. Here the human imagination objectifies its creative powers as the creative powers of woman.

The mirror space of the underground, which adds another layer of meaning to the world, has this surplus additional world of meaning that it creates, transformed into fantasies of plenitude focused on the maternal body of woman. Through the underground the fertile body of woman is made to embody subterranean truths, and in doing so the Kaliai create a hermeneutic structure where they always displace and subvert the public meanings of the world they inhabit by being able to introduce another layer of meaning to the world. The fertile body of woman opens a gateway to the fertile world of displacement and multiplication. I am suggesting that the world of plenitude opened up by the feminine and the underground also should be seen in terms of the multiplicity of meaning that is opened up by spaces of alterity—by the ability to add a layer of otherness to the world that, in its distance, allows the world to be reduplicated.

THE REPRODUCTIVE POWERS OF WOMEN IN THE EARTH

The displacement and condensation of desires for cargo into the figure of woman were accompanied by a certain eroticizing of desire that I now want to analyze. Censure claimed that in America a woman created the living standard of whites. As we saw earlier, when God ran away from the Kaliai, he came to America, where he made friends with a "rubbishman" ostracized by other whites. This white rubbishman was later to give his sister to the god of Papua New Guinea, and it was through her that the cargo of whites was created. Posingen explained it like this:

> Before I storied to you about this, that the Big Man ran away from us. We chased him away, and he found this rubbishman who was washing sago. . . . The American went and brought this child [his younger sister]. She stood up, this woman stood up. She became Tamasina, and she threw her hand and worked America to have a good sit-down. America is out, it has come up clear. This woman, she stood up to be their Tamasina. . . . She was not a black woman. She was a white woman. She was the sister of this rubbishman, of this poor American. He gave his sister to the Big Man, and this Big Man gave his power to this woman, and she threw her hand like I storied to you. When she threw her hand all sorts of cargo came up.

In his cult rituals Censure tried to find a woman who would stand up next to him and reenact this scene of what had happened in America, where a female Christ stood up next to the runaway god of Papua New Guinea. As his cult declined, Censure found it increasingly difficult to get a woman to come and reproduce this scene. This was partly because one of Censure's interpretations about what had happened in America involved physical intimacy and indeed sex between the god of Papua New Guinea and the female Christ. Posingen reviewed his father's predicament by describing what happened in America like this:

There the Big Man worked it as we spoke before. I think that if there was a woman here, who stood up with strength alongside my father, then he would have been able to work it the same as in America. . . . If a woman [who was to be his Jesus] came, the two would salute [*ruru*] each other, and then Father would hold all the different parts of her body. He would hold her body, like that part underneath her crutch, her hair, this hair of this something of hers [vagina]. Father would hold all these things. When he held them, it is like this, he was giving her power, he was giving her power inside her spirit and her body. When he had finished, the two would again salute [ruru] each other. They would bend down toward each other and then straighten up. The woman would then stand up and throw her hand, and she would be speaking at the same time. When she spoke, it was expected that something would come up. You asked us about this, and we are explaining its way. If there was a woman who would have worked strongly with my father, then it would have been enough for them to have worked it the same as in America, that is, when the Big Man went to America and worked this woman. This woman did not belong to the underground, this American woman . . . she belonged on top.

Father Janssen and the kiaps who patrolled the Kaliai bush saw the sexual aspects of Censure's cult as an expression of Censure's deviant desires. Although I would not want to deny the realization of personal gratification on Censure's behalf, it is also a question of the symbolic functioning of a space of procreation in which Censure's desires came to mediate and participate in the desires of his followers for the birth of a new world.

Censure emphasized that it was only through his coupling with an above-ground female Christ that he could create a new world. At the beginning of Censure's cult, when the Wind of God had yet to come up, Censure appointed two women to be female Christs who would stand for the living of Papua New Guinea. These women were Censure's *mankimasta,* which is the *Pisin* word for the Melanesian domestic servants in European households. The women were expected to cook, fetch firewood, fill up water containers, and generally look after Censure. They were told that if they worked well with Otit, on the Last Day they would become true Tamasinas and stop simply being pictures of underground Christs. Initially, Censure did not give individual cult names to the women he appointed to be his female Christs; he just referred to them as "Tamasina on top" who were to be doubles (poroman) of the "Tamasina down below." Later, when the Wind of God came up, it informed Censure that the underground had too many women, and they required more above-ground poroman to mirror and reduplicate their numbers and identities. It was then that the cult increased the number of Tamasinas who were to work for Papua New Guinea. These women were sometimes called *skulmeri* (schoolgirls), and at the height of the cult in the early 1970s the skulmeri included five women from Benim, three from Aikon, four from Angal, four from Gigina, and five from Meitavale. Many coastal villages also gave Censure women to be his Tamasinas; two were from Ketenge, one from Taveliai, four from Pureling, and three from Gilau. These girls were coastal people's way of securing their rights to future cargo. Monongyo described it all like this:

> Those along the coast that came carried pigs and speared them.
> This was so that everything of theirs [cargo] would stop good until the
> time when something wanted to open up and come; then they would re-
> ceive all this [cargo] from Censure himself. All those who were strong
> [in their belief] and who had given their Jesus to Censure [their daugh-
> ters], well, something of theirs would also go straight. Now supposing
> that they did not steer, they did not straighten [give] a Tamasina to-
> ward Otit, then they would have nothing. Later they would have to
> come buy the law of the Tamasina and then receive cargo.

In his rituals Censure tried to get all these above-ground Tamasinas to transfer their strength and power to one of their representatives who was to act as a double for a true mother of creation in the underground. On the Last Day, when the ground was to move, the most powerful of the underground female Christs was to come to the surface and give her knowledge to her above-ground poroman, that is, to the woman who was ritually and intimately coupled with Censure. This above-ground woman, who was also the representative of the other above-ground Tamasinas, would then become the real Christ-Tamasina of Papua New Guinea and would stop being simply a picture of the most powerful of the under-ground Christs. The underground mother would pass on her power to her above-ground double, who in capturing the power of the underground was expected then to distribute it to the other Tamasinas in Censure's cult, that is, to women who had earlier in the ritual passed on their power to her. Circulating among women, these are forms of empowerment in which living women empower an above-ground representative to mime and cap-ture the fertile power of an underground mother that is then redistributed to above-ground women. Living women here come to be reempowered through the mythic space of a past embodied in a maternal earth that only their bodies can capture, replicate, and redistribute. A whole economy of procreation is being created here. The gifts of women between men (from male cult followers to Censure) are built around the secret flows of power between women in a surface world that is always more than itself because of women.

MOTHER EARTH

Censure sometimes spoke of the original fertile powers of the earth as a stone. He claimed that beneath the island of West New Britain lay Stone Sakail, and there the true mother of creation resided. Before Censure's cult, Stone Sakail was said to lack power, and this was marked by its sleeping in a horizontal position. When Censure found some circular symbols at the lake called the Glass of God, Stone Sakail moved into a more powerful upright position.[4] This occurred because the Wind of God revealed to Censure that the island of Sakail had the underground name of a woman, Lungu. Censure called this name, and Stone Sakail moved into an upright position to reveal a woman underneath. Posingen gave me this account of this process of naming and reclaiming the hidden feminine power of the earth:

> The Wind [of God] came up and named it, he [Censure] then called its name and this stone stood up. . . . Its boss was sleeping underneath this stone, underneath its base [*as*]. Well, this boss, all sorts of *kaikai* [food, a euphemism for cargo] came up from this stone's *as*, from its boss. Its boss, she has the name Lungu. She sleeps underneath the *as* of this island of Sakail, this stone. All right, this woman, food comes up from her. She is human, but when you go toward her head, it is cement. It is not as though she is human over her whole body. No, for the power of God has made her like this. He gave her this something, that is, of woman whom food comes up from. She is human on the side that all food comes up from, but toward her head she is cement. Her *as* is like women's, and food works at coming up from it. It comes up from this stone of the Big Man, for this stone now stood up, and a woman is now inside, and she is the boss of the underground, down below. All food comes up from this woman. Well, now the wind [of God] came up to Censure, and this stone came on top and stood up.

Here the generative powers of the earth are assimilated with the generative powers of woman, which produce a figure that is half stone and half woman. In part, the radical alterity of this woman's body is a way of figuring the alterity of a future world and the alterity of a European world of production. This mother earth story also reveals the hybrid nature of women's identity, that women's powers of reproduction become the mythic terms for thinking about other processes of production and reproduction—those involving food and cargo. Through naming this underground mother, Censure seeks to capture her power. He brings the hidden fertile powers of the earth and of woman into the order of language. Here woman becomes a metaphor for a power of fertility that exceeds and stands outside men but that men must also reveal, capture, and socialize through the naming, disclosing power of language.

In part the hiddenness of women's reproductive power in the earth and in the future resonates with those hidden interior processes of reproduction that occur inside women's wombs. Women's bodies are good to think with, for they embody secrecy and indeed the procreative power of the hidden. As an objectification of hidden creative processes, woman's body can be deployed to think through all those unseen forms of production and creation that whites hide. Through children that move from their unseen interiors to the outside world, women come to embody and enact the power of disclosure.[5] They become a way of realizing the creative power that lies in secrecy, the procreative power that lies in processes of concealing and revealing.

UNDERGROUND DESIRES

In his rituals Censure tried to capture the reproductive powers of this original underground mother by appointing a woman to represent her. More specifically, through his having sex with this above-ground representative, he sought to release the powers of reproduction residing in this mother earth figure. These fertility rituals led to Censure's arrest in 1971 and again in 1973 for "the attempted procurement of underage girls." In 1973 a Situation Report on the Kaliai area instructed patrol officers to inform villagers that "other instances of law breaking will not be tolerated and the people are [to be] advised not to have orgies as these too are likely to result in legal repercussions." In a report he submitted to the administration Janssen (1970) described Censure as suffering from a sexual complex. Likewise, Patrol Officer Pattison, in his Patrol Report for 1973–74, wrote: "The man is obviously demented and the trend of his 'stori' gives the impression that he is a pervert. However, he maintains a remarkable level of control over the cultists."

Many villagers told me of Censure's sexual relations with the young

women who were given to him in order to buy the law. Septireh claimed
that his niece from Benim became pregnant by Censure. Today many
people are simultaneously amused and outraged at what they now see as
Censure's tricking them so he could have sex with their young women.
After 1973 Censure found it increasingly difficult to find women willing to
perform the sexual rites of his cult. Fathers were reluctant to allow their
daughters to be Tamasinas, for they suspected Censure was trying to
marry them without paying a bride price.[6] Censure's wife also was jealous
of these female Christs, and she would chase them away by picking fights
with them. Censure's appearance also frightened many women, especially
his refusal to wash and the mucus that used to run continuously from his
nose. Censure was searching for a woman who would accept him in his
ugliness in much the same way as the hero Akrit in Kaliai stories was
accepted by women who saw beyond the dirt, flies, and pus on Akrit's
skin. However, faced with continual female rejection of his person, toward
the end of his cult Censure persuaded his son Sengelo to take his place in
the ritual that involved physical intimacy with an above-ground Tamasina.
Censure did this partly because a woman that he had found to act as his
female Christ was from his moiety, Little Bird, whereas his son belonged
to her appropriate marrying moiety of Big Bird.[7]

Censure tried to perform the ritual coupling of his son with this female
Christ at Meitavale's telephone door, Mount Silo. Censure spoke to his
son and said that he and this Tamasina were to "kiss," and from this would
come the new law of existence. Sengelo, however, was embarrassed and
also afraid of the complaints that would come from the woman's relatives
if the new law of existence did not come. Yet his father persisted: "That's
all right, the two of you just try it, just try it and we will see. Your tongue
is to go and the woman's tongue is to come, and the two [of] you are to
eat each other's mouths [kiss]." Censure was trying to reenact what the
woman in America had done when the law came up there. However,
Sengelo, much to his father's anger, remained embarrassed. For in addition
to kissing, the ritual also involved sexual intercourse; indeed, the mixture
of semen and vaginal secretions was referred to as the water that would
create the cargo. I asked Monongyo to clarify this talk about water and
cargo:

> Its meaning is like this: they will work it like that, they will kiss the
> first time, they will pull each others' tongues. When this is finished,
> they will work it as they will [have sexual intercourse]. The woman will
> want to, then the water will want to pour out. Then the cargo will spill

out. They will work it again, pull it again, and it will pour out again, and cargo will be spilled out everywhere. It is like this, all the cargo comes up from Jesus, from this woman, from Tamasina. The cargo does not come up from the man, but from her alone. [I asked, "From the body of this woman?"] From the mountain, what is the name of this Tamasina at Stone Sakail? . . . She is the true mother [of the cargo], Stone Sakail. All right, when it comes to us of Papua New Guinea, we of Papua New Guinea will work it as we do, but it follows her.

Here Monongyo explained how sex with the above-ground Christ also mimed and enacted sex with the underground mother who was the true source of cargo. The procreative fluids that spilled out of the woman's body in the ritual were also spilling out of the underground mother's body but as cargo.

Censure in fact developed a whole secret erotic metaphoric discourse around the underground body of this fertile mother. He would tok bokis (talk secretly, metaphorically) to his close followers, telling them that when the age of cargo finally came up, and "you were wandering about and you come up to this woman, then you will come up to her with a key, and you will shoot it inside."[8] After telling me this, Posingen informed me that in reality this mother's body was covered in vaginas and that his father's talk about a key was really tok bokis for having sex with this woman.[9]

> He spoke like this, that with this woman, on this side and on that side, all over, there were vaginas, all over her skin. If you were a man carrying a key, you would go up to her. Father would speak like this, he would say "key", but father would also say that he was working talk-picture and that it was not a key but a man [man's body]. A man would go and "shoot" [sut, i.e., penetrate] one side, he would shoot one of the vaginas. To us men, father would reveal this, but to all the women he would not say anything about this. This talk belonged to him, this was his tok bokis, that a man would go and "shoot" her and from this all sorts of things would spill out, it would not be play [there would be lots of cargo]. One man would be shooting one side, and another man would be shooting another side. But when he [Censure] went to the women, he would say that the man was carrying a key to open some-thing and everything would spill out. He would work this sort of tok bokis to women about the key, but when he came to us men, it was different—he would say, "You men, if you wanted to come up and work a good existence, then you would sut this something, and when it

opened and something spilled out, it would not be play." Father would
tok bokis about this all the time.

Here we have a supereroticized woman who is shared by men. Having
more than one vagina, she is able to incorporate more than one man and
produce more than for just one man. Here a whole sexual economy of
desire is developing around cargo, where the desire for cargo is figured
and realized as sexual desire.[10] It would be a mistake to reduce these sexual
fantasies simply to the unconscious desires of an individual, Censure;
rather, they also speak to a whole world of culturally formulated desire.
In particular, the underground speaks to the underground desires of men
for an accessible, readily available form of sexuality that can fulfill all their
desires. The repression of sexual desire is used for figuring the repression
of all other desires, such as for cargo and the white man's lifestyle. Making
available a supereroticized woman becomes the image for realizing in an
attenuated way all people's other desires. We see in these fantasies the
reworking of sexual desire that the desire for European goods brings. In
these underground images of a supersexualized femininity we have the
eroticizing of property and of all other desires that come to be modeled
on male desire, especially men's desire for women. Here cargo is eroticized
and feminized, whereas woman in turn is objectified and merged with the
desire for cargo. Here two forms of fetishism involving women and commodities are merged to create a new erotic life for things and a new objectification of sexuality (cf. Hyde 1983).

Here what needs to be explained is why Censure and his close male
followers found it difficult to declare in front of female followers the explicit contents of their sexual fantasies concerning the true underground
mother of creation. It is almost as though women would problematize the
objectivity of these images by recognizing the underground desires of men
that lurk in them. I do not think it was a concern for women's sense of
modesty that led Censure to conceal from women the meaning of the
"key" that was to be inserted into the underground mother's body. I am
suggesting that the underground objectified and gave voice to the fantastic
contents of men's desires and that men sensed that it would be problematic
in front of women to make the hidden repressed voice of male desire stand
for the repression of all other desires.

Censure's superprocreative underground Christ was said to be "the true
origin of how food comes up; it all comes from her." All the other underground Christs were second to this Tamasina—they were her workers. I
was told she was Stone Sakail and that all the references to a stone lying

beneath West New Britain were just public talk-box about her. One reason she was called Stone Sakail was that her skin was like "cement."[11] Posingen described her like this:

> Her skin is like cement, but her vagina is visible, and all the men will go shoot it, and it will be like Father said, everything will work at spilling out. . . . Her skin is like stone, like cement, but down below she is human. Her *as* [genital area] is not covered. If a man comes up to her and shoots her, pulls it out, then cargo will spill out everywhere. This Tamasina, this woman, who is the true origin of everything, her name is Stone Sakail, her name follows the name of the stone. This woman she is Stone Sakail.

Censure often spoke publicly of a buried stone that needed to be unearthed and stood upright. This was talk-picture about unearthing this woman so that she could come to the surface of Papua New Guinea. On one occasion, at the telephone door at Meitavale, a ritual was performed that required followers to unearth a huge buried stone—representing Stone Sakail—so that the underground Tamasinas and this original mother could come into Papua New Guinea. Posingen explained that while this stone slept, the law was blocked, but when it was turned, everything would be revealed: "That's right, everything—all knowledge, all forms of schooling—that you whites possess and which makes you all sit down good will come up when we turn the Stone Sakail and make it stand upright. Then all the laws that you whites sit down with will come up to us in West New Britain." However, it was partly a woman's body that was also to be unearthed and turned in this ritual. The underground mother had to come up clear and be stood up the right way. Then, it was said, something would be "switched on," with rice, meat, and everything else coming from her: "It will come up from this woman who is Stone Sakail." To outsiders Censure spoke of Stone Sakail, but to insiders, especially men, he spoke of a woman's body covered in vaginas. Posingen spoke of this woman as "the Boss of Bagehpu," which is the secret name for the original ground from which people were created. There is a theme of incest in this imagery, for this woman was also the mother of humanity. As Posingen put it, "Our come up [origin] stands up, and a man will go and sut [shoot] it, and from this things will spill out. Everything will be sealed-blocked, until a man goes and shoots her, and then things will spill out. This all takes place at Stone Sakail."

The ritual unearthing of this stone was partly the unearthing of a common sexual body between the races. I was told how men would have to pay for the law, and then they would acquire the right to shoot this female stone-human. It was emphasized that whites would also have to pay:

> A man will go shoot her, and cargo would then come out. If it was an Arawe man or someone from somewhere else, it would be the same. Now supposing all the white men come, then they too will have to pay for the law in order to be able to work this. When they worked this [the pay], then they could shoot her again, and there would be enough cargo for all of us. It is then that we will all be able to sit down good together. It will be the same for all you whites as it is for us native people.

The sharing of a common mother, and the sharing of a common terrain in the body of this stone, defines a unifying space in which the races meet and start to become each other. It is the buying of sexuality, of a common woman, that brings the races together. This woman is not the image of a pure gift; she is the law that has to be bought for the cargo to come up. It is the law of access to woman's sexual body that provides the law of access to the body of cargo. Posingen claimed: "When they buy the law, then cargo will come up. Whites will come and receive their cargo, and we will do the same. We will then be the same, all of us will be the same. There will be enough for everyone."

The common contract underpinning access to a woman's body draws the races together in a common commerce that is also to some extent positioned as outside the present world of money and commodities. Woman's body here mediates another form of creation but also another economic system in which commodities come to be mediated by the gifts needed to purchase sexual rights to a woman. The bush Kaliai will own this woman, and their understanding of the globe's future dependence upon them is that all ethnic groups and races need to give gifts to gain access to this primordial mother. The world of commodities and of global power comes to be reduced to an indigenous paradigm of power, which is the benefit accruing to men from bargaining for control of a woman's sexuality and her reproductive powers. The globe is reduced to a huge bride-price system in which the Kaliai control the ultimate productive woman after whom men lust. [12]

I have so far emphasized the gift element in this future world of global commerce that trades in woman. Yet Censure's attempt to make woman provide the global terms of world exchange also has a touch of the prostitution of the underground. Although the payments are small in relation to the cargo that spills out, and this makes those payments like token gifts, an element of commerce remains in these transactions that were meant to take the Kaliai beyond the existing world of commerce. The underground mother's body was to some extent to be sold by the Kaliai to male Kaliai and to strangers. Here the Kaliai's understanding of their future global centrality is that of a world of token commerce that engages their underground world. The Kaliai have unearthed and revealed their underground in order to trade it in a way that makes its fertile powers accessible to all. They do not seek to hide or monopolize this woman but will exchange for access to her, and in doing so they will create a world of racial and ethnic equality. In this analysis I have emphasized the word token because, although there is a buying of the law, this does not obey the laws of a Western marketplace. Rather, it takes the form of a token price that becomes a gift that subverts the world of commerce that regulates the circulation of commodities. Here the world of commerce is redeemed through woman. She provides an alternative economy to money, the law that everything is free. She is the law of *marimari* (pity, mercy, kindness). She provides a means of escaping the existing world of commerce but partly through that world of commerce becoming married in a token way to the powers of reproduction that she provides. The globe here becomes assimilated to some archaic truth about the feminine. There is an attempt here to embrace the world of global exchange in a way that makes one's underground truths accessible to all. Yet the underground language of male desire provides the common terms of global exchange. The unearthing of its common primordial feminine objects provides the conditions of exchange for uniting men in a common sexual currency that trades on the libidinal investments men have in cargo and in their sexual desires. The underground is a powerful metaphor that allegorically codifies the unconscious processes through which human desire is realized. That unconscious is not a black box or an instinctual reservoir of existing desires; rather, I see it as embodying and exploring those repressed psychic processes that are inscribed, constituted, and tormented by the codes of gender and race.

PRODUCING A NEW LINE OF PEOPLE THROUGH THE UNDERGROUND

So far I have explored how Censure's understanding of cargo's production was bound up with his feminizing the earth's procreative powers and with his developing an erotic discourse in relationship to an underground supersexual, superprocreative mother. However, Censure's feminizing and eroticizing of the underground took other forms, including his having sex with and impregnating some of the other underground female Christs. Indeed, Censure claimed that some had carried children for him in the underground. As we shall see, Censure sought to repopulate the earth with a new race, born not from the separation of the living from the dead but of the marriage of these two realms.

Censure's sexual liaisons with underground women were at the telephone holes where he used to ring for female Christs to come to him. He would stand up at these "doors belonging to God," look, and laugh toward the underground women before spitting at them. He was flirting with these women before impregnating them with his spit. Censure claimed that from his spit came a new line of people down below. One reason Censure took on the task of schooling the underground was that this new line of people was unaware of his new law. Posingen explained that this new line had emerged from

> some of the magic spit he used to do, when he spat at the "doors." This spit of his was, he said, his power. This spit, he worked it at the telephone. This spit would go and turn into a man or into a woman. These people would then come up and be schooled. It was like this: we finished our school with this line of people that we call "the spit of magic." When my father finished schooling this line, he then began gathering together all our ancestors [for their return].

Posingen likened Censure's spit to the spirit of God and the Angel Gabriel, who was believed to have come up to the Virgin Mary and entered her so that she carried Jesus. Like Christ, the children from Censure's spit were sometimes said to have no father. On other occasions Censure was spoken of as their father in the same way that God is Christ's father. Censure here reenacts the imagery of the Bible, becoming God in the process of making the underground the source of his virgin births. The children that resulted from Censure's sexual affairs with underground women were to be his allies in working his new law. Posingen put it like this:

> This spit of Papua New Guinea would go down below, and later they [the children] would come back to Papua New Guinea and would work in helping Papua New Guinea. . . . It is like this. Later when Father wins this sit-down [existence] of ours, this something that they talk about "the Last Day," when the ground moves, then all these children will come up on top, and they will be his line. His spit will become his line, and they will stop on top in Papua New Guinea and teach everybody. That will be their work, schooling all the people of Papua New

Guinea. It is like this: Papua New Guinea on Top does not have plenty
of people because it does not have enough women. So this line will
come on top and occupy this place on top and teach everybody. They
will school us in all these things that you know, how to work food—the
way you [whites] all do.

Censure's spit was a way of repopulating the earth. The children from
Otit's spit would belong to Papua New Guinea on Top, which was seen as
not having enough people.[13] This ascribed depopulation of the nation also
paralleled the cult's loss of followers. Censure's fertility ritual sought in
the earth the mothers of the future, that is, those procreative powers that
would let the living remultiply. We saw earlier that it is only when the
above-ground has the same numbers of women as those below ground that
the cargo will come. The plenitude of the lifestyle of the white man here
is associated with another form of plenitude, that of attaining more people
and in particular more women. A new line of more powerful mothers will
produce a new line of Melanesians who have mastered the white man's
knowledge.

Through the underground mothers of the past, through these female
Christs, the cult searched for a new line of people to replenish the living.
Through marrying one's past, having sex with it, Censure sought to discover the grounds for the future. The fertile terrain of the past provided
the imaginary conditions for owning and controlling one's future but also
for remaking the identities that are to occupy and institute that future
world. In the new line of children born of sex between the present and the
past, the living and the dead, there is something about the necessary nature of the imaginary past in forming the boundaries of identity and of
any new sense of self. The creative constitutive power of the imaginary
past is sexualized. The underground space of the feminine here is an imaginary space of fertility where the powers of the human imagination delegate
to the figure of woman their own creative constitutive effects.

Also a new sort of subject is figured as emerging from the living reconstituting themselves through reclaiming the creative space of the past.
When he spoke to underground women, Censure emphasized that the new
children of their union were to belong to him and the surface world and
not to them and the underground:

It is like this: I will give this spit to you all, to all you women who
are being schooled, and you will carry a new *kru* [offshoots], a new
line. All you women will become pregnant and children will then go
down [be born]. My spit will go down, and a new line of children will

also go down. This new line of children will not belong to Papua New Guinea Down [the underground]. They will be my line, they will belong on top, for I belong on top. I belong to Papua New Guinea, and I worked this spit, and you carried them all, and all this line of mine must later come back on top to Papua New Guinea. They don't belong to youse.

In the underground Censure was producing a new line of national citizens who approached the knowledge and competence of whites. Here the underground mirrors that very transformation of subjects, and especially of children, that the state and church are trying to produce above ground. We see here the way the civilizing project comes to be indigenized, as it comes to be internalized and mediated by the traditional creative spaces of the underground past and of women's bodies. The discourse of nationalism, which is partly a discourse about producing new sorts of subjects, was embraced, and through his cult Censure sought to produce more effectively these new educated, national subjects. Indeed, Censure's resistance to the state and the church was one of claiming to have more effective ways of making Papua New Guineans resemble whites. He held the true *lo* (law) of Papua New Guinea, which had come up from the Wind of God rather than from the transformative pedagogic projects of government, schools, missions, and development. Here people embrace the project of coming to be remade, and their resistance becomes that of more effectively producing that project as their own. Kaliai villagers did this by mediating this project through their understandings of metamorphosis and transformation as bound up with woman and death.

In Censure's cult feminine reproduction became the mythic language for thinking about all production, including that constitution of the boundaries of the world and of selfhood provided by the project of becoming white. Through the feminine space of death the Kaliai were to be reborn and educated through a civilizing process they had made their own and that they had internalized into the very earth that marked and established the conceptual boundaries of their being.

BRINGING THE UNDERGROUND TO THE SURFACE

One major crisis that Censure faced occurred when people started leaving his cult; he then lost the female followers who were central to his rituals and cosmological project. One of Censure's solutions was to turn to underground women to provide the personnel that would work with him on top as the female Christs for Papua New Guinea. Posingen explained that women were plentiful in the underground, so Censure and those special women known as the Wind of God started dividing up the underground women so that some would now come on top to work for Papua New Guinea, whereas others would continue working for the underground: "On top did not have enough people [women, Tamasina], and so they [underground women] would send some on top to Papua New Guinea, and then they could poroman all the women of the underground." Here women of the underground get reassigned to take the place of those above-ground women who had operated as doubles or poroman of underground women. The underground here starts to provide the copies or duplicates of itself in the surface world. It starts to mirror itself back to itself. In the underground a woman would turn to another and say, "You go on top and stay in Papua New Guinea, and I will be your poroman." Those that came on top to Papua New Guinea were said to be coming to the side of Censure, whereas the others were said to "stay with the true mother, Tamasina; they would stay down below." We see here the importance of processes of ritual coupling; the surface world and the underground must mirror each other's ritual labors. When this breaks down because women are leaving the cult, it is resurrected in the fantastic form of the underground's provision of women for the surface world to engage in its mirroring of the underground. We see here the autonomy assigned to the underground and how the depth of meaning it provides is that of the necessity of coupling an image to its reality. The underground women require their doubles this side of the grave, they want to come to the surface, and they need above-ground women to "draw" and "paint" them and their labors. The underground has to be captured by coming to be evoked and copied in the mimetic gestures of women's bodies, for the fertile power of mimesis will allow the surface world to pull toward itself the labors of the underground. The underground women reportedly told Censure:

> "We of the underground, we are plenty, and there is this something [cargo] that we would like to give, but who is there truly on top who could hold it and pull it on top? They are not there. If we were to give this something there are no women standing on top who could pull it on top." All the women of the underground used to speak like that and also the Wind of God that used to school them all.

Here the inability of the surface world to create a new world was transformed into the loss of women's bodies, which Censure tried to solve by bringing some underground women to the surface to become pictures of the other women left below. At this point the imaginary world of the underground comes to be more fully folded back upon itself, as it enters the world of the living to provide the personnel to act as representations and copies of itself. We see here the captivating power of the human imagination and the self-sustaining worlds of mirrors it can create. Yet this mirror function was intimately married to the reproductive figure of woman. Indeed, the underground and above-ground became more permeable when the figure of woman stepped out of the mythic space of the underground past in order to remirror herself in the world of the living. Here the dead mime the living miming the dead, so that they—the dead in the underground—can again copy the living. This interchangeability between the underground and the surface world makes creativity reside in the very permeability of these boundaries and in the labors of mimetic reconciliation that come from one world's acting as a double for another.

We need here also to treat seriously the process whereby underground Christs were divided into two gender camps—one belonging to Censure and the other to the underground mother. The interface between past and present, living and dead, underground and surface is a sexual procreative interface. The creative interface of the mirroring of two worlds is eroticized, and this partly speaks to the pleasure and desires that can be projected into the imaginary space of the underground and onto all labors of doubling, onto all those points of conjuncture at which differences meet and become paired (Bachelard 1983).

We also have to ask why images of the underground are bound up with woman and secret metaphors of her sexuality and procreative power. When Posingen spoke of his father's cult, his discussion was often about how its public talk and ritual work were really talk-box for something else in the underground, and this hidden reality was the truth about woman's power to create. Posingen often spoke of an above-ground meaning that had another underground meaning, of a public meaning that had a different meaning when you carried that meaning down below. The underground here is a fertile repository for secret meanings, for concealed productive truths; it is a womb for dark meanings that are not obvious but often metaphorically implied. I see the underground as objectifying the fertile doubling power of metaphorical meanings, a way of talking about the productive relationship between a world of surface meanings that always contains within itself more than itself (this is woman's pregnant body). This engendering metaphorical relationship between outside and inside meanings is displaced and reobjectified as a relationship between the visible and the invisible, light and darkness, surface and underground.

This interface between worlds of meanings is sexualized and rendered procreative.

Performances by the living, which were addressed to the underworld, brought to the surface the desires that men had projected and objectified into an underground realm of supermotherhood. A touch of Oedipus exists in this longing for the underground mother and in the transformation of all desires into the model of men's desires for a supersexual, superprocreative femininity. The underground here voices and objectifies the underground fantasies of men with all the libidinal investments and pleasures that the world of fantasy is capable of bringing. Yet this world of fantasy also denied its fantastic nature and instead sought to realize and objectify its presence. The repression of fantasy here takes the form of denying itself as fantasy, for the underground is an imaginary space that denies its imaginary existence. As the underground loses its believers, it attempts to keep alive its magical presence in the living world by sending female Christs up to the living to act as pictures of itself. Here the underground creates the world of pictures in the surface world in order to secure and mark itself off as real. The underground for the Kaliai is not an imaginary space. We in the West are the ones who tend to fictionalize other worlds, treating them as ideal and bodiless. For the Kaliai the underground is a real space that requires the artifice of the living to capture its magic and reality. Through the process of transforming the surface world into ritual pictures—that is, into a performing platform for representations that refer to realities in the underground—the underground secures its reality while rendering the living as idealizations of itself.

Censure adopted one other solution to solve the crisis of not having a Tamasina; this was to transform himself into a female Christ. He declared himself a woman so that he could become the female Christ of Papua New Guinea who was going to mirror the true underground mother. Posingen quoted his father as saying: "They are all running away, and I will not have a woman to come stand up strong, so I will turn [change] and be Tamasina." In the next chapter I will focus on the theme of androgyny. I will start with Censure's cult, but I will also look at how other cargo leaders took up this powerful mythic theme of androgyny as an apparatus of transformation for breaching the divisions and stabilized identities of the existing world.

Chapter Six

Androgynous Imagery, Sexuality, and the Procreative Powers of the Imagination

> And when you make the inner as the outer, and the outer as the inner,
> and the upper as the lower, and when you make male and female into a
> single one, so that the male shall not be male and the female (shall not)
> be female, then shall you enter (the Kingdom).
> Gospel of Thomas, quoted in Eliade, *The Two and the One,* 1979, 106

I want to start this chapter on androgyny with a story about an intellectu-
ally disabled Kaliai man who was said to have married a child belonging
to the *tewel* that live in nearby mountains. Tewel, the angry ghosts also
known in Pisin as tambaran and in the local languages as **mahrva,** are said
to have short arms and are never sick. They are sometimes said to be
people who have suffered a violent death, and their souls hang around
seeking vengeance upon the living. Although in Kaliai culture the tewel is
a form of otherness, it is also a possibility of what it means to be human.
Villagers who are selfish, greedy, and do not share with others are said to
be tewel, or mahrva. The Kaliai believe that a tewel will sometimes swap
its child for one of their children and that this tewel child can be recognized by its constant hunger and crying. The Kaliai tell the following story
about one such changeling, the female child of a tewel that was left with
them.

> Time passed, and the child started to talk. This child grew
> quickly—this tewel child. It grew quickly in terms of getting fat, but its
> crying went on and on, and people started thinking. All the big men
> spoke to the mother: "This child is not yours. We think a tewel has ex-

changed children, she has taken your child and left behind its child. This is why the child cries so much. Now look, you can see its hands/ arms, they are those short ones." As the child grew, it ate large and not small amounts of food. All kinds of foods had to come continuously for her to eat. This girl's name was Merisa. She grew up to become a woman, she developed breasts; she worked gardens, and she cooked food. Time passed, and people spoke: "This woman cannot go and marry a good man." We will give her to a *longlong* [ignorant] man." This man's name was Narung. . . . They both came and lived with us [the Mouk]. This woman never became sick because she was the daughter of a tewel. She died nothing [that is, of natural causes, or not having had children]. She did not carry one child, she died nothing. After they buried her, her poor husband ran away to us at Aikon. [He told us,] "My wife died and we buried her. I felt so sad for her so that I have run away to you." My father spoke: "That's all right, you stay. When your sorrow for your wife is finished, you can go back." [*Narung replied,*] "Oh no, I want to stay here."

He stayed with us for one year. . . . He would go break *baibai* [cycad nuts] . . . and wrap them up, putting one bundle here and another bundle there. Then he would say: "Wife [*meri*] go get the baibai and put it in the water, so we can go now, we are already hungry [i.e., we have stayed long enough]." He always worked like this. He alone would do this work, he had no wife around. He would talk *nating* [nothing] to himself alone. He would tell his wife to do things, but then he himself would go do them—do this and that. He would do all these things. When the baibai was ready, he would sing out to his wife: "Wife let us go get the baibai so we can uncover it, and all the big men can eat." He would talk like this, and then he himself would go get these things. [He would tell Merisa,] "You go turn the stone and pull the baibai up from the water." [He would reply in her voice,] "But where is the leaf? You go get the leaf first." He would go get the leaf and the cane. Then [assuming his wife's role] he would go turn the stone and pull the baibai up.

He would talk like this to his wife, yet it was not his wife, it was only himself. He himself would send himself out to all his orders. He was the husband and wife at the same time. *Em i bungim em tasol* [He gathered them together]. After he covered up the baibai, he would talk, he would talk as a woman, the wife would talk: "Narung, shall we eat here, or shall we go back to the village?" Then he would reply: "Ah, we will cook some first, cook a few, and eat a few first, and then we will carry some back to the village." He would then change places [*wife speaking*:] "All right, well, go get some firewood." He would go get the firewood, light a fire, put some stones in it, and then put the baibai in the fire. [*Husband speaking:*] "Hurry and turn the things so they are done quickly, the sun is close to setting." [*Merisa speaking:*] "Do not worry, they are nearly done now, and we will go." He worked at changing his own voice. . . . He would send his wife to get something, and then he himself would go get it.

Here a man loves his wife so much that after she dies he keeps her identity alive inside himself. He does not relinquish his identity, but he takes on her domestic chores and even her voice. This story shows us someone internalizing and coming to occupy the place of the other—both a female otherness but also the tambaran other, for Narung's wife is the child of a tewel. Narung overcomes the pain and sorrow of separation brought on by death by internalizing the deceased other into himself. Some psychiatrists might see in this story the pathology of a multiple personality disorder, but I want to argue that contained in the pathos of this moving story is precisely that imaginary dialogue with the other that all human beings require in order to be themselves. In the case of Narung the other is doubled over, operating as both the otherness of woman and the otherness of a child of the dead. I see this story as speaking about the domesticated monstrous feminine, a theme that can be found in some other bush Kaliai stories that speak of a tambaran, or *masalai meri* (wild monstrous woman), who is captured, brought into the village, smoked on a fire, and gradually taught to speak and work gardens. This masalai meri will later marry and become the founding ancestor of a line of people. In the case of Merisa, the wild femaleness integrated into the social order does not begin a new line, but she becomes integrated into her husband's identity; so close and necessary does she become to his existence that he refuses to part with her. As I see it, the power of this story, the reason it is told, lies in its speaking and acting out the imaginary relationship that every man has with woman, in which he needs to become or to internalize woman in order to be himself. Narung simply makes manifest the psychic structures that underpin all existence; where some internal miming and voicing of the other are needed in order to be oneself (H. Mead 1934; Sartre 1948, 1975). The monstrosity of the feminine other here alludes to the danger of becoming lost in the boundaries of the identity of the other. The monstrous wife here represents both the gift and the act of terror that the other poses to the boundaries of one's existence.

I want to argue that the story of Merisa is not so extraordinary but is simply an extension of that imaginary dialogue with forms of otherness that everyone needs to sustain to render all life meaningful. This need, which is often invisible or normal, can become explicitly reworked in certain historical circumstances (like the colonial context) that involve their own negotiations with otherness. Indeed, one of the main points of this book is that this general need to occupy (and even to domesticate) the space of the other in order to be oneself is a central feature of cargo cults. Occupying the outside space of the other becomes central for reclaiming and extending control of the boundaries through which a self maps out the borders of its identity(ies). Mimesis is never simply a process of passive copying and of becoming the same; instead, mimesis articulates and explores the freedom to remake and transcend existing stabilized structures of identity by internalizing the corporeal schemes of other identities. This is a process of trying on and exploring the possibilities for being a subject. Through mimesis people develop alternative second identities to inhabit: they transgress the boundaries of themselves, and they transgress the boundaries of social orders predicated on building certain stabilized identities around certain stabilized corporeal schemes.

So far I have focused on how mimesis works to appropriate and destabilize those processes of becoming white that emanate from European-inspired institutions. I argued that mimesis does not so much deny the processes of becoming white as that it internalizes the process by embedding in it the familiar framework of one's Melanesian culture such that it also empowers the past in the process of moving people into their reworked white future. I want to continue to analyze this ambiguous mixture of modernity and the past but focus now on how the mythic world of primordial androgynous ancestors came to be mimed as a way of becoming white. One image of the creative past to which Kaliai cult leaders returned was that image of androgynous creative beings that was central to Kaliai myths about the origins of men's house tambarans and of the existing social order. In Kaliai cargo cults the process of going back to a world in which sexuality had not been fully dichotomized was often the language used for going to a world that did not have strict racial dichotomies. As I have argued, Kaliai cargo cults often associated the blurring and overcoming of gender identities and inequalities with the blurring and overcoming of racial identities and inequalities. Here the body of the other sex provides a way of destabilizing all those meanings and social frameworks built around unambiguous classifications of bodies into clear dichotomies.

In his 1979 analysis of the androgyne, Eliade wrote about the process of becoming both male and female as "the total reversal of values." He rightly saw it as a process of going back to the beginning, "a regression to the primordial," and by this he meant a return to that more ambiguous time before the processes of Creation created the differences that make up the categories that order the world (114).[1] In this chapter I analyze how the otherness of the white man's identity and his alternative social order came to be mediated by the exploration of alternative forms of bisexuality whose generative potential resided in their being mythically figured as prior to the emergence of the cleavages and secrets that created and now make possible contemporary social order. Through taking on the identity of the opposite sex, certain cult leaders created a line of flight; although the line of flight often mimed European processes for becoming white, it did so within an alternative indigenous mythic vision of processes of metamorphosis and transformation. Here we are going to be analyzing the process of creating Creation and the role of the opposite sex in providing a space of alterity through which the colonial task of being remade can be refigured and seen in a different creative light.

KORIAM AND THE FEMINIZATION OF MEN

From what my informants can remember, the first cargo cult that played with the androgynous imagery of the mythic past in order to realize the future was the Koriam cult of the early 1960s. In Chapter 1 I pointed out that this cult had a major influence in the village of Benim. There men dressed up like women and exposed to real women the secret masks that men controlled. Widespread in the Kaliai bush is the view that the masks of traditional Kaliai society are a punishment given by God to the black man before God ran away to whites and gave them His true valuable secrets. As Posingen put it:

> Tambarans are now possessed by men. We hide them from women. The reason for this, I think, is that God is still punishing us. We were *bikhet;* God ran away, and He gave us this something. However, He did not give it to make men happy. No way. It is a punishment for buggering up men because they were unresponsive to His talk. This something hides, if it were to come up "clear" [i.e., into the open], all humans would be destroyed. This something is not something good, it is His punishment. He spoke: "You were obstinate towards me, now when this something comes up, you must hide it well; if you do not hide it, you will die."

Traditional masked ceremonies acquired new meanings as they became part of the racial interpretation of the Fall offered in cargo cults. The deceptions and trickery of masks that underpinned traditional gender inequalities came to be figured as the punishment given to one's race. In the context of European cultural hegemony, bush Kaliai society's need for masks is seen as people's entrapment in lies from which they cannot escape. Men in particular have been given the punishment of having to hide a lie and their participation in a lie. Utopia comes to be seen as a world without gendered secrets, without the engendering qualities to which secrets give rise. Posingen told me this was why Benim villagers exposed their masks to women: "They exposed them so that a good law could come inside them all. Now this something [masks], in the Bible they say it is sin and that it should not be worked. For this is something no good, which is hidden from women. It must be revealed so that good customs can come up. Koriam worked it, and this came up."

Before exposing the masks, the men of Benim put on the grass skirts of women, cut coconut shells in half, and put them on their chests to symbolize female breasts. They held cordyline leaves and waved them as they came out, performing dances ordinarily reserved for women. As they did so, the men chanted: "We are all women now, we are all women now." Posingen gave me the following description:

> The work of Koriam came up to Benim; people had heard his talk, and they worked a meeting of all the big men at Benim. They worked a big feast, and this was to be the work for exposing tumbuan. Tumbuan was to be revealed, and all the big men put on grass skirts like all the women, and they came outside saying: "We now have come up like women. This power of us [men] can now come up for you women to see." The man who was inside Varku threw Varku outside, and some of the young women saw it, but some of the old women were scared, and they covered their eyes with grass mats; others stayed inside their houses.
>
> They [the men] put on coconut shells, so their breasts could stand up and be similar to the breasts of women. They came outside carrying a [cordyline] branch, like this, saying, "We are all women now, we are no longer men." They put on all the clothes of women, for this something tumbuan and Varku was now revealed, so they worked this. They had all become women now [ol i meri pinis na] for something was now exposed. Before they were all men when this something hid.

Here men equate the loss of their secrets with a process of disempowerment that they experience as their feminization. The paradigmatic image for feminized men is provided in Kaliai myths that state how, at the original beginning of society when no masks existed, men had breasts that they used to nurse children, whereas women had beards. In putting on coconut-shell breasts and exposing the masks to women the men at Benim were miming and seeking to recapture this original androgynous time of equality when men did not dominate women through the terror of monstrous masks. The exemplary Kaliai model for a world without power is an androgynous world that is also the world before God ran away from the Kaliai and gave them the punishment of masks. In Kaliai cargo cult mythology the secrets that sustain the white man's power are seen to have emerged alongside the secrets that sustain the black man's power over women. Indeed, people seek to create the world of white existence by abolishing the secrets that sustain the gender relations that make up their social order. I see the Koriam cult as reworking the disempowerment of Melanesian men brought by colonial contact; here the colonial experience of feminization is revalued and positively embraced by being assigned an original creative force. This merging of the androgynous world of myth with the feminization processes of colonialism is made possible because both offer the promise of a utopian world without secrets and the monstrous inequalities that secrets create.

CENSURE AND THE PROCESS OF BECOMING WOMAN

I want to turn now to some more recent cults that I have information about in order to analyze how people's sense of the future is mediated and realized by the way they appropriate and internalize the body of the other sex as their way of modeling the alterity of the future on the alterity of a creative past. In particular, I want to look at androgynous imagery in the Censure cult. At an early stage in his career Censure declared himself to be a woman and in fact to be the female Christ who was going to deliver a new existence. Later in his career, when he was dying and had few followers left, Censure started to have underground women enter his body. As Censure lay on his bed, they would speak from his mouth to his family. I want to look at the specific ways in which Censure took up this process of becoming woman.

In Chapters 4 and 5 I described how Censure searched among his followers for a female Christ who would reenact what had happened in America, where he claimed a woman created the new existence enjoyed by whites. At the beginning of his cult Censure was successful in getting women to be his Tamasina. However, later these female Christs were said to have been chased away by Censure's wife, many were frightened of Censure's intentions and appearance, and their fathers suspected that Censure was trying to marry their daughters without paying a bride price. As Monongyo explained it:

> The thinking of some men started to foul, and they no longer had
> good knowledge, and they thought this man [Censure] would marry
> them all [the young female Christs] for nothing. All right, they then
> stood up and ran away with their children. One man ran away with his
> child and then another. It went on like that, until they [all the female
> Christs] were all finished, and we then sat down nothing. We, his family,
> stayed with him.

After Censure's arrest for "the attempted procurement of underage girls," his cult declined rapidly, and he found it difficult to get a woman to stand up as a Tamasina for Papua New Guinea. It was then that Censure declared that he would become this woman, that he would be the female Christ for Papua New Guinea. Posingen explained it like this: "Plenty of people started leaving us, until my father and us were left behind. He spoke: 'It doesn't matter, I alone will pull this food [the cargo]. I will be the Tamasina of Papua New Guinea and pull this food.' He spoke like this, and he worked this promise of his, but he died and there is nothing now." Here Censure takes on the role of the fertile woman missing from his cult; he becomes the female Christ who will complete human existence. Having proclaimed woman the true creator, Censure had to become her if he was to complete his internalization of the powers of creation as he imagined them. Theresa saw it like this: "We were counting [naming, assigning] all the Tamasinas down below. Now they wanted those on top [cult women] to come to be their *poroman*. They [above-ground women] came, but they did not stay, for they came and ran away. So Censure stood up and said: 'All right, I alone on top will stand up for Papua New Guinea as its Tamasina. I will work with the women down below.'" Here Censure becomes a double of the feminine; he starts to reflect and internalize underground identities that now surface in his identity. He becomes the embodied mirror of his mirrorings of the feminine underground. For Censure underground women are the true sources of creation that have to be captured in a field of representation that comes to be focused on him, that comes to require that his identity be radically refigured to embrace and embody their creativity. In his lust for these women and in his lust for the powers of creation that they embodied, Censure was willing to divide up and fragment his identity to keep alive within himself that which he desired to continue to exist outside himself.

Part of the internal division and fragmentation of Censure's identity came from his having to encompass both genders, for he had to school not only both men and women but also both moieties. Here we need to remember that Little Bird (**Piraou**) is gendered female, whereas Big Bird (**Bogi**) is gendered male; according to Posingen, Censure's femaleness came from his belonging to Little Bird.

> This talk has its source with this, that in the story [myth of origins]
> Piraou is female and Bogi is male. Well, Father is Piraou, he is female.
> Well, when he wanted to stand up this work of his, he never had some-
> one else to be his poroman. . . . It is like this: this woman Piraou went
> and found her line, and her brother went around and found his line.
> For this reason all the line of Piraou is female, and all the line of Bogi
> is male. It is because of this that now this talk-box came up, and Father
> would say, "I am a woman—I am not a man." It is because the story
> [myth of origins] goes like this.

In traditional culture some significant creative heroes like Kowdock belong to the female moiety of Little Bird. The two moieties are associated with left and right, which are also gendered female and male, respectively. If a men's house has to be shared, Little Bird will sleep on the lefthand side and Big Bird on the righthand side. This spatializing of gender difference came to be internalized and mapped out in Censure's body. Monongyo explained it to me like this: "He worked it like this: it was half to the side of women and half to the side of men. The half side that went to women went to the left side, and the half side that went to the men went to the right side. He worked it like this, the two of them worked it like this, he and this Tamasina [underground mother]." Here we see that Censure is a mirror double for an underground female Christ who is bifurcated in the same way. When I queried Monongyo about this, he again emphasized to me that this female Christ did not belong to one moiety but to both— Little Bird was on her left side and Big Bird on her right. This female Christ was appointed by Censure to work both gendered moieties in the underground; she was to reproduce his androgynous labors down below. As Monongyo put it:

> He marked it so that she alone would work. She would work to the
> side of women and to the side of men, to both sides. Now, Father [Cen-
> sure] had to work on top, and this Tamasina had to work down below.

She had to work like him, like how Father told her. This woman also
had to work it, half male and half female, for she had to school all her
line [Little Bird], and later she would have to turn and school all Big
Bird. She had to work the same way. Father worked like this on top,
and this Tamasina had to work like this down below. In her work she
had to follow the position of Father. It is not as though she could work
some other kind of position to that of Father. Her position had to follow the position of Father. Father had to work it first, and this [the ritual work] went down below, and they then followed Father, all the underground. It is not as though the underground could work something
different to that which Father was working. If they did this, then things
would not come up all right, things would not end good.

In encompassing both the male and female, Censure and this female
Christ encompass both sides of the social order. This female Christ, who
is androgynously bifurcated in the same way as Censure, can be seen as
the objectified form of Censure's female side. It would be possible to see
Censure as also an objectification of her masculine side, only we should
remember that Censure is spoken of as appointing her. Indeed, she mirrors
his dilemma that he has no poroman or paired equivalent in the Big Bird
moiety to share and reduplicate his labors. Posingen explained it like this:

It is like this: he alone stood up this work. Now supposing there was
a Big Bird to join Little Bird [i.e., Censure], and the two of them could
work it [the ritual work], then it would be all right. Little Bird could
teach its line, and Big Bird could teach its line. This is the reason that
there is this talk that half his side is male and the other half is female.
Its meaning goes back to this: he alone stood up this work so he had to
work toward the female side, that is, Little Bird, and he had to work to
the other side, the male side of Big Bird. Now this underground Tamasina, she had to work it the same way as well. Half her side was female,
and the other side was male. The reason why they said half the side was
female was because this is all Little Bird and the other half side that is
male goes to all Big Bird. Its meaning is like that. But if another person had stood up with Censure, then he [the other person] could teach
all Big Bird, and Censure could teach all Little Bird. If two people had
stood up, then they would not have to work this other thing [divided iden-
tities]. For one person would school his line, and the other man would
school his line. But no Father worked it differently, and its meaning is like
this: it is like a man who straddles [kalapim] a stream. [I ask: "He would
speak like this in picture-talk, is that right?"] Yes, he would be straddling

a stream, he would be working on one of its sides, on this side of the water, and he would also be working on the other side of the water.

I was told that most people in the cult knew of Censure's claim that he was both male and female and that this was mapped out on the left and right sides of his body. A number of ex-cult followers from different villages independently told me of Censure's claims to being a woman.

Part of Censure's internalization of the feminine came from his receiving his knowledge from certain underground female Christs known as the Wind of God. Censure started to take on the identity and persona of these female Christs. Whereas other cult followers had a double, or poroman, in the underground who was the same sex as they, this was not the case for Censure, who had female Christs as his poroman. This information came up while I was discussing why disputes among cult followers acted to block the *lo* (law). I was told that when you buggered up an aboveground person, you also injured their spiritual double in the underground who would also have to be offered compensation; otherwise, the underground double would block the cargo. Theresa told me of a time Censure and his lieutenant Amulmul fought: "I started thinking about Censure so I fastened this pig of mine to go buy [compensate] this poroman of Censure's down below. I straightened her, and it was finished." At this point her husband, Posingen, interjected, saying: "It is like this Amulmul was crossing God, the God down below. It is like this: he was crossing the Tamasina down below. So for this reason this pay was worked." Posingen went on to tell me that Censure's poroman were those underground Tamasina who were known as the Wind of God. Before this, I had always thought of the Wind of God as not having gender, but Posingen clarified the relationships here like this:

> It is like this: the Wind of God is a woman. A woman stands up as
> the Wind of God, who always speaks to Father. . . . The first time,
> Lydia [of *Bikpela Pisin*] stood up as the Wind of God. Arego [of *Liklik
> Pisin*] also stood up as the Wind of God. All of these women were the
> Wind of God who spoke, and Father heard them. . . . It was not
> enough for a man to stand up as the Wind of God. . . . Now all the [un-
> derground] men just work; they worked along with Otit, but it was the
> women who stood up as the Wind of God.

I was also told that the knowledge known as the Wind of God was like what the Bible called the spirit of God. All the other underground women did not know the Wind of God, nor did they know the special *tok ples* language that Censure said was English. Censure received his knowledge from the women known as the Wind of God, and he used it to school other underground women. Here the underground comes back to itself via the detour of those above ground, and women come to be schooled by women (the Wind of God) but via the mediation of an above-ground man who starts becoming the voices he is relaying. This is how Posingen explained it: "This talk place [Censure's English] stops just with the Wind of God, it came to my father who learned it, and Father then returned it back down below [to other underground women]. Now down below, they all didn't know it [with the exception of the Wind of God]."

As Censure became older, he also started to become ill, and this was thought of as the underground women wanting to pull him down below to join them. Censure's illness was thought of as the female Christs invading his body where they did damage. I was told how Censure's soul would leave his body, and then a female Christ would appear in his mouth and speak. In the Kaliai area, although sick people do become possessed by masalai and take on the identity of animals, those who act as shamans do not practice becoming possessed by another person and talking as that person. Censure was seen as unique in this. It was said that when the underground women "wanted to come and pull his Wind" Censure would pass out. His body would become stiff like a corpse, and he would hardly be breathing as the women came inside and started speaking. They would tell people where Censure had gone: "Father is still hearing a court at Balito, he is still there"; or "Father is still schooling all the women at Balito." The voice that came to Censure's mouth had the same pitch and intonation as a woman's voice, and in particular it had the voice mannerisms of a *misis,* a white woman.

> Now with all the women of Papua New Guinea, if they talk, they talk strongly. But this woman who started to talk here, she was not like that. She was a misis from the underground, they are like that, like this woman. It was not as though it was like my father. Now with all these women on top, when they talk, they talk strongly; now this woman, when she came, she would talk truly easy [gently]. His [Censure's] talk would die, and she would start talking saying: "In a little while Father will come back; it won't be long now." After a while she would say: "Father has come back now." When she spoke like that, Father would get up and call out for smoke and betel nut. He would say: "I left completely, I went over to that area, to go to a court in that area, over what this man did."

We see here in part the underground objects of Censure's desire, a black woman remade in the image of a white woman. It appears that the voice of above-ground women is too harsh to be the creative voice of the underground female Christs who, though they might have a black skin, have incorporated into their bodies the gentleness and grace of a white woman. Censure speaks in the remade voice and persona of black women. He takes the vocal gestures of a white woman and uses them to mediate images of alterity by projecting them onto an underground black femininity that he in turn internalizes and objectifies as the underground voices of his trance persona. I was told that the underground had already achieved the white man's lifestyles and that was why the voices of underground Tamasinas were like those of a misis. The production of new hybrid identities is being experimented with; a new form of woman is coming to be created. My interpretation is that these underground voices are objectifications and amplifications of the civilizing process to which people have been subject. Through the underground Censure appropriates the civilizing function, exploring its magic and fecundity; here the transformative power of the civilizing process comes to be rendered as the magical creative voice of woman. The domestication of male subjects is perhaps also being explored and objectified in Censure's trance, when the gentle voice of a white woman comes to inhabit a black male body. Perhaps the civilization process as a process of feminization is coming to be spoken here, yet it is also becoming diverted by being associated with and relayed through the creativity of the feminine in traditional Kaliai myths of matriarchy. There is a marrying together of images of empowerment: that coming from tradition, which associates creative labor with the feminine and the androgynous, and that coming from Europeans, which associates cargo with gentility and the civilization of subjects. Paradoxically, the image of feminine empowerment becomes the image of racial empowerment, with the elevation of the voice of woman becoming partly its masculinization in the body of Censure but also its whitening.

When those living underground wanted Censure to attend certain trials, they would send women "to pull his Wind" so that he would go down below to them. These women would send an illness up to Censure when they wanted him to go and school them. The women who resided in Censure's mouth were said to have been carried by Censure's sisters in the underground, and these women were thus of the same moiety and bloodline as Censure. They were his matrilineal body—the feminine side of his identity within this kinship system in which men transmit their totemic-moiety identity not to their children but through their sisters to their nephews and nieces, who share the same matrilineal body as they. Posingen told me two such women were called Dodomu and Ilaten: "It is like this, his sisters carried them. Now it is not enough for some other meri [women] to come and watch from his mouth. No other Tamasina could do this, only his *kandere* [nieces] could come and stay in his mouth and talk." When I asked why Censure's kandere were given this task, I was told that they were watching over him while his breath was taken from him: "They would stay so they could *kis* [receive, capture] his wind; it was also so that they could give wind to their father [Censure] so that he would not go completely. So that he could sleep like he was. They would come, sit down, and watch inside his body, and when he came back and went inside his body, then they would go out again."

The other interpretation that I was given for Censure's illness was that his body was being farmed and used as a garden by underground women. Earlier I described how Censure refused to wash his skin and how this dirt was referred to as *kaikai* (food). The underground women would come collect this food from Censure's skin, as well as from inside his stomach, and they sometimes injured him. Censure's sickness came from his internalizing the feminine. The women were feeding off him by using the inside of his body as a garden. Indeed, some started pulling food from his body, the very food that Censure was eating to keep himself alive. Posingen explained to me:

> This sickness is like this. . . . He spoke *tok piksa* like this, that all the women would go inside him and wash all the dirt inside his body. They would gather this dirt. They would go inside his stomach, and because of this blood would come up. He was then defecating blood. He spoke: "This sickness of mine, all the women from the underground are working food inside my skin, inside my stomach." We would give him large quantities of food, but it would not remain inside his stomach. All the women from the underground would come inside his stomach, and they would pull it out.

On other occasions Censure referred to his ritual laws as his garden. It was said that when Censure worked his ritual laws and sweat came up to his body, this sweat was blood that female Christs would come to gather, for in eating it they also acquired Censure's knowledge.[2] Censure and his family were especially worried about the women feeding on his insides; they were worried when he became ill that the underground Tamasinas would pull him down below and put a stop to his garden. Censure promised his family that seven or eight years after his death something would come up. The underground female Christs were said to have been shamed by the above-ground women's rejection of Censure, and so they wanted to pull Censure down below by giving him this illness that would end his above-ground life. They also volunteered to take on the intimate task of becoming the female Christ who would work with Censure as his poroman and help him deliver the new law of existence. They were said to like *laikim* Censure, a word that in Pisin has connotations of sexual desire, and they wanted to pull him down into the underground to reside with them.[3] Rejected sexually by the women above ground, Censure turned his desire to be desired to the underground women. There is in Censure's project a certain narcissism of the male subject who loves himself through the imaginary figures of his thoughts, who wants to be desired by the imaginary idealized objects of his desire. Posingen informed me how the underground women had spoken to Censure, saying, "It is like this: all the Tamasinas down below like you, and they want to open the law. They want to pull you down below, and then they will work the law to come back on top. Now all the Tamasinas on top don't like you. Now look, you speak to them all, but they are just afraid." When he was ill and unconscious, Censure and his family interpreted this as meaning that Censure was attending underground courts to explain why he had no female Christ. Posingen explained it to me as follows:

> He would be courted for this reason, he would have to go down and say that he did not have a Tamasina to stand up on top and poroman [befriend, pair off with] him, for Papua New Guinea. He would go and have to straighten all this talk. He would have to say for what reason he did not have a Tamasina on top, for Papua New Guinea. All the women in the underground were cross, and it was for this reason, because they would try hard, and when they looked up there was no woman for Papua New Guinea, there was no woman standing up there who was working. When they looked up, they just saw my father alone, and so they wanted to pull him so that he would leave, so that he would die.

Censure to some extent comes to be consumed by his imaginary lovers who are literally eating his insides. He internalizes them, and they in turn internalize him. In this mutual inhabiting of each other's bodies there is also a tension and a mutual cannibalization of identity going on. Posingen told me that the women of the underground were cross at the way Censure had been rejected by other women, and for this reason they worked at cutting his body, at cutting his stomach:

He had no Tamasina on top, so all the women down below became cross, and they came and buggered him up like that. They [the Tamasinas] would come all the time. Now when he used to "die" [become unconscious], he would lie asleep, and this woman would come and stop in his mouth, and she would say what it was all about. She would speak it out, saying: "Father does not have a Tamasina on top, so we will pull him down below, so that Papua New Guinea will have nothing. Who else is going to stand up [in the place of Censure]? We will pull him down below, and he will school us down below, and when it is our time and we are ready, then we will come back to you all."

As Censure lost more and more of his followers, and as he became too ill to perform new songs and dances, he moved the new laws of existence, his garden, into his body. I was told that when the women came to clean Censure's skin, "they were working the law of kaikai [food]." Censure told his family: "This skin of mine is dirty, but later when all the women come to clean it, it will come up as food." While this was being related to me, Theresa interjected to say it meant that all sorts of cargo was going to come up from this. Censure died in 1988, and he was not buried in a traditional horizontal position but vertically. A hole was dug in the shape of a chair, and Censure's corpse was seated on it. Censure had instructed his family not to backfill this hole with dirt because he wanted his flesh and blood to decompose in a way that allowed the female Christs to continue coming to collect blood, flesh, and knowledge from his body. Posingen described this as a form of Holy Communion that would clear the head and thinking of the underground women, giving them their new knowledge:

> The law was on his skin and for that reason they came to take all kinds of laws and all this something, like his meat. They would then work it so that new knowledge would come up to them all. Knowledge for those down below would come up from all the meat of my father. They would work it like that so that good knowledge came up to them all in the underground. In the talk-picture that came to us of Papua New Guinea, they would say that this was kaikai. However, when it goes to the underground, its meaning is like this: that they all said that they wanted to eat the meat of Otit so that they had more knowledge. He was cleaning their knowledge through this, like us when we now receive *Oikaristia* [wafer, bread of Holy Communion] and wine and they [priest speaking as Christ] say, "You eat my meat and you drink my blood so that you are strong, and you will have a good life." It is like

that in the Bible, they talk like that. "You will eat the meat belonging to me and drink my blood."

These underground women were also using Censure's corpse to make cargo. They farmed his body like a garden up until the last moments of his corporeal existence. Censure was literally eaten up by the female specters of his imagination that internalized him as much as he internalized them.

MELO: BECOMING WHITE AND MALE

I want to turn now to look at another cargo cult that also deployed processes of androgynization as weapons in a colonial struggle to abolish the differences of race. This cargo cult was begun in the late 1970s by a woman called Melo, who, along with many of her followers, had been part of Censure's cult. This cult never reached the size of Censure's at its peak; Melo's remained a relatively small cult based in the village of Boimangal, and it drew in some supporters from the villages of Aikon, Salke, and Doko Sagra. Melo's ability to start her movement was partly made possible by Censure's claim that a female Christ would reveal the new law of equality. Like Censure, Melo reread the Bible in terms of traditional Kaliai myths of matriarchy that posit women as the creators of social order and power. In her dress, gestures, and mannerisms Melo started miming traditional Kaliai myths of matriarchy, which claim that in the beginning, when women discovered the secrets about tambarans, women had beards and no breasts. Melo took on these images of masculinized femininity. She cut her hair and glued it to her chin to form a beard. She also used vines to tie her breasts in ways that denied their protruding feminine nature. She refused to carry things on her head like other Kaliai women. Instead, like Kaliai men, she carried everything on her shoulders and walked ahead of other women. This is how Monongyo described her behavior:

> With these breasts of hers, she would get vines and tie them, so when we looked at them, they did not look like breasts were there. No, they would be flat like those of us men. When she walked, she would come up to all the big men of the village, she would not go to the women's houses. No, she would insist on going inside the men's house. It went on like this, and all the big men saw her and said: "This is a big man here, you must be quiet. All you young men, you cannot come inside [the men's house], the big man has come, and you must all walk outside." When the big men talked like this, this woman [Melo] was

truly happy. Now supposing they spoke: "Ah, you are a woman, you go back to the [women's] house! Look all the other women are in the married houses!" She would respond: "Who is that who is a woman? I am a man." Melo would respond back like this. We could not call her Melo, we had to call her *unisman* [honest man]. It is like this, she is a person of law.

Melo's claim to the status of a man was recognized by some Kaliai men who went so far as to incorporate her into men's secrets about tambarans. During tumbuan ceremonies Melo would go into the men's house and put on a mask and come out dancing with it. I want to argue that in Kaliai myths the alterity of another time was often paradigmatically figured as a primordial time of androgyny. Further, bush Kaliai cargo cult processes of androgynization embodied the utopian desire for an ambiguous open form of time that had not been fully overdetermined by the emergence of clear divisions into the social arena.[4] To repeat the androgynous past was to repeat and recreate a world before the formation of rigid hierarchical differences.

Melo did not just take on the identity of a Kaliai man; she also often took on the identity of a white man. When Melo arrived in a village, she would inspect it like a European patrol officer and issue reports on its state of cleanliness. In her gestures she mimed the powers of inspection that European kiaps regularly exercised. In her village she would tell people to sweep an area that had rubbish and to cut grass in an overgrown area. Like Europeans, she was especially strict about cleaning up dog or pig feces. She irritated young men and other women by ordering them to remove any feces. This position of power that Melo claimed over young men and other women led to many complaints, and it was one reason she was forced out of her village. She and her female companion had to go live in garden houses outside the village where they continued working their law. Yet for a number of years Melo had many male supporters. For example, she had a male secretary (*kuskus*) who would write down in Pisin all the talk, customs, and rules of her cult. Those who disobeyed Melo's orders were threatened with expulsion and told that they would not be able to enter the new law of existence when it came. Individuals who feared missing out on their cargo could buy off this pigheadedness by giving shell money to Melo. Monongyo gave me this account:

> She would say: "Now you must truly believe, when you look at me
> like this, then you must believe. All right when I am at my village and I
> speak, there is not one man who will sack [disobey] my talk. If he sacks

my talk, then it is not enough for me to kis [incorporate] him, his sit-down will not come up all right. He will just remain as he is, he will re-main behind. When everything comes, I will distribute it, and you will all come to me. But some others who have said that they will stop [i.e., not join the cult], they will receive nothing, there is not one thing that will come up to them." [*Monongyo explaining:*] It is like this they would not receive cargo or money.

Melo consistently worked at assuming the identity of a man, and people condensed and projected their desire to be different sorts of people into Melo's desire to be a different person. Melo's dissatisfaction with her posi-tion in life became a metaphor for the Kaliai's dissatisfaction with their position in life, and this was why Melo acquired followers. She split the men into two camps, those who opposed this new position of respect and power acquired by a woman and those who saw the revaluing of this woman as a means of revaluing their existence. Monongyo described to me how on one occasion Melo and her followers went from Aikon to Moluo to see the cargo cult law of Mapilu and Malour. She was reported to have said, "I want to check out this line of men. Are they working it the same as me, or will they leave this road and go astray [*abris*]?" When Melo arrived at the village, the leaders of Moluo spoke: "Ah, the big man has come." Even though there was no dirt around the village, all the women rose and started sweeping. Other people made sure there was a good bed in the men's house for Melo to sleep on. People were careful not to call her by her name, for this was disrespectful and would provoke the angry reply: "I am not Melo, do you think I am something nothing that you can call my name Melo? I am your big man. Why are you calling me like that? Do you think you could find someone else the same as me? You must call me 'unislaw' [honest law], only then would something come up so that our existence becomes the same as whites."

Melo saw the social acceptance of her transgression into new bound-aries of identity as part of the remaking of the world. People's struggle to acquire a new way of being in the world was explored and condensed in Melo's exploration of new ways of being a person. Here one form of transgression becomes assimilated to other forms of transgression. A woman's taking on the identity of a man becomes equated with the Kaliai process of taking on the lifestyle of whites; the refiguring of the gender hierarchy promised a refiguring of the racial hierarchy.

Melo claimed that by transforming herself into a white man, she would gain respect and influence among whites, who would then listen to her requests for cargo. Monongyo put it like this:

> She thought of the white man's law, and she wanted to become like him—like a *masta.* She wanted the big men to think that she had become like a white man and that she would make good work come up to their village. In time, they would come to have things like a car and all other things. She spoke that she would work it like this: that her talk would go to the white men, and they would hear her talk, and they would send all of these things.

Modeling herself on white men, Melo also adopted the practice of having other women as her domestic servants. She would sing out for them to bring water and food. This often made other women angry, but Melo would respond by saying: "You must work it like this, so my stomach is all right. You must not work toward me like I am a native; you must work like I am the number one [leader] of you all. You must work good food, like this, so I can eat, rest, and think about the talk of the come-up [new existence] belonging to us." Inside her house Melo had a kitchen helper, a *kukboi,* whom she would order about as though she were a European: "You break the pawpaw, get rid of the seeds and skin and put it on a plate for me to eat." Melo's kukboi did the cooking and cleaning. After she had finished eating, Melo would sing out: "Ah, *mankimasta* [Melanesian domestic servants in European households] come and take away the plate." The plate would be removed, washed, and put away. Melo might then ask her mankimasta to find a cup and bring it with water so she could wash her hands, just as Europeans wash their hands after eating something messy. Whereas other villagers used the bush as their toilet, Melo ordered that a latrine be built for her exclusive use. Inside her house Melo created a pillow using pieces of cloth and a piece of timber. She built her bed a long way off the ground to keep her skin clean like the white man's. Monongyo explained:

> Their [Melo and her female companion's] bed was not like this which we are sitting down on, it was *antap* [high off the ground]. During the night they slept antap, it would not be good if they slept down below, and the dust of the fire worked it so their skin was covered in ash. Their skin had to stop antap, so that it was clean all the time, so it was clean like that of yours. It was not allowed for dirt to go on top of it. In the morning she washed her hands, washed her legs, washed her

eyes, and then she would throw away the clothes of yesterday, and she would put on new ones, a new shirt and clothes. No, she did not put on clothes, she put on the shirt of us men.

Melo was imitating European habits of cleanliness. She also used to sit down on top of people's bodies, claiming that she was now sitting on a comfortable European couch. Inside her house she also built a European-style chair and table using vines and bush timber. There Melo would sit like a European man, and with her legs crossed she would receive people for consultations. Monongyo gave me this description:

> She worked it like this: whenever people came, they would sit down on the bed, but she would go and sit down there—on the chair. She would sit and put her legs like this [crossed legs]. This marked the sit-down of a masta. Where she sat down, there were planted behind her three pieces of wood for supporting her back. When she sat down, she could lean back like all masta and talk to all the people: "You all have what sort of worry?"

When traveling in the bush, Melo would navigate like a European, using pretend binoculars made from carved pieces of wood. She also built a make-believe camera and made people decorate themselves before lining up to be photographed. She claimed that when the photos were developed, people would see themselves with the new white skins that they were to acquire. Monongyo described how

> She would make people stand up for a while and then tell them: "You can now be happy. Later I will wash [develop] this. When the film comes back, you can see these photos of ours and be happy. Now you must decorate yourselves good. You will see your skin, and it will be as white as that of all white men. It will not come up black, like us na-tives. No way!" Their skin would come up white, like all you whites, and then they [Melo's followers] could be happy.

I asked Monongyo if Melo said anything about how the photos would represent people's hair or whether they had any thoughts about this. He replied: "The hair would not be like ours, it would look like that of yours. They [people in the photos] would come up like all whites, and then all kinds of something [cargo] would come up." Melo told people that if they did not get their photographs taken by her "then it would not be enough for their skin to change and for them to come up like all masta; they would stay as *ol kanaka* [natives]." Those whose skins remained dark would become the natives of the new race of white men, and their black skin and subordinate position would remain with them forever. Like other Kaliai cult leaders, Melo presented her work as people's last chance to earn the right to enjoy a European lifestyle. Her photos were not just representations but a means of producing a new white body for people. Monongyo explained it: "Yes, the photo would change their skin. For it is like this with this photo of theirs: she would wash this photo, and after she washed it, their skin would come up good. Now supposing some people were afraid and she was not able to photograph them, then their skin would remain black."

Here European chemical notions of development get married and transformed into notions of having one's symbolic identity washed with all the notions of moral purity, baptism, and rebirth that this contains. For the Kaliai a photograph captures one's tewel, or **ano,** which is how people refer to the soul and second skin a person will inhabit when they leave their first skin or body. Melo's camera promised to reveal and capture this second skin that was the future identity that a person was to inhabit when the new law of existence was won. Using Melo's camera, people stared at themselves through the lens of a European cultural artifact that promised to redeem their problematized identities. In a sense, Melo's camera embodied and objectified the redemptive pedagogic projects of European hegemony, which is people becoming white by seeing themselves through European eyes. The magical power of the camera fetishized and appropriated the transformative pedagogic project of European cultural hegemony. It condensed the process of becoming white into a material object that embodied the gaze and representational practices of European culture, which could now be appropriated by Melanesians. A new way of developing the Melanesian subject was offered by the camera; it allowed people to develop themselves differently by developing differently the white gaze that captured them.

Melo's camera allowed the Kaliai to mime European forms of mimesis—they copied the processes of copying belonging to Europeans. Indeed, they searched in their miming of European mimesis for a way of transforming a representation into reality or, more accurately, for a way of representing foreign representational practices so that they realized the foreign culture they embodied. European representational practices were displaced and reconstituted so that they became part of a magical cosmology that understands a representation to be the spiritual essence or soul of the objects it portrays. The alternative image of reality offered by European technology promised an alternative world that, for the Kaliai, was not simply the promise of an ideational world of representation but a real world to which the representation referred. It is a question of photographing oneself into existence, of taking the mimetic representational practices of European culture and casting them under the spell of an indigenous system of magic that is able to draw a soul and a reality from a representation.[5]

Melo was experimenting with the boundaries of various identities, and she tried to use the power of a technological European gaze to produce new corporeal schemes for her followers. This belief in the creative magical power of the camera corresponded to a certain truth, and that concerns the way all identity is constituted through a process of seeing oneself through the eyes of others, including all their techniques for capturing and accentuating the process of seeing. I believe that what makes the mechanical eye of Europeans so powerful is that these technologies of surveillance are simultaneously technologies of memory and as such fit into a traditional culture of mourning and memory of the dead. What also makes the mechanical eye of Europeans so powerful is that the transformative creative power of machines is married to the field of viewing bodies, such that the field of vision offered by the camera becomes experienced as transformative. Moreover, in the photos it produces the camera does offer people alternative ways of seeing their bodies—it does displace their identities into alternative spaces. This displacement is experienced as magical, for it corresponds to that displacement of self that a new existence will bring about.

Melo in her actions and gestures was also experimenting with developing new hybrid forms of identity that blurred the divisions of race and sexuality. Earlier I pointed out that Melo's refusal to subordinate herself to other men drew upon traditional Kaliai myths about how in the past women were the dominant sex. Melo's autonomy from men went further than this. Though she had a husband, she refused to have sex with him, claiming it would damage her law and she would not be able to deliver a new existence. When her husband tried to have sex with her forcibly, she told him: "If you do that, then the law won't come up." Initially, Melo's husband heeded her warnings, but later he raped her. She told him he had broken the law and that he could no longer live in the same village as she. Her husband did leave, but later he became sick and died. Many suspected he was sorcerized by Melo's followers for what he had done. After her husband's death Melo started traveling around with women whom she called her wives; one of them was Aikele's wife. Melo was beaten a number of times by men who accused her of using love magic, like a man, to attract female lovers.

Even before she left her village, Melo had so taken on the identity of a man that she demanded a wife. She carved a penis out of a tree called Bola, tied it with a string to her body, and used it in sexual relations with her wives. One woman who became Melo's lover told her relatives how Melo had warned her: "Supposing we two sleep together and I throw my penis, and it comes to your vagina, you cannot be startled." Melo used the process of internalizing and assuming the body of a man to sustain the process of becoming white, and vice versa—she used the process of internalizing the white man's identity to sustain the mythic process of becoming sexually other, of recapturing the creative androgynous past. People's experience of their bodies is central to their experience of themselves and the world. The body is the site of one's identity, its minute gestures encode a whole social order that governs its etiquette and rules for interacting with others. Indeed, when people want to recreate themselves and their world, they often do so by recreating their experiences of their bodies. The way people can most radically reexperience themselves and thus reexperience the world is by internalizing the body of the other into their interactions and practices. Monongyo gave me this description of the alternative social world that Melo created around herself by using her claims to a new corporeal identity:

> She came up like a masta, this woman. . . . She would say, "Ah, you give me a kukboi." She spoke that she would be her wife: "All big men you give me a kukboi." . . . Everything, like food or water, or something like her trousers, all these things of hers, this woman would have to wash and look after them and cook food for her. She herself [Melo] would not cook. . . . . This woman would wash her clothes, wash her trousers, these long trousers that we men wear. . . . When it was sunny, this woman would carry these things and go wash them. When they were dry, she would put them away. She would also straighten her bed.

We have in this miming of the minute aspects of Western domestic behavior the appropriation of the otherness of the future through the appropriation of the otherness of the past. The process of being engulfed in the identity of a European man, this mimetic fusion and involvement of racial identities in each other, is also associated with the reliving of an androgynous past world that mimetically fuses and involves the different gender identities in each other. The magic of mimesis here lies in capturing the distance of the past so it can be used to capture the distance of the future and so that its ambiguous gender identities can be used to destablize and merge together existing racial identities.

IMOKEH'S SEXUALITY

In the Kaliai bush one other aspiring cargo cult leader has embraced sexuality and the opposite sex to try to create a new world. This man is part
of the New Tribes Mission, and he has asked me to conceal his identity
by calling him Imokeh-Bloweh, which in tok ples Aria means 'Imokeh cut
it'.[6] I will refer to him as Imokeh. Imokeh's wife often scolds him for working a cargo cult even though he has not attracted any followers. Many
cargo cult leaders watch Imokeh closely, for they suspect that he does have
the potential to start a new *stori* (cult organized around a narrative about
secrets) that might succeed in revealing the new world. When I visited
Imokeh in November 1994, he told me how he went to family-planning
classes organized by the New Tribes Mission and how he had bought some
of their literature, which spoke about how the eggs of women fuse with
the sperm of men to create children. He claimed that while "studying"
these European ideas about procreation, it came to him that his relationship to God was of a similar sort in that he expected God's semen/spirit
to impregnate him and lead him to conceive a child that would be the new
talk he would carry. God would give His sperm in the form of a spirit to
Imokeh so that he could carry God's new child, which Imokeh could then
give to everybody else:

> This thinking came to me, for me to ask God that He would give
> His spirit to come to me. All right, this thinking came to me, and I
> worked at praising God with my thoughts that he would give me what
> was in this book about the happiness of marriage, where the eggs of
> women and all these little things that belong to men, which get up chil-
> dren [sperm], the two of them would join together to form a child. I
> was studying this while I was lying down and I was praying to God. I
> thought like this, that the spirit of God will come inside me, and it will
> work inside me like the egg of woman and the water of a man when
> they join together. This spirit of God would come like the water of a
> man to me, and this spirit that stops inside of me would become like
> the egg of woman, and the two of them would join and work together
> and get up one good spirit inside of me.

We see here the feminization of a man who sets himself up to be insemi-
nated by God to become His vessel. We also see here the spiritualization
of procreation, where the sperm becomes analogous to the spirit of God
that entered the Virgin Mary, only now the child that is born is a new
school of thought. The desire for a new black Christ here is realized as a

process of internalizing and reforming in one's body the European notion of God, and the most powerful image that Imokeh has for this incorporation of something outside that transforms and creates something new is woman. We see here again how the process of becoming white is a process of men becoming women in order to give birth to a new Christian self, a new voice. As Imokeh put it:

> In terms of my thinking, this spirit of God will come inside of me and will work with my spirit, my body, my blood, and all the different parts of my body, along with my thoughts and my knowledge, all of this will come up and be like the egg of woman. I alone will become the egg of woman, and God will come like the water of a man, the spirit of God will come like the water of a man, and it will work inside of me and get up a new child, like this something that comes up to me [Imokeh's vision, hallucinations] and which I use to talk to all men about the name of Jesus. This new child is like this, it is the new knowledge which has come inside of me and which I will start and use to school all the men and women. This is the new child. I saw this, and I asked Him for it and before it did truly came up to me [his visions]. This is what has formed my belief, and I believe strongly in this: that later this child will come up, and it will show me as it did the previous time. This child that came up to me, came up to me in talk and strength, in talk and power. This here is my child and God's child together.

Imokeh is widely suspected by many bush Kaliai of being mad, and he too suspects that this might be the case. This madness is seen by Imokeh as a form of divine madness that allows him to see God, the dead, and all that is blocking the coming of the Last Day. Similarly, Censure and others spoke of Censure's visions as a form of madness. Indeed, the women to whom Censure referred as the Wind of God were also called by the Mouk and Aria word for madness, **mangamanga.** In 1993 Imokeh had told me that his madness had been brought on by an injection that the New Tribes Missionaries gave him for cerebral malaria. He told me he was unsure whether the missionaries deliberately gave him his mad visions so that he would find the secret or whether they gave them to him to block him from discovering the hidden truth of how the Last Day was to be realized. In November 1994 Imokeh told me that another, truer reason for his madness had to do with his wife's refusal to sleep with him, which forced him to masturbate. He saw himself as losing his strength through masturbation, as depleting himself, and he also saw this as a sacrifice. He spoke of his semen as his present to God, which he gave with the expectation that God would reciprocate this gift with cargo. He also told me how the semen that fell onto the ground would recreate the ground and the bush and give rise to a new existence:

> All these dreams and all these things that I have been seeing [visions], that God has been showing me, the true *as* [origin] of all this, it has to do with me alone. This *as* is like this, it is like this . . . my wife did sleep with me, but sometimes she was weary [*les*] of me. Plenty of times, plenty of times, she was tired of me. When I asked her to sleep with me . . . she would become cross with me, and I wouldn't be able to sleep with her, so I would go off by myself, and I would make it so that my water [semen] spilled nothing, nothing onto the ground. All right, this something now, this work of mine [his masturbation], now it has stood up all this something, all these kinds of dreams, and all these things that I used to see. . . . It is like this: they came up from this water of mine that I was using, that went loose nothing onto the ground. It is like this: I have lost it so that later this something that I have lost will pay all men and women of the ground so that they can come up [with a new existence].
>
> In my thoughts, it was like this: I was giving this to God, I was giving it back to God. It was my present. It is like this: the work that Jesus made, I was copying it. Coming up to it through this.
>
> All right, my wife worked this sort of custom to me, so I worked this, so that everything, all the plants, all the people would come up from this work, from this work that I was making. It is like this; I was giving it back to God so that later God could give it back to me.

Imokeh went on to point to a passage in the Bible that says, "Everything that has come up, it has come up from the hand of this one child." Imokeh claimed that this hand was not just referring to the hand of Jesus but also to the work of masturbation that Imokeh was performing with his hand.

Imokeh has spent a great deal of time traveling along streams in the Kaliai bush, removing *pipia,* that is, leaves, sticks, and other obstacles that might block the flow of his semen downstream and into the outside world. The streams were unblocked to allow his semen to flow into the sea so that all the other countries could be remade. The sea would spread his semen everywhere and allow it to reach all corners of the globe:

> It is like this: it [the semen] would come down into the streams, and when I went around getting rid of the dirt [pipia] in the streams, it was

so that this water [semen] would run with this other water, and it would
go all the way to the sea, and from there it would spray to all the
areas. . . . All the time I was getting rid of the dirt, I was working a
road for this [his semen].

There is more than a touch of megalomania and narcissism in Imokeh's
visions. His desires for cosmic centrality cannot be removed from his madness. Indeed, I see madness as consisting partly of this urgent desire to
recreate the world such that an individual radically overvalues the process
of creation that resides within him or her. Human beings' creation of
worlds of signs and phenomenal worlds is displaced into the euphoric
experience and desire to create the material world anew. Imokeh is a New
Tribes Mission follower, and the mission's fire-and-brimstone vision of life
has influenced him to some extent. He told me that after his semen recre-
ated the earth, all the bad people and their customs would be "cooked,"
and only the good people would be left behind: "With this here, with all
these new things that are going to come up, it is like this: later God will
cook [incinerate] all the bad customs and all the customs of the ground.
He will cook them, and something new will come up. It will come up from
this water [semen]. It will be all good customs and all good things that will
come up from this, later on, on the Last Day."
   The New Tribes Mission's talk of the Last Day has revived the millenarian desires of cargo cult believers. The mission tries to dampen these desires by telling its converts that the Last Day cannot be hurried up, that it
has its own time. Yet people are not happy with this notion that they
should be resigned to a world that disadvantages them. When Imokeh
started having visions, he would visit graves and waterfalls and wait for
the dead. He tried to blend traditional Kaliai notions of the underground
with Christian imagery; however, since the coming of the New Tribes Mission, Imokeh's visions have increasingly become focused around knowledge that is coming not from the dead but from the spirit of God. Whereas
in the case of Censure the Wind of God came from the underground and
was used to reempower the space of the past, this is increasingly not the
case with Imokeh's vision. A process of spiritualization is going on in the
Kaliai; the American missionaries are pressuring people to edit the dead
from their conversations, visions, and dreams. This has not really been
successful in abolishing millenarianism in the Kaliai bush, but it has
helped to reconstitute its language.
   The relationship of cargo cult followers to the New Tribes Mission is
ambiguous. Many believe that the missionaries are trying to help them but

that the missionaries have been forced by the government of Papua New Guinea to trick people about the true reason for their presence in the country. It is said that if the missionaries did reveal the secret knowledge in the Bible of how whites were getting their existence, the missionaries would be kicked out of Papua New Guinea. The missionaries are seen as forced to collude with the Papua New Guinea government, which today is held partly responsible for blocking the cargo and the knowledge of how to acquire it. Imokeh told me he thought that the politicians just wanted people to be underneath and dependent upon them:

> My thinking is like this: that all white-skins [New Tribes Mission missionaries] are not enough to talk out clearly to us about all their customs in their country. For our government has stood up and placed a strong law [prohibition] in our country that all the men from other countries who come inside cannot story to us about all the kinds of customs of their countries. It is like this: some of your countries have come up free countries, they have come up rich, but not us. I think that our government thinks that we have to lift up the names of all those who have stood up and been marked as party leaders for us. They think that they alone will come up as big men, they alone will be rich. We will just be underneath them. We will work underneath them.

Imokeh's statement describes a broader process in which bush Kaliai villagers have made their conversion to the new mission into a critique of those Melanesians who control the state. Many cargo cult leaders see the missionaries as giving them cryptic messages that they must decipher. The missionaries are seen to be doing this so that they can reveal secrets while escaping from government criticism and expulsion. Indeed, Imokeh believes that this was why the missionaries gave him the medicine, so that he could start having visions that would reveal what the New Tribes Mission wanted to say but couldn't:

> My thinking is that they are afraid of the government of PNG so they are hiding it. They hid it and gave me this medicine. They gave it to me until I started feeling that this medicine was working in me, and this kind of sickness [his visions] started coming up. My thinking is that they wanted to hide things, and they used this medicine to change all the blood and all the different parts of me inside, inside my body, so that I would out the talk [reveal the secret], and when the government tried to check who had revealed things, it would just find me. It would not be able to find them.

The other reason I was given for why the European missionaries could not reveal the secret of cargo was that the Kaliai were still being punished for what they had done to God when they chased Him away. Imokeh explained to me the thinking of other New Tribes Mission followers:

> Their thinking is like this: that we stop with all the pigheaded customs of this ground, and they [American missionaries] are not enough to out the true talk to us. They [New Tribes Mission followers involved in a secret cargo cult] said to me: "We live with pigheaded customs, we live with darkness. Our eyes are still covered in darkness, and for this reason we cannot know. It is for this reason that they work at tricking us."

In Chapter 7 I will be looking more closely at people's relationship to the New Tribes Mission and how a clandestine cargo has been operating inside the new mission. But before I do that I want to explore two other cargo cults that arose after Censure's cult in the Moluo-Robos area. Although I will be moving away from the theme of androgyny, one cult still had a desire to find a new way of using woman to give birth to the new age through the mediating links her procreative powers could establish with the underground.

Chapter Seven

Mimesis, Transgression, and the Raising of White Children

The Other is no longer first a particular existence which I encounter in the world—and which could not be indispensable to my own existence since I existed before encountering it. The Other is the ex-centric limit which contributes to the constitution of my being. He is the test of my being inasmuch as he throws me outside of myself towards structures which at once both escape me and define me; it is this test which originally reveals the Other to me.

Sartre, *Being and Nothingness*, 1975, 245

After the villagers of Moluo and Robos left Censure's cult in the early 1970s, many joined two new cargo cults led by Malour and Mapilu. Like Melo, these two cargo cult leaders were accused by Censure and his followers of copying Censure's work. Mapilu's cult was the largest and the first of the two new cults to emerge, but because a few families still practice it secretly, I will analyze it later as a way of leading into the next chapter's discussion of cargo cult beliefs operating inside the New Tribes Mission. Mapilu is a leading figure in the New Tribes Mission cult, and in 1993 he informed me that the missionaries had instructed him not to speak to me. Many villagers and I saw this as an attempt by the missionaries to cut the flow of information I was then receiving concerning the cargo cult motives that had fueled the rapid conversion of Catholics to the new mission. Most of my information about Mapilu's cult comes from ex-cult members; this is also the case with Malour's cult, which emerged in the late 1970s. Malour's cult lasted only a few months, and because of this I don't have as much information on this cult as I have on other Kaliai cults. Malour's cult, which was based in the village of Moluo, did not have time to elaborate itself around different events, issues, and crises. Except for Samaga,

Septireh, and the line that was to form the village of Doko Sagra, most Moluo villagers joined the cult.

In Malour's cult we again find a concern with mimesis and the processes of becoming white, with people struggling to refigure the world by pushing the boundaries of their identities into the corporeal schemes occupied by the European other. The power to create the world anew came to be associated with the process of occupying that space of alterity provided by the body and cultural existence of the white man who, in being copied, was also changed. We are dealing here with processes of self-transcendence and with the ritual dimensions of creation that came to be inscribed in the processes that mime the minute gestures, mannerisms, and speech patterns of Europeans. Throughout this book I have emphasized that in all societies the body is a site of identity and cultural order and that people's experience of their socialized bodies is a crucial site through which they apprehend the world as ordered (cf. Foucault 1977; Grosz 1994; Jackson 1983; A. Strathern 1975; B. Turner 1984; T. Turner 1980). Cargo cults used music, singing, and dancing in their rituals to recompose people's bodily experiences and to mediate a sense that the order of the world was changing radically. Bush Kaliai cargo cults did not treat the body as a static inert medium of objectification; instead, the symbolic reworking and transformation of the body's habitus provided a powerful medium for enacting utopian processes of social transformation that anticipated people's desire to experience themselves as other than themselves.

The utopian desire to reform self and world, which was often played out as the process of assuming the racial identity of one's rulers, to some extent played out the hegemonic logic of Western practices of pacification and Christianization. Certain pedagogic practices and models of self-formation had been offered to the local population as instruments of liberation from the prison of a violent cultural past. These Christian and secular state techniques for forming moral subjects were often authorized through a discourse that constructed people as living in moral darkness and in need of spiritual enlightenment. In the Kaliai area this moral critique of the black man was internalized and reproduced in local cargo cults. All the Kaliai cargo cult leaders I know were proud of the way they harangued the local population for following their ancestors' ignorant, dark ways. In taking on these colonial-inspired tirades, cargo cult leaders saw themselves as seeking to morally retrain the minds of their followers. In effect, cargo cults became vehicles for extending the moral hegemony of a civilizing discourse that originated in European culture and the pastoral practices of church and state. The cargo cults appropriated Western pastoral techniques of self-formation and made the moral reformation of the Melanesian subject into a local affair no longer under the exclusive direct control of church and state. Here people resisted these institutions by partly taking over their role of moral governance, which they incorporated into their communities and into their new sense of self. The cult run by Malour in the mid-1970s is an example of this process.

Like many Kaliai cargo cult leaders, Malour made speeches in which he yelled at his followers in a manner that people equated with the proselytizing behavior of kiaps and missionaries. In appropriating the language and style of European moral critiques, Malour also appropriated the moral technology of self-development pushed by whites, which he then used to police his congregation with calls for them to become better kinds of subjects. Like Europeans, Malour sometimes used images of celestial future consequences to establish the need to strive for moral perfection in the present. Malour told his followers that when his law was successful, a ladder would come out of the sky, and everyone would have to climb this ladder. Those who had been obedient would be able to climb up the ladder leading to God and the white man's lifestyle, but those who had been disobedient would slip off. A woman called Amkou, who was part of this cult, recited Malour's speeches to me:

> [*Malour speaking:*] "Women you must all listen to your husbands, so that when this ladder comes down, your legs will be able to climb up this ladder. I will show you this ladder, I have written it in my book." He would then show us its mark [symbol]. [*Malour speaking:*] "Now supposing your leg slips on this ladder and you fall down, then you will remain seated down below, but your husband will have gone on top of this ladder, and he would have left." He spoke to us like this: that it was to come down onto the ground and people would climb up and leave. But if a man went on to the ladder and it was slippery, then he would fall down and he would forever remain there, he would never be able to go up. For this would be a person who never listened to talk, he would be a person who had beaten his wife and children. Papa [God] would say to this man: "You are pigheaded and cannot climb onto my ladder. My ladder is for people who have clean insides. All of you, whose stomachs [emotions, motives] are dirty or who work at stealing, or work trouble, will not be able to climb my ladder."

Amkou informed me that the cult required husbands and wives to talk gently to each other and to their children. People's thinking was said to be "Look, they have shown our ladder to us, what shall we do so that we can climb up this ladder?" The ladder image was especially used by men to police their wives; they would turn to the women and say: "You women, you must obey our talk! Look, the symbol [*namba*] of something belonging to us has been shown to us by this man." Here a Christianized image of the future was used to police not only obedience to cult rules and leadership but also gender power relations. The cult placed an enormous moral burden on women by requiring them to adopt strict forms of deference to male authority in order to achieve the heavenly world of the white man's lifestyle. Along with forms of domestic obedience went a strict code of dress that required women to stop wearing the European clothing that most women were then wearing. Women were instead always to wear traditional grass skirts. Malour told women that if they were calm and obedient, their deceased fathers would see them and take pity on the fact that they were not wearing good Western clothing: "If you are a woman of anger, then everything belonging to you [your cargo] will not come. If you sit-down good [behave], then your father will see you, and something will start running like water. Your father will start to worry about you. He will say: 'My child is not wearing something good, my child is wearing all sorts of broken things, so what is to happen?'"

Here the desire for cargo becomes the structure of value within which the moral framework of sociability is recast. Domestic relationships and interactions come to be policed by the world of the dead, which looks upon the living and determines its sympathy for them in terms of their goodwill toward each other. The omniscient gaze of God is now relocated to the more familiar gaze of one's parents. They take on the judgmental, policing role of God. The hegemonic gaze of the white man, as mirrored through the eyes of his God, is displaced into the domesticating gaze of one's parents, which offers in its intimacy the promise and hope of negotiating access to a better future. The process of internalizing the judgmental penetrating look of whites and their God into the eyes of one's parents can be seen as an attempt to find in the other world a sympathetic set of eyes that might start to glaze over with feelings of empathy for the plight of the living.

This process of internalizing God's moral gaze into the watchful look of one's parents also worked, I would argue, to familiarize and bring closer to people a system of surveillance that problematized their moral identities. In part, behind the omniscient moral gaze of the dead and God, hid the eyes of Kaliai men, who were scrutinizing the moral details of their wives' labors. The outside eyes that followed the living were the displaced eyes of men who sought to reform the world morally by developing a system of surveillance and discipline focused on women. In this context Malour set his wife up as the exemplar of woman; she wore grass skirts from morning to night, every single day. The wearing of grass skirts became a ritual law imposed on women. If Malour saw female followers wearing European clothing, he would refuse to leave his house and come out into the village square to speak to people. Indeed, he would publicly criticize and shame women who wore clothing. Amkou told me of the fear and guilt that gripped many women, how they would publicly confess that they didn't always wear grass skirts, and they wondered what was going to happen to them.

This moral policing and disciplining of women extended to their relations with children. Amkou quoted Malour as telling female followers: "You women, when the children cry, you must hurry up and give them breast milk. If they say they are hungry, then you must hurry and cook so they can eat and we can all sit-down [live] with good talk. Later, your sit-down [existence] will come up really good." Here the world of maternal duties assumes a moral significance for the whole society's future. The everyday domestic world of women becomes morally recoded as needing to produce for the dead the image of a harmonious loving household that contains no bickering. Amkou described to me the turmoil women felt as the most minute aspects of their behavior sought to create and fulfill a moral contract with the dead. She told me how women would be seated in the village square listening to Malour, and they would confess: "It is true, we beat our children. They are hungry, and then they cry, and we beat them, because we become angry with them. So what is going to become of us now? What can block our stomachs [feelings] and allow our stomachs to remain easy [calm]?" The cult here establishes and exploits those forms of moral inadequacy that haunt all women's sense of themselves as good mothers and as worthwhile moral subjects. The desire for cargo is used to bolster ever more scrutinizing forms of moral evaluation by men over women; men's better management of women becomes the moral means for achieving a new, better future.

Throughout this book I have argued that, like European Christianity, Kaliai cargo cults helped create and sustain the very problematization of identity that they offered to overcome. Moreover, through their advice and practices for becoming the ideal moral subject, Kaliai cargo cults displaced the pedagogic process of becoming white into ritual practices and techniques that existed outside the direct control of church, state, and Europeans. Cult leaders diverted the process of copying and becoming like the white man by fusing it with indigenous local forms of knowledge dealing with the dead. Malour's cult transferred the moral hegemony of discourses of enlightenment and Christianization to a local context in which people began to develop their distinctive pastoral powers for forming and caring for themselves as moral subjects. Villagers began to experiment with newly appropriated techniques of self-reformation that often involved producing a critique of their moral darkness. The existence of moral darkness was read into the most minute disturbances of everyday life (not listening to one's husband, arguing with one's wife, not feeding one's children quickly, and allowing them to cry too long). Cargo was the language of value within which followers internalized into their "stomachs" and everyday struggles a moral critique of themselves that allowed them to rework more fully the discourses and practices for rendering themselves as morally reborn in the white man's image (as harmoniously constituted subjects).

Septireh, who was in the village of Moluo when Malour began his work, told me how Malour would visit graves to talk to the dead and so as to "*kis* [acquire] the law from all the big men [ancestors]." He described one such occasion when Malour went with Kulo to the village cemetery, and there Kulo reenacted the conversion experience expected under Christianity, only now with respect to his ancestors:

> All right, he took Kulo, and the two of them went and stood up there at the graves. Now [at first] Kulo didn't hear anything, but Malour heard them [the dead]. Now Kulo, he thought this something was true. They came back here, and they were singing out, they sang out, and we all went and gathered there. When we saw Kulo, he said, "Brothers, I went and I shook [with fear]. Me and your brother went, and I shook no-good [a great deal], I didn't have any talk. I will now come up like the wife of my brother for then I didn't have any talk [he is referring to the reputation of Septireh's wife as a quiet woman, a woman with no talk]. I will now be like a Christian man. . . . Now at this time I am not enough to work one sort of talk containing anger or to talk hard to my children or to beat my wife, or to talk behind the back of another person. No, my hand, you see it, my brothers? My hand has died. My hand died today, during the night. Tomorrow I will be different, my mouth will be blocked, and I will stay like that."

We see here how the processes of pacification, civilization, and Christianization come to be refracted through the dead, an operation full of paradoxes for, although it simultaneously brings these hegemonic processes

close and renders them familiar, it also transforms them and makes them
something different from what they are for Europeans. As we shall see
later, Malour went a great deal further in copying the gestures and personhood of Europeans. He even referred to himself as a king, and he used
the title of queen for his wife and a deceased female child with whom he
communicated.

MIMESIS AND THE BODY OF THE WHITE MAN IN MALOUR'S CULT

Malour's cult began when the leaf of a balbal tree was blown by the wind
onto his breast. At the time Malour was inside his house, thinking about
this leaf when it landed on him. He rose excitedly and showed it to others,
who then started copying down its marks. Amkou describes this occasion:

> We brought a mat, and he drew on it the marks of this balbal [leaf].
> He drew all the marks found on all these leaves belonging to the bal-
> bal. He then spoke: "You must all believe in this something; where do
> you believe this came from? I do not know where. I was asleep when it
> came onto my breast. This something is just like when people write and
> send it [a letter]. It came and slept on top of my breast, and now I hold
> it. You must all believe in it, and you must all copy the writing of this
> something, and you must follow it." He spoke like this about the leaf of
> the balbal. We all thought this something was true, for we wondered
> how this something came to sleep on top of his breast. All of us men
> and women believed in this balbal leaf, for the house was totally closed
> off, so how could this something come inside? We said, "I think this
> man is going to work us so our sit-down [existence] finally comes up.
> Before, Censure tricked us, then Namore and Mapilu tricked us, now I
> think this man has found this thinking, and it has come from Papa
> [God]."

Malour saw this leaf as a letter from God, and he claimed it had come to
him because he did not steal or work other sorts of trouble. Malour's cult
soon took on a new twist when his young daughter died. Instead of burying her in the local cemetery just outside the village, Malour buried her
next to a large stone close to his house. Around her grave he planted deco-
rative flowers. There he and his followers would go and pray for Malour
to receive "talk" and money from his daughter. Amkou described these
occasions: "Malour would come down from his house, go to this grave,
sit down, and pray. I am not clear about all these prayers. He would work

talk first, and then a new person would come and pray. Well, the soul of this child would come up to her father and mother. She would come up at night secretly to her father and mother [so as to give money and talk]." If followers were sick, Malour would advise them to pray at his daughter's grave, telling them that tomorrow their illness would be gone. He would say to a sick person, "You go speak about it at the grave; your strength can be found at the grave; you must go sit down and pray at the grave." Amkou told me that people confessed their transgressions at the grave:

> Now supposing today I worked some sort of cross talk to my children or to Leo [her husband], then I would go in the afternoon and confess this. I would go sit down and speak like this: "Papa, today my stomach was hot toward all my children, and I sacked [disobeyed] the talk of my husband, so I am talking clear about this to you so that you can help me. So you can *raus* [expel] this sin of mine, and I can go and live well."

Malour tried to school his followers in European forms of knowledge; he emphasized to them, "You must all be strong on knowledge." Though he did not know how to read or write, Malour handed out pieces of paper, and he tried to school his followers in penmanship. Most of Malour's followers did not know how to write, and they simply scribbled down all sorts of marks, which Malour then inspected and graded (cf. Worsley 1957, 97). Amkou described these school lessons like this: "We would all start writing about and about [in haphazard ways]. He would come and look at these and say: 'Your writing has come up like this [gives a mark]. Theresa's has come up so much, Leo your writing has come up so much.' He would work at correcting this something of ours. . . . He was copying all the teachers." Malour's followers believed he was schooling them in the new knowledge that would come with the lifestyle and cargo of whites. In addition to imitating European teachers, Malour inspected his village like a European kiap. He would stroll around his village, whistle, and use postures that people saw as foreign and indeed the same as those of Europeans. He would stroll about on his toes like he was wearing boots, his two hands would be on his waist, his neck would be stretched out, and he would turn from side to side inspecting everything. With this unusual posture Malour would repeat English phrases like "How are you today?" Paul, who had been a member of this cult, gave me this description:

> Now with their boss [Malour], he would be walking around like this. He would yell at his line that they must hear his talk. He would walk

about on his toes, looking upward with his eyes. He was a young man, but when he yelled there was not one big man who would reply back. He was a rubbish-young-man-nothing, but when he spoke all the big men sat down quietly. This walkabout of his was not like ours, it was like the walkabout of all *misis* when they put on these shoes of theirs, they walk around in a similar way. This shoe of theirs, that is up and down [high heeled]. We natives, we do not walk about like that.

Paul told me that Malour held meetings with his followers in *Pisin* and that he appointed secretaries who were responsible for writing down in books the messages he received from the dead:

> He would sing out to his secretaries, and they would come and start writing. His brother Paulus was schooled at the community school and so he had this knowledge [of writing]. When he gave talk to this man, he was able to write it down. He would say, "This piece of talk of mine, you must give it to our line. It is not enough for me to give talk to them. I just will sit down, and you, Paulus and Akatung, you must give the talk to all our line. I am not enough to talk. I will wait and speak only when the law is about to break."

Malour also had two servants to do his household chores. Like Melo, he was imitating European domestic life. Followers were invited to come and eat at Malour's house, and they would do so in individual family groups. The communal feasting of traditional Kaliai society was replaced with the more individualized European-style dinner invitations. Paul described how Malour would remain standing while his guests dined, which to me suggests the etiquette of a restaurant owner or an anxious dinner host:

> Malour would mark a day for everybody to get together. He would order some people to cook and some people to go hunting. All the food was to go to Malour's house. All the food for the feast went to Malour's house. A man and his family would go inside and eat. When they had finished, another man and his family would go inside and eat. The Boss would just be standing up and looking. When they had finished eating, another group would come in. It went on like this until everyone had eaten.

In addition to the persona of boss and teacher, Malour took on the powerful European persona of a healing Christ. Paul recounted how everyone would be seated under a hot sun in the village square, where they were

learning the new laws of their existence, and there they also watched Malour heal the sick:

> They [followers] would all sit down under a huge sun, and their boss
> would talk to them about the kinds of law that they would have to fol-
> low. If someone was sick, he would go to Malour, who would come up
> like Jesus. I saw this, and my wife saw it. He would hold somebody and
> say that their sickness would now be finished. If someone had a sore,
> he would hold it. One of my sisters had a sore on her leg. Malour had
> two names, Boss and Teacher. Well, Teacher came to look at the sore.

Paul went on to describe an occasion when everyone was seated in the
village square and a plane flew overhead. Cult followers turned and asked
Malour who was coming in the plane. He looked up and said: "Ah, bas-
tard, my old mother!" Puzzled, people asked him again who it was, and
he replied: "Oh, it is just my old mother, she startled me. I thought it was
someone else, but no, it is mother." On other occasions when a plane flew
over, Malour would raise his hand and say: "Ah, sorry, you can all go on
top; later I too will be flying on top." Malour was claiming that when his
law succeeded, he too would fly in a plane. When Malour spoke to planes,
his words were addressed to his deceased mother to whom he would say, in
English, things like "I will see you next time." Malour often spoke broken
English, and his followers mistakenly thought that he knew English.

We are dealing here with the way people play with structures of self-
identity and with the way the internalized other is refigured inside the self.
It is impossible to be a self without a vision of the other whom one internalizes and responds to. The other is not simply outside but, as Sartre
pointed out, always inside the self as one of its constitutive moments with
which it exists in dialogue. In the colonial and neocolonial context the
empowered position of this other swaps places with the self in order to
engulf certain individuals who enjoy the experiences of power that come
from miming the identity of those who dominate them. We are dealing
with how people internalize images of alterity and what lines of flight and
becoming are authorized through the process of becoming other. The alienating other provides the terms for going beyond the boundaries of oneself; people are internalizing the other as a way of familiarizing themselves
with and overcoming the alienating structures of colonialism. The way out
of the mirror gaze of the colonial double is to become this mirror—to
walk through and into it in a way that allows you to appropriate its imaginative space. People set up this mirror function and perform the gestures,

rituals, and commands of the other to displace its presence by becoming its presence.

I would argue that the process of familiarizing and internalizing the white man appropriates his alienating gaze, but it is also true that it relocates the alienating gaze inside indigenous societies where it empowers the cargo cult leaders who mime the critiques and harangues of missions and state officials. Mimesis is both a means of overcoming the alienating structure of race relations and of reproducing those alienating structures in the individuals and communities that internalize the new enunciative boundaries through which they now form their new sense of themselves. No subject has a relationship of pure self-possession, all subjects come back to themselves through the mediation of cultural categories, and in the contemporary situation the categories through which one reflects and forms oneself are provided partly by Western culture. People's sense of self-identity comes partly from internalizing the discourses of church and state, which often criticize the bush Kaliai. People appropriate these critiques; in doing so they extend the hegemony of state and church ever more fully into the local area, which they also do by confirming that they "misunderstand" or have reread the messages given in order to discover their true hidden secret.

Although Malour often claimed his thinking went only to the Big Man—God—it was not like that, for he and his followers often spoke to the dead. Amkou told me how Malour informed his followers: "Where do you think all your fathers who have died have gone? They are waiting, they are working cargo for you all, and it is waiting for you. You must all be strong." Sometimes someone like Malour's wife would ask him to contact a special deceased relative. Malour would then be left alone in his house, and after a while people would hear tapping and whistling inside the house, noises interpreted as made by the dead. Later Malour's secretaries would come and write down any information Malour had received from the dead. Amkou told me how Malour's secretaries would say: "This sort of talk has come up to our boss, and we can now give it to you all so you can live well. You all must not steal. You, young girls, must behave yourselves; you, young girls, must be strong at school [the cult's moral school]." On other occasions "talk" would come to Malour in the form of a spirit. His voice would change, and his secretaries would recognize this and come running with paper to write down any messages. These were often denunciations of the *longlong* (ignorant) culture of Kaliai ancestors. Malour would say:

You must work it like this [cult work]: you must be strong, and you
must get all sorts of things to come to us. We will see it with our eyes,
and we will live well and be happy. Before, all our ancestors sat down
longlong, but we the new line want to try hard to find the thinking that
will allow us to live like all masters. For our existence is no good. We
work hard in our gardens, our mothers fill up the water containers,
break firewood. What time will our sit-down change so we can sit-
down good ? Are we to sit-down longlong all the time like this?

Like Censure, Malour situated his cult in opposition to the past and as
representing a new generation that was trying to discover new ways of
thinking about the world. Yet this process of becoming white, which re-
jects the prison of the past, also embraced the dead as a way of escaping
the alternative of total imprisonment in white culture. Like Censure, Malour rejected development as the road to the white man's existence. This
brought him into conflict with the committee members of the local government council who lived at the nearby village of Doko Sagra; they reported
Malour's cult to a visiting native kiap. Although these committee members
had their own cargo cult beliefs, they were not happy about continuously
having to do government work that others chose to ignore. We can see
here the way people become governmental subjects, how they take on the
policing role of administrative structures, reporting their relatives to the
administration for failing to fulfill the new disciplinary routines that start
to form the borders of their new civilized identity. For many Kaliai villagers the process of pacification is embodied in the discipline of setting aside
certain days for agricultural work, development work, and church work.
Those at Doko Sagra who were officially in charge of policing the formation of new subjects and a new society through this disciplinary process
of becoming felt threatened by the alternative processes of becoming white
that Malour was proselytizing. We have here competing ways of becoming
white, where those empowered by the administration's version of this process feel undermined by its appropriation by those without formal authority. At the local level people compete with how they are to mime white
culture and its processes of becoming white. Some seek to reclaim a degree
of dignity and autonomy from this process of whitening themselves, which
they do by getting their dead to participate in the task of civilizing and
disciplining their descendants.

When a visiting kiap came to Doko Sagra and was informed of the
cargo cult by council committee members, he proceeded to Moluo where

Malour lived. There he asked Malour why he had buried his daughter close to his house and whether he expected to receive law and money from her. The kiap tried to shame Malour by repeatedly calling him *malas,* the Pisin term for a common species of timber tree (*Homalium foetidum*). He also alleged that Malour had married his wife to other cult leaders, that is, made her sexually available to them, which was not true. The kiap then threatened to jail Malour and his secretaries, which made the women cry. During the night the kiap came up with a compromise, a new form of punishment that required cult followers to dig up the body of Malour's daughter and replant it in a new grave. Paul gave me this description of how the next day they unearthed this decaying body, which had been buried for only three to four weeks: "Even though people didn't have spades, they used their hands to dig; it was like they were dogs. They dug and dug, until they came up to the coffin. They carried it to the top. This was their punishment. Flies were everywhere; my own family had run away, they were afraid of the flies and the smell." After this punishment Malour never sought to start his cult again. Instead, he, like many other Kaliai cargo cult leaders, joined the New Tribes Mission.

MIMING WHITES THROUGH ONE'S CHILDREN: THE MAPILU CULT

One accusation that the kiap made against Malour was that he was going back to the traditional Kaliai custom of burying the dead close to where people slept. Throughout Melanesia the dead are the source of magical knowledge and power—and what can often be found in cargo cults is a fusion of the magic of contacting the dead with the power and knowledge of whites. According to Williams (1923), people in the Vailala cult of the 1920s claimed to have run into dead relatives who had turned white. This was also the case in the Kaliai area, where dead relatives with white skins often appeared to people in dreams and even while people were awake. I want to explore this appropriation and reworking of the process of becoming white by turning to the cult that started before Malour's, the Mapilu cult, which was organized around certain spirit children who had white skins. In the afternoon villagers from Robos and Moluo would gather together to sing and give food to Mapilu's children, who would eat it inside their parents' house. A huge *haus kiap* (kiap's house) was built for these children at Maldung on the River Angal, where Moluo and Robos villagers were then living.

These spirit children were said to have come up from the menstrual blood of Mapilu's wife, Paname. Here the polluting blood of woman was revalued to become a hidden source of procreation. This blood produced a new line of white-skinned children who would provide villagers with access to white society and power. Paul, who was Mapilu's *kuskus* (secretary), explained the origin of these children like this:

> When his wife menstruated, she would bury the blood. She would dig a hole, like a grave. She would dig around in the bush and other places, she would work at putting this blood there. This blood later came up to her as a person and spoke: "Mother, what do you think this something is that you work at burying? It is me here, it is me, Michael Ross." This was her first-born child. Now with her second born, another blood came up, and he spoke: "I am Johnson." A third one came up, and he spoke: "I am Bullet." So there were now three of them, and they worked at giving talk to their mother and father. Only they could see them; the rest of us could not see them.

Paname had a fourth spirit child called Semrengen, who was not as pleasant as the others and with whom I want to deal separately later on. Although Paname, through her children, was the source of cult knowledge, her husband controlled cult meetings and activities. Paname was said to have been blocked from public speaking by her children, who informed her: "Mother you cannot talk, when the law breaks open, we have marked this as the time for you to talk."

The three spirit children—Michael Ross, Johnson, and Bullet—became the conscience of the community and part of its desire for a new moral order. They would come and say: "Mother, you must speak to all the men that they cannot be cross with their wives, they cannot hit their children, they must sit-down good." Followers were instructed not to steal, lie, or commit adultery, for if they did the spirit children would see them and report them to their mother. This policing of misdemeanors by white spirit children displaced the moral pedagogic gaze of church and state, kiap and priest, magistrate and catechist into a domain that allowed people to own their moral policing. We need to recognize that these children are white, and it is the perceived moral gaze and critique of European institutions that is located in these spirit beings, who nevertheless also represent an attempt to reclaim some autonomy and responsibility for the production of ethical subjects.

Before the arrival of Europeans, people had many of the moral values they now claim Europeans provided, but in the contemporary context a certain form of amnesia often operates: people sometimes pretend that their grandparents were ignorant of all morality. Within this hegemonic rendering of memory and history, cargo cults often operate to reclaim a moral conscience grounded in compromised terrains and figures of alterity. In their cults people came to familiarize that idealized moral policing that Europeans and Western institutions claimed and that villagers projected onto Europeans. Mapilu's white spirit children to some extent worked to further internalize white hegemony, transforming it into a familiar offspring, a moral gaze with which people could live. I see these white spirit children as people's alter egos—in Freudian terms their new superegos. They are an objectification of people's newly created white consciences, that is, they are a way that people come to own the new European-informed moral gaze that continuously watches over them. These new children represent the birth of a new structure of guilt. A new mode of self-reflection comes to be fetishized and objectified as the gaze of their remade hybrid offspring.

Here the pedagogic transformations that are making people white— that is, other than themselves—are projected and more perfectly realized in spirit children who internalize whiteness into indigenously derived bodies. Through these white spirit children people realized the desire to become the other and to look at the world through those cultural structures of alterity provided by the body and look of the other. One's children here are one's ideal form as other; they represent the other as an object of desire to be internalized—if not into oneself directly, then into the future form of one's bodily being in one's children. That people came to police themselves morally through spirit children who had become their white conscience was not an imaginary phenomenon totally removed from the "real world." It corresponds to certain everyday interactions that I witnessed in the field. Children would sometimes criticize their parents and grandparents from the standpoint of development, church, and government. Patrol Reports are full of observations by kiaps that the administration must look to the young for support for its policies, and this group often provided it in practice. In terms of Kaliai parents, they often associate the position of the government with their children, whom they nominate for appointments to Western institutions. I see Mapilu's white spirit children as a way of objectifying, of reflecting allegorically, on those processes that are part of Christianization, pacification, and development—the processes within which children can become the moral guardians of communities by aligning with Western institutions, discourses, and pedagogic practices.[1] The incorporation of one's spirit children into one's policing conscience was a process that reenacted in a refracted form the internalization of policing that came from raising children reared on internalizing the gaze of church and state. The creation of certain kinds of new subjects by European-inspired pedagogic processes took the refracted allegorical form of a new race of white spirit children. It is significant that it was not people's living children who would bring the future utopia but those children associated with the traditional Kaliai space of power—the dead. The world of the past also came to be reborn and revitalized through the process of its becoming white. At the same time the white man and his processes of becoming were also made something other than themselves.

Paname was unable to have children, and in part her spirit children fulfilled her desire and that of her husband for children. Their personal desire came to participate in the desires of their community for a better life. There is a complex relationship of interdependent wish fulfillment, wherein Mapilu and Paname's desire for children becomes entangled and merged with the collective desires of a community for a new world made up of a new kind of indigenous subject. Mapilu's followers expected to turn white when the new law of existence arrived. The white spirit children can be seen as projections that anticipate people's new future identities. People believed they would acquire the cargo, existence, and skin of the white man when the spirit children came to live with them; they would become like these children. These children served to objectify ways of being both white and Melanesian other than those offered by state, church, and Europeans. Mapilu's cult was started and led by the young of bush Kaliai society; it represented their desire to become white while hanging onto the world of the dead belonging to their parents. Mapilu and his wife were young when they began their cult, and many young people like Paul held prominent cult positions. I see the white spirit children as externalizing and reworking those internal pedagogic processes of becoming that were focused on Kaliai children. Kaliai elders still often accuse the young of forgetting their traditional culture—its myths, rituals, songs, and techniques for making bark cloths and shields. The young are sometimes accused of becoming too much like whites and of being too controlled by white culture. In part, Paname's spirit children embraced and celebrated the project of becoming white, but these children were also ways of exploring the tensions and contradictions of this project. As we shall see, one of these children, Semrengen, was a bad-tempered white brute.

Ex-cult followers saw Paname as copying that part of Censure's cult that involved Censure's begetting spirit children in the underground. Amkou put it like this: "When we went to Censure's *stori,* Censure spoke

about his children Sen Les, Sen Seuve, and Sen Kilok. She came, and
she copied from this man [Censure], this talk of his." What distinguished
Mapilu's and Paname's spirit children from Censure's spirit children was
that they came from Paname's carefully burying her menstrual blood.
Mapilu told his followers that this care shown by his wife toward her blood
was also why these children spoke exclusively to their mother and not
to him:

> You all look at my wife, her children have come up to her. I just re-
> ceive talk from Paname, all talk comes from Paname. All these men,
> they bring their talk to their mother, and then she gives it to me so that
> I can speak about it. But I do not receive talk from my children. For
> Paname, she behaved properly toward them. When her sick-moon
> came, she planted them all, and because of this the children now come
> up to their mother and not me.

Other women were expected to copy Paname and carefully bury their
blood so that they too could produce a new race of benevolent whites.
This reflects the notion of producing a moral obligation with spirit beings;
the original care shown to them was to be reciprocated in the future. The
maternal relationship becomes the ultimate bond of debt that can be projected into the outside world of the dead and into the world of a white
future to tie these spaces of alterity to the world of the living. Women, as
mothers, became the great mediators. Women's capacity to create relationships between living communities (as in marriage) was now deployed to
create relationships with the inaccessible communities and lifestyles inhabited by whites and the dead. Women's procreative powers are what sustain
and make the future possible. This capacity for women to create the next
generation becomes the focus of utopian idealizations of what is possible.
Women's control of the future comes to be transfigured into the moral
burden of creating a new benevolent race of children; although they inhabit the spirit world, they owe their identity and form to their mother's
care of their broken bloodied bodies.

Mapilu and his wife had been part of Censure's cult, and on one occasion Censure visited them and gave their new cult his blessing. Many
people saw Mapilu's reliance on Paname for knowledge of the world of the
dead as copying Censure, who also received his knowledge from women
(although in Censure's case it was underground women). Underpinning
both cults were traditional Kaliai myths of matriarchy that tell of how
women discovered the basis of a new social order. Mapilu's cult borrowed
Censure's reworking of traditional Kaliai mythology and especially Cen-

sure's view that only the procreative body of woman could create a new social order.

Another point of similarity between Mapilu's and Censure's cult was the importance attached to snakes. The spirit children who resulted from Paname's menstrual blood would appear as snakes. According to Amkou, "She [Paname] spoke that they, all her children, changed their skins like snakes. She spoke that their skin had come up like the skin of a snake, like snakes change their skins, and we see it lying around in the bush. She spoke that they turned into snakes, they came up like pythons, and later they would change again and become human." Mapilu's followers often collected snake skins, believing them to be the shirts of Paname's spirit children that they had shed on their way to catch a plane to attend meetings in Australia. Mapilu informed his followers that Paname also went with her children to these meetings in places like Sydney. Paname would spend a great deal of time absent from the village, and when she came back in the afternoon, sometimes her hair was stylized in ways that people considered unusual and that they associated with the hairstyles of white women. Paname would say that she had just been to Australia, and there her hair had been cut like a misis. Amkou remembered these scenes like this: "When she styled her hair like this, it made us think that her story was true and that she had gone to Sydney, and they had cut her hair there. . . . When we heard a plane, she would get up and say: 'Look, that is them there—Michael Ross, Johnson.' [*Paname speaking to the plane:*] 'You all go around on this plane to Sydney, later I will board it at Brisbane.'"

Brisbane was the cult's name for a rock formation found at a local waterfall. This formation had four protruding pieces that were said to be the four engines of a plane called Lolomeh. Paname claimed that this huge plane did not always remain stone and that her children used it to take her to Australia, often against her wishes. Amkou gave me this account of Paname's law:

> She would not stay good in her house, she would go foul about in the bush. After a while, in the afternoon, she would come back to the house and say: "Did you hear the plane cry?" We would say, "Ah yes." [*Paname responding:*] "Me, oh bloody shit! This Bullet, Michael Ross, and Johnson, they pulled me and we went. They fouled me, and we went to Sydney. These three men—I don't know what sort of people they are. I wanted to stay here but they were strong [persistent]."

Mapilu supported his wife's claims to have traveled to Australia, saying it was important work, for she had gone to receive law. He complained that she was always coming and going at the expense of her need to rest. He called on other women to do his wife's domestic chores—chop firewood and fill up the water containers—so she could continue to make these important overseas visits. Amkou told me how sometimes, when Paname came back with her unusual afternoon hairstyles, she carried the yellow sap of a certain tree, which she said was medicine from Australia.[2]

> She would put this sap in a shell, and she would dress the sores of the young children. At this time they had plenty of sores and they were sick. This woman would carry this medicine, and she would say: "The medicine is here. They took me, and I went to Sydney, and I have brought back this medicine." All the women would get up and say: "Our nephews [the white spirit children], their custom is very good, for they acquired medicine and gave it to their mother who carried it back." Everybody would be really happy over this "water" [sap] of this tree. She would say: "You all come, and let me dress your sores." When they dressed the sores, they did not cover them with something; they just painted them with this medicine.

At the waterfall where Paname would catch her airplane, followers often gathered to perform feasts.[3] Paul described this site and its cult significance like this:

> This waterfall is, as I said to you before, it has a four-engine plane called Lolomeh. The rock has a shape that resembles two engines over here and two engines over there. This place she called it Brisbane. It also has a small creek that spills over, and its name is Jordan. We would drink from this small creek, and we would wash our sores in this small creek. If someone was sick, they would drink from this small creek. She would get up and say: "This huge plane, you now see it lying down there, but you wait, later you will see things differently."

Near this plane were other significant cult features: a stone that was shaped like and referred to as a tractor; on top of the waterfall were sedimented layers of stone that resembled stacked timber; a small stream that carried yellow sediment into the larger river was referred to as a toilet; and a round stone was said to be a ball belonging to the spirit children. At the waterfall was also a stone that had two round circles known as *namba* (mark, symbol) and to which people made speeches requesting cargo. One circle was for Little Bird followers and another circle for Big Bird followers.[4] Paul explained: "I, who belong to Little Bird, would speak to my

The stone tractor of Mapilu and Paname's white spirit children. The hole in the middle marks the place where a driver sits.

mark; and you, of Big Bird, would speak to your mark. You could not mix them." These marks were said to be similar to the round circles that Censure discovered at the Glass of God. At their waterfall Mapilu's followers decorated themselves and sang cult songs. Those who belonged to Little Bird would sing on one side, and those who belonged to Big Bird would sing on another side. The cult's songs contained the name of the spirit children, and they were often songs of sorrow. One song contained the words "Michael Ross, I have fallen down on a wrong belonging to me; Michael Ross, I have fallen down on sin." These songs were similar to songs in the Catholic Church; both involved people internalizing and owning their sin. However, in Mapilu's songs the request for redemption was not to God, Jesus, or Mary but to a spirit world of people's own making over which people felt they had more control. After singing, individuals would come forward and call out "the names of all these boss who gave this talk to Mapilu and his wife." Paul described how he went and sang out: "Michael Ross, Johnson, Bullet, before we went and saw Censure's namba, but now it is good that one belongs to us, close to us, on our ground, and we can come and see it like this and be happy. You will get up this law of ours, it will come up to us, of Robos and Moluo, and we can then sit-down [rest with a good existence]. That is all Michael Ross, Johnson, that is all my talk."

These speeches had an element of regional and linguistic nationalism.[5] The speeches were made by Aria speakers who were asserting their identity and autonomy from Mouk speakers, whose underground sites the Aria had visited when they had been in Censure's movement. Paul's speech also involved his saying: "Before I was longlong, and I went and saw the namba of all the Mouk at Meitavale, but now my namba, of us Aria, is straight on our ground, I have come to see it like this. I'm going to kill this small pig of mine at our namba, I want you [spirit children] to come up and live with us so that we can live together." After Paul finished speaking, his wife went and made exactly the same speech, and other people did likewise. At the waterfall site where pigs were killed, some pork went to cult followers and some went to the spirit children. Paname would put some pork in a pot and would call out to her children: "Youse, at night, come to us and eat this something of yours." I was told the children would come and eat the soul of the pork and that the food that remained would be eaten secretly by someone else, like Mapilu and his close supporters.

In terms of performing cult rituals, Paul informed me how Mapilu always abstained from singing: "He would never sing, he would just walk. . . . He was the boss, and it was not enough for him to sing or to carry anything. He walked about like; he would always come walking like this." While saying this, Paul impersonated a white man walking with his hands behind his back. Paul laughed and told me that Mapilu was here copying the relaxed body postures of whites.[6] Like Malour, Mapilu strolled around his village as if he were a kiap inspecting it. Occasionally, he would stop and order people to tidy things up. Mapilu also took on the role of a military commander. Like Batari and Censure before him, Mapilu drilled his male followers in European forms of military dressage. They were required to march and fall into orderly straight lines; sometimes the men would be holding the long stems of pawpaw leaves as their muskets. The men also went on military maneuvers. They were divided into two groups, and when one group fired its "muskets," the other group fell onto the ground, trying to dodge the other's bullets. Leo described his participation: "He worked us like this. We worked it and worked it, we did not rest. Every morning we would learn this. He said: "Later, if any fighting comes up, you will be trained. When you go into the fighting, you will be able to dodge the bullets." I asked Leo whether Mapilu had informed them with whom they were to fight, and he replied, "No, he did not reveal the people we would be fighting against, he just worked at training us." The men rapidly became sick of having to train every day under the hot sun, so Mapilu switched to training women and children. He would march them with "a teacher" in front and a teacher behind them. The teachers would be carrying a stick, and if they threw it to the right, those marching would follow it and go to that side. If the stick was thrown to the left, everyone would march to the left. Along with marching, women were made to wear traditional grass skirts and sing songs. Mapilu told them those who did this would be rewarded when his stori succeeded. He also warned them: "But if you women just sit down, and this stori of mine wins and the law breaks open, then you women will not know what to do with yourselves. I am learning you so that you will all have knowledge, and when this stori of mine comes up, then you will already have the knowledge."

Here the repetitive learning of a law that comes from white society guarantees people access to the white man's existence. My experience of cargo cults is that they explore and search inside the ritual forms of the white man's culture and identity for the concealed premises of his being and existence. In doing so, cargo cults often treat the implicit and the unstated as a hidden form of knowledge that needs to be made explicit by their naming and designating this secret or, alternatively, by their ritually enacting and occupying the implicit rules governing the white man's personhood and culture. Cult followers are not mistaken in seeing the disciplined bodily routines and gestures of whites as the secrets to a Western lifestyle. Certainly, whites pride themselves and lead others to believe that a civilized existence comes from copying forms of discipline they believe the black man needs. This transformative power of discipline was what cult followers were trying to grasp but through their understanding of transformation as coming from a world of magic, where to mime something was also to magically capture its soul or essence. Here two different views of ritual as transformative intersect to produce all sorts of experiments in identity and corporeality. The ritual labor of mimesis means different things in the disciplinary pedagogic cosmology of whites than it does in the magical cosmology of the Kaliai. In part, what allowed these two forms of mimesis to intersect was a common concern with incarnating new forms of order through ritual; in both, the ordering framework of the body was made central to the constitution of social order.

BLOOD AND THE DISCIPLINING OF WOMEN'S BODIES

Mapilu's cult was heavily involved in producing new bodies and a new social order through its management of women's bodies. More specifically, the new order and its new subjects were to be delivered through new forms of control over women's menstrual blood. Amkou gave me this description of how female followers took on new forms of moral responsibility toward their blood:

> Now with us [women], when the sick-moon came up to us, we would work it good. Some of us would go wash it by the river, but some of us would carry a mat and put it underneath our beds so that when the blood went down, it would gather on a mat. There it would gather until the sick-moon was finished. The women would then take this mat and anything else they had used, and they would bury it. They would also get cordylines and plant them around this blood. This woman [Paname] spoke to us to do this. This was a mark. We worked it good with all this blood, so that all these children of ours [from this blood] would not come and cut our necks.

Paname informed women that the way they treated their "sick-moon" would determine what sort of white spirit child it became. She told people to watch out for whites coming into the Kaliai bush, for they could be her children. She outlined certain personality traits that would enable people to recognize the different children. When visiting kiaps traveled through the Kaliai bush, she would study them to see which child they might be. If the white person was good natured, she might claim he was her child Johnson, who had come up from blood she had carefully buried. But if the white person was angry and had red eyes, she would suspect he was her child Semrengen, who came from blood that she had unthoughtfully thrown away. It is significant that the child with an indigenous name was the violent angry child and not any of the children with European names. Amkou gave me this account of Paname's speeches to women:

> She said that Semrengen was not a good person, that if he came up here, he would just cut the throat of some person. [*Amkou voicing Paname:*] "Sorry big men, my mouth is sore from this man Semrengen. This man's customs are no good. If you see him coming as a kiap, or as someone else, it is this man alone. This man will be in front and, if he was to come up here, his eyes would be completely red." She spoke that with Semrengen her menstrual blood had been thrown away [rather than carefully planted]. . . . She spoke like this to all us women: "All women, now supposing you have a sick-moon, then you must bury it, you cannot throw it away, for if these men come up [the spirit children from the blood], then they will come and cut all of your necks."

I see this account as voicing in a refracted form some of the apprehension and fear people feel about those official processes of becoming white that are applied to their children. But instead of accusing their living children of having this monstrous possibility as part of the process of their becoming aligned with white culture, the fear was displaced onto the white spirit children who threatened to cut the necks of the mothers who mishandled the blood that created them. This narrative warns of the dangerous possibilities that reside in those processes that are rendering people white and that are threatening to create mishandled children who are selfish and have no respect for their mothers. One reason bush villagers gave for their reluctance to send children to high school was that once they acquired Western-style jobs, they would no longer think of their parents. The spirit child Semrengen is a monstrous warning that speaks to that culture of alienation between parents and children brought by the process of becoming white. In Mapilu's cult women were responsible for managing and overcoming these potential distances between children and parents that were assimilated to the distances between Melanesians and Europeans and those between the living and the dead.

Through the control of their menstrual blood women were taught and encouraged to produce a new race of white men with good-natured temperaments. This new race of whites was also more familiar whites, for as the offspring of bush Kaliai women they were people's close relatives. We have here the production of new hybrid identities, children who cross the boundaries of being white and black and who travel between the dead and the living, as well as between Australia and Papua New Guinea. The perceived polluting body of woman created these new mediating figures. Her sick-moon became an alternative violent form of birth that created the conditions for a new social order. I would argue that the outsideness and transgressive nature of menstrual blood made it an appropriate symbol for capturing that which was outside and transgressed the indigenous social order—namely, a European existence. The polluting body of woman provided that excess of meaning that could be managed and reincorporated to produce an outsideness that was familiar. It is here a question of a white order to which people have ties. The familiar outsideness of women's bodies promised to render many other forms of outsideness also familiar and close.

Like Censure's cult but in a different way, the Mapilu cult criticized people's ignorance about the true procreative powers of women's bodies. Women were seen as the bearers of an alternative, unacknowledged source of creation. Their bodies carried a hidden form of procreation not recognized by the living, which was their spilled menstrual blood. Paname used Christianity to support this position, telling her female followers:

> You must work it good toward this blood, for these children have been sent by God. It [a child] came but it broke, and the blood came out. Now you cannot think that this is just empty blood. No, it is all children. We sleep together with our husbands, and this child has broken and come up like blood. Now you must work it good and plant them all. . . . Now with these sick-moons, you must work it good, for when they all come up [as children], you might see that some have red eyes and are cross. You might think that they are children that you carried and that died, but, no, it is this blood that you threw away. So you all better watch out. . . . Now this man Semrengen, I saw him that time I traveled around on the plane with all the children. I saw that the eyes of this man were totally red. Now if he was to come here, I think he would probably cut me, for I threw him away. Now what is to happen? If he comes up, what is going to happen? . . . Now you all look, my children have all come up like a kiap, and some others have gone on a plane and are coming here. Now if you see my child, Johnson, he will be tall, and his custom will be good.

Mapilu's wife's desires for children led her to fantasize certain relationships with these spirit children, and those relationships incorporated the desires and fears of her community. Her dramatic living out of these relationships provided an arena within which her community could allegorically mirror and act out its psychic struggles. Mapilu and Paname were not just out to deceive everyone but were also actively deceiving themselves, as their desires became subsets of the desires of others. Paname's desires for children led her to hallucinate their presence and even to interact with them. Locked inside her house, she would talk, laugh, and scold her children.[7] Later, to her husband she would describe their height and mannerisms: "Mapilu, this man—Johnson—he is as tall as you, your child is as tall as you." Paname needed to experience the reality of these children by getting other people to accept their reality. She would tell her followers how three of the children were happy to eat from a common dish, except for Semrengen, her last-born child. Paul informed me:

> He was a no good man. If he was to come and see that they were to all gather at one plate, then he would become cross, he would throw all the plates about. Semrengen would say that his food belonged to him alone and that the food of the older ones belonged separately to them.

> He did not want to eat together with these other men. He would come
> and cry. His mother would story to us like this. He would throw around
> the plates inside the house. We could hear all the plates banging
> around.

Inside her house Paname impersonated her children and even their access
to European forms of knowledge. Although not able to play a guitar, Paname would pluck away secretly on the guitar strings, telling her followers
that it was her children playing. While she did this, she would scold her
children, saying, "Hey, you cannot play the guitar!" or "Play the guitar
properly!" Sometimes Paname would address her followers outside, saying: "All the *manki* (young men) want a guitar, they are cross, and they
are throwing around the plates and the food. The guitar must come." Paname would take the guitar and give it to her children, saying: "Here is
this something which you have been crying over, take it and go play it."
While Paname secretly played the guitar, her followers would perform European dances in the village square. The dances were of the sort people
had seen on the coast and in city hotels. Today people burst out laughing
at how they danced in anticipation of who they were to become. I asked
Paul what sort of dances they did, and he showed me one they called the
twist, saying, "They were the dances of you masters." I asked him if a
man danced with his wife, and he replied, "No, everybody would dance
individually. People would roll their eyes around. All those who knew how
to dance would dance good, but the rest would be working all sorts of
things. The work of this man [Mapilu] was very funny."
     On one such occasion Samaga was sitting down listening to this music
when he felt like eating some betel nut. He rose and went inside Paname's
house; as he did so, he heard shuffling noises and Paname cried out: "Hey,
Michael Ross, Johnson, and Bullet—why are you not playing the guitar?
Your grandfather has come inside. . . . Why are you afraid? This is just
your grandfather coming to get his betel nut." As Samaga went inside, he
saw Paname throw the guitar away; she, however, pretended to scold her
children for not taking better care of it. From this time on Samaga and
others from Moluo became disillusioned with Mapilu's cult.
     Perhaps the most radical of Mapilu and Paname's experiments in mim-
ing European customs occurred when the cult sought to abolish the taboos
and avoidance relationships between in-laws (cf. Worsley 1957, 128). Mapilu directed this aspect of his cult at the young rather than the older generation. The older generation were not as willing to take on the experiences
of shame associated with becoming familiar with one's in-laws. When tell-

ing me about this experiment, Paul was half amused and half embarrassed; he started by saying: "I have thought of something, but I'm afraid because it is no-good-altogether." He then described how they worked a big feast of taro and pork that their in-laws attended:

> They said the custom of shame was finished, and the custom of one stomach was what we would now sit-down with. We now ate with our *tambu* [in-laws], and we sat down with the custom of one stomach, which is like yours—of all you masta. . . . They said: "Shame is now finished, and now we will reside with one stomach like all masta, we will no longer work at having shame or anything like that." This kind of custom where someone like you would think no good [be jealous] about your wife with me and I would think no good about my wife with you, this kind of custom would be finished, we would now sit-down good. We would sit-down with one stomach, all no-good thoughts would go, and we would all sit-down like all you masta. Mapilu told us: "It is like this, if I came up to the misis in your [a white man's] house, she would give food to me and I could eat with the misis."

Mapilu characterized tradition as a culture of jealousy, and he used the white man's culture to provide the model of a more open society, one not torn apart by all those suggestions of impropriety contained in traditional taboos. At the feast people put pork in their mouths, then cut off a piece, and offered it to their in-laws. These gestures of physical intimacy were extremely problematic for many people, especially in a culture that continuously speaks about sex through metaphors of eating. Amkou describes how many women felt:

> All the men worked this long table, and there all the men together with their tambu were to eat. All the women with their tambu were to eat together. Man! We wanted to die. Who was it who wanted to be friendly and eat with their tambu? All the women were afraid. All the men spoke: "You cannot be afraid, for later our sit-down will be like all masta." He [Mapilu] stood up and spoke: "Why are you afraid of all your tambu, for you know that all masta do not work it like us? You all know that the sit-down [existence] of all masta has come up for this reason because they have the custom of one stomach [unity]. Now all you and your tambu must sit down and be friendly and eat together." Andrew, I went and sat down with my tambu, and we shook hands. Aehhhhh!

He [Mapilu] spoke: "You must work it like this so that all your shame goes, and the law can break open and then we can sit-down like all the masta."

Before with all the big men, there was not one person who would sit down with his tambu. If someone sat down with his tambu, he would be speared. But this man [Mapilu] came and did this, and we spoke: "I think this man is working this stori and it is true. Now look, we are eating with our tambu."

The last few lines of this discussion reveal the way people associated the act of transgression with the act of creation. The process of transgressing existing social relationships was experienced as a set of self-validating truths by which people experienced themselves as creating and living a different order of experience. The cult set about performatively enacting the new social order, and this miming of whites, this miming of difference and alterity, gave people the experience of finally living in a different time. The process of assuming the habits of Europeans became the magical act of self-transformation that would deliver the cargo and new identities, and this required men to grant greater trust to women. New codes of sexual conduct, as well as a new, less possessive and suspicious way of thinking, promised a new world of ethics in which Melanesians could finally inhabit the civilized norms of Europeans that seemed and also claimed to promise so much.

MIMESIS AND CARGO

Cult followers often waited for signs of their cargo at a small hole that Mapilu referred to as Bulil. A small stream that flowed into this site was referred to as Power. At Bulil water flowing underground made noises similar to a generator's. This hole belonged to the white spirit children. Women would visit this hole and wait until dawn for signs of cargo. A few men were dispatched with the women to make sure that what the women claimed to have seen was not made up. Paul told me how the women were hoping for the dead to show them "pictures" of the promised cargo:

With the ants carrying their eggs, they would say: "This is rice here." [Another woman speaks:] "What are they showing?" [First woman replies:] "They are showing rice to us all." [Yet another woman speaks:] "Well, get up the songs, get up the songs." It would go on like this until another ant walked in front of this hole, and they would say: "Oh look, there is a car going there, there is a car." . . . If there were two [ants]

and one was traveling in one direction and the other in another direction, they would say: "Oh look, two cars are avoiding each other." . . . .
At dawn all the women would put on new paint and new grass skirts,
and they would come back singing. When we [men] heard the women
singing, we knew that they had seen something, some kind of mark. If
there was no singing and they were just walking about, it meant that
they had not seen a mark.

When told what the women had seen, other followers sang out with joy.
The ants were understood to be the souls of dead people who were showing the living a picture of the future. For people these microscopic events
at the Power hole signaled that the spirit children would soon come to live
with them. We have here a culture that seeks to capture reality through its
image; it searches for magical signs and reenactments of what eludes
people in the present. People are continuously miming or looking for copies of the objects of their desires. Most traditional magic in the Kaliai area
takes the form of miming the object that you seek to capture or create.
For example, certain chubby-looking insects that float on water are used
in hunting magic to capture pigs; the insect's body is said to be like a pig's
body. To catch a cassowary people use a slender-looking insect that floats
on water and has long legs like a cassowary's. Taussig captured well the
magical logic of mimesis when he wrote:

> For this is where we must begin; with the magical power of replica-
> tion, the image affecting what it is an image of, wherein the representa-
> tion shares in or takes power from the represented—testimony to the
> power of the mimetic faculty through whose awakening we might not
> so much understand that shadow of science known as magic (a forlorn
> task if ever there was one), but see anew the spell of the natural where
> the reproduction of life merges with the recapture of the soul. (1993, 2)

To some extent the colonial and neocolonial context is made up of a struggle between competing ways of rendering and channeling the creative formative labor of mimesis. People know the official forms of mimicry that
Europeans want them to assume, but people also do not trust the mimetic
road for becoming white that Europeans are mapping out. In cargo cults
a more traditional view of ritual and mimesis, which taps into the power
of the dead, comes to intrude into European rituals and culture, giving a
new interpretation to the imported pedagogic forms of mimesis and copying put forward by missions and government officials. In taking on the
pedagogic process of becoming white, cult followers also redefined the

mimetic terms and performances for making themselves white. The experience of becoming white came to be mediated by more localized understandings of alterity and mimesis that gave a magical dimension to colonial processes of transformation. In effect, colonial processes of social change came to be interpreted through a whole series of indigenous frameworks for figuring and realizing change. People searched inside their culture for tools of transformation and metamorphosis that would allow them to use ritual representations to control and direct the changes around them. Here another form of mimesis, which is predicated on alternative local understandings of processes of becoming, intrudes into those forms of change authorized by Western culture. I see the conflict between colonial authorities and cult followers as emerging from the intersection of two competing forms of mimesis that come to redefine each other's processes of copying and becoming.

MIMING WHAT WHITES WANT TO HEAR: SUBJECTIFYING THE WORLD OF SPIRITUALITY

Mapilu's cult came to an abrupt halt when a tree branch broke off and killed a small girl. She had been marching and singing cult songs. Many of the girl's relatives, even those who were cult followers like Leo, wanted the cult's leaders jailed. Leo claims that they did not go to the administration because Mapilu was able to temporarily persuade them that the girl had not really left but had simply joined the white spirit children in a better life. Leo described these events like this:

> He [Mapilu] said, "You cannot cry." He was holding the stomach of the small girl, and a plane went overhead. He spoke: "Mother, you cannot cry, she is traveling in the plane. Look, all the line [the spirit children] have now come. They have come to take her, they have come to travel around with her first, so you cannot cry." He was holding the stomach of this small girl, and he was . . . saying: "You all cannot cry, you all cannot cry." But she was already dead, for her brains had come out. . . . When the plane came over head, he said: "Look, Johnson has come, I think he will take her in the plane, and they will go to Sydney. I am not too sure what will happen, but she will go and be judged by Papa [God], and she will either die completely or she will come back." He worked this talk to us, and it cooled the stomach of the mother of this small girl. She fastened her stomach, and she stopped crying. The father of this small girl came, he was carrying a spear. He did not come

to the village, he sat outside. His stomach was totally hot. All the men went up to him and said: "You cannot come cross, ignore it, for you will block our road [of cargo]. You cannot be cross, just sit-down and leave it."

When the girl's father did come, Paname was able to persuade him not to press charges. Amkou gave me this description of what Paname said to the girl's father, who was also Amkou's brother:

> This woman [Paname] came, and she worked at greasing [persuad-ing] my brother. She said: "Father [a term of respect], you cannot worry. She has gone, but she is going to sit-down well [with a white life-style]. She has gone, but she will come back to you." She worked at greasing the girl's father and mother like that. She spoke: "She [her soul] is still traveling around, I am not sure but perhaps tonight she will get up, or it might even be during the day today." She worked at speak-ing like this, and we sat down looking at the girl. Time passed, her stomach started to swell up, some of us started saying: "She's not going to remain with us, her brains have come out." Leo said: "Tomorrow we will carry her back to the village." All of us carried this small girl back to Moluo. We planted her and there was not one person who went back to the *stori* [cult]. It was finished. He [Mapilu] alone remained and kept working this stori of his, and he tried to pull us back. But it has not turned out like that.

At about this time a European kiap arrived in the Kaliai bush. He found out about the cult and the girl's death, and he took Mapilu, Namore, and Paul to Gloucester. Paul prides himself on how he avoided a jail sentence by shrewdly giving the assistant district commissioner a strict Christian interpretation of Mapilu's ideas about spirits. The commissioner asked Mapilu: "What is this talk that you are making, that your talk comes up free, that your talk comes up as a spirit?" Paul claims that Mapilu did not understand the question so the commissioner asked him: "Paul, how is it that the father of this story says his children came and gave a story to him, that they came up like a spirit? What is the meaning of spirit, what does it mean for something to come up spirit?" Paul acted out to the commis-sioner a Christian interpretation of spirituality that had the effect of interi-orizing and subjectifying the world of spirits. Mapilu's ideas about spirits were presented falsely as the subjective presence of God's gift inside the self: "This man [Mapilu] said: 'This talk that I am working, it is not as though I am working nothing, it came up in my thoughts, it is spirit. God works spirit and it came up. With all of us, including whites, all of us who are on the ground, spirit works inside us individually.' [Paul then turned to Mapilu and said,] "You must talk like this to the kiap so that he understands." Paul spoke not about the white spirit children from Paname's menstrual blood but of how spirit is what God gives everyone in their thoughts for working everything. According to Paul, the assistant district commissioner agreed, and he instructed them to think and talk like this: "The big man worked thoughts which allow us to work all sorts of work." Paul and Mapilu were then told that they no longer had "court" and could leave. Paul, who now is a catechist in the Catholic Church, sees himself as having schooled Mapilu in what Europeans wanted to hear: "If I did not give him this small piece [of talk] to work, then the three of us would have been jailed." We have here tactics of evasion—people mime to Europeans the reassuring narratives of incorporation that Europeans want to hear. However, people are secretly working other narratives that keep alive the idea that spirits have a certain objectivity, even if it is receding.[8] European disciplinary structures are predicated on subjectifying the world of spirits; they introduce a form of spirituality that locates the processes of creation inside thoughts that emanate from a form of divine subjectivity. People recognize what whites want, and they struggle to give the appearance of allegiance to the spiritual world of whites while all along trading in other forms of spirituality that keep alive the objectivity of the dead.

Mapilu is still working his cult, only now he does so secretly inside the New Tribes Mission, which he joined around 1987. He pretends to the European missionaries to be interested only in the Bible and the talk of God, yet secretly he and his brother-in-law Namore are trying to contact the dead. Namore and a number of other families have gone to live with Mapilu at the Brisbane waterfall site where their cult was once centered. Recently, Namore came up to his sister Amkou and told her:

> Amkou you must hear my talk. If you hear my talk and follow me,
> then your sit-down will come up. Now if you do not listen to me and
> you stay living with your [other] brothers, then I am sorry, sister, about
> your sit-down. You will look at me, sister, and you will cry [out of envy
> for his new good existence]. Where I work this garden, at the waterfall,
> you will later see a house [referring to a house of cargo]. An iron-
> roofed house will come up.

One major change in Mapilu and Paname's cargo cult is that whereas people once often referred to this cult as Paname's stori, they now almost always referred to it as Mapilu's stori. Ex-followers claim that when the cult first began, Mapilu and Paname sometimes competed and argued over cult leadership. From a position of hindsight one New Tribes Mission follower saw the small girl's death as God's punishment for their disunity:

> With this here, they [followers] said that in the beginning this
> woman [Paname] found this something and that the two competed over
> it. Mapilu wanted to go ahead of her, but his wife wanted to go ahead
> of him. The two became jealous of each other and fought, and then
> with this something [the accident] the Big Man worked it so that a
> branch killed this child. Everyone courted them and this something is
> now finished.

Today Mapilu is in charge, and this corresponds with the increasingly patriarchal vision of Creation into which people have been incorporated, especially since they joined the New Tribes Mission. Although the cult has moved away from traditional Kaliai mythological rendering of woman's creative labor, it has nevertheless still remained immersed in other traditional mythic schemes, like that of Akrit whom Mapilu now copies. Mapilu, like Censure, has adopted the practice of not washing and of wearing poor clothing. Paul told me, "He is not a person who washes or who combs his hair. Only occasionally does he wash. When we were gathered together recently at Namore's place, he was not wearing good clothes or trousers. No way! He was not wearing a good singlet or shirt. He was wearing only a tiny piece of cloth. Even when we went to church, he would be wearing just this. His wife was the same. All her good things remained unused."

Mapilu was seen to be exploring those ambiguous forms of identification belonging to the rubbishman, Akrit, who in traditional myths wears a dirty skin that conceals a lighter cleaner identity. Akrit is a powerful trope for many cargo cult leaders, who see in this figure of doubleness an image of those transformations and instabilities that they would like to realize in themselves. Amkou gave me this description of how she and others were urged by Namore, who is her brother and Mapilu's righthand man, to notice: "He [Mapilu] does not wash or comb his hair or wear good clothes. You all look, is he wearing good clothes? He is wearing old broken clothes. You all look, has he washed? We all wash and comb our hair. This man we cannot know, but I think he has already thrown his hand out [to work cargo and money]." Amkou went on to explain that the large sum of wealth, for which Mapilu had thrown out his hand, was believed to have already gone to an American New Tribes Mission missionary for safekeeping. In the early 1990s people often said that the New

Tribes missionaries were building a huge warehouse of cargo for Mapilu at his remote waterfall site.[9] One of the missionaries, Tom, had been saving money for Mapilu. One Sunday he preached the virtues of saving, and he used Mapilu as an example of how someone could end up owning a store. Those who heard this lecture blew it out of all proportion and believed that a huge store would soon be built at Mapilu's inaccessible waterfall site and there helicopters would deliver cargo. Paul told me that Mapilu secretly believed that Tom was his first-born child, Michael Ross:

> Tom comes and says he is from America, but when it comes to his [Mapilu's] side, he thinks like this: "This child that I work at finding, he has come, he is here Michael Ross." With this here, everyone knows and thinks this: "Before this man killed a pig, he killed a pig at Bagai for Tom." They shot this pig and spoke: "We want you to take this school of America and bring it to us." Mapilu killed this pig, and Tom worked the school at Kwako, and he then carried this school and brought it on top to Para-batne because of Mapilu, because he killed this pig for masta Tom. Its meaning goes like this [Paul voices Mapilu's thoughts]: "Something that I worked before at trying to find it, well, it's here now, I have found it, this here is my child Tom." This is his thinking. For when Tom came on top, he spoke: "Mapilu, when I go to America to rest, you too must go to your camp [waterfall site]." Everyone heard it like that, but when it goes to him [Mapilu], to his thinking, then he will turn it like this: "This man has told me to go live alone so that all my cargo will come. A mechanic will come work my house. I think Michael Ross is this person here, Tom." This is his thinking.

A flag flies at the village of Para-batne (close to Bagai) where Mapilu and Namore go each Sunday for a church service run by the New Tribes Mission. When Amkou and Leo visited Para-batne, they were told: "You see this flag here? Soon it will be standing up in that area over there [the waterfall]." It was explained to them that this flag did not belong to all the villagers but only to Mapilu: "You all look: this man's [Mapilu's] flag has come but not ours. These flags come only from all white-skins, so why is it that this man has received this flag?" Leo and Amkou claim that the flag was seen as a sign that Mapilu was succeeding in capturing the favors of whites and that this was why some families were now following Mapilu and going back to work gardens at the cult's waterfall site. The New Tribes Mission, which set up the flag at Para-batne, was seen to be secretly endorsing Mapilu's cult. Even the writing that the missionaries put up on the black board was seen to have a secret code, and people were told by

Mapilu and Namore to go look at the writing and to think a great deal about it. The writing was said to contain secret names, and when the missionaries rubbed out the writing, they were seen as trying to conceal this clandestine code so that they were not jailed or expelled by the government of Papua New Guinea for revealing the hidden new law. The bond that people have to the New Tribes Mission is partly framed as that of a secret complicity that has to be maintained against the government and other whites, like the Australians, who are seen to be not interested in helping Melanesians but in keeping them repressed. Indeed, part of the reason some New Tribes Mission converts refused to stori [provide cult and traditional information] to me was that I was from Australia, the land of the bad whites, which was further confirmed by my opposition to the New Tribes Mission, the Americans, the good whites. In the next chapter I will explore more fully the cargo cult logic that underpins people's incorporation into the New Tribes Mission.

COLONIALISM, MIMESIS, AND PROCESSES OF BECOMING

Throughout this book I have been arguing that people return to their present realities through the mediation of that which is beyond. In the Kaliai bush, people's understanding of this "beyond" often took the form of the dead and whites who were accessed through the mimetic faculty. The ability to revise the present came from transcending its borders in journeys and visions that produced a new world of shared meaning concerning the outside realm that was to ground the solidarity of the project of becoming other than oneself. No subject has a relationship of pure self-possession; all subjects come back to themselves through the mediation of a boundary that throws into relief the present and the identity structures upon which the present depends. People are redefining the present and their place within it by refiguring their understandings of the outside and by entering into new imaginary relationships with that outside. Writers like Ricoeur (1979, 1991), Derrida (1987, 1994), Serres (Serres and Latour 1995), and Deleuze and Guattari (1987) have spent a great deal of time analyzing how a world is given its concrete self-presence through those images of distance that create its horizon and sense of placement. Only through the detour of the outside, through relaying meaning through the postal effect it provides, can the realizing effects of self-presence and self-possession be generated.

The shared sense of contemporaneity, of living the same space and time, is generated from a shared sense of what lies outside that space and time.

Indeed, when societies want to redefine themselves, they often do so by redefining that boundary through which they figure worlds of otherness. People's imaginary relationship with the outside underpins their imaginary relationships with each other, so much so that when people want to re-formulate their relationships with each other, they do so through re-forming their intersubjective understandings of what exceeds their immediate grasp—be it the past, the future, the dead, Europeans, or places like Sydney, Brisbane, America, and even heaven and hell.

The cargo cults that I have been analyzing were not seeking to go back to a static traditional culture that they often criticized. Instead, they were partly movements of cultural reform that sought the modernization of tradition within a framework that simultaneously indigenized the process of modernization. These movements sought to restage traditional culture, using as their background the powerful moral critiques that Europeans had made. That critique and its primitivist assumptions were internalized by people, producing alienated subjects who hated the past for that moment of its savagery that they read into themselves. It is within the framework of this internalized self-critique that cargo cults emerge to provide experiments in forming new moral identities, in providing new ways of ethically caring for the self. Although Kaliai cargo cults often appropriated the moral rhetoric of Europeans to authorize a critique of the ancestors, the cults were not a straightforward incorporation into European hegemony. Instead, the cults were more interstitial, with people using both European and traditional culture to situate themselves between the past and the future. People reread the past to give it a future, and they reread the future (that they were shown by Europeans) to give it a past that was their own. People's ownership of the future came from grounding it in their myths, that is, in creating it as the destiny of a story of origins that they held. Through the pedagogic crusades of state officials, the outsideness of Europeans had come to be associated with the future, so much so that people could come to own their future only by first owning their sense of Europeanness, that is, their sense of themselves as other than themselves. It was not simply that people were seeking to become whites, for they were also remaking what it means to be white. They were, to use Deleuze and Guattari's 1987 phrase, deterritorializing the process of becoming white by making the white man become other than himself too.

Like many other Melanesian groups, the Kaliai have a long tradition of people internalizing otherness by becoming the animals in their environment. Traditionally, people would dress in the plumage of birds, the tusks of wild boars, and the canine teeth of dogs, and they would devour the fat of snakes to take on the beauty, emotions, and qualities embodied in these creatures. In their rituals people would play and extend the boundaries of the human form by making their bodies the dwelling place of another life form. This process of becoming other than oneself was a site of power, wherein warriors and shamans moved into animality in order to use its violence to subdue the world and others. A sense of control and order came from the process of internalizing forms of otherness. Indeed, Kaliai social order was modeled on the differences between various animals, birds, and plants that in traditional myths were said to be the first beings that turned into humans and carried the totemic matriclans that make up the existing moiety system. Through their mothers individuals acquire a totemic identity that links their body to these primordial forms of embodiment. What I want to emphasize is the normality and centrality of those deterritorializations and reterritorializations of identity that made up the social order. The white man's existence came to be part of this culture of appropriation in which people dressed themselves in the identity of things other than themselves, not only to remake themselves but also to remake those other things.

All human subjects constitute themselves by internalizing and responding to the gaze of others. In cargo cults this assimilation of the other reaches a form of theatrical self-identification in which people's corporeal gestures become identified with those of Europeans. All human identities are formed through mimetic labor, through the internalization of cultural schemes for the body that initially reside outside the body. I have sought to explore what sort of subject positions are produced by the processes of colonization, pacification, and Christianization. What sort of compromised identities and what sorts of experiments in identity allow people to live with the compromised, ambiguous structure of their lives? In bush Kaliai cargo cults the inner world of pedagogic transformations brought by Western institutions came to be played out in the person of spirit beings and cargo cult leaders who, though black, had moved into becoming more or less white. In miming Europeans cargo cults leaders were objectifying this process of coming to be colonized by foreign gestures and moral norms that were also potential sources of power for placing oneself differently. Cargo cult leaders often came to dwell in the world differently; their contact with the outside world of the dead and whites came to radically refigure their sense of reality. They often dwelled in a world of hallucinations in which their desires took the form of fantasies lived as real events.

That all existence is through and for the other is the intersubjective basis of all forms of hegemony in the domain of class, gender, and race.

People make themselves known to themselves by the way they make the other known to themselves and by the way they make known the other as knowing them. The white spirit children and the cargo cult leaders who became like whites were attempts to control and own the white gaze through which people constituted their hegemonic sense of self. Seeing oneself through white eyes that had been familiarized was a way of objectifying that internalization of self-domination that took the form of villagers' seeing themselves through a white conscience that they had made their own.

In Kaliai cargo cults strategies of resistance did not take the form of seeking to eliminate the white man and his civilizing mission and its disciplinary practices. Instead, strategies of resistance entered into a parasitical relationship in which they fed off the dominant culture, reconstituting its rituals and symbols to make them work for other local causes. Here people's resistances and misreadings could also become part of their incorporation. Yet there were limits of official tolerance to this mutual symbiotic relationship in which the civilizing process partly proceeded through its failures to fully realize itself, which is to say that it depended upon all those minute appropriations and reconstitutions that localized and perverted its hegemonic hold. We need to note those corruptions of meaning that rendered state and church intolerant of appropriations to which they ordinarily turned a blind eye or dismissed as misunderstandings and ignorance. At certain points those local borrowings no longer constituted a means of relaying the civilizing process through misreadings but now constituted a perversion of it that interrupted its passage and hegemony. We are dealing here with processes of Christianization and Westernization as a structure of flows and interruptions. Colonizers and colonized negotiate the limits and the terms of the parasitical relationships that determine who feeds on whom and in what manner. Anthropological notions about adjustment movements do not capture accurately this compromised state of accommodation and assimilation. In changing the traditional local categories that order the world, Europeans produce a turning of categories that destabilizes and renders ambiguous the very corporeal grounds of one's identity, and it is perhaps this that is encoded in people's miming of whites and in notions of white spirit children.

Cargo cults are made up of empowering performances in which otherness is dramatically internalized; this involves a whole labor of creative copying in which the body becomes a space of exploration, a domain where other forms of identification can be taken on board and creatively reworked. Cargo cults involve the ritualization of politics, a process of creative labor focused on the assimilative qualities of the body, which takes new identities into itself but quotes and marks them with the traces of past forms of identification. The new compromised ways of being a subject brought by Western pedagogy can be objectified and creatively played out in cargo cult notions of spirit children and in mimetic performances that destabilize identities and the power relationship encoded in and through bodies.

Chapter Eight

Kaliai Cargo Cults and the New Tribes Mission

I do not know if I thanked you enough for the paper about the Old Testament stories. Do you think you could find out for me if it is permitted to take the fires of Hell allegorically? It seems impossible to believe that eternal physical torture can ever be inflicted on any one. Yet I am sure all the priests here believe in a literal interpretation . . .

Hubert Murray, letter of July 26, 1935, quoted in West, *Selected Letters,* 1970, 183

This chapter focuses on the New Tribes Mission, which arrived in the Kaliai bush in 1984. It analyzes the new American mission's attempts to transform and eradicate not only the collective memory of the traditional past but also the more recent collective memories created by cargo cults. I want to explore how people took up the radical project of remaking themselves as subjects who would achieve liberation through a massive act of forgetting. The significance of the New Tribes Mission is that it put back into the hands of whites those pedagogic processes of self-formation that involved a moral critique of the darkness of tradition. Converts came to adopt the new missionaries' demonization of bush Kaliai culture in part because it was in accord with some of the Kaliai's own critiques. Villagers internalized and repeated to the new American missionaries the very images of demonic caricature that the missionaries required so that they could missionize in good faith.

The conversion project of Christianity often requires subjects to read themselves as evil, and in the bush Kaliai area this was not hard to achieve, for warfare, widow killing, sorcery, and monstrous masks had cast a shadow of darkness onto people's souls. The history of people's contact with missions had left them with a legacy of guilt and anxiety about themselves as moral subjects. Like the cargo cults before them, the new American missionaries exploited this colonial legacy. They also amplified and accentuated its grip on villagers by adding to this legacy their demonic version of a born-again Christianity haunted by the devil and the fires of hell. It would be no exaggeration to say that the new missionaries were obsessed with and captured by the very images of evil that they projected onto others. The new missionaries not only helped to create and keep alive the very images of evil on which their mission was founded but they were also overjoyed to find native subjects who had already accepted and internalized into their self-images these "correct" Christian demonic caricatures of themselves.

In part, the hegemonic capture of the bush Kaliai by the New Tribes Mission was made possible by cargo cults that had popularized the image of a punishing god who gave black people their culture as his punishment before he left for America. The new missionaries were mainly from the United States, and they brought similar narrative structures of divine retribution that confirmed to people the necessity to read the world and its events in strictly moral Christian terms focused on an avenging God. When earthquakes damaged San Francisco in 1989, the American missionaries used the opportunity to point out that this was God's punishment for sin. Bush Kaliai villagers seized upon the new mission's emphasis on a vengeful God, which they fused with their cargo cult understandings of how God was punishing Melanesians for their original *bikhet* (pigheadedness) toward Him. When I was in the field in 1994, converts reproduced this moral discourse by claiming to Catholics that the recent destruction of Rabaul by volcanic explosions was God's punishment for their sins. One Catholic villager described to me the claims of his relatives in the New Tribes Mission:

> They say that it [Rabaul] was a place of humbug, a place for killing people for no reason. There people stole, and there they everywhere had sex with women. They say that because of this Rabaul was buggered up, because of these wrongs. Now another talk of theirs is that: "Supposing the Last Day comes up, then we [New Tribes Mission converts] will all go to Jesus and youse [Catholics], the ground will turn along with you all and you will be gone." I said: "That's all right. I am the food [*kaikai*] of the fire [hell], and you should not worry about me. Forget about me, I will stay outside [the New Tribes Mission]." I worked this talk, and they said: "How is it that we work at talking, and you don't hear us?" They then worked at crying and spoke of this fire

that just lit up at Rabaul: "You see it? Youse [Catholics], who are the mothers of darkness, you see it! Youse are pigheaded, now look at it! This something has covered up all the places, and they are all finished."

What we have here is more than just people internalizing the coercive moral rhetoric of missions. Here cargo cult appropriations of Christianity, which focused on a punishing God, come to be reconfirmed and revoiced by a new mission that has appropriated and reempowered these cargo cult messages of punishment in ways that have allowed these messages to be reappropriated yet again into new cargo cult voices focused on the new mission. The contemporary hegemonic context of Papua New Guinea is made up of such reciprocal borrowings, wherein parasite and host often swap places in quite complex and convoluted ways. Here hegemonic relationships become ones of mutual appropriation; cargo cults and missions feed off each other's appropriations of themselves, as well as off each other's appropriations of each other's appropriations. The appropriations are mutual and circular, creating a spiral whose directions and curvatures are struggled over. The New Tribes Mission and the cargo cults feed off each other's interest in the Christian theme of punishment, with each struggling to use this theme for their own purposes of social control, empowerment, and autonomy.

SATAN AND HELL IN THE KALIAI AREA

In 1986 during my first period of fieldwork the New Tribes Mission had yet to set up church services. At the time I heard no mention of Satan or the punishing fires of hell. When I returned in 1990, villagers who converted to the new mission spoke frequently of Satan and hell. Many saw my interest in traditional stories as fouling them from the road of God and pulling them back to the dark ways of the past. Converts took up the new mission's condemnation of traditional customs, which were now referred to as Satan's laws. With respect to gardens and hunting, converts no longer used spells that called upon renowned deceased gardeners or hunters for help. Instead, people prayed to God for help. Some converts started to see the underground world of the dead as the place of *pekato* (sin, hell). These converts concluded that the underground world of their ancestors must be the underground world of hell where their ancestors were now burning as their punishment for rejecting God. This new demonic vision of the underground maintains the objective reality of the traditional world of the underground dead by merging it with the reality of the external spaces posited in Christianity that were intended to displace traditional spaces of death. Alongside these syncretizing strategies, which seek to merge different geographies, are other uncompromising views that totally reject the existence of all those external powers and spaces of alterity posited by the ancestors—those belonging to *tewel,* masalai, tambaran, and the dead. Some converts refer to these rival domains and forms of power as the lies of ancestors who came under Satan's spell. The world of the past is a huge demonic fiction created by Satan, who now becomes the only permissible image of objectified evil. Whereas before, in dreams and in the bush, villagers would run into an ancestor, tambaran, tewel, or masalai, whom they would regard as real, some now refer to these extraordinary beings as Satan's illusions and tricks.[1] There is an attempt here to subjectify the world of the past, to interiorize and deny the objectivity of the spaces and realities that people can engage with outside themselves and use to refigure their sense of themselves. One young convert told me tambarans did not exist and that there was nothing at graves, that the latter were empty places he was not afraid to visit at night. Many young New Tribes Mission followers told me how they now ate food from masalai places.[2] In doing so, these converts were assuming a radical new relationship to the spaces around them. They were placing themselves differently from their parents. They were remapping the boundaries of their identities by using the power of God to enter and violate the forbidden respected terrains of the past. This process of conquering one's fear of masalai sites was conceived of as a process of conquering Satan's hold upon one's mind and self. It was celebrated as disciplining one's mind to think differently from the satanic ways of one's ancestors.

In the Mouk language area, an American missionary, to whom I will refer as Sign, was influential in using ideas about the devil to generate mass conversions to the New Tribes Mission.[3] He adopted an uncompromising fundamentalist type of proselytizing, hitherto unknown in the Kaliai area but soon taken up by converts and made their own. In 1990 Sign told me proudly how villagers had cried when confronted with the "fact" that their ancestors had died in sin for not knowing God. These tears were seen as proof of the sincerity of people's conversion and that people were remembering the new sermons of a born-again Christianity. Catholics and New Tribes Mission converts told me that Sign had informed villagers that their ancestors were burning in the fires of hell for not knowing God and for having sinned against His laws and that this was why people were crying. To further impress upon people the need to give up Satan's ways, Sign showed villagers videos and drawings of hell and the dead burning for their sins. Catholic followers gave me the following account of the campaigns of terror that the new missionaries and their followers used to get them to convert: "Now they [New Tribes Mission] have worked a picture that we [Catholics] are in darkness and cooking in fires, while they remain all right. They have seen our souls cooking in fires, but their souls are good. We have seen this picture on paper."

It was not only Catholics and the old men of tradition who were subject to these campaigns of terrors but also cargo cult followers. Sign advised them to stop using the cult names that Censure had given them, for these were Satan's names. Censure's son claims that Sign informed him that his father was burning in hell for the lies that Censure had put people through in his cult. In short, Satan and the fires of hell were used not just against tradition but also against the culture of syncretism in which people had incorporated Christianity into their local narratives and landscape. When Sign first arrived in the Mouk area, he encouraged people to come and story to him. Some Mouk leaders went and gave him one of their most significant stories, that of the black Moses-Christ figure Titikolo. To get people's trust Sign initially copied down these cargo cult stories and even pretended to agree with them. Later, however, he was said to have burned these stories and to have denounced them as Satan's trick. I was given this account of these events:

> Before, all the people storied about Titikolo and he copied it down
> into his book, but later he burned all these papers and said: "You must
> all now follow me, and I will work this [his mission]. All these other sto-
> ries that youse enjoy working, they are not true, they are Satan tricking
> you all. These are not true stories, they are the lies of your ancestors,
> they are the law of Satan, they are the law of darkness." It occurred like
> that, and he burned these papers and stood up this church of his. He
> burned all these papers containing our stories; the stories of Bowl and
> Nangile. He lit them in front of everybody and said: "You cannot live
> with this anymore, you cannot follow this thinking of yours anymore.
> It is the lies of your ancestors. It is not a true origin. You must forget
> about this and come inside my Bible school, and you cannot keep this
> thinking and mix it with the Bible. You must finish with it altogether."
> It is all finished now. He turned their thinking, and they have now
> given it up.

There has been considerable historical work done on how the devil was used in campaigns against evil in European culture (Russell 1981, 1984, 1986). It has been argued that during the great witchcraft crazes of the

fifteenth century, the church and the upper classes used the devil to police
the unauthorized reworkings of Christianity that formed a large part of
popular folklore culture (Ginzburg 1983; Monter 1976; Trevor-Roper
1975). On the colonial frontier the devil is still doing the church's policing
work. Just as in the European witchcraft craze—which used Satan to police the folklore culture of the poor that mixed Christianity with shamanism, magic, and sorcery—so the New Tribes Mission has used Satan
to police and cleanse people of these same hybrid practices. The rise of
satanism in West New Britain has been part of a similar moral campaign
of fear that has used the devil to purge villagers of their pagan beliefs and
especially of their tendency to reproduce those pagan beliefs inside folklore forms of Christianity.

Despite these similarities, the rise of satanism in West New Britain has
also been very different from that of fifteenth-century Europe, and this is
mainly because the New Tribes Mission has used seemingly nonviolent
tools to produce the fear that incorporates and transforms subjects. No
blood is spilled in its campaigns of terror. Here I agree with Nietzsche
(1886, 140) that in the modern world it is not so much that violence and
cruelty disappear but that they become spiritualized: "Almost everything
we call 'higher culture' is based on the spiritualization and intensification
of cruelty" (see also Adorno 1979, 231–36; Foucault 1977).

In the moral campaigns of the New Tribes Mission the devil was partly
a metaphor for pagan culture. He personified the rivalry that pagan culture posed to official Christianity. Yet the devil's destructive form also encompassed the ability of pagan culture to fuse and disguise itself as Christian. The devil's power to deceive allowed his deceptions to take the form
not only of pagan beliefs in supernatural beings but also the form of cargo
cult beliefs that led people astray from "true" Christianity and into more
localized understandings of a black Christ or God. In a published defense
of the New Tribes Mission two missionaries at Gigina have stated that
their aim in the Kaliai bush was to replace syncretism with Christianity:

> The cultural awareness training that is required for all New Tribes
> Mission missionaries, includes a discussion of the tendency of all
> people to interpret any message through their own cultural grid. Great
> care is taken in all of New Tribes Mission's teachings to prevent syncre-
> tism. . . . In their [the missionaries'] teaching, they directly addressed
> cargo philosophy. They did not want to leave any room for the Mouk
> people to assimilate Christianity into their cargo cult beliefs. (Brunn
> and Zook 1990, 183, 185)

Satan was more than just a metaphor for the undomesticated wildness seen to be embodied in pagan beliefs about masalai, tewel, and tambarans. He was also a tool for controlling all those new localized forms of Christianity that escaped and threatened the totalizing control of whites by miming allegiance to Western culture. The mixing of pagan and cargo beliefs with Christianity was what the new missionaries sought to control by denouncing it as Satan's law of darkness. Faced with the new mission's demonization of their beliefs in a black Christ or Moses, many cargo cult leaders now claim to have abandoned their *stori* (cult and secret narratives). However, what has often happened is that these leaders have transferred their millenarian hopes to the New Tribes Mission, from which they also conceal their new cargo cult interpretations and expectations concerning the new mission.

CARGO CULTS AND THE NEW TRIBES MISSION

When the New Tribes Mission arrived at Amcor, hundreds of bush villagers flocked to help them build an airstrip. People worked without pay, and many expected that planes would later bring free cargo for them. It was said that those who did not help build the airstrip would miss out on the coming cargo. Villagers from Aikon, Angal, Benim, Gigina, Moluo, and Salke all went to Amcor, and many refused to disperse even after the airstrip was built. In 1985 the administration became concerned with what it saw as a cargo cult developing around the new mission, so it sent a kiap to investigate. He tried to break up this new large gathering but was only partly successful. Many villagers refused to leave, or they left only to later build camps close to Amcor. At the end of 1986 they were joined by other Mouk villagers living closer to the coast—those at Aikon, Boimanga, Onamanga, and Salke. The villagers of Salke even deserted the cash crops of coconut and cocoa trees that agricultural officers had been trying to establish. They, along with other converts, pulled their children out of community schools at Bolo and Bagai run jointly by the Catholic Church and the government. These schools were accused of teaching false knowledge. Two children were also pulled out of the high school at Kimbe to come and join the new school of America that would save the Mouk. Even those Mouk working on distant plantations were told to come because something was now close to happening, and they would miss out on it if they continued to stay away.

From the time they first arrived at Amcor, the American missionaries were incorporated into cargo cult beliefs. Some villagers cried when they saw the new missionaries because the villagers thought they recognized long-lost relatives who had been transformed into white people. Much of the clandestine cargo cult that has developed around the new mission in the Mouk area has focused on the American missionary Sign. At one stage, money was collected and given to Sign to buy the law of America. Sign's Christian millenarian preachings about the Last Day and the New Age of Christ have revived the millenarian beliefs of many ex-cargo cult followers who have been waiting anxiously for the end of this world and Christ's return to his Mouk homeland. Many converts accuse the Catholic Church of neglecting them and of hiding the true Bible from them (see Janssen 1970, 1974). Some converts blame the pope personally for blocking the cargo and the new law of existence. Today many see the Bible of the Catholic Church, which is written in *Pisin,* as full of lies. They also see the Bible, which the American missionaries have translated into Mouk, as containing different truths about Christ's return and his coming new age. The translation of the Bible into the Mouk language was seen as authenticating the Mouk's centrality to God, and it has served to sanctify a newly emerged form of ethnicity that has blended the sacred boundaries of the new mission with the fixed grammatical rules within which the missionaries have codified the Mouk language.[4]

Many Mouk speakers, including converts, complain that the way the missionaries speak Mouk and the way they have translated the Bible is not in accordance with how the Mouk actually speak. People complain that the white man's Mouk is too long and heavy on their tongues, and by this they mean that the formalizing of grammatical rules by the missionaries does not take into account all the shortcut exceptions that make language pleasurable and fluid. Yet many converts also equated the literacy classes of the New Tribes Mission with the need to learn this new way of speaking Mouk that had come from the redemptive space of America. Many saw this new, "more correct" way of speaking one's native language as also correcting their thoughts. Discussing the role of missions in the development of new regional languages in the former Belgian Congo, Fabian pointed out that their role in the formation of grammatical rules was part of the moral disciplining of subjects:

> The involvement of the missionaries in the control of language was
> no coincidence, nor just a side-effect of their role in education. The aim
> of colonial rule was to establish and maintain power; to be able to do
> this on the level of "symbolic" power was vital to that rule's success.
> Missionaries were essential in this. Watching over the purity of Chris-

tian doctrine *and* regulating correctness of grammar and orthography were intrinsically related as two aspects of one and the same project. (1986, 83)

The linguistic translation project of the New Tribes Mission has worked to reconstitute the boundaries of people's identity, with converts using the mission's privileging of their language to downplay kinship, exchange, and ceremonial relationships with adjacent language groups. Moreover, the translation into Mouk of the Bible's millenarian message (about the Last Day and Christ's return) came to be seen as vindicating the Mouk's cargo cult longings and expectations of a new age. The newly translated Bible was seen as empowering the Mouk with the possession of a new sacred text from the land of America to which their god had run away. There was a sense of closure in American missionaries' returning to the Mouk—that is, returning to the original land of God—the alphabet that the Mouk lost when God ran away from them.

Part of the New Tribes Mission's success in the Kaliai area came from its recruitment of personnel from America.[5] Since World War II many cargo cults throughout Papua New Guinea focused on Americans as the good whites, as opposed to the bad whites—the Australians—who are characterized as having been interested only in working Melanesians hard and in "pulling money" from them (cf. Chowning 1990, Lawrence 1964). Contemporary bush Kaliai cargo cult stories tell of how, when God ran away from the Kaliai, He went to America and gave everything to Americans. Many Kaliai believe that God, Christ, and the dead reside in America. Many are waiting for the black God whom they wronged to return and to bring the new law that will *stretim* (straighten, collect) their existence. When the American missionaries did arrive, telling people that Christ was coming and they were bringing His law, people's existing millenarian expectations and understandings of America were confirmed.

Throughout Papua New Guinea memories of the Second World War have served to validate cargo cult understandings that there are other, more equitable ways of organizing human affairs than the coercive selfish laws of the Australians. The old men of the Kaliai area, who fought alongside U.S. soldiers, remember the law of America as the law that everything is free, for they were freely given European food and clothing. They remember the African American soldiers who wore the same clothes as whites and ate European food. They remember and tell of how the bush people were treated as equals by the good whites, the Americans (see Thurston 1994, 201–202). They do not remember the discipline and subordination to whites that were part of the war; instead, the old men remember and emphasize the utopian dimension of their relations with Americans. Cargo myths have blended with these war memories to form a powerful horizon of expectation into which came the American missionaries, who have reinforced this horizon of expectation with their own millenarian redemptive view of their missionizing.

In the early 1990s the New Tribes Mission instituted an adult literacy program that fueled these millenarian expectations. It revived cargo cult beliefs about how the Mouk had originally possessed the white man's knowledge—such as writing and the alphabet. Villagers saw the American missionaries as now returning this lost alphabet to its original possessors. In 1986 I was taken to rock shelters at the headwaters of the Banu River and shown where Titikolo had painted the "A, B, C" (alphabet) before he left and gave it to his friend, the rubbishman in America. On another occasion I was told:

> He [Titikolo] put marks [the alphabet] on the stones around rivers, he wrote various things. It is like this—plenty of people believe in this writing. This writing is like that belonging to a person. I don't know how to write, and I wouldn't be able to write on stones. But how is it that this writing is on the stones? Who does it belong to? Our grandparents told us he went to Siasi, and then he went to America and came up to this rubbishman—this was a man whose father had died, and everyone else didn't like him.

When the literacy classes of the New Tribes Mission started, they were attended by many old men, some well over sixty. These old men struggled desperately to learn the alphabet in the belief that, if they could learn to write their names, they could later sign the forms that would give them access to cargo. People saw the new lessons they were given as the new school and law of America. The new discipline of the classroom and of Bible reading at home took on the connotation of a new ritual law that would produce a new sort of moral subject with the right to share in the white man's existence. Here converts revoiced, in a reworked form, the mission's view of the transformative pedagogic effects of writing, namely, the ability of writing to produce a new sort of improved subject. Converts seized upon the Western utopian promise of education, not only in terms of its promised practical knowledge but also in terms of its promise of a new sort of utopian existence made up of new more moral selves (see Swatridge 1985). The pedagogic projects of whites have a millenarianism, albeit an institutional form of millenarianism, and people seized upon this transformative utopian goal, for they recognized it as being like theirs.

At the beginning of 1994 many converts were predicting the age of cargo would come when Sign returned from leave in America with the final translation of the Bible that he was working on. Relatives in the new mission told Catholic villagers: "The ground will now finish, you know. The Bible will turn it. When our *boi* [companion] Sign goes and comes back, then I think something will come up." Nearly everyone in the Kaliai bush has left the Catholic Church, which now has a strong following only in villages near the coast. Catholic villagers often told me how they were "greased" by relatives to join the new mission, for something was now close to happening. One man recounted to me the emotional appeals of his relatives, who would say to him: "We are really worried about you, and we cry for you. Things are now close to happening. Look, our brother Sign—he has gone [to America]. When he comes back, I do not know, but something will come up then. All the time now, your mothers cry over you, they cry over you." Catholics told me that their relatives would cry for them because they were going to burn in hell and miss out on the cargo. Many people have found it difficult to resist the emotional on-slaught of their relatives' crying continuously for them. Posingen gave me this account of the blasphemy and humor that he used to resist his rela-tives' tears.

> They [his relatives] cried, but I do not believe them. I would believe
> if they had stood up and had seen someone go into the fire. . . . They
> all cry. If they want to purge [*raus*] their big darkness [*tudak*], then they
> will work a huge cry. They will be truly sorry and cry. I asked them:
> "You all cry, but what is the meaning of why you cry?" They came and
> greased me, saying: "Man, this something [their crying and beliefs] is
> true grease, this law of ours is grease." But I felt it [what they had to
> say], and I replied: "What true area is grease? This area where you have
> sexual intercourse—is that the area that is grease?" [Posingen was refer-
> ring to the sexual seduction of women, including his daughters, by New
> Tribes Mission converts.]

SIN AND THE PAST

Converts now remember the time before the arrival of the American mis-sionaries as an age without ethics. All the traditional rules of hospitality and etiquette have been forgotten, and what converts selectively remember is the murderous past of war, sorcery, and the guilt from breaking the necks of widows. Although people were under the influence of the Catholic Church for two generations, many converts claim that they were totally ignorant of God and that it was the New Tribes Mission that first brought God to them. This is also how the American missionaries like to characterize their missionizing, for it helps them to undercut the Catholic Church's accusation that the missionaries have stolen Catholic followers.

One reason people gave for converting to the new mission was that it offered better techniques for producing moral order. For many years in their cults villagers had been engaged in the project of making themselves into new moral subjects, and often this was equated with the project of renouncing everything to do with tradition. The new mission confirmed this project, and in this it was different from the Catholic Church and the government, both of which had a policy of selectively preserving tradition. The new missionaries instructed Kaliai villagers to give up their traditional dances, songs, and ceremonies, for these only had the effect of stopping people from thinking about God, and they brought back the transgressive disordering desires of the pagan past.

The New Tribes Mission has tried to hide its repression of tradition from government officials. I asked Catholic villagers about the mission's public assertions that it had not stopped traditional customs and that this was simply the spontaneous action of Kaliai villagers. Referring to the most powerful of the missionaries—Sign—I was told: "He is lying. He is afraid of the government of Papua New Guinea, and so he lies and works this sort of talk." A New Tribes Mission follower claimed that Sign would humiliate publicly those who attended traditional ceremonies: "If a man goes and sings Mirmir [a local festival involving songs and dances], he will really shit himself. When they pray inside the church, then he [Sign] will really 'kick around' those men who went to this *singsing* [festival]." While I was being told this, another man interrupted to say:

> If they go work Mirmir, then they are working sin; if they go to any
> rituals, like to the feast of the tumbuan, then they are working sin. If
> they run into such a feast on the coast, then they cannot eat this food;
> if people offer it to them, they will refuse it. If they eat it and come
> back, then Sign will cross them, saying: "This food belongs to sin, why
> have you gone and eaten it? Do you think this food is good food? It is
> food-no-good; it is the food of darkness; it is the food of Satan. So why
> have you gone inside and eaten it?" He will work this kind of talk for
> the food of Varku and all other things. [I ask: "Did you hear him work-

ing this talk, or is it other people working this talk?"] No, it was him,
just now, when he was running the church. This is his law for running
this church, and it is why everybody truly believes.

During his sermons Sign would question Kaliai big men about traditional
customs, saying: "This something is sin. Are you going to pull back sin?"
Here shame and humiliation in front of the congregation are used to break
down ties of kinship and hospitality that might draw people back into
traditional ceremonies. The traditional ceremonies threaten the new mission because they assert and map out an alternative sense of community
to that provided by the mission. When I asked Sign about his opposition
to tradition, he told me that the way people had practiced their ceremonies
was sinful. By this I and others believe that he meant the secret food belonging to the tambaran that men eat at the expense of sharing it with
their children, wives, and other female relatives. The New Tribes Mission
has a domestic pedagogy; it sees its educative task as including the moral
domain of family responsibilities to which it seeks to give form by restruc-
turing those aspects of traditional culture that cut across and subvert the
intimate shared space of the nuclear family. Men have always had a great
deal of guilt about eating the tambaran's food secretly. Traditionally, this
guilt was alleviated through the practice in which men were permitted to
give some meat reserved for the tambaran to their families if they told
their family it was the tambaran's vomit, that it had overeaten and thrown
up this food. The American missionaries have successfully tapped into this
traditional sense of guilt and have offered to alleviate it with an alternative
culture that is free of monsters and guilty secrets.

The missionaries have taken men's experiences of guilt and have used
them as part of a general condemnation of tradition. Although many traditional *singsing*—like Mirmir and Sia (a dance)—do not involve secret
eating by men, these too have nevertheless also been condemned as sinful.
When I asked followers why, they criticized traditional ceremonies, claiming that singing and dancing provided opportunities only for flirting and
courting the opposite sex:

> They say the singsing of Mirmir has the sin of darkness. It is dark-
> ness because we stand up and sing and humbug [flirt] in front of all the
> women, and all the women put on grass skirts and dance around
> us. . . . Its meaning is like this: if we go to church, then we can only fol-
> low the law of God. If we work these other kinds of things belonging
> to humbug, we will pull back these customs of our ancestors, and then
> we will no longer be hearing the talk of God.

Melanesia has a long history of missionaries who object to the sensual pleasures and eroticism in Melanesian dancing.[6] This has partly to do with the problematic relationship of the missionaries to their own sexuality. Yet the missionaries are not mistaken in assigning a sexual dimension to traditional dancing. Coastal villagers still compete during feasts. Visiting young men dance in a way that is meant to seduce as many young women as possible from the host village into eloping with them. Men also tell stories of more secret forms of transgressions—married women who sneak off during ceremonies to fulfill a desire for someone other than their husband. In their choreography Kaliai dances often celebrated the seductive, strong, agile body of a warrior able to dodge spears. Dance ceremonies fused eroticism with war, teaching the skills of warfare through the seductive techniques of dance. Speaking about his grandparents, Posingen told me, "When they learned people to sing and dance Mirmir, they truly learned it so that later when something no good came up [war], then they could dodge the spears." Today men have internalized a sense of guilt about using dance ceremonies to attract women. Instead of celebrating and competing for seduction on these occasions, converts denounce them as working humbug: "Sign speaks that these singsing are something belonging to humbug. This is true, the new law of Papua New Guinea goes to this." The austerity and moral discipline of traditional pagan ethics are now often seen as being nonexistent. The past was simply a time of wild excess that is now to be domesticated through the discipline of daily church attendance and Bible reading. The latter disciplinary practices are celebrated as offering new techniques for producing reformed subjects who can remember their moral obligation to live an ordered existence free of the disruptive effects of seduction and eroticized desire.

CARGO CULTS TRY TO APPROPRIATE THE NEW TRIBES MISSION

When the New Tribes Mission first arrived in the Kaliai area, many cargo cult leaders claimed credit for their arrival and saw it as proof of their ability to establish a new relationship of help with the dead. The cargo cult prophets—Censure, Mapilu, Kail, and Watna—all claimed that the arrival of the Americans proved that they had successfully contacted the dead. When the new missionaries started preaching the Bible, Censure used their preachings to prove the correctness of the biblical knowledge that he had given his followers but that he claimed to have acquired independently from the dead.

Initially, Censure tried to use the New Tribes Mission to revive his cult, but he later turned against the new missionaries when they took his remaining followers and denounced his cult. He then blamed the Americans for blocking the new law that they were supposed to bring. Censure warned his followers that the new law of the white man—*Longmaelong*—which he had been working, had come close to arriving: "Longmaelong has come and filled up Mount Silo. . . . Kilok is holding it, he has pulled it to us and put it there." Censure warned the villagers of Benim and Gigina, who were then still occasionally visiting and participating in his ceremonies, that if they broke completely away, Sen Kilok would send some *masta* to come and work another kind of law that would be a false law. Censure told these villagers that the New Tribes Mission was their punishment for deserting his cult and that the missionaries were only pretending to bring the new law, whereas they in fact were blocking it. For that small group of relatives that remained loyal to Censure's memory, this has proved to be true. They accuse the new missionaries of acting just like other whites, in that they are interested only in fouling Melanesians with a false law meant to distract them from developing their own law. These accusations use the desire for the material living standards of whites as the language of objectified value within which to articulate a struggle around the need for the bush Kaliai to develop an autonomous black theology. Cargo and commodities are here the fetishized language of value within which a number of other struggles and processes are voiced.

To some extent the fetishized nature of cargo conceals these other contested social and cultural struggles. Yet this fetishization of cargo, its transformation into the language of all value, also reveals the commodification of social relationships within which people and their forms of value have come to be encapsulated. This commodification of relationships is reworked in cargo cults as people giving a moral dimension to the values objectified in commodities. To borrow an insight of Marilyn Strathern's I would argue that different conventions of reification exist, some are central to the gift economy, and these can work to conceal "the extent to which the things that people make stand over and beyond them" (1988, 167). For Strathern the Melanesian emphasis on the social relationships embodied in objects also entails forms of mystification: "One would understand as constraints, then, the symbolic conventions by which social relations are indeed the overt objects of Melanesians' dealings with one another" (1988, 167). Like Strathern, I see reification as central to the production of different social orders, and in the postcontact situation it is partly a question of how different conventions of reification intersect and rework each other's processes of fetishization.

In cargo cults the forms of value embodied in commodities come to be viewed through symbolic conventions in which social relationships with the dead are reified as the source of knowledge and the source of objects of wealth and power. One person who approached the New Tribes Mission in these terms was a woman called Kail. She tried to use the new mission's arrival to recruit followers to a cargo cult that she had been working alone in the village of Benim. She told the other villagers:

> It was because I spoke and rang Papa [God] that the New Tribes has come. . . . The New Tribes came because of me. They are carrying a good custom for working our sit-down. You must all hear their talk. When their school comes to Benim, then you must all go and hear its talk so that you all believe and come back toward me. I will then give this talk belonging to me and extend on theirs so that your sit-down comes up good.

Kail danced happily as she made these claims, saying: "You see it, it is because of me, it has come now. You did not listen to my talk, but it has come now. Yewhi! Yewhi!" Kail claimed those who continued to be pigheaded, by rejecting her beliefs, would remain poor forever. She told villagers, "Look! This something that I was always speaking about, it has now come up. It has come now, so you all get ready. . . . You cannot wander about, you must all sit down good in the village; keep it [the village] clean and work good houses. This something [the new age] is now coming, it is coming and later you will be all sitting down good. Those of you who have not been listening to my talk will stay behind, but I will go ahead." Like other cargo cult leaders, Kail took up the administration's rhetoric that stable, tidy, well-ordered villages were a moral prerequisite for achieving a new existence. Using this official rhetoric, she warned villagers not to fall back into the wandering, undisciplined, ignorant habits of their grandparents. Through internalizing and revoicing the harangues of kiaps and missionaries, cargo cult leaders appropriated the redemptive role of moral critique that Europeans and their institutions have always used to problematize and capture Melanesians.

In terms of the New Tribes Mission, not all the cargo cult leaders who joined the new mission were completely happy with its abolition of custom, and this was certainly the case with Kail. She would sing and dance traditional songs in front of her house and say, "Our songs Sia and Mirmir, you cannot lose them, they are our custom. . . . Bring a drum to me. You all say that this church of ours which has come has made you all afraid [of tradition], but Sia you cannot lose it, for this is our custom. God himself gave this law for us to sit down with. It belongs to us, so why are you all afraid of it? If you all remain afraid of it, then you are all being pigheaded."

Kaliai cargo cults have often been critical of tradition and have on occasion called for its abolition. Yet they have also always seen the traditional world of the dead as an alternative form of power that whites hide. Kail was noted for using traditional garden magic to make taro grow, and this magic relied on calling the names of dead ancestors who had been good gardeners. In knowing garden magic, which is normally men's knowledge, Kail was seen as unusual and was said to be working things like a man. In front of her relatives, Kail would perform the military-like exercises of police officers and soldiers. Beneath her bed was a hole in the ground that was her telephone and wireless for talking with the dead. Inside her house she would put food on a bed for the dead to come and eat its soul. Kail always wore grass skirts, and those she changed out of she would hang up in her house. When asked about this, she replied: "This something is the come up of us all, the grass skirt is our origin." By this Kail was referring to the fact that the grass skirt covered the vagina through which everyone was born. Monongyo explained to me:

> She would not throw them [the grass skirts] away; she spoke that
> they were the mother of us all. They were the mother of us all, and for
> this reason she would never throw them away. She spoke like this, its
> meaning is like this—if everybody heard her talk, and she worked and
> worked it, then it was up to the wish of Papa, and he might send down
> a law. It was then this something [the grass skirts] could be thrown
> away.

Kail was never seriously taken up as a cult leader, yet she nevertheless illustrates the attempt to appropriate the transformative project of the New Tribes Mission and to assimilate it to existing cargo cult understandings about the transformative power of the dead.

Although some converts claim publicly to have totally given up their traditional beliefs, in practice this is not always the case. When someone becomes sick, sorcery explanations are sometimes used or strongly hinted at; when someone dies, converts will quickly lock up their houses and not go outside at night for fear that an angry ghost might be nearby; and when a child becomes lost in the bush, I have heard converts blame the influence of a masalai or tewel for having made it *longlong* (disoriented). These folklore beliefs are still closely enmeshed in people's thoughts and feelings, and they are what sustain the clandestine cargo cult rereadings of the New Tribes Mission's project. Another cargo cult leader who tried to use the

New Tribes Mission to revive his cult was Mapilu, who was recently beaten up by converts because he went back to using traditional taro magic in his gardens. At the end of the last chapter I pointed out how ex-cult followers who were close relatives of Mapilu claimed that Mapilu saw an American missionary at Kwako as his spirit child. Mapilu and his brother-in-law, Namore, have found it difficult to reestablish their cult, for they are watched closely by the missionaries and their teachers. Partly to avoid this close scrutiny, they have recently moved farther inland, back to the waterfall site that had been the center of their cult. Throughout the Kaliai bush the New Tribes Mission has been very effective in setting up a system of intelligence gathering; teachers report all transgressions, including nonattendance at church services, to the Americans. Some villagers suspect the Americans of then reporting transgressors to God. One convert described this new system of moral surveillance like this:

> Now at this time we go to church every Friday, Saturday, and Sunday. We as individuals believe strongly in going on top to Papa. . . . All right, we all watch out good. Now, at this time, each person will boss his own skin [moral cleanliness]. Now supposing a man fouls in the bush and loses his church [*lotu*] for two or three weeks, then they [the teachers] will record his name in a book. When Sign comes, they will point to this man who was pigheaded, show his report to him, it will come up to Sign. And Sign will do what to him? He will either talk to him, or he will send it [the report] to the Big Man [God]. The law now is like this.

Here the American missionaries come to realize the godlike qualities of omniscience that they preach. The system of moral surveillance and reporting they have created is meant to be internalized by individuals and become a new religious conscience, what a Freudian would call a new superego. Yet in the process of occupying the exemplary center of this surveillance system, the missionaries have acquired some of the omniscient godlike qualities that they have instituted. Indeed, Catholics told me how their relatives in the new mission claimed that Sign could hear everything said outside his presence: "Before, they [converts] used to say that if we spoke, then with our talk, Sign would have already heard it." Here the Bible's image of God's omniscient gaze comes to be repersonified and lived out in the center of the new system of moral surveillance and reporting that Sign has used to capture, police, and transform the bush Kaliai. The missionaries have appointed teachers to different villagers, and their effect has been to transform the bush Kaliai area into a vast panopticon that focuses an omniscient moral gaze on the missionaries who start to take on the godlike qualities they institute.

Currently, the most creative individuals of bush Kaliai society—its shamans, dreamers, and visionaries—are the most scrutinized and repressed. Their attempts at syncretism are stopped as soon as they are publicly voiced. In losing their control of Christianity to the teachers of the New Tribes Mission, these creative individuals have also lost control of those techniques for forming subjects that Christian guilt is so good at providing. The new mission has recentralized and returned to the hands of Europeans all those processes of self-formation that the cargo cults had appropriated from Christianity. Today people are torn between a desire to liberate themselves from the tudak ("too dark," great darkness) of tradition and the alternative belief that they might in fact be empowered by these dark secrets. Cargo cult leaders, like Mapilu and Namore, want to hang on to their waterfalls and underground sites. In doing so they are looking for a way to repossess the spatial conditions for forming their sense of themselves by controlling the outsideness that shapes the horizon of the future. In seeking to keep control of that which is hidden but determinative of the boundaries of visible existence, these cult leaders struggle to control the means for creating identities and policing everyday lives. The choice between the New Tribes Mission and the cargo cults is not a choice between policing and nonpolicing but a question of who polices whom and what geographies of alterity will be used to mediate those policing structures.

The clandestine attempts by villagers to keep the underground alive has a long genealogy in the Kaliai area, and its effect has always been to immerse people in a secret, underground, doubled existence. Indeed, I would argue that Kaliai cargo cult stories about the underground gain their power because they resonate and reproduce, inside narrative, that hidden doubling of existence that cargo cult followers enact in practice when they hide their secret truths and rituals from church and government officials. The hidden other world of cult activities creates, mimes, and reobjectifies the hidden other world of the underground posited in cult narratives. Hiding from the gaze of whites, developing their secret alternative truths about the Bible and God, cult followers enact that alternative secret underground existence that they posit to exist in their narratives. There is in all these complex structures of mirroring and doubling, where the human imagination objectifies and projects its operations into the contents of its fantastic narratives, the lived experience of a double existence created from living secret worlds of underground meanings. The underground here is not just

a metaphor for the unconscious but also a metaphor that mimes, displaces, and reproduces in narrative the doubled existence of concealment
lived out in people's practices.

REMEMBERING THE PAST

Although they are required to believe exclusively in God's power, many
New Tribes Mission followers find it difficult to totally reject all beliefs in
masalai sites and underground spaces belonging to the dead. Traditionally, a shared memory of events at special sites underpinned the identities
of communities and their ownership of the surrounding environment.
People have sought to rework some of the stories about these sites as a
way of hanging on to a sense of shared history that can also be very personal. For example, some New Tribes followers still believe the story of
how the mother of one their leaders fell into a stream and ended up standing in the village square of an underground village. The dead who lived
there started quarreling over whether this woman should stay and live with
them. In the end she was sent above ground, back to her husband. New
Tribes Mission converts have modified this story to add the Christian gloss
that it was God who spoke and sent her back. In the new reworked story
God's power does not completely obliterate the remembered power of the
dead, but He appropriates from them their benevolent merciful qualities.
The dead lose any redeeming characteristics, whereas God comes to be
remembered as the one who saves people from the misfortune generated
by their past, a demonic past that wants to hang on to them. Such reinterpretations have resulted in the increasing Christianization of people's collective memories, with God's power now set up in opposition to the traditional power of the dead, whose menacing actions He counteracts. The
new story of God's saving people from underground sites revoices that
salvation from their past that Christianity seeks to enact by getting people
to forget the knowledge of their grandparents. People have found it difficult to forget all the extraordinary stories dealing with their grandparents;
instead, people reenact in their new stories the contest between the world
of the dead and God that people experience inside themselves.

   Although many converts claim to deny any reality to the powers of
alterity posited by traditional culture, in practice the New Tribes Mission
has needed the remembered power of masalai, tewel, tambaran, and the
dead in order to establish the greatness of God's power. If these traditional
figures of alterity had no power, what point and need would there be for
God's benevolent intervention? In practice, the incorporation of people

into Christian hegemony has often been predicated on sustaining memories of rival spaces of power that have to be tamed and subdued. At the local level Christianity sustains selective memories of ancient powers, and it keeps alive the menacing alternative to God's power, which He then restrains and subdues. The pacification and domestication of subjects comes to be objectified as the pacification and domestication of their landscape and its monsters. The hegemonic process of forgetting is never complete and total, for Christianity requires a particular memory of the past and of the landscape in order to objectify and mediate its conquest of subjects through conquering the sites and spaces that mediate people's identities (Lattas 1996b).

CHRISTIANITY AND PARADOXES OF MEMORY

It is a mistake to see memory and forgetting as opposites; rather, they are often two sides of the same process. Indeed, what we have in the Kaliai area is the paradox of people's needing to remember what it is that they need to forget. Here the moral requirement to forget subverts itself by keeping in consciousness a memory of what has to be expelled and repressed from memory. The politics of memory and forgetting in the Kaliai area are full of these sorts of ambiguities and paradoxes that give a certain instability to the process of cultural repression. These paradoxes and ambiguities are not accidental, for they also sustain and make possible the success of missionizing.

With respect to sorcery, people interpret the missionaries' condemnation of sorcery not as a denial of sorcery's power but as their needing to forget and give up this "black power" they had previously possessed. People say once they do so, God will be obligated to protect the bush Kaliai from the sorcery of others (especially those on the coast) who refuse to give up the evil satanic powers of tradition. Lay preachers gather converts for the New Tribes Mission, not by denying sorcery's power but by claiming those who join the new mission will be protected by God from sorcery's reality. At a large meeting on the coast in 1990 a teacher in the New Tribes Mission, Warenga, claimed that sorcery would destroy coastal villagers, for they had sinned against God, but that sorcery could no longer harm the true believers of the New Tribes Mission:

> This is our talk. It is clear, it is our talk. If a man tried to kill me,
> do you think I would die? I say this because sorcery has been tried, and
> it was not strong enough. I also drank bleach, but it too was not strong

enough. I also drank fish poison, but it too was not strong enough.
Look, I have won over these three things, they were not strong enough.
Councillor, it all has to do with belief. We Christians [New Tribes Mission followers] believe in one God, in the ten laws of God. Because we
believe, this something [sorcery] does not have the power to grab hold
of us. However, youse [Catholic followers on the coast] have all broken
God's ten laws, and because of this, sorcery destroys you. The cause is
with you. [Other New Tribes Mission followers call out, "Enough,
enough!"]

The European missionaries are embarrassed by such excessive eulogies to
God's power, but they also turn a blind eye to their teachers, who have
been recruiting followers using these claims. When I challenged Sign about
the claims of his teachers, he told me that it was true, a knowledge of God
would result in the eradication of sorcery. Here a convenient ambiguity
about how sorcery will be abolished by Western culture allows the new
mission to feed off people's painful experiences of sorcery and their desires
to have its reality ended. Indeed, underpinning the growth of the New
Tribes Mission has been an antisorcery movement, the latter having also
been a feature of all bush Kaliai cargo cults (cf. Marwick 1975). Although
the new mission seeks to abolish traditional beliefs and customs, it also
requires and keeps alive this traditional world of fear from which it
offers protection.

   One traditional form of sorcery (muso) from which the new mission
offered protection involves the ability of women's bodies to pollute and
destroy men. The new mission did not destroy traditional ideas about feminine contagion; instead, converts saw the new mission as giving men
God's power and strength so that they could withstand the dangers of
women's bodies. Male converts often boasted to Catholics how they now
had the power to drink water from those parts of streams where women
crossed and how they could eat mushrooms and other food found along
paths traveled by women. Such ideas and practices were attempts to develop a new social order involving a different spatialization of gender relations. There also was an attempt here to develop new corporeal schemes
for male identity—to develop a new Christian male body capable of with-
standing sexual contact with women as well as the dangerous revenge of
women. The latter was often summed up traditionally as the ability of an
angry wife to pollute her husband's food with menstrual blood. The power
of the new mission was built on developing a new folklore culture in which
its teachers acknowledged traditional beliefs like the polluting power of

women and then negating this power through God's power and the gift of His strength to men in the New Tribes Mission. This new contract between male converts and God undermined those traditional forms of deference to woman's bodies that once acted as a brake on overt forms of male violence in domestic relationships. Indeed, the most violent attacks on women that I heard of in the field involved New Tribes Mission followers. All social relationships map themselves onto bodies and space such that new forms of sociability also require new bodies and new forms of emplacement. The new Christian male body's relationship to women and space was no longer governed by the pollution beliefs of the past and the need to pay deference to the power of woman that was marked on the terrains she crossed. The traditional pollution beliefs surrounding women were a way of objectifying and spatializing women's power to create and a way of forcing men to acknowledge and go around the power embodied in women. The reemergence of a patriarchal God in the bush Kaliai area involved not only getting rid of all the female Christs whom Censure had placed in the landscape but also empowering men's bodies such that they no longer had to spatially acknowledge women's presence and power.

SUBVERSION FROM WITHIN

Despite its repression of traditional practices and beliefs, the New Tribes Mission has also selectively used traditional beliefs as the basis for incorporating itself into communities. Before the new mission came, the Catholic Church also had a policy of building its support around respecting and using tradition. Thus Catholic priests were encouraged to pray at village grave sites, for this would introduce villagers to God by blending church and indigenous understandings of the sacred. Along the Kaliai coast some Catholic churches are painted with traditional designs, and during Sunday services people sing hymns in the local languages of Lusi and Aria. Outside one Catholic church at Lavoure stands a carved post of a figure that is half snake and half human. It is Moro, whom coastal villagers see as their black Jesus who ran away from them (see photo on page 77).

Despite its seemingly intolerant Protestant fundamentalism, the New Tribes Mission has also adopted a certain logic of strategic incorporation that amounts to a logic of subversion from within. The new missionaries have used their mastery of the local language to get people's trust and to get across their fundamentalist message. Individual missionaries also seem to have used strategic lies to incorporate themselves into communities and into the cargo cult narratives that dominate many people's thoughts.

When they first arrived at Amcor, the new missionaries asked Mouk big men to come and tell their stories. Those who went gave Sign the story of the trickster god Titikolo, who is known for changing his name as he visits different communities. I was told how, when Mouk storytellers recited Titikolo's different names, Sign opened up his copy of the Bible and replied that these names could all be found in its pages (cf. Valentine 1955). Paul, the son of one of these respected storytellers, gave me his father's account of this meeting: "They [Mouk storytellers] told the story, and Sign said that all these names are here in the book [Bible]. [*Sign speaking:*] 'This story is true, the names of this man are here.' If they continued the story again but a different part, they were told: 'It is here, the name of this man is here.' If they storied again, whatever they called, all the different names, were said to be there. [*Sign speaking:*] 'The names are here!'" In 1986 another storyteller, Nangile, told me that Sign informed these storytellers that one name was missing from their story, and if they could provide this name, the new law would come. Nangile went on to tell me how he and his relatives would lie restlessly awake at night, trying hard to remember what name they might have lost.

On another occasion in 1986 at the village of Bolo I and others were told publicly by a man from the neighboring Lamogai area how an American missionary had held up a piece of cloth and informed Lamogai villagers that if they could name its creator, the law would break. These sorts of reported actions have confirmed to Catholics their belief that the new missionaries have been exploiting cargo cult beliefs and are secretly running a cargo cult themselves. Other information that I was given by Kaliai villagers was of a similar sort—that the new missionaries were actively trying to incorporate themselves into local narratives, including cargo cult narratives. I was told how the missionaries had even tried to insert themselves into the generative time of people's past. Paul told me of the time his father, Bowl, gave genealogies to Sign, who then informed Bowl that he (Sign) had been born at the same time as Bowl's ancestor, Ikoun.

> He [Sign] said what my *kandere* [maternal uncle] just said. He said: "Ah, Bowl, I think we two are the same *pisin* [moiety]—Matagel [a totem and clan of Big Bird]." . . . He spoke: "Do you know of the time they carried me?" Bowl answered: "No." He [Sign] then spoke: "No, you do, you know they carried me at the same time as they carried your grandfather. When they [the women] were pregnant with me, they were also pregnant with Ikoun. When they gave birth to Ikoun, they also gave birth to me." He said that the two of them were brothers.

[*Sign speaking:*] "Ikoun is my brother. You must not believe that I belong to this [present] time. No way, I belong to the true past."

Many who joined the new mission regarded Sign as one of their returned
ancestors, an association reinforced by the speed with which Sign learned
to speak the Mouk language. All this had the effect of indigenizing the
mission's power and to some extent subverting it, for the missionaries were
now used to validate and sustain the very world of the living dead that
people were told to forget. Indeed, as I mentioned earlier, when the missionaries first arrived, many people cried because they believed they recognized deceased relatives. Today some people see the missionaries as having
detailed knowledge about people's ancestors that the missionaries acquired from their Bible. Here people's memories of their past come to be
validated and shared with the memory spaces of the Bible, and this becomes people's way of incorporating the missionaries into the local kinship system. A number of Catholics accuse the missionaries of trying to
capture converts by incorporating people's kinship system into the Bible.
Two friends gave me the following account of how Sign went about collecting genealogies from their parents and relatives. "It is like this. If I follow
my story [genealogy] and go back and back to my *sting* [first ancestor], if
I come up to my sting and then go beyond it, I come up to Papa, God. It
is like this: if I storied and came up to my sting, then Sign would say: 'I
really think you know, for the names are here' [Sign points to the Bible].
    It is difficult to know to what extent people are reinterpreting their
interactions with Europeans to fit their desires and to what extent the
missionaries might be strategically seeking to colonize and incorporate
people's memories of the past into the Bible. My feeling is that both have
been happening recently in the Kaliai bush.
    The perception that Sign knew the names of the first Kaliai ancestors
has contributed to an understanding of him as physically close to God
and the origin of things. This is a perception that, villagers report, Sign
has encouraged in other ways. An old man told me that when he and
others went to tell their stories to Sign, he told them they should speak
the truth; Sign then pointed to three wires attached to his radio, claiming
that one wire went to America, the other to Australia, and the third to
God. The old man asked me whether Sign's claim was true, and he was
visibly shaken when I told him it was not.
    Initially, Sign audiotaped the stories of Mouk big men as a way of
getting their trust by showing interest and respect for their meanings.
These storytellers saw the narration of their stories as a gift that would

open up the white man's road to cargo (cf. Berndt 1962). Later some of these storytellers refused to story to me. They saw me as competing with Sign for the collection of stories and did not want me (because I am from Australia, the land of the bad whites) to get ahead of the mission from America that would deliver the cargo. The ironic thing is that, as discussed earlier, Sign later turned against these storytellers and reportedly told them that their stories were the lies of their ancestors whom Satan had tricked. Sign informed people that they were no longer to live with these stories and that they now had to go to the church and school he would be starting. He also warned Mouk villagers not to mix their cargo cult stories with his Bible classes.

Despite their public claims to the contrary, many converts have not really given up their cargo cult notions that Christ was one of their original ancestors and that he is still punishing them. They still expect him to return and forgive them. Many converts remain apprehensive about accepting the mission's view that Christ was a white man who did not originate in the Kaliai area. When no one was around, one convert told me, "God is not a white man, God is a black man. Our ancestors chased him away from us, and he went and worked your sit-down to come up all right." The American missionaries have been showing people videos of the Bible, and these have often contained a white person as Christ. New Tribes Mission converts have tried to reconcile these films with their cargo cult narratives by using various explanations of how color processing must have "washed away" the color black, leaving Christ looking like a white man.

THE MAGIC OF CRUCIFIXIONS

In addition to showing villagers videos of Adam and Eve, Moses, and Christ, the New Tribes Mission has tried to control the cargo cults and foster a "true" culture of Christianity by using dramatic plays to reenact biblical events such as the crucifixion of Jesus. Converts perform crucifixion rituals at Easter and also to mark the conversion of Catholic villages to the new mission. When the village of Moluo converted, a person was tied to a large wooden cross that was brought into the village to mark its turning away from sin and darkness to the world of light and knowledge. The teachers of the New Tribes Mission justify these new rituals as ways of implanting the messages of Christianity firmly in the minds of those who are unclear. Yet these rituals are also interpreted by some people through their memories of cargo cult rituals that were performed to bring back Christ and the dead. The miming of Christ's crucifixion, which was supposed to instill in a people a memory of what they owed to Christ, a memory of their debt to him, was often interpreted within another vision of mimesis: to reenact something was to capture its original power and presence. One convert told me, "This picture [crucifixion ritual] that they are all working here, it is a picture, but I think it will go to something true. But where will it come up, where? It came up to Jesus at that time, but I think they are still working it [the rituals] on your side [in the land of whites]."

When this ritual was performed each Easter between 1990 and 1994, converts informed their Catholic relatives that Christ would soon be coming, and they would urge their relatives to convert, lest they miss out on the cargo. The crucifixion rituals involved hoisting a man onto a wooden cross; around his neck was placed a plastic bag containing red plant dye said to symbolize Christ's blood. At the foot of the cross stood two women who represented the Virgin Mary and Mary Magdalene. A man would come and use a spear to pierce the bag. When the blood spilled out, the two women and the audience would cry for the blood that was washing away their sins. One convert explained why Sign had taught them this ritual: "Yes, he schooled us in following this. He schooled us in this so as to purge [raus] sin, to raus sin through this blood." This convert spoke of his Catholic brother-in-law as living in great darkness "for he did not see the picture of Jesus [i.e., the crucifixion ritual], so that this blood could go down and change him, so it could get rid of his sin." During one crucifixion ritual, an ex-convert told me, a spear was taken away from him and given to another man, because there was a fear that instead of piercing the bag, my informant might actually perform the crucifixion and spear the man on the cross. Other Mouk converts told me of the strong fear they had that this man might feel the need to kill Christ again to properly cleanse the Kaliai of the sins of their pagan past. In the Aria village of Robos a teacher in the New Tribes Mission told me that many new converts were frightened when they first saw this ritual because they were not sure whether they were going to perform a murder that would reenact the cleansing murder of Christ. New Tribes Mission followers have told me they expected something to come up through this ritual. It is unclear how people expected change to occur, but what is noticeable is that for many converts the underground begins to disappear as the realm that will remake them. Posingen described to me the claims of his relatives in the New Tribes Mission: "I want to talk about this picture [ritual], when they work at shooting Jesus. All the people believe it, and they talk like this, that this is not talk-picture [an allegory], that they are working something true, this is something true."

After this ritual was performed, many people cried. In particular, people cried for the blood that was now cleansing them but had not cleansed their close relatives and ancestors. One convert explained it to me:

> All these men who cry, its meaning is like this: they kill Jesus, and his blood is spilled and it goes down—his blood goes down and changes all those people down below [the congregation, audience], their bikhet, they all say "sin." They all kill Jesus, his blood is spilled, and it purges all the sin of all people. The picture [ritual] goes like that. All right, this blood of Jesus that is spilled, it washes all this line who have gone inside the New Tribes Mission. This picture of the blood of Jesus will purge their sin. Well, when this happens, everybody thinks plenty because they say, "The picture of Jesus, we have speared it, killed him, his blood has come down and changed me, and now when I die, I can go good on top to the hand of Papa. But my grandparents, my mother, my brother, they did not see the picture of Jesus, and they have gone to live in the fire." They cry over this.

The work of redemption here contains the pain of coming to be separated by one's salvation from the world of one's grandparents. Through these crucifixion rituals people explored emotionally the moral distancing of themselves from their grandparents. They suffered through the blood that washed them but had not washed their ancestors. The spatial separation of heaven from the world of the ancestors was a metaphor for a process of nonreconciliation with the cultural world of the past that the New Tribes Mission has inaugurated. Yet people's tears also marked their difficulties in living with these cleavages and especially with the idea of coming to be permanently alienated from the deceased relatives who loved and reared them. A number of converts have found it difficult to live without the comforting presence of the dead, and they have been secretly bringing their dead to come and reside with the Americans at Amcor.

LIVING WITH THE DEAD THROUGH PHOTOGRAPHS

Hyland's 1990 articles in the journal *Catalyst* made the case that a cargo cult was running within the services of the New Tribes Mission.[7] Mission representatives at Amcor denied this (Brunn and Zook 1990) and claimed to have successfully substituted Christianity for syncretism. In fact, this was not the case. For many converts the new mission has become the focus of their clandestine relationships with the dead. One Catholic told me how his close relatives in the New Tribes Mission had claimed that converts who died would sometimes come back and reside in the houses of the American missionaries, where they would eat Western food, like rice:

> They [New Tribes Mission relatives] spoke about this poor fellow who just died, and they were crying over him and said that he had already come up to David [an American missionary at Amcor]. They said to me: "Why are you crying? This man has come back, and he is eating rice here [in David's house]." This is the talk of all of them. . . . This talk, I heard them talking it, and I said to them: "That's all right, I just want one of them [the dead] to come up to me so I can see him, and then I will come inside." They said: "He has come up, and he was given food. David gave food to him. He then put aside the plate and left."

Some converts believe that their dead relatives live inside Sign's house. Sign rarely allows villagers to come inside his house, and this has helped generate a sense of mystique around it. The house contains photos of people who have died, which has confirmed people's understanding of this as a space belonging to the dead. Photos and representations are referred to by the word **ano,** which is the same word people use for soul. I was given the following explanation of how the missionaries' photographs had captured people's souls:

> When they are around, Sign takes their photo. Later, it comes up as a picture, which looks like them. They [relatives in the New Tribes Mission] look at the picture and think that all the people who have died have come back here. . . . When they walk about, they get their picture taken. Like when she [a woman who was flown to a hospital but later died] was sick, they [the missionaries] photographed her. When she was brought to the plane, they photographed her. When she was about to die, they photographed her. When she died, they worked her picture [photo] to come up. Now they think that this woman who died has now come back here. They all think whites have a way of "stealing [capturing] you and me through photos." When they get us on a photo, they have a way of changing, of turning it, so that when I die they get my ano [soul] to live, but my body remains behind.

I was told that when this woman died, Sign told people: "You can go bury her, but she has already come to live with me." Unsure, I asked people where she was living, and they replied: "She lives with Sign himself at Amcor. She lives inside Sign's house." Converts told their Catholic relatives: "She does, and so do plenty of [dead] men and plenty of [dead] women. This old man Ikoun also lives with Sign inside the house." When Catholics started crying for the dead woman, their New Tribes Mission relatives said they should not do so, for she was already living with Sign: "Youse do not know, but we [converts] know. She is there. You are sorry for her and cry, but we worry only for the time she acquired food and she gave it to us, and we think about her and cry only a little. But you do not know [about death], so you cry a lot over this worry. You do not know about the *as* [hidden cause] of this."

Some New Tribes Mission converts speak of a taboo about entering a room at Amcor mission in which all the souls of the dead live. Catholic relatives were told: "This room is truly taboo. We can hear them talking, but we cannot see them." Through photographs Europeans have captured people's memories of the dead as well as the cargo cult culture involving the dead that now is focused on Sign. Converts claim Sign invites them to come and hear the dead talk: "When they [the dead] want to talk, Sign will say: 'You all come, you all come, and hear the men who are going to talk. The old man Ikoun will come to speak, the wife of so and so will come and talk, the wife of Argus will come and talk.'"

Martin, a teacher in the new mission, told his brother in the Catholic Church how he had attended this gathering of the dead, but too many dead people were gathered there so he was unable to hear them clearly. However, he did hear one of them say, "We want you to get all our line so that they can see us and we can see them." One person told me that what people had heard played back were audiotapes of deceased relatives: "They record the voices of all people, play it, everyone hears it and thinks that it is the talk of all the dead speaking now." What I find interesting is the way people's presence is captured and reproduced through European technology, and this is reappropriated by the bush Kaliai to reproduce the living souls of their dead. The traditional understanding of a representation that captures and participates in the reality to which it refers was clandestinely practiced inside the New Tribes Mission to refigure all its recorded images involving the dead.

In the houses of the missionaries, posters and pictures of biblical heroes like Jesus, Moses, and Jacob have also been interpreted as representations of dead relatives. I was told of a mechanical humanlike contraption inside Sign's house that people alternately interpreted as Jesus or as one of the dead. These interpretations of Western cultural artifacts keep alive the

Kaliai dead; people merge their deceased relatives with the icons and representations of power held by whites. The Bible and its mediation by the American missionaries transformed the spaces they inhabited into domains of power that could be appropriated and joined to the living world of dead relatives.

My feeling is that people also transferred the land of heaven to the houses and buildings of the Americans at Amcor. When the missionaries told people not to cry for a dead person, for that person was now alive in a good place—namely, heaven—this was interpreted to mean that the missionaries had personal knowledge of the whereabouts of the recently deceased, that they had seen him or her and for this reason could speak so knowledgeably of the dead person's whereabouts and state of existence. Villagers even speculated that the missionaries had helped give the deceased their new good life. One of my respected Catholic informants told me:

> In terms of my thinking, they [converts] are not talking true. I think
> it is like this: Sign worked this church to go down, and he revealed all
> kinds of thinking to come up to them all. Well, now they have put all
> this talk inside with this thinking of theirs, when they say that "a man
> who dies will come back again. If you and me die, we will come up to
> him [Sign]. If we die, we will come up to him, and later we will go in
> there, in this room [a secret taboo room in Sign's house]. We will go to
> Sign first, and he will speak to us." It was like this with this child of
> Ivan's, who died just now. . . . They say he came up to Sign. Ivan was
> working at being sorry over this child of his, and Sign said to him:
> "What are you sorry for? This person [the deceased child] has come
> and is living here. This man is sitting down here. You cannot worry,
> your stomach can no longer be no good over this child of yours. He
> has come to live in a good place, so leave it. You must go and work
> and be happy." Well, now, Ivan no longer worried. He was happy over
> his child. He said to me: "Your nephew [the deceased child], we went
> and ran into him, and he is there."

I see people, all people, as distorting the world to fit their desires and that this is just as true for the missionaries as for the bush Kaliai. Underpinning people's distortions of the talk of the missionaries was a strong desire by bush Kaliai villagers for an accessible form of heaven so they could keep the dead close to them. Although death has been increasingly Christianized by the New Tribes Mission, people have clandestinely sought to displace their desired world of the dead into their most concrete visible

symbol of utopia, the houses of the missionaries. This has partly worked
to deify the missionaries and the European cultural world they have created around themselves. It has also had the effect of regrounding the space
of death in a concrete locality to prevent it from coming to be formed
exclusively into a transcendental heaven that would radically separate the
living and the dead.

THE NEW GODS ON EARTH

To a large extent, converts to the New Tribes Mission live out their identities through amplifying the power of the mission that has incorporated
them. They have started to deify the new missionaries, and one form this
has taken is to make the missionaries participate in those notions of a
punishing God that the missionaries have been promulgating. In the early
1990s a storm destroyed many houses at the coastal village of Kandoka,
and two women were killed by lightning. Converts told their Catholic relatives that the American missionary Sign had destroyed Kandoka and that
this was the punishment he exacted because Kandoka did not join his
mission, although it had indicated an interest in so doing. What made the
moral position of Kandoka villagers worse was that they gave the pretext
of having traditional custom work as their reason for not joining. It was
explained to me:

> When Kandoka was destroyed, they [New Tribes Mission converts]
> all said it was because Kandoka had deceived Sign to go down there,
> but when he went down, they changed their talk and did not go inside
> the church. All right, Sign then made it so that a tide came up and de-
> stroyed Kandoka, broke all their houses. . . . The reason was that all
> Kandoka said they would go inside this church, but they were deceiv-
> ing Sign. He went down with a huge line, they all went down, and then
> they [Kandoka] changed their talk and said: "Forget about it. Youse go
> back, we have big custom work, the work of our ancestors." So Sign
> went back, then Sign went down a second time. The third time he did
> not go down, all his line went. It was when they came back, that it hap-
> pened—the tide came up. They all say Sign worked it.

Here people amplify their self-righteousness and self-importance by amplifying the power of the white men who have incorporated them. People
identify with their masters, deifying their masters as a way of celebrating
the new personal forms of power that have captured and transformed
them. The missionaries are here experienced as omnipotent and as taking

on the vengeful personality of the God they preach. The developed coast, with its preference for tradition and its reputation for drinking, theft, and sexual immorality, comes to be punished for rejecting the project of moral reform. This narrative replays the story of Katika (see Chapter 1). Katika tried to get the Kaliai to come to his church, and when they rejected his moral school, he punished the Kaliai by running away to America. Sign has taken the symbolic place of Katika; he is seen as bringing back the moral knowledge that the Kaliai originally rejected. The fear of not re- peating the pigheadedness and sins of their ancestors was why converts were initially very strict about attending church services every morning and afternoon. Today the cult has declined in intensity; services are held about three times a week, and some members miss even these.

For at least the last fifty years people have been reared on the cargo cult story of how they had originally possessed God, His knowledge, and the white man's lifestyle. Their crime was their refusal to listen and to subordinate themselves to the moral requirements and discipline of His church, and so He took His knowledge to strangers. When Samaga and Septireh gave me their version of this story, they told me that Titikolo was this original teacher and that he caused a flood to destroy the huge men's house in which everyone had then lived. Samaga and Septireh also told me how the iron and cement remnants of this building could still be found at the headwaters of the Aria River:

> They say that he worked a church, and he asked all the people to
> come to it, but all the people were bikhet. It was here, where I spoke
> about before [the headwaters of the Aria River]. They were bikhet
> there, in this area, where the cement and iron can now be found. He
> came from there to here [Kaliai area], and he then went to youse
> [whites] and worked a school in America. Later he put a school in En-
> gland and then in Australia.

People's adoption of the evangelical message of the New Tribes Mission was made possible because villagers had already internalized cargo cult narratives of the moral and material consequences of their original rejec- tion of God's word. People embraced the new mission's project of moral reformation as a project involving their welcoming and loving the desire to be changed, even if, and perhaps because, this also involved one's subju- gation. This desire to be dominated is what Foucault referred to as "the fascism in us all, in our heads and in our everyday behaviour, the fascism that causes us to love power, to desire the very thing that dominates and exploits us" (1982a, xiii). I believe Melanesian history has to be approached through what Foucault called a "genealogy of problems, of *prob-lematiques*" (1984, 343; 1982b), and this would be a history of the different ways the self has been problematized. We are dealing with modes of sub-jection in which the domination of subjects emerges from the way they are ethically positioned in relationship to themselves. The asceticism and puritanism of the New Tribes Mission represents the emergence of new forms of self-scrutiny and an intensification of that civilizing project that saw itself as pacifying and subduing a traditional culture of violence. With respect to Europe, Foucault has analyzed the history of the different modes of objectification through which human beings are produced as subjects. He has explored how those processes of objectification often work to divide individuals from themselves and from others (Foucault 1982b, 778). I have sought to analyze how changes in the narrative struc-tures of mission discourse have worked to appropriate and ethically repo-sition bush Kaliai people's relationships to themselves and to others.

All relationships are mediated through the forms of objectification pro-vided by narrative. The coming of Western processes of Christianization, pacification, and development has changed the narrative frameworks within which individuals conceive of themselves and others. The objectifi-cation of subjects within the New Tribes Mission discourse of sin con-firmed relationships of self-alienation and self-hatred that previous forms of Christianity had established and that had been localized and internal-ized into cargo cult pedagogic practices. Indeed, the New Tribes Mission has been feeding off those structures of self-alienation that previous forms of Christianity had internalized in Kaliai subjects, who in turn had repro-duced those forms of self-hatred and self-castigation in the redemptive moral projects of their cargo cults. The reproduction of pastoral care and responsibility over a congregation requires that a congregation read itself as sinful and in need of the redeeming care of a teacher. Earlier, I argued that Kaliai cargo cults took over this Christian technique for producing the desire for pastoral care. The Kaliai also obtain a strange sort of plea-sure in reproducing these "dividing practices" that offer to help people escape the world of darkness and enter a new world of light. Even as Christianity condemns people, it establishes its seductive capturing power over them by promising to heal the very alienation it produces in them.

DEVELOPMENT, CHRISTIANITY, AND REGIONAL FORMS OF NATIONALISM

Part of the New Tribes Mission's success has come about because, like Kaliai cargo cults, it has created a new regional ethnic form of nationalism from the project of moral redemption. In particular, the translation of the Bible into the local languages of Aria and Mouk has introduced a sacred dimension into those languages and into the classrooms where villagers learned to read and write Mouk and Aria. Before the mission arrived at Amcor, coastal villages had monopolized church and state educational resources. Coastal villagers provided the pupils who went to high school to become politicians, public servants, businesspeople, and artisans. The new mission's Bible and literacy classes gave the Mouk a new form of pride and even gave rise to claims that the Mouk would now become the missionaries who would morally transform the whole of Papua New Guinea. Some people even claimed that the Mouk would be sent to the land of whites to convert the Europeans who did not believe in God. Many young men who were appointed teachers in the New Tribes Mission were sons of cargo cult leaders, and wherever they went they tried to stamp out everything to do with tradition. In addition to capturing nearly all the Kaliai bush, these young teachers traveled to the south coast of West New Britain to convert people from the Catholic Church and to the new mission. Although the New Tribes Mission likes to present the bush Kaliai as never having been literate in any language, the young men who became its teachers had attended community schools at Bagai, Bolo, and Salke. These young men have used the authority conferred by their knowledge of the Bible to displace the old men of tradition from leadership positions. Today the teachers of the New Tribes Mission mediate disputes in villages, plan activities, and provide moral guidance.

The New Tribes Mission transformed the absent god of the Kaliai into an absence inside people's souls that came from not sufficiently knowing and believing in God's power. By knowing God through the familiarity of their language, the joy of His plenitude would fill people up. This spiritual joy in redemption has come to be fused with people's pride in the new regional forms of ethnic identity to which the new mission has given rise. Ceremonial exchanges, new marriages, and everyday contact with Catholic Anem, Lusi, and Kombei villagers have been denounced as having contact with people of darkness.

A new regional identity has emerged around the new mission; it maps its boundaries by denouncing the Catholic Church and the government for not having sufficiently transformed the bush Kaliai into moral subjects. Here resistance takes the paradoxical form of criticizing the state and Catholic Church for failing to change the bush Kaliai into Europeans. Many parents, who had sent their children to community schools at Bolo and Bagai, pulled them out once the family converted to the new mission, claiming that these were the false (*giaman*) schools of the government and

Catholic Church from which nothing would come. The bush Kaliai used the new mission as an opportunity to create a new identity that affirmed its resistance to previous controls over people's lives that were experienced as having delivered nothing. As discussed earlier, some villagers, like those at Salke, rejected participation in development projects, and they abandoned their coconut and cocoa groves to live farther inland, away from the close scrutiny of government officials on the coast. When development officers for the proposed Kandrian-Gloucester project came to Bagai, one convert held up his Bible and told them this was to be their food (kaikai) and not business. In short, contrary to its desires, the mission was hijacked by people to sustain a millenarian project that used religion to resist community schools, the Catholic Church, the state, and development projects.

Although the European missionaries have been encouraging the establishment of stores, New Tribes Mission followers have used the authority of their renewed Christianity to resist full participation in the market economy. Those who have established stores have been accused of charging high prices that will damage their afterlife. I was given the following account of how converts reacted to one member who charged prices higher than other storekeepers: "All the men spoke that this man who works a store will later feel it in heaven, for he is stealing money." People were angry that this storekeeper charged two kina for rice instead of the usual one kina. Many converts spoke of money as something belonging to Satan, for it led people to forget God. I was told: "This person is no longer thinking about the work of Jesus; he has lost thinking over this, and he is working something according to his own wishes. Later he will feel it." People complained to this storekeeper in these terms: "This store, you must work it so that it goes to the church. We do not sit down with the customs of the past so that you can work it as you are. This is something belonging to the ground, it is not something that will help you go to heaven; money will not help you go to heaven."

The new missionaries have advised people about how to run stores and what prices they should charge. On their advice all the stores at Angal and at Popmu had notices that no credit was allowed. This caused much division, with those opposing the notices saying: "We are not whites that we should write a notice which says that this store offers no credit. We are not whites—whites follow their own laws, and we of Papua New Guinea have to follow that belonging to us, we have to follow our custom." One New Tribes Mission convert, who did allow credit at his store, gave this moral justification for his generous actions: "Boys, this is something belonging to the ground, it is not something true, it is not something you could carry up to heaven; when you die, it just disappears."

People are trying to find new, more moral forms of commerce, that is, a way of engaging themselves as moral subjects in the new relationships brought by business. The new evangelical emphasis that the Mouk should focus on the righteous road leading to their death has been used to undercut attempts by the missionaries to further incorporate people into capitalist exchange relations. The missionaries have introduced goats, ducks, and fish, and these have been taken up by people not for commerce but for subsistence purposes. Villagers have also been reluctant to grow and sell cash crops like cardamom, which the missionaries have been pushing. The pursuit of money and the commercialization of one's existence is something people oppose as satanic (cf. Taussig 1980). In 1994 one convert told me how the government wanted to keep out all the good whites and let in just the businesspeople. I was also told that only the word of God, given in the true language of the Mouk, would create the new existence of whites:

> Youse [Europeans] came and schooled us, and some of youse do believe and do work for the Last Day to come and for Jesus to come up. However, we look at your laws, those that are worked in books, and you say that these laws of yours will make our sit-down as good as your sit-down. However, the law of God says that He alone will school us with the laws belonging to us. He will school us in our true language so that we can win. He will come and give these laws to us, He will give us our church, Jesus himself will come and give it to us, and only then will we win the sit-down which youse have. However, with your laws we are not enough to win them, nothing will come from that. We will work it and work it, and it will just go on like that. . . . It is like this: all the true laws belonging to us, Jesus will come down and give it to us in our language and with our church, and then we will win. We will then be able to win in business, in the knowledge for working business. We will then be able to win it, and we will have the same customs as you whites. Our existence will be the same.
>
> But through your laws this will not come about. You look at this Bible of ours that the New Tribes Mission works at schooling us in. They say: "This is your Bible, this is your language, and you will now be able to work business." But no, all these people who have tried these business have not been able to win. They have been able to win small pieces of money, but the sit-down that you have, no way! It's too hard. It's because of the talk of your government: "Papua New Guinea is to stop underneath, it is to stop underneath the government of Australia." It is like this: we are like rubbish, your government says that we are rubbish.

Here we can see that the Mouk embraced the New Tribes Mission because they saw it as delivering to them their own lotu (church), something
that the cargo cults had also been struggling to develop with their notions
of a black Christ, Jesus as a woman, and Noah and Moses as Kaliai ancestors. The resistance of New Tribes Mission converts to development, the
Papua New Guinea state, and Australian colonialism has come to be
phrased in the same Christian language of the Last Day and Christ's return that was central to earlier bush Kaliai cargo cults. This overlapping
use of the same concepts by mission and cargo cults has produced the
ambiguous situation in which people resist through their further incorporation in, and allegiance to, Christian messages that are made to resonate
with all sorts of underground connotations.

INDIVIDUATION AND THE NEW TRIBES MISSION

As in bush Kaliai cargo cults, some converts to the New Tribes Mission
cult experimented with sociability and identity. One initial form was an
attempt to abolish the matrilineal moiety system and to move more fully
toward European patrilineal forms of identification. The missionaries
have contributed to this process of social experimentation by seeking to
abolish the strict avoidance taboos governing relationships between in-
laws. I was told how on one occasion Sign urged someone not to be embarrassed and to call the name of his *tambu* (in-law). This informant went on
to equate these practices with the way converts now practiced European
forms of etiquette, such as knocking on doors before entering and asking
politely to use something before taking it:

> I do not know about you [whites], but we have our tambu [in-law].
> My wife's sister is my tambu. I cannot call her name. But Sign has
> come and abolished this. This goes now to the side of white-skins. If
> someone goes to someone else's door, they knock. This goes to the cus-
> tom of white-skins. If there is a saucepan, and it is outside, you can
> take it only if you ask. When they [relatives in the New Tribes Mission]
> told me about this, I told them they took some customs from the
> church and some from the customs of white-skins.

We see here European ceremonial customs of respect coming to assume
sacred—indeed, biblical—proportions. People saw European forms of etiquette as the new moral law that would reform and remake them. Adopting European etiquette was seen as adopting new forms of moral discipline and understandings about property that would allow people to

escape the corrupt familiarity of the pagan past. The new rules instituted by teachers in the New Tribes Mission included the rule that only a person who owned a garden could get food from it to give to a visitor. Converts came to assert more individualized forms of property as preferable to the immoral license and familiarity of traditional kinship relations. Since 1994 these rules have not been followed to the same strict letter as they were previously. Today Catholic relatives point to this as a sign that the New Tribes Mission cult is declining. They also point out that converts often now swear and sing out to relatives to go to gardens to pick food for themselves. I was told:

> Before, I could not go get taro from someone else's garden; only the person who owned that garden could go get it and give it to me. Now, at this time, people are starting to give up this talk of theirs. Now they sing out and say: "Go get the taro from the garden." And they will go and get it. This promise of theirs which they first worked has been given up. Before, only if you climbed your coconuts and brought them down and gave them to me could I eat them. However, now they will tell you to climb these coconuts and eat them, but often they are not even their coconuts.

During one intense phase in the early 1990s followers of the New Tribes Mission tried to abolish bride prices.[8] This was resisted by many mothers and fathers who demanded some compensation for rearing their daughters. The compensation they received often took the form of secondhand European goods like plates, clothes, and trousers, or a token bride price of ten kina. In 1990 the villagers of Moluo gave me the names of ten girls who had been married for ten kina, and villagers complained bitterly that this did not compensate relatives other than the parents. On the coast Catholics related to New Tribes Mission converts told me of their anger— when one of their daughters married, they shared the bride price with relatives in the New Tribes Mission, but these relatives gave back nothing when their daughters married. Numerous complaints to government officials led New Tribes Mission followers to go back to the official bride price of fifty kina, which was set by the local council government. I was told that Sign used the story of Adam and Eve in the following way to get rid of bride price payments:

> Our customs for working children to go inside the men's house and for working shell money to buy women, all these things, these are sin. . . . He [Sign] alone would denounce [kros] these customs. He

would go back to the beginning of us all, our origins from Papa, from
Adam and Eve. He would say: "With Adam and Eve it was not the
case that some man purchased the child of another man. No! God
alone worked them." He says that we must follow this. If we buy a
woman with lots of shell money, then this is sin.

[*Another man interjects:*] He says we are stealing, stealing something
belonging to another man. This man uses this talk, and it is not
straight in my thinking. I worked this talk that we spoke about earlier,
about the pain of the mother, and I say: "Did God look after this child
and make it big? True, he gave it, but looking after it is a lot of trouble.
When you are small, you urinate on your mother, you urinate on her
skin, you urinate on her clothes, you defecate all over her skin, and it is
the same with your father. The two look after you when you are sick
and you come up big."

New Tribes Mission followers have also developed new marriage customs such as writing letters to parents asking for a bride. If a parent refuses, those requesting a bride might refer to God as the true Creator of
the child and ask the parents: "Is this your child that you can block and
tie her up?" I was also told that Sign frowned on women in the new mission who married Catholic men: "It would be all right for women of darkness [Catholics] to marry into the New Tribes Mission because they would
join the church, but it would not be good for a New Tribes Mission woman
to marry a man of darkness. No, this woman must pull the man to come
inside the church. If a man of darkness marries a New Tribes Mission
woman, then she must pull him in so that he begins to be schooled."

It is hard to know whether Sign is actually making these rules or
whether his deification leads converts to refer to and sanction all rules as
coming from him. However, it is also impossible to live in the Kaliai area
without running across these new rules. My feeling is that Sign knows
about the new rules, and he turns a sanctioning blind eye to them and
even encourages them. Today those who criticize the new missionaries do
so partly because, like earlier Kaliai cargo cults, they too have been claiming that Jesus is coming back, and yet he has failed to materialize thus far.
In 1995 Sign and some villagers at Amcor became involved in a big dispute. The villagers angrily told him that he had been lying to them about
Christ's coming and that they had waited patiently long enough. Some
people's anger is especially directed at the culture of sin and guilt that the
missionaries have developed around them. One Catholic villager denounced Sign in the following terms:

This man is a liar. He has taught everybody to see everything as sinful. He says that the food belonging to us, of Papua New Guinea, has sin, that it is the food of Satan. Manioca, taro, and sweet potato is all the food of Satan. I think Sign is working a cargo cult. If someone later comes and asks him about certain talk, he will say: "I do not know about this, it is everybody else saying it." But he is lying, there is no one standing behind him who would work this talk.

CHRISTIAN HEGEMONY AND WHAT IT MEANS TO EAT OFF ONE'S HOST

In this chapter I have explored how people internalized and reworked the coercive moral rhetoric of the New Tribes Mission. I argued that early cargo cult appropriations of Christianity, which were focused on a punishing God, came to be revoiced by the new mission, which reempowered these cargo cult messages of punishment in ways that allowed the new mission's message to be again reappropriated into new cargo cult voices.

People's cultural domination is created out of such two-way borrowings. It is made up of mobile parasitical relationships in which parasite and host often swap places in quite complicated, roundabout ways. Here it is not just a question of the host's (New Tribes Mission's) drinking the parasite's (cargo cults') blood but also, in the process of doing so, drinking back its own blood (Christian doctrine), which had originally been internalized into the parasite (cargo cult). The blood of Christian doctrine comes to circulate and form some unusual economies of meaning. The New Tribes Mission has fed and grown off cargo interpretations and expectations of itself, whereas the cargo cults have tried to feed covertly from the millenarianism of the new mission—its talk about the Last Day and Christ's return—that the cults have assimilated to their millenarian pastoral projects. Today, when the cargo cults drink from the New Tribes Mission, they do so not just in a simple direct way but partly through the process of the new mission's having been set up as secretly recognizing and sanctioning the cargo cult messages of the past. In this scene of exchange there are multiple refamiliarizations with oneself through the medium of the other.

I have been arguing that the new mission was made to voice cargo cult appropriations of Christianity in a way that allowed the mission to also appropriate the cargo cults. I see the present structure of hegemonic relationships as made up of relations of mutual appropriation in which host and parasite feed off each other's appropriations but also feed off each other's appropriations of each other's appropriations. The metaphor of host and parasite has certain advantages in terms of grasping the shifting flows of this interpenetration of self and other. However, this is also a specular relationship in which identity emerges not simply through the mirror of the other but also through appropriating and mirroring back the other's appropriations and mirrorings of oneself. There is a struggle to repossess and control the mirroring terms that mediate the specular relationship that makes identity possible. Mirrors come to be caught within mirrors, echoes within echoes, producing forms of epistemic murk in which it becomes difficult to discover where the official voices of European missions end and those of local Christianity begin (Taussig 1987). Both pleasure and anguish exist in the resulting ambiguities and instabilities of meaning. Villagers insert their desires and personhood into that specular relationship of domination provided by the gaze of Europeans, and in doing so they remake the meaning of the gaze of whiteness that judges and creates them.

Throughout this book I have explored how cargo cults took on the role of producing a new sort of society that had internalized the white man's norms and his cargo. This process of reproducing oneself as white was often mediated by white spirit children, or ancestors who had turned white, or cargo cult leaders who mimed Europeans. What has happened in the contemporary context is that the American missionaries have used the fires of hell to try to reestablish Western control over the world of the dead and over those spaces of alterity that mediate the transformative mimetic labor of repositioning oneself, the world, and the process of becoming white. However, not everyone has been happy with this loss of control over the empowering spaces that position identity, the past, future, and present. I know of two shamans in the Kaliai bush who recently claimed to have traveled to hell and who came back denying the presence of any incinerating fires there. One shaman claimed that all the talk about Satan's fire was really referring to fires inside volcanoes and that volcanoes were really doors to the dead. The other shaman came back declaring that what people were referring to as a fire was really the welding sparks of a giant shipyard where those who had committed sin were sentenced to hard labor. These shamans sought to put out the fires of hell by transforming them into other domains of meaning that kept alive the laboring world of the dead. These shaman can also be seen as struggling against the recentralization in European hands of forms of pastoral power, which the fires of hell were helping to accomplish. The politics of space that these shamans were waging represented opposition to a particular coercive technology of social control, which was taking over the terrains of a black theology.

These two shamans are, however, the exception; many converts have gone further down the road of Christianization. Some converts now deny traditional stories of people being captured by the dead or having their souls stolen by masalai, claiming instead that Satan really did these things. It was he who caused a certain woman to fall into an underground village, and it is he who today captures the souls of children when they become sick. The objectification of evil, which traditionally took the form of the world of the dead and masalai, is Christianized here; instead of getting a shaman to dream that he is rescuing a person's soul, converts now pray to God to get Satan to release the person he has captured. The personification of evil in traditional culture comes to be displaced and colonized by the personification of evil in Christianity. The struggles between the shaman and the ghosts of the dead, tambarans, tewel, and masalai come to be assimilated to the struggle between God and Satan. The hegemonic power of the New Tribes Mission has come from the reality it accords evil. Rather than denying its objectivity, it refetishizes and reobjectifies it. In doing so the new mission transforms the struggle against the past into a demonic struggle to embrace the saving power of God. Here traditional topographies and figures of evil (focused on masalai places, waterfalls, mountains, and graves) come to be displaced and personified in the figure of Satan, whose dwelling place of hell starts to collapse and deny the specificity of the localities of tradition. A certain deterritorialization of people and memory is occurring as villagers become incorporated into the orthodox imaginary topographies that belong to Europeans. The attempt to localize Christian topographies and biblical heroes is what the scorching fires of hell are policing.

Throughout this book I have been analyzing the cultural incorporation of processes of cultural incorporation. I have focused on the alternative forms of emplacement offered by tradition and the dead that hold out the promise of inserting an improper place into the dominant culture and its forms of emplacement. In the case of the New Tribes Mission we are dealing with camouflaged forms of allegiance that hide people's transgressions; we are dealing with the forms of euphemism that people develop to conceal and articulate an alternative world of meaning within the dominant culture. Here people embrace the task of othering themselves, of remaking themselves, but they also seek some control over this process by secretly making this othering process something other than itself. The civilizing process of becoming white comes to be recast and rendered livable by making it into a process that the dead can also secretly inhabit. We are dealing here with those artful forms of double reading that allow people to simulate compliance while reusing the dominant culture for other ends. Cargo cult followers insert themselves and their desires into a borrowed culture that they poach, transform, and combine with their traditional culture to make the dominant culture into a space that not only they but their dead can inhabit. Indeed, the Kaliai have thus far been able to find a livable space for themselves in Western culture only by first finding a livable space for their dead. It is the dead who socialize and make livable the borrowed worlds of white-skins with their transformational pedagogic practices. People reinvent the civilizing process by making it partly their own, and this is part of their project of making themselves at home in a context in which their identities and their world have both been severely problematized.

Yet home and self-possession also require travel; they can be achieved only through the detour of problematization, and these narratives of travel, self-alienation, and self-possession are reinvented in cargo cults. The process of coming back to oneself, the exterior terrains, the mirror structures that make journeys of self-discovery and self-transformation possible are continuously reworked in extremely ambiguous pastoral practices of caring for the self. The hybrid character of these practices of self-formation means that their political and historical effects are by no means obvious or singular. Certain levels of complicity and resistance, dependence and autonomy, reside together in complex struggles to become white that also reinvent the meaning of whiteness in the process of assimilating it to oneself. In all of this there is often a certain objectification of self and community through the new value structures provided by commodities and the moral meaning of whiteness. Both cargo and white skins become part of people's moral revaluing and rethinking of place, the past, the dead, and themselves. These new forms of objectification create new forms of mirroring that merge with those traditional forms of mirroring that were located in the dead, in double-skinned bodies, and in underground geographies. We are also dealing here with the creation of new histories through the creation of new geographies, through the project of inventing, crossing, and tying together new spaces. The contested nature of space is a contesting of history, for what is history if not these narratives that join together divided terrains, identities, and categories? The terrains are ways of spatializing, objectifying, and reuniting the categories of sociability.

It was not simply whites who brought to Melanesia processes of self-alienation, for these were also an element in traditional stories of a masalai, sorcerer, or tewel's stealing a person's soul. Christianity, with its images and narratives of the Fall, sin, and the devil, brought new forms of self-estrangement, of not being at home with oneself. Cargo cults poached upon and reinvented these Christian narratives and images of not being at home in the world as part of the appropriation and reinvention of pastoral practices of self-possession and self-formation. The struggle to occupy a place can take place only through a simultaneous struggle to occupy all that is out of place, for there is no place without a sense of what is out of place. The struggle for utopia is a struggle for the emplacing quality of the out of place. If people were and are still attracted to the New Tribes Mission, it is because it offers powerful forms of self-estrangement that also promise powerful forms of self-possession. The secret struggle here is to possess oneself through the alienating techniques of others, which one secretly makes into vehicles for repossessing the dead and oneself through the dead.

Notes
Glossary
Bibliography
Index

Notes

PREFACE

1. In this book when they are first mentioned in a chapter, I have used italics for Pisin words and boldface for native Kaliai terms belonging to Mouk and Aria. Some frequently used Pisin terms, such as *masalai, tambaran,* and *tumbuan,* I have treated as English terms that have become part of the specialized vocabulary of Melanesian ethnography.

2. Villagers at Aikon, Doko Sagra, Onamanga, and Salke were initially too scared to tell me anything about the dead, claiming that they did not know or had forgotten what their grandparents had said. My experience of fieldwork is that knowledge comes only from within a relationship that you develop with people. The more you know, the more people tell you; here knowledge also is a mechanism of social incorporation. The disclosure of information was often phrased as a gift that was more and more forthcoming when villagers saw that I had no intention of denouncing them or making fun of their stories and when they saw that I had demonstrated my commitment to communities by returning to them.

INTRODUCTION

1. Kaliai villagers constantly use the *Pisin* terms *waitskin* (white-skin) and *blak-skin* (black-skin). Along with their English equivalents, I also use these terms to capture people's perceptions of present relationships as grounded in bodily differences.

2. Satan was also sometimes revalued by cargo cults to become the alternative god of Melanesians who stood opposed to the god of white men (Lawrence 1964; Worsley 1957, 32, 111–13; cf. Taussig 1980). Although Satan was not taken up by bush Kaliai cargo cults, some coastal villagers see their trickster god, Titikolo, as the bad god of Papua New Guinea who might nevertheless return to help them. There is a history of the devil and of trickery in Melanesia that remains to be written and that would be partly a history of a politics of inversion. In some places Hitler, Germany, and the Japanese were embraced in a similar way (M. Mead 1966, 191; Valentine 1955; cf. Kaplan 1995). Some of the Batari cult's military commands were spoken in German, which supports Worsley's point that German could be "favoured as an anti-Government tongue" (1957, 98).

319

3. Father Janssen described Kaliai villager's grasp of Christianity like this:

> Lotu [church] is a *lo* [law], i.e. a powerful secret, which is only known in various degrees to the Holy Father, the bishops, the priests and perhaps also to some catechists. But these men do not reveal the secret, they use only pictures when they talk about God, grace and the last day. In this present cult [Censure's] movement there were even rumours, that the bishop had told the newly trained catechists, not to tell everything which they had learned. (1970, 17)

Janssen claimed that Catholic Church notions of the mystery of the sacrament and God's grace were merged with cargo cult notions that the church hid its meanings and that the church used *tok piksa* [talk-picture; allegorical talk] to disguise its real truths. Janssen saw this as a confusion:

> It is very difficult for the people to convert themselves from magic to Christian beliefs. It is hard for them to understand, that Christianity (God, grace, last day) is not a secret, that could be revealed, but a mystery that underlies human existence, that should motivate man's personal and social behavior, and that will bring human fulfilment only in connection with secular activities, not always on earth, but, as Christian hope expects, at a time afterwards, at a day and in a way only mysteriously indicated in the sacred scriptures. (1970, 18)

Janssen's subtle distinctions here are far from clear, and in the field such explanations would have only reinforced cargo cult hermeneutic practices focused on the church's secret, underground meanings.

4. When I asked Censure's family whether the English word *censure* was part of Censure's name, they seized upon it as the right meaning, although they had been unaware of it. They claimed that Censure was probably aware of it, for he was said to know English even though he didn't.

CHAPTER 1. TRADITIONAL BUSH KALIAI SOCIETY AND
THE ARRIVAL OF *OL WAITSKIN*

1. The following figures from patrol reports in 1973 give some idea of the different degrees of incorporation into cash crops at the time of Censure's cult. The six coastal villages of Gilau, Kandoka, Ketenge, Lauvore, Pureling, and Taveliai had planted a total of 59,529 coconut trees, while the bush villages of Aikon, Angal, Bagai, Benim, Gigina and Moluo had planted only 6,664. Whereas Kandoka had 12,977 coconut trees, Benim had 187 and Gigina 260.

2. A number of philosophers have pointed to the important role of houses in the construction of human identity and sociality (Bachelard 1969, 3–73; Heidegger 1971; Casey 1993). Melanesian anthropologists have also documented and analyzed stories about houses as the scenes of a primordial sociality (Landtmann 1927, 15–16; Mimica 1981; J. Weiner 1991). In the Kaliai bush, men's houses were traditionally modeled on birds and frogs and were given womblike connotations.

3. Austronesian speakers find it hard to learn Anem (Thurston 1987). Anem-

speaking men who have married Aria-speaking women often complain that their wives and children have not learned Anem. This is especially problematic, given that they see Anem as the first language of humanity.

4. Marriage between members of the same moiety is spoken of as marrying one's own blood and mother. It is also a form of symbolic homosexuality, a marriage between groups gendered the same.

5. In the early 1990s a Malaysian company began cutting timber in the Kaliai bush. Its royalty payments have further discouraged villagers (especially those at Denga and Bolo) from undertaking the arduous task of cutting copra. The recent construction of a network of roads by the Malaysian timber company has not changed bush people's attitudes toward cash crops. Indeed, bush villagers see timber royalties as a way of acquiring the few Western goods they need without resorting to cash crops. Many bush villagers opposed the coming of the timber company as another white man's trick. Its logging operations have created a "law and order" problem, which is theft and violence in a context of massive corruption in which people can do little to remedy their dissatisfaction with low royalty payments and environmental damage. This book does not examine the impact of the Malaysians because they have not been incorporated into cargo cult stories. A different sort of politics has emerged in regard to the Malaysians, and it does not involve the same mythologization. This contrasts sharply with how people at about the same time did incorporate the American New Tribes Mission into their cargo cult myths and relations with the dead.

6. Janssen (1970, 6) claimed that four Catholic and two Anglican catechists joined Censure's movement, along with two teachers, two councillors, and numerous *komiti* (council committee) members.

7. Kaliai villagers sometimes use these Pisin terms interchangeably. They tend to use the term masalai (**pura**) for named sites that house certain ancestral figures of change. They use the word *tewel* (**ano, mahrva**) mainly for ghosts who seek to eat the living. They also use tambaran (**mahrva**) for angry ghosts and for certain primordial, superhuman cannibals like Boku.

8. Gloucester Patrol Report No. 4 for 1969–70 listed three schools in the Kaliai Census Division with 164 students at Kaliai village, 179 at Salke, and 75 at Bagai. After a fire destroyed the school buildings at Salke, the aid post and community school were rebuilt at Bolo.

9. Steve Feld (personal communication) has informed me that in Southern Highlands Province and Western Highlands Province there are stories about soap as the condensed skin of whites. Here the rubbing of soap into black and white bodies voices the same ambivalences and suspicions of commodities as cannibal substances. A similar analysis could also be done of numerous Papua New Guinea newspaper stories about human flesh being sold as meat in urban markets (Lattas 1993).

10. The villages of Boimangal and Onamanga were not listed in official census documents. They had broken away from the villages of Aikon, Angal, and Salke. In the late 1980s the breakaway villagers returned when everyone converted to the

New Tribes Mission. It was then that Aikon and Salke moved farther inland to become the new villages of Popmu and Sarangtu, respectively.

11. Likewise, the villagers of Bagai, Doko Sagra, Moluo, and Robos who converted to the New Tribes Mission pulled their children out of the community school at Bagai, claiming that the Catholic Church and government, which ran this school, had failed to change their lives.

12. The conflict between bush and coastal villagers is also played out in terms of each accusing the other of using magic to work continuous rain, which damages their crops. In 1986 I heard bush villagers claim that their gardens had been damaged by magic from coastal villagers who were angry about giving pigs and shell money to the cargo cult leader Censure. Some bush villagers blamed Censure himself for their poor gardens, claiming he was working magic to punish them for having deserted his cult. In short, the health of gardens is a way of objectifying social relations.

13. In the late 1980s young men from the Kaliai bush were taken to Port Moresby to negotiate with Malaysian timber contractors. Those who went complained about eating soft Western food, like the Australian breakfast cereal Weetbix, which caused them to get diarrhea and feel sick. Their solution was to demand to be taken to the markets in Port Moresby where they bought "Papua New Guinea food." The young men contrasted soft debilitating Western food with the "strong" food they normally ate, which was cooked in open fires. Whenever I had diarrhea, people would attribute this to the softer foods that I ate, and I would be offered baked taro or manioc to strengthen me.

CHAPTER 2. THE EARLY HISTORY OF CARGO CULTS IN
THE KALIAI AREA

1. Melanesian people have a long history of using binary opposites to think through their relationships with whites. Sometimes this figures in cargo cult myths as the different destinies of two brothers who become separated and alienated from each other (Lawrence 1964; Pech 1991). Lawrence documents how in Madang District there was originally the notion of the Germans as the bad whites and Australians as the good whites; then the Japanese became the good whites in opposition to the Australians, and finally the Americans became the good whites, while the Australians continued to be seen as the bad whites blocking the road of the cargo.

2. Wagner (1991, 334) collected the same story in New Ireland, which indicates that some bush Kaliai cargo cult beliefs were part of an underground regional folklore culture that existed alongside the plantation economy.

3. The traditional bush Kaliai punishment for this crime was to cut Varku's footprint (a cassowary's footprint) into the woman's hair, sever her head, and throw it out of the men's house into the village square for the women to collect and bury.

4. Cargo cult accounts throughout West New Britain incorporate current re-

gional conflicts. The Kombei are unpopular because of their reputation for sorcery and because of the political power they hold in national and provincial governments. On the West New Britain island of Bali, villagers claim that when their god, Luangeh, ran away to America, he did so because his wife from the Kombei area disobeyed him; she came back from gardening and spied on his secret serpentine body.

5. This exchange of racial identities, which Batari spoke of to McCarthy, can be found in bush Kaliai accounts of how, when the dead want to return to Papua New Guinea, they disguise themselves by changing the color of their skins. Posingen claimed they did this by immersing themselves in different drums of water. He heard this explanation from those running the cargo cults in the early 1970s, and he later asked a visiting kiap if it was true. Beliefs like Posingen's worked to subvert the stability of black and white identities by rendering them ambiguous and interchangeable.

> Those like us [Melanesians], they will go to one water which is in a drum. There are two waters, one water here and another water over there. Now suppose we are leaving, say, if we wanted to go and come back to our village, then we would go and leave this drum which is ours and would go to the drum belonging to you white men. We would go down into it, and our skins would change white, and then we would come to Papua New Guinea and travel around. After a while, when we wanted to go back, then we would go and wash in our water, and our skins, which are black, would come back and we would remain like that.

6. Kaliai myths speak of plants becoming human and starting certain matrilineal totemic lines. I also collected two stories of children who died on distant plantations and then plants sprouted up where they had died. Parents later brought these plants back to their home villages and planted them as memorials. Both plants were red—one was a red cordyline, the other a taro plant with a red tuber—and the red in both was the children's blood. Censure also spoke of plants that had a secret human presence.

7. The millenarian promise offered by institutions can be seen in a letter sent August 8, 1966, by the district commissioner to his field staff in West New Britain about finding a solution to cargo cults:

> The long range solution I feel is only by way of better education and more sophisticated administration through such organisations as Councils. We may not be able to do a great deal in quickly changing traditional thought patterns but we should be trying to find ways and means to influence the people to greater endeavours in their own interests. We should make it quite plain to them that such activities as cult activities hinder rather than engender progress, that in many respects they have fallen behind many other areas considered in the past as more primitive.

8. In 1964 Koriam Urekit was elected to the first House of Assembly. Two years earlier he was on the New Britain District Advisory Council and an observer to the legislative council in Port Moresby.

9. Many anticolonial millenarian movements in Africa also operated as anti-sorcery movements (cf. Fields 1985; Mcleod 1975; Richards 1935).

10. The government had information about Aikele's cult activities as early as 1962 when complaints were made by a teacher, John Salkie, of Aikon village. He claimed that Aikele had said, "[If you] do this work, all right, you can see your fathers and mothers who died before" and "You all know we have more cargos [sic] coming from our fathers and mothers who died before but the white people are stealing them." Those who had told Salkie of Aikele's claims refused to repeat them to government officials, who in turn refused to believe Salkie and charged him with spreading false rumors.

11. This information was provided by the ex-luluai of Malasongo village, which was partly made up of Mouk villagers who had migrated to the Bariai coast. When a patrol ran into this ex-luluai at Benim village, he claimed: "I must live on my own land, or otherwise, when Aikeli's law is broken, I will not share any of the cargo." Aikele's law was said to involve paying a tax to gain a share of the cargo:

> When the time comes, we will all go into our houses and lock the doors, there will be twenty-four hours of darkness, accompanied by thunder and lightning. When the sun returns, we can all leave our houses, and the cargo will be there. There will be cars, trucks, cycles, radios, and the other things that you Europeans have. The whole of New Britain will be flat and there will be plenty of roads for the cars.

12. Moluo villagers deny deliberately burning these coconuts, which they say were destroyed when dry grass caught fire accidentally. They do admit to cutting down young seedlings when they left so that the villagers of Robos could not "humbug" on the fruits of their labor. A patrol report dated December 12, 1967, claims: "[Of] 4,000 coconuts seeds which were sent by the District Agricultural Officer at Talasea for planting, only 800 were found and the rest were consumed by the people."

13. Aikele also tried to pull villagers from the Kandrian side into his project. Villagers at Bagai, Moluo, and Robos trace their descent to the south coast (from where they today receive some timber royalties). A letter, dated January 6, 1966, claims that Aikele collected taxes from four Kandrian villages: "These were Asa-watne and Pau who contributed £6 altogether, Ourin £1 and Gergering which gave £7 but then asked for it back. The money was returned." The administration thought the money was for development purposes at Bibling Ridge, and Aikele had often reassured government officials in those terms, although he nevertheless continued the development along different lines. Aikele became opposed to the administration's attempts to develop new forms of governmentality. At Kulwango village in Rauto the patrol officer at Kandrian accused Aikele's followers—luluai Kulo and twenty other men—of interrupting polling for the first House of Assembly election. At this time some competition existed between Koriam's movement and Aikele's. A letter dated May 27, 1964, and entitled "Confusion by Luluai of Molou," recorded that Kulo made a speech that drew on people's understandings

that New Britain had been created first, but it had lost God's "school" (moral teachings and knowledge). God then tried to give his school to other Melanesians, but they too were pigheaded, and so God went to America. This school was now coming back, and it would come through Aikele's work rather than through council government and elections. Kulo was quoted as saying:

> This European is working for the election but it is an election for a Council only. This is only a Council and you people cannot go to it. You must come to the other work that Aikele has found for us and not this Council. You must come on Aikele's road. I want to get money from you and give it to Aikele and work a road for us. (A sum of £7–3–0 was collected and handed over). This is a strong meeting. New Britain came up first and later we were made. We came up first and God gave school (education) to us. We were big-heads to God's talk. We ignored the school so God then built a bridge to New Guinea and placed his school there. The New Guineans in turn ignored the school so another bridge was built to Papua and the school was transferred to there. In turn the Papuans ignored the school and the bridge to transfer the school was then built to America. In America, one man heard the word of God and built schools and thus learning came up from America. God later took the school to Japan and it is now starting to came [sic] to Australia and New Guinea again. (Patrol Reports, Gloucester, 1964)

Unaware of the full resonances of this speech of Kulo's, the patrol officer noted: "There appears nothing adverse in the speech made by Kulo and it was explained that is [sic] merely a confused idea of how learning came to different parts of the world with a religious context."

14. Patrol reports in December 1966 claim that Aikele collected $134.75 Australian. The administration took this money and deposited it into a Commonwealth savings account. People still ask about this money.

15. This is a well-known Kaliai motif belonging to the initiation ritual of the tambaran Mukmuk. There an initiate squats between the legs of his maternal uncle, who is beaten across the stomach with a cane. Later the uncle will receive shell money for the pain he "ate." Aikele was assuming this caring ritual relationship with his kiap, and it carried the expectation of compensation for hardship received.

16. Throughout the Kaliai area people are spoken of as having two skins. When they die, their outer skin is left behind, and the person goes to live in an inner second skin. This second body is also what people travel around in in dreams, and it is this second body that masalai capture and eat. Only now, with the arrival of the New Tribes Mission, are people increasingly taking up the Christian project of spiritualizing this second body. Yet, even so, many New Tribes Mission followers find it difficult to conceive of a soul, the animating force of the self, as something without corporeality.

17. Many Kaliai villagers tell the story of an original teacher-god called Katika whose pedagogic functions are today performed by catechists. Katika kept calling villagers to attend his church, but they chose instead to go hunting and to their gardens. At Bolo one lay preacher told me:

Katika was at the village of Botogoigoi. He worked *belo* [rang a bell], but everyone was bikhet. It is still like this now. People did not want to *lotu* [go to church]. They took their children and axes and went to their gardens. Katika stood up and ran away. He was tired of their habits. He was tired of our bikhet. This is why now there is not one thing which has come up before our eyes. You see this *morota* [sago palm leaves used for thatch], it is everywhere. If we had heard his talk, then something [of significance] would have come up to us. This boss who gave us our customs, we came up at the same time as him. If we had heard his talk at the beginning, then something, cargo, would have come up by now. But he has gone. Katika left, he ran away.

18. These stories can also be used by members of this educated elite as an explanation for their powerlessness, incompetence, and corruption. Recently, when I asked the secretary of the local landowners' timber company about the lack of any significant benefits from the timber project, he replied cryptically that I must know the reason for this, for I had heard some of the stories of the big men.

19. Versions of this story can be found in the Madang area, Siasi Islands, south and north coast of West New Britain, and on Bali Island (Lawrence 1964; Pech 1991; Pomponio, Counts, and Harding 1994).

20. I heard this version of Titikolo in 1986 at Salke village before it converted to the New Tribes Mission. Today the new mission has become a vehicle for distributing American anticommunist rhetoric. One American missionary, Sign, supports certain national and provincial candidates sympathetic to his mission by labeling their opponents as communist. His converts have taken up and reproduced these evaluations.

21. Janssen (1970) noted that followers used the word *stori* to refer to myth and genealogy but also to their movement and its work. People were called upon to come into the stori. Referring to Censure, Janssen noted, "We may say that he sees in the story a revelation of the '*lo*' [i.e., a secret order of existence]" (1970, 31). The word *stori* was also used in the sense of "secret power," as when people said that if they worked their stori, it would create the white man's lifestyle. When I was in the field, people mourned the fact that all their stori [cargo cults] had "fallen down" (collapsed, ended), and they wondered who would be strong enough to start a new stori. Storytelling was an activity, a revealing magical practice.

22. Censure told his followers: "I am not enough to wash this dirt of mine on my skin; for on all these different [bodily] parts, there is food" (*kaikai*). Censure spoke of his ritual laws as a "garden" that followers would work to produce food: "Our garden is all right now, it won't be long before we are eating." When kiaps arrived and denounced the cult, they would often emphasize the need to concentrate on gardens, but for cult followers, who had been schooled in Censure's "talk-box," the kiaps were telling them to focus and work their cult rituals hard. As Posingen put it:

> The kiaps also called it this [a garden], they would say: "You must stay and look after your garden until your garden is good, and then you will sit down good." The kiaps spoke like this: "If you are strong with this garden of yours, then after a while, when your garden is all right, then you will sit down good

with it." Now this "talk-picture," this "talk-box" about the garden, the masters would be working "talk-box," and my father would also be working "talk-box" back.

23. For Censure all the different myths of origin involving masalai and totemic beings meant that there were too many branches (*i gat planti rot tumas*) in Kaliai genealogies (Janssen 1970, 3). Although he did not fully take up the monocausal schemes of Christianity, Censure was influenced by its boasts of simplicity and clarity and by the seemingly greater explanatory power of its totalizing schemes.

24. Censure's major opponent was Councillor Sela, who also had a secret cargo cult. Sela had an old German coin dated 1875 that he claimed was dropped from the sky by a sea eagle. This was a magical coin that would deliver money to Sela. It was also said that Sela performed other miracles, such as acquiring tobacco and betel nuts from thin air. Initially, Sela had half-believed Censure's stories but later, according to Janssen (1970, 5), "He went to Meitavale, abused the people[,] and pulled the post of the cult flag out." Committed to his position as councillor and afraid of losing it, Sela became convinced that the new law of existence would come from his coin and council government. He confided to one friend at Bolo village that he might have to trade in his coin to acquire the new law. Although he denounced Censure's movement as a cargo cult, Sela sought to create a rival movement that recognized council government as a magical transformative framework. Janssen captured this ascribed magic of state structures when he wrote, "When cooperatives and councils were introduced a few years ago, some people used words like 'agenda,' 'law,' 'rebate' and 'cheque' in a ritualistic sense, as if these were the new magic spells to a quick and overall socio-economic welfare. . . . There is hardly any secular thinking and understanding of legal procedure and economic methods" (1970, 16).

25. Censure claimed that when his father died, he went into the underground and married a woman called Mesona, who carried Masta Ellem. The government officer Sisley was seen as Censure's *kandere* (nephew) Sen Seuve (Janssen 1970, 6). I too was seen as coming from the underground.

26. Sisley 1970, 4. Posingen explained to me the cult's rejection of schools, aid post, taxes, and business as the rejection of the white man's law and the discovery of their own:

> Father thought that this law belonged to all the Australian men, and he was not enough to put it inside his law. The law belonging to him was about him finding a new sit-down for Papua New Guinea, for us alone. We wanted to find a sit-down for ourselves, and these laws belonging to all white men, we left them. We would not let people go inside them, like go to the house-sick or whatever. We wanted just to stay here and for Father to get up this [law] here. When the time came and we won it [a new existence], then we would receive a new school belonging to us. We would not go inside that belonging to all Australian men; that was finished.

27. These secret names also had the power to end sorcery. Sorcerers who joined the cult and recited the names would have their heads made "clear" so that they

would no longer think of injuring others. Through the power of a new language, followers sought to reeducate themselves and create a new sense of moral community. Posingen described the cult's school as reenacting the mission and government's moral pedagogic projects but in a more powerful and thorough cleansing manner: "It is like when we go to the Bible and the law of government about not stealing and damaging something belonging to someone else or damaging their name. This school of Senlaw and Senfor would clear away this something, it must break the thinking of all men and clear their thoughts."

CHAPTER 3. PUNISHMENT AND UTOPIA: DEATH,
CARGO CULT NARRATIVES, AND THE
POLITICS OF THE UNDERGROUND

1. According to Janssen, coastal villagers "were supposed not to go back to their villages at the beach, but to settle at their old places in the bush" (1970, 7). The cult began to elaborate itself around some of these coastal locations, recreating people's sense of home and place within the new framework of their stori. Janssen (1970, 25) detailed how, at Taveliai, Censure visited a cemetery where Father A. Hayes was reported to have found the money that allowed him to build Kaliai Mission Station. There for the first time Censure saw a coconut tree that had red flowers and that he claimed was a picture of a married woman belonging to the underground. He claimed that another red flowering coconut tree at Pureling was a picture of a young unmarried woman. Pureling villagers also showed Censure a stone believed to contain gold, and he told villagers to clear the surrounding area so that the gold could come up. At Kariai two betel nut trees that spontaneously sprouted in the village square were said by Censure to have been moved there by his stori and that before they were to be found at Sinai near the *raunwara* (pool known as) Jordan.

2. Villagers say these newspapers were brought by a "kiap," but patrol reports say they were brought by a Jehovah's Witness stationed at Kimbe. The newspapers at Aikon were taken away by a visiting kiap, but at Moluo and Robos they were not confiscated.

3. This insight is also absent and not used by Lindstrom in his previous book on cargo cults on the island of Tanna. Indeed, though Lindstrom was analyzing discourse, he rejected analyzing "the ontology of Tannese cultural understanding" (1990, 8). As he put it: "I do not much care about the details of what the Tannese say, nor about the structure in which they encode what they say."

4. Sisley (1970, 3) was misled about this stone's being called Nazareth, which was instead the cult's name for a small pool adjacent to the Glass of God. Posingen claimed that this large stone would turn into a city when the Kaliai bush changed and became flat. At the raunwara called Nazareth there were also other significant stones like the large stone that held back the water, "God's Money," or "Bank." On another large stone were the three *namba* (marks, signs) of the three genera-

tions that Sisley mentioned. Nazareth also had underground rooms, and nearby was a cliff that Posingen spoke of as a ladder: "The ladder comes down, it goes over to Mountain Sinai and Galilee and heaven, where they all meet."

5. An example of this is the sticks that cult followers carried; they represented and were to turn into guns when the new law came. For Monongyo these sticks symbolized a new world of equality:

> We worked the picture of it so that this stick would go to something true. All these guns, we would later hold them, like those belonging to you white men. With the guns, all of us together would hold them. This is the meaning of the stick. It did not belong to fighting or finding game, but that we had to come up the same as you white men. This [ritual law involving sticks] had to come to us natives so that the same thing which goes to you whites could now come to us natives. When we won this work [the cult], then we were to sit down like youse.

6. The phrase moni dabol was an amalgamation of Pisin and tok ples languages; it embodied the new hybrid domains of meaning that people have become and that would redeem them.

7. People asked for cargo in ways that denied its worth. They used antonyms in asking the dead for a grass skirt or an old broken knife. I was told, "They would throw talk-box to this something, but it was really about this something of theirs which would come up when we sat down good. . . . They would talk-box to *pipia* [rubbish], but something good would come to them all."

8. People often speak of West New Britain Province as though it were an island in its own right, which indicates the objectifying mythic power that administrative boundaries can assume.

9. The analogy here is to steep forest paths where the roots of small plants hold the ground in place. When these plants are cut, the ground crumbles away, creating dangerous slippery surfaces.

10. Cult names for things like posts, beams, and plants were often the indigenous name with the prefix *senlaw* added. For example, the traditional name for *post* was **krangar,** and in the cult it become *senlaw-krangar.* The cult's school was similar to the school belonging to the male tambaran Varku. He taught initiates new names for things, and those names were often the indigenous name with the prefix *sen.* When learning the cargo cult's school, the new names were repeated with the same intonation and rhythm used by Varku when he schooled initiates in his new law. Censure modeled his cargo cult school on the lessons of male tambaran cults. He learned how to learn in a certain way.

11. In his report on Censure's movement Sisley gave this description of the cult's ritual laws:

> When a village arrives for the first time to join the cult the people are divided up into their particular "Pigeon" Groups and then begin to be "schooled" by Napasisio. A normal days [sic] activity being as follows. Rise at 5 am and spend two hours singing various chants requesting the ancestors mentioned to return and help the people break through the knowledge barrier thought to be

why the white man is so fortunate. After this there is a short break of half an
hour and then the school begins. For this the people are divided into their "Pigeon" Groups and spend the next three to four hours chanting the names of various ancestors and saints of the Catholic Church. This is to teach people about
their ancestors so that on the last day they will be able to greet them and together go forth into the new society where everybody will be equal. This idea to
them meaning that they will have the knowledge, supposed wealth and luxuries
of the white man.

After the "schooling" the people spend the afternoon resting and collecting
food until 5 pm when a further two to three hours are spent singing. This pro-
gramme happens everyday and is to be carried out by the coastal villages when
they return to their homes. (Sisley 1970, 2–3)

12. These mirror structures reenact the binary logic of the moiety system,
which requires two separate interdependent groups that perform the same rituals
as the basis of their exchange relations.

13. This argument draws on Levi-Strauss's insight (1979) about the analogous
nature of binary opposites; how people think through one opposition using the
familiar terms of another opposition.

14. Serres 1982b, 45. Serres argued that incest is also a rejoining of that which
was disconnected: "Incest describes a loop that turns back upon itself towards a
previous crossroads and strongly reconnects the spatial complex" (1982b, 48).
Some local villagers accused Censure of an incestuous relationship with one of his
daughters. These accusations cannot be dismissed as malicious gossip directed at
undermining Censure's standing. I also received them from a respected magistrate
at Bagai who accompanied a European kiap who had publicly confronted Censure
on this issue. What needs to be explained is why Censure's work should have been
so readily associated with suggestions of, if not actual, incest. I see the cult's desire
to dissolve the separate categories of same and other in the field of race as repeating this logic in the field of sexuality and kinship. Here incest repeats and
enacts the same transgressions of difference and taboo that are desired in the field
of race relations.

CHAPTER 4. RACE, GENDER, AND GEOGRAPHIES OF
           GUILT: CHRISTIANITY AND KALIAI MYTHS OF
           MATRIARCHY

1. When the villagers of Benim left Censure's movement, they formed their
own movement led by Watna. It borrowed heavily from Censure, with Watna appointing two female Christs (one for each moiety) to deliver the new law of existence. It is said that Watna "buggered up" his law by sleeping with the female
Christ of Big Bird who was closely related to him; she was his step-sister. While
seducing her, he reportedly told her, "You cannot talk; this is law here that I am
here giving." Watna predicted that by marrying his sister the law would come;
when it didn't, he predicted it would come from their first-born child. When the

cargo still did not come, he told his disillusioned followers it would come from the next child. When the cargo again failed to arrive, Watna lost his followers and they and he joined the New Tribes Mission.

2. This lime powder container has a bulge at one end that is spoken of as its testicles, whereas the lime powder inside is often jokingly referred to as semen. In effect, Kewak symbolically broke her brother's penis and by implication the phallus of all the men who ran away from her tambaran. Kowdock is an important cultural hero throughout the Kaliai area. A mountain close to the village of Pureling is his men's house. He made the first stone axe and gave men the task of building fences and cutting down huge trees so women would admire men. Kowdock is spoken of as a person who "sacks" other people's talk. Out of an acute sense of his individuality (em yet) he changes existing states of affairs even when they are favorable.

3. Metaphors of female procreation also feature in official state discourse. A Patrol Report for 1975–76 mentions that fifteen hundred people attended Independence Day celebrations at Kaliai. There the officer in charge of Gloucester gave a speech entitled "Papua New Guinea is born now out of her mothers [sic] womb. An era towards struggle and hardship and hard work for every one of us here now."

4. Septireh told me how white kiaps would lecture men that they were no longer to throw spears or hit their wives with objects; they were just to hit them and "swell them up with their hands." In reality, traditional forms of violence toward women were moderated by the presence of brothers, unfinished bride-price payments, and the intervention of respected older women.

CHAPTER 5. SEXUALITY, REPRODUCTION, AND THE UTOPIA OF MIRROR WORLDS

1. Today nearly everyone has a scathing opinion of what people agree was Censure's sexual exploitation of female followers. People now laugh at their credulity and at Censure's adeptness at exploiting their desires. Those who joined the cult briefly say that they just came to try it to see if its work was succeeding as was being claimed. Those who stayed longer point out that Censure made obedience to him a moral test that would lead one who failed it to be perpetually lost in the dark ways of the past. Many ex-followers still think it is possible to find someone who will "out" the law for Papua New Guinea. Though they are critical of individual cargo cult leaders, they are still firmly committed to cargo cult beliefs.

2. These roads, which were cut out of the surrounding red clay soil, were like bitumen roads. They led down to the surrounding rivers of Meitavale and then invisibly on to Port Moresby, Rabaul, Brisbane, and Sydney. Taxis and trucks— vehicles that would later carry cargo—were reportedly seen running briefly along these roads.

3. Patrol Report No. 2 for 1972–73 had this to say about Censure's cult: "Although it is maintained primarily by the Bigmen, it was interesting to note that

several of the most important women seemed to take a more active role than is usual." In 1986 I noticed that many women in the cult were extremely well versed in cult mythology and doctrines. These same women claimed that many women who had once been followers wanted to return to the cult, but their husbands were stopping them. Many men I spoke to blamed their wives for pulling them into the cult. Although this blame has a rhetorical element to it, I feel there is also an element of truth that corresponds to women's supporting and taking up the ideological revaluing of woman that Censure was promoting.

4. When cult followers visited the Glass of God, they made speeches asking Stone Sakail, which was also referred to as God's island, to rise: "Now that we have come up to our number, we will come up to it and call this island of His [God's], and it will go on top."

5. I owe this point to Judy Lattas, who is working on reinterpreting Hannah Arendt's understandings of the public and the private, the visible and the invisible, in terms of the labor of women's bodies.

6. The marriage of many women to one man features in stories about Akono, whom Censure seemed to be copying in his refusal to wash and in his assuming the persona of the rubbishman.

7. Monongyo explained their predicament to me like this:

> This woman was a Tamasina, but Sengelo here he was taking the place of his father. It is like this with his father, all the women, all the Tamasina, they all came, but they did not work good like they should have. They all spoke: "This rubbishman, what is to happen? Will my skin have to go against his?" All the women, their talk was like this, they were afraid, afraid, afraid, afraid, and they all moved away. There was just a few of us left behind at this time. He [Censure] then spoke about this [other woman] Tamasina, who was the same pisin [bird] as him, that she should come and instead work it with his child [son].

8. Part of this imagery of the key also involved the metaphor of this underground woman's body's being like a post office where men would go with their keys and open the particular boxes allocated to them. A new way of marking and ordering the procreative powers of woman, of allocating them between men, drew upon Western spatial images of ordered shared terrains of individual property:

> The post office has all these numbers [referring to post office boxes that are lined up and numbered], a master will go and look at his number and put the key and take his messages [pas]. With another master it will be the same. Now, with this talk-box that Father worked about this woman [underground mother], it is the same as the post office. If I was to go, I would look for the number belonging to me, and I would put the key there and take any messages and anything else. With all of us men who would go, each would have their number. It is not enough for us to go and to mix, it is like the post office that is here [at Kimbe]. It is not enough true for one master to go and open another [box] with his key. With this something we all have an individual number. You would go and shoot inside your key. . . . We would go and put a key, put a key, and some-

thing then comes up. It spills out from her, and we would receive it. The meaning goes like that.

9. Censure's image of an underground Christ with vaginas all over her body resonates with a Catholic Church painting that I saw at the village of Bagai. I do not know whether Censure ever saw this painting, but it depicts Christ's body as covered in bloody wounds that have an elliptical shape of the kind used in Kaliai iconography as an image of a vagina. Here in Catholic iconography Christ's disempowerment at the hands of state authorities was rendered as the feminization of Christ, a theme to which the Kaliai could very much relate.

10. I want to distance my analysis of eroticism and sexuality in cargo cults from Lindstrom's 1993 analysis of cargo cult desire as love. Though he competently analyzes the ethnocentric universalistic assumptions about desire made by the West, Lindstrom reproduces the trap of those assumptions by never exploring the ontology of indigenous Melanesian desires and their historical transformation.

11. In Kaliai folk tales the cannibal ogre Boku is known for his superhuman strength and his skin of "cement." The underground mother's body resonates with this, and as such she partakes of an original monstrous presence, of an archaic time when bodies and people were other than their contemporary depowered form.

12. Posingen and Monongyo differed about how the law was to be bought. Monongyo believed that the law could be bought only with the gift of a woman to Censure. He believed that the woman who was covered in vaginas was really talk-picture for all the women who were given to Censure as gifts to buy the law. Posingen was not so certain that the law could not be bought with pigs and shell money, for many people did give these to Censure to secure their right to cargo.

13. The Kaliai have an acute sense of themselves as lacking in numbers. This is partly a sense of having lost people through sorcery and also a result of people moving away to work as contract laborers in distant areas. People's image of Australia and America is of lands that overflow with people, because the successive different generations of the dead have accumulated there.

CHAPTER 6. ANDROGYNOUS IMAGERY, SEXUALITY, AND
THE PROCREATIVE POWERS OF THE
IMAGINATION

1. Eliade's view of the androgyne as a return to a homogenous oneness does not fit neatly with Kaliai notions of primordial time, which maintain a logic of pairing. Although myths of origin play with the inversion of gender terms and their partial effacement, they do not completely abolish the male-female distinction but render each bisexual in a different way. The androgynous nature of primordial men is different from the androgynous nature of primordial women, which is to say that women with beards do not equal men with breasts and can do so only through the formal mathematical models of a structuralism that abolishes the concrete images of bodies. In Kaliai myths the partial effacement and blurring of

sexual difference is more its reconstitution in an original primordial time made up of masculinized femininity and feminized masculinity.

2. Monongyo spoke like this about the women who were internalizing knowledge through eating Censure's bloody sweat:

> He didn't used to wash, and his skin used to come up dirty, and something like "food" used to be on it. He alone would be working the law [ritual dances], and sweat would come up. It was then that all the women of the underground would come to receive knowledge from him. Its meaning was like this: that they would come and receive it [sweat-food-knowledge]. They would fill up with it and leave. They would look at it [sweat-food], and they would get knowledge from it. This something, its meaning is like that.

3. When Censure failed to find a woman to be his Christ, the underground women began increasingly to insist that he join them in the underground, that the law be "broken" (released) there —down below—rather than on top. The underground women would say to Censure:

> You must come to us. If you want to try it, like you are, then come down to us, down below, and work it here and the law will open up here—down below— and then go on top. You know, you on top, in Papua New Guinea, do not have a true door [a female Christ]. If you want to try it, how will you do so? It is not enough for a *pasim* [a way of life] to come up. Supposing Papua New Guinea was strong, and you tried it and the law came up to Papua New Guinea, then it would pull us, and we would come on top. Now you look, youse are not enough to pull us up. Now if you had someone like us, then we would be able to open the law. The law must open then, from down below and come on top to Papua New Guinea.

4. The Koriam cult's desire to end racial inequalities by putting an end to the tambarans, which are used to mediate gender inequalities, is still a pervasive theme in the Kaliai bush. It was also something that Censure emphasized when I visited him in 1986 (Lattas 1992c). And it was why New Tribes Mission followers gave up using tambarans.

5. Censure also "photographed" his followers. He would line them up at his telephone doors so that they could be photographed by the dead. He would say to his followers: "You all stand up good so the men at the door can photograph youse. You all must stand up straight you cannot lie about. . . . If you want to work the law, then do this well so they [the dead] can photograph you all." Here the new law of existence is the process of seeing oneself through the gaze of the white man, which comes to be indigenized and assimilated to the photographic gaze of the dead. The hegemonic gaze of the white man is being appropriated in the eye of the camera and is displaced into the more familiar gaze of one's deceased relatives.

6. Imokeh is also the name of a masalai snake that in Kaliai myths gives to the living certain species of taro and sugarcane, as well as the designs on his skin, which the Kaliai now paint.

CHAPTER 7. MIMESIS, TRANSGRESSION, AND THE RAISING
OF WHITE CHILDREN

1. In Catholic villages young men have gained all the positions in the local landowner timber company. They are also appointed to council government and to school and church organizations. The New Tribes Mission has further perfected this process by appointing young men to be the moral guardians of communities. In the 1970s these young men learned to read, and today their access to the Bible provides them with the authority and respect to organize village affairs.

2. Amkou claimed that Paname would leave the village before anyone had awakened, and she would return later in the afternoon. Amkou described Paname's travels and deceptions like this:

> She would run into people like Matagel who were putting out nets, and they would give her a small piece of cassowary meat. When she brought it back to us, she did not speak correctly about it, telling us that all of Matagel gave it to her. No! she would say that her children gave it to her. She would come back carrying this cassowary meat, and her husband would get up and say: "All mothers cook some food, do you think this woman has been traveling close to us? You all know that she has gone somewhere and come back. I think she has gone to Sydney and come back." Her husband would speak like this, and everyone would be extremely happy. I too was happy when I came new to this work. I thought: "I think this woman is working a true story, Leo let us go inside this story." I spoke like that, and Leo then said, "Let us go." The cassowary meat that this woman carried back was shared out. She spoke: "You all eat, and you cannot talk much about it, just eat it." Her husband would also speak like this: "You all know this something has come from Sydney." Mapilu rose and spoke like this: he said that this cassowary meat had come from Sydney [Amkou laughs]. Paname then spoke: "Mapilu tell all the big men that they cannot talk plenty about this cassowary, for all the owners of this something will come and sit-down close to us and watch us. Now if people eat just a small portion and complain about this, then talk will come up over this. I alone will receive cross talk from this line, from all the children Bullet, Michael Ross, Johnson, and Semrengen."

When we finished eating this cassowary, she then said: "Mapilu, you stay in the village, I'm not going to stay in the village. All this line says that I have to travel around, that I have to catch a plane. You stay in the village and give talk to everybody. I am not enough to open my mouth, this talk [of mine] will have to remain for later. You alone Mapilu must talk." Paname was not enough to talk; they had blocked her mouth. She spoke: "With me, they have blocked my mouth. I cannot talk, you alone must give talk to all the big men, not me. My time has not yet come. When they say I can talk, I will. But if they say: 'Mother, you wait,' then I will wait, I will hear their talk." Her husband came and told us about this.

3. Paname warned people not to cut down trees in this area for it contained her uncle's wireless. He used it to ring the dead at the Brisbane waterfall to let

them know that followers were coming. The dead would arrive, bringing chairs to sit on, and they watched the cult's ceremonies.

4. Paname would leave her followers and go look at these namba. If they were clean, she would come back singing, and her followers would be happy, for this was a sign she would return with good talk. According to Paul, followers visited their namba to check on the moral state of their moiety and thus their likelihood of getting cargo:

> When we went down there [to the waterfall], we really decorated ourselves with shell money, grass skirts, and paint around our eyes. All parts of our bodies were covered in paint. . . . Our hair would be covered in decorative leaves. We would go down this huge hill singing. When we came to the bottom, Mapilu would say: "Little Bird go over there, and Big Bird youse all go over there. Sit-down quietly, keep the mouths of all children closed, and we will sit-down and wait for all the big men to come—Michael Ross, Johnson, Bullet, Semrengen. All adults, you all know the ways of this man Semrengen, he is a man no good. He will come, and he will be cross, not with us but his poor mother will receive the cross." During this time we would all be sitting down, and there would be no one talking, we would just be looking at all these numbers [circles] on the stone. We of Little Bird would look at our number. If it was clean, then it was all right. But if it was dirty, then we would say: "Oh, we have a wrong [fault, crime] here, look our number is not clean."

Mapilu would also claim credit for cleanliness of the namba of each moiety, claiming it was because he always came to see them. As in Censure's cult, people would sing out to the spirit beings, saying, "Michael Ross, Johnson, Bullet, Semrengen—we have come to see our namba, and when we go back to Moluo then this namba of ours, you must take it and follow us and come up to Moluo. There we will gather together and the law belonging to us will break open, and we can then rest." While speaking, people would look at a huge stone in the river. To get to this area where they made these speeches to the dead, people would walk across an area referred to as a bridge. Censure's cult also involved people walking across a bridge, which was the narrow firm ground that people crossed to avoid the swampy ground that led to the Glass of God and Lake Nazareth. This thin, firm, bridging ground can be seen as a spatial metaphor for the cult itself and its bridging of the distances between the dead and the living, Europeans and Melanesians.

5. Paul told me that Mapilu forbade people to sing using the "neck" [voice styles] of other language groups like the Ibanga and Mouk. He emphasized that songs had to "follow the neck of all Aria."

6. Samaga and Septireh claimed that the Benim cargo cult leader Watna also copied Europeans' gestures. According to Samaga, "He would get sticks and put them into the holes of crabs and then to his ear, like that, he would then listen. He would listen, but who was talking? I think they [Watna and his followers] were all just lying. Now supposing a [dead] person was talking, then he would nod his head like this. Now supposing there was one talk that was grease-too-much, then he would work at laughing like this." While his brother showed me how Watna

laughed, Septireh pointed out, "He would laugh like all you masta when you gather together at a club house and youse drink and eat. He was laughing like youse when you sit in a chair."

7. When a garden house was built for Mapilu and Paname, it was not built like everyone else's with open sides; instead, it was totally sealed off with leaves. Inside was a table to hold the food belonging to the spirit children. Amkou gave me this description:

> When we brought the food, Mapilu would go outside and talk, but Paname would get all the plates and bang them around. She would say: "Aeh, Aeh, I think it is because the food does not have any meat, and that is why all the plates are being thrown about." [*Paname, now speaking to her children:*] "You all eat—tomorrow some meat will come for youse, all the men will find it." She would work this talk to her children so that we would think this story of hers was true. They would hide inside the garden house, and they would trick us by banging around the plates and spoons. She would speak softly to her children: "Just eat, just eat, your father will talk to all the big men. She would speak loudly and softly, and we would all think that her children had come and were speaking to their mother.

8. Although Catholics accord the dead and spirits a certain externality, they do not see them as totally independent of people's thoughts, for today it is said that because people no longer think and believe in the dead and spirits, they no longer come up.

9. When Mapilu's cult was new, he made his followers clear an area and build two large houses with many interior rooms like European houses. These were referred to as the *haus kiap* (government officer's houses) belonging to Michael Ross, Johnson, and Bullet, who were later expected to store their cargo there. The area around these houses was kept clean and planted with flowers.

CHAPTER 8. KALIAI CARGO CULTS AND THE NEW TRIBES MISSION

1. Traditionally, masalai had the power to capture people's thoughts by hypnotizing them into believing in a world that did not exist. In Christianity this capacity to deceive is assigned to Satan, and it leads, as Foucault pointed out, to a focus on problematized subjectivity: "For Christians, the possibility that Satan can get inside your soul and give you thoughts you cannot recognise as satanic, but that you might interpret as coming from God, leads to uncertainty about what is going on inside your soul. You are unable to know what the real root of your desire is, at least without hermeneutic work" (1984, 361). For Foucault, what goes with Satan is a whole culture of self-scrutiny and self-interpretation. In the bush Kaliai area this took the form of converts who stood before a congregation and confessed publicly their secret embittered thoughts and their hidden desires, something that disturbed some of the old men.

2. One ex-convert explained the beliefs of converts like this:

With masalai sites, they say they are not masalai sites but something belonging to Papa. Papa worked this something when He worked the ground, but it is
not a masalai place. They are not afraid of it, for the Bible says that God
worked everything, it is His work and there are no masalai. Crayfish or fish,
which we say are masalai, they will say that it is our food, that God put our
food in this area. And they will eat it, they will eat the things from masalai
places. Everything has been created only by God.

3. I have chosen the name Sign for this missionary because it resonates with
his real name, which carries cargo cult connotations of marking, symbolizing,
and foretelling.

4. After the New Tribes Mission started its Mouk literacy classes, Anem-
speaking women from the coast who had married Mouk speakers were scolded
for speaking Anem and for teaching it to their children. Other languages were
referred to as the languages of darkness, which stood in opposition to the reformed
clarity of a Mouk language that had come back from America.

5. Later the New Tribes Mission recruited an Australian to initiate development projects, such as introducing goats, ducks, and fish. Converts claim that Sign
sent this person away because he was pushing business and taking people's
thoughts away from the church. The good American missionary was seen as opposing the corrupt world of business pushed by an Australian missionary who was
not as close to God as the American. Again, we see here the way everyday interactions are made to reenact cargo cult mythic paradigms of history.

6. Images of wild excess in dancing disturbed early missionaries but also early
government anthropologists like Chinnery, who thought it appropriate in his report on his patrol in southwest New Britain to quote the Reverend G. Balmer of
the Lutheran Mission. The latter criticized the dance Sia, which can be found
throughout New Britain, in the following terms: "Natives who waste their time,
their property, and their food in unrestrained dancing will not be able to do enough
work even to find tax money for the government; and while they remain slaves to
wild unrestrained dancing it will be impossible to elevate them in morals, economic
conditions, or culture to a higher level" (Chinnery 1925). Dancing was here positioned as subverting the desire to create a new sort of moral subject whose labors
would be directed not to kinsman and ceremonies but to the state, its taxes, and
the marketplace.

7. Hyland spent a few days in the Kaliai bush when he was under contract to
the local landowner timber company to conduct an environmental impact study
that never has been implemented properly.

8. In December 1995 a big man from Popmu boasted how he had "won" because he had just married off his two daughters without a bride price; he challenged other men to meet his sacrifice. Converts here compete not through ceremonial feasts but through giving up rights to women in a moral project that seeks
to emulate the white man's more civilized existence and treatment of women. However, my experience of this is that it has also devalued women and produced some
quite shockingly violent attacks on women.

Select Glossary of Frequently Used Melanesian Pisin and Mouk Terms

---

PISIN TERMS

as   (E: arse*) backside, foundation, base, basis, bottom, origin, cause, source, reason.

as ples   birthplace; home ground; home villagers.

bikhet   (E: big head) to be pigheaded, stubborn, disobedient, conceited, obstinate.

Bikpela Pisin   (E: big pigeon) the moiety of Big Bird, which is gendered male and often said to have originated from a cassowary or a sea eagle.

bisnis   (E: business) cash crops and trade stores.

blakskin   (E: black-skin) a native, a Melanesian.

boi   (E: boy) companion, native laborer.

em yet   he himself, he was in charge; he alone was important.

Glas bilong God   (E: Glass belonging to God). A pool discovered in the headwaters of the Aria River by Censure's female followers and thought to be the mirror, binoculars, and looking-glass of God; the place where Melanesians originated from coconuts and where some dead and other underground spirits resided with God.

haus kiap   the government officer's house; a guest house in a village that was built to accommodate visiting kiaps while they were on patrol.

kaikai   food, but in Censure's cult also a euphemism for cargo.

kandere   (E: kindred) relatives on the mother's side—uncle, aunt, nephew, or niece.

kina   a clam or oyster; also the name and icon for the currency of Papua New Guinea.

kis   (E: kiss) to get, receive, take, capture, incorporate, accept.

kukboi   (E: cook boy) kitchen helper.

---

* Words in parentheses that follow the designation E: are the English words from which the Pisin words are derived.

339

kuskus   clerk, secretary, or bookkeeper.

Liklik Pisin   (E: little pigeon) the moiety of Little Bird, which is gendered female and is often said to have originated from a kingfisher or from a bird known locally as a kowdock.

lo   (E: law) law, custom, rule, habits, routines, and ritual obligations; in cargo cults the *lo* is often a ritual or magical secret or a hidden alternative order of existence.

longlong   madness, stupidity, foolishness, ignorance, confusion.

lotu   church, religious worship.

luluai   a village headman appointed by the administration.

mankimasta   a Melanesian domestic servant in a European household.

masalai   an ancestral being that inhabits pools, streams, rocks, and trees. In the Kaliai area a masalai is seen to have the power to change into a human form and today into Europeans. Illnesses are often attributed to a masalai that has captured the soul of a person. In his dreams a shaman will travel to a masalai site to rescue that captured soul.

masalai meri   a female masalai or a masalai that has taken the human form of a woman.

masta   white man, a European.

meri   woman, girl, wife.

misis   (E: Mrs.) European woman, single or married.

moni kina   kina currency.

namba   (E: number) number, mark, sign, symbol.

pas   (E: pass, past) letter, note, or message; to go past someone or something, to get ahead, or to arrive first.

pasim   (E: fasten) to tie something, block it, obstruct it, hold it back.

pekato   sin, evil.

pikinini   child.

pipia   rubbish, dirt, leavings, refuse; in many Kaliai cargo cults a euphemism for cargo.

pisin   (E: pigeon, pidgin) a bird, any bird; also can refer to the language of Melanesian Pidgin.

ples   (E: place) village, region, area.

poroman   (E: foreman) comrade, companion, partner, mate, likeness, model, exemplar; in Censure's cult one's poroman was one's underground double, an underground namesake from whom one expected cargo in the future.

raunwara   (E: round water) lake, pool.

raus, or *rausim*   to expel, purge, remove, drive away.

ruru   to salute, pay respect through some gesture or ritual action.

sindaun   (E: sit down) to live, behave; existence, conduct, way of life.

singsing   a festival that includes dancing, singing, and often feasting.

skul   (E: school) to instruct, learn, give advice; a lesson.

stori   (E: story) myth, genealogy, parable; in the Kaliai area a narrative about the secrets underpinning existence; also can refer to the movements that organize around such narratives. All Kaliai cargo cult movements refer to themselves as a *stori*—people come into and join a stori, leave the stori, and then the stori falls down (disbands).

sut   (E: shoot) to shoot, penetrate.

tambaran   an angry ghost or primordial superhuman being that tries to eat humans; also refers to masks, bull roarers, and bamboo wind instruments that belong to the men's house and with which men perform secretly in an attempt to trick women and children into believing that these instruments are real beings. When a tambaran comes up from the bush, it requires a feast of pork, taro, and other food to lure it into the village and appease its anger.

tambu   small pieces of shell that have been cut, bored, and strung on a string to form shell money; can also mean to make something taboo, to abstain from. It can also be a term for certain relatives with whom one avoids close contact, such as one's sister-in-law or brother-in-law. One's in-laws are also often referred to as one's tambu.

tewel   (E: devil) a ghost that seeks to eat the living; also the word for *soul* or a picture or representation that resembles an original.

tok bokis   (E: talk-box) secret talk, or cryptic, allegorical talk.

tok piksa   (E: talk-picture) talking through images, pictures, and examples, that is, allegories, metaphors, and parables.

tok ples   A native language, mother tongue. Censure also sought to create his own *tok ples,* his own new native language for Melanesians.

tudak   (E: too dark) very dark, night.

tumbuan   a masked figure that dances. Men are inside the masks, which are among the secrets of the men's house. The designs of various masks are given to the living by deceased relatives during dreams. Individuals can also purchase the right to use certain designs from other villagers who own the designs.

waitskin   (E: white-skin) a white man.

MOUK TERMS

ano   soul, picture, reflection, ghost.

dabol   see pages 123-24.

bogi   sea eagle, totem of the male moiety of Big Bird.

dongen   ghosts of murdered widows that often come back or remain behind, seeking revenge upon the living.

mahrva   see *tambaran.*

muso   sorcery.

piraou   kingfisher, the totem of the female moiety of Little Bird.

pura   *masalai;* also the term for white man.

silasila   the fenced enclosure that men build to hide themselves while they are putting on the masks and eating the food sent by women to feed the masks.

tumno   maternal uncle or mother's brother.

Bibliography

Adorno, T. 1979. *Dialectics of Enlightenment.* London: Verso Edition.

Allen, M. R. 1967. *Male Cults and Secret Initiations in Melanesia.* Melbourne: Melbourne University Press.

Althusser, L. 1971. *Lenin and Philosophy and Other Essays.* London: New Left Books.

Anderson, B. 1983. *Imagined Communities.* London: Verso.

Bachelard, G. 1969. *The Poetics of Space.* Boston: Beacon.

Bachelard, G. 1983. *Water and Dreams: An Essay on the Imagination of Matter.* Dallas, Tex.: Pegasus Foundation.

Bakhtin, M. 1981. *The Dialogical Imagination.* Austin: University of Texas Press.

Bamberger, J. 1974. "The Myth of Matriarchy: Why Men Rule in Primitive Society." In *Women, Culture, and Society,* ed. M. Z. Rosaldo and L. Lamphere. Stanford, Calif.: Stanford University Press.

Barth, F. 1975. *Ritual and Knowledge Among the Baktaman of New Guinea.* New Haven, Conn.: Yale University Press.

Basso, K. 1984. "'Stalking with Stories': Names, Places, and Moral Narratives Among the Western Apache." In *Text, Play, and Story,* ed. E. Brunner. Washington, D.C.: American Ethnological Society.

Basso, K. 1988. "'Speaking with Names': Language and Landscape Among the Western Apache." *Cultural Anthropology* 3 (2): 99–130.

Bataille, G. 1985. *Literature and Evil.* London: Marion Boyars.

Bataille, G. 1987. *Eroticism.* London: Marion Boyars..

Battaglia, D., ed. 1995. *Rhetorics of Self-Making.* Berkeley: University of California Press.

Bercovitch, E. 1989. "Mortal Insights: Victim and Witch in the Nalumim Imagination." In *The Religious Imagination in New Guinea,* ed. G. H. Herdt and M. Stephen. New Brunswick: Rutgers University Press.

Bergson, H. 1991. *Matter and Memory.* New York: Zone Books.

Berndt, R. M. 1962. *An Adjustment Movement in Arnhem Land.* Paris: Mouton.

Bersani, L. 1990. *The Culture of Redemption.* Cambridge, Mass.: Harvard University Press.

Bettelheim, B. 1955. *Symbolic Wounds.* London: Thames & Hudson.

343

Bettison, D. G., C. A. Hughes, and P. W. van de Veur, eds. 1965. *The Papua-New Guinea Elections, 1964.* Canberra: Australian University Press.

Bhabha, H. K. 1994. *The Location of Culture.* London: Routledge.

Bloch, E. 1970. *A Philosophy of the Future.* New York: Herder and Herder.

Bloch, E. 1995. *The Principle of Hope,* vol. 2. Cambridge, Mass: MIT Press.

Bourdieu, P. 1977. *Outline of a Theory of Practice.* Cambridge, England: Cambridge University Press.

Brunn, D. and M. Zook. 1990. "Cargo Displaced by Christianity in Kaliai." *Catalyst* 20 (1): 182–88.

Burchell, G., C. Gordon, and P. Miller, eds. 1991. *The Foucault Effect : Studies in Governmentality: With Two Lectures by and an Interview with Michel Foucault.* Chicago: University of Chicago Press.

Burridge, K. 1960. *Mambu.* London: Methuen.

Bynum, C. W. 1982. *Jesus as Mother.* Berkeley: University of California Press.

Bynum, C. W. 1992. *Fragmentation and Redemption.* New York: Zone Books.

Casey, E. 1993. *Getting Back into Place.* Bloomington and Indianapolis: Indiana University Press.

Castoriadis, C. 1987. *The Imaginary Institution of Society.* Cambridge, Mass.: MIT Press.

Chinnery E. W. P. 1925. "Notes on the Natives of Certain Villages of the Mandated Territory of New Guinea." *Territory of New Guinea Anthropological Report 1.* Melbourne: Government Printer.

Chinnery E. W. P. "Certain Natives in South New Britian and Dampier Straits." *Territory of New Guinea Anthropological Report 3.* Melbourne: Government Printer.

Chowning, A. 1974. "Disputing in Two West New Britain Societies: Similarities and Differences." In *Contention and Dispute,* ed. A. L Epstein. Canberra: Australian University Press.

Chowning, A. 1990. "Gods and Ghosts in Kove." In *Christianity in Oceania,* ed. J. Baker. Lanham, Md.: University Press of America.

Chowning, A. and J. C. Goodale. 1965. "The Passismanua Census Division, West New Britain Open Electorate." In 1965. *The Papua-New Guinea Elections 1964,* ed. D. G. Bettison, C. A. Hughes, and P. W. van de Veur. Canberra: Australian University Press.

Clark, J. 1989. "The Incredible Shrinking Men: Male Ideology and Development in a Southern Highlands Society." *Canberra Anthropology* 12 (1 & 2): 120–23.

Clark, J. 1992. "Madness and Colonization: The Embodiment of Power in Pangia." *Oceania* 63 (1): 15–26.

Clifford, J. 1988. *The Predicament of Culture.* Cambridge, Mass.: Harvard University Press

Counts, D. E. A. 1968. "Political Transition in Kandoka Village, West New Britain." PhD. diss., Southern Illinois University. Ann Arbor: University Microfilms.

Counts, D. E. A. 1971. "Cargo or Council: Two Approaches to Development in Northwest New Britain." *Oceania* 16: 228–97.

Counts, D. E. A. 1972. "The Kaliai and the Story: Development and Frustration in New Britain." *Human Organization* 31: 373–83.

Counts, D. E. A. 1980. "Akro and Gagandewa: A Melanesian Myth." *Journal of Polynesian Society* 89: 33–65

Counts, D. E. A. 1982. *The Tales of Laupu.* Boroko: Institute of Papua New Guinea Studies.

Counts, D. and D. E. A. Counts. 1976. "Apprehension in the Backwaters." *Oceania* 46: 283–305.

Dalgleisah, D. N. 1970. "Appendix A: Cargo Cult Activities in the Bagai Area, Kaliai Census Division." *Patrol Report,* Gloucester Files, Papua New Guinea.

de Certeau, M. 1988. *The Practice of Everyday Life.* Berkeley: University of California Press.

Deleuze, G. and F. Guattari. 1987. *A Thousand Plateaus.* Minneapolis: University of Minnesota Press,

Derrida, J. 1979. *Spurs/Eperons.* Chicago: University of Chicago Press.

Derrida, J. 1987. *The Postcard.* Chicago: University of Chicago Press.

Derrida, J. 1992. *Acts of Literature.* London: Routledge.

Derrida, J. 1994. *Specters of Marx.* New York: Routledge.

Donzelot, J. 1980. *The Policing of Families.* New York: Pantheon.

Douglas, M. 1966. *Purity and Danger.* Harmondsworth, England: Penguin.

Dufrenne, M. 1973. *The Phenomenology of Aesthetic Experience.* Evanston, Ill.: Northwestern University Press.

Eliade, M. 1979. *The Two and the One.* Chicago: Chicago University Press.

Elias, N. [1939] 1978. *The Civilizing Process.* New York: Urizen.

Evans-Pritchard, E. E. 1937. *Witchcraft, Oracles, and Magic Among the Azande.* Oxford, England: Clarendon.

Eves, R. 1996. "Colonialism, Corporeality, and Character: Methodist Missions and the Refashioning of Bodies in the Pacific." *History and Anthropology* 10 (1): 85–138

Fabian, J. 1983. *Time and the Other.* New York: Columbia University Press.

Fabian, J. 1986. *Language and Colonial Power.* Cambridge, England: Cambridge University Press.

Fanon, F. 1965. *The Wretched of the Earth.* London: MacGibbon & Kee.

Fanon, F. 1968. *Black Skin, White Masks.* London: MacGibbon & Kee.

Feld, S. 1982. *Sound and Sentiment.* Philadelphia: University of Pennsylvania Press.

Fields, K. E. 1985. *Revival and Rebellion in Colonial Central Africa.* Princeton, N.J.: Princeton University Press.

Foster, R. 1992. "Take Care of Public Telephones: Moral Education and Nation-State Formation in Papua New Guinea." *Public Culture* 4: 31–45.

Foster, R. 1995. "Print Advertisements and Nation Making in Metropolitan Papua New Guinea." In *Nation Making*, ed. R. J. Foster. Ann Arbor: University of Michigan Press.

Foucault, M. 1967. *Madness and Civilization.* London: Tavistock.

Foucault, M. 1977. *Discipline and Punish: The Birth of the Prison.* New York: Vintage.

Foucault, M. 1978. *The History of Sexuality,* vol. 1. Harmondsworth, England: Penguin.

Foucault, M. 1982a. "Preface." In *Anti-Oedipus,* G. Deleuze and F. Guattari. New York: Viking.

Foucault, M. 1982b. "The Subject and Power." *Critical Inquiry* 8: 777–95.

Foucault, M. 1984. "On the Genealogy of Ethics: An Overview of Work in Progress." In *The Foucault Reader,* ed. P. Rabinow. New York: Pantheon.

Fromm, E. 1961. *Marx's Concept of Man.* New York: Ungar.

Gillison, G. 1993. *Between Culture and Fantasy.* Chicago: Chicago University Press.

Ginzburg, C. 1983. *Night Battles.* New York: Penguin.

Girard, R. 1986. *The Scapegoat.* Baltimore, Md.: Johns Hopkins University Press.

Goodale, J. 1985. "Pig's Teeth and Skull Cycles: Two Sides of the Face of Humanity." *American Ethnologist* 12 (2): 228–44.

Grosz, E. 1989. *Sexual Subversions: Three French Feminists.* Sydney: Allen and Unwin.

Grosz, E. 1994. *Volatile Bodies: Toward a Corporeal Feminism.* Bloomington: Indiana University Press

Guiart, J. 1951. "Forerunners of Melanesian Nationalism." *Oceania* 22 (2): 81–90.

Halbwachs, M. [1952] 1992. *On Collective Memory.* Chicago: University of Chicago Press.

Hamilton, A. 1989. "Bond-Slaves of Satan: Aborigines and the Missionary Dilemma." In *Family and Gender in the Pacific,* ed. M. Jolly and M. Macintyre. Cambridge, England: Cambridge University Press.

Heidegger, M. 1971. *Poetry, Language, and Thought.* New York: Harper & Row.

Heidegger, M. 1977. *Basic Writings.* New York: Harper & Row.

Herdt, G. H. 1977. "The Shaman's 'Calling' Among the Samba of New Guinea." *Journal de la Societe des Oceanistes* 33: 153–67.

Herdt, G. H. 1981. *Guardians of the Flutes: Idioms of Masculinity.* New York: McGraw-Hill.

Herdt, G. H. 1987. *Sambia: Ritual and Gender in New Guinea.* New York: Holt, Rinehart and Winston.

Herdt, G. H. and F. J. Poole. 1982. "'Sexual Antagonism': The Intellectual History of a Concept in New Guinea Anthropology." *Social Analysis* 12: 3–28.

Herdt, G. H. and M. Stephen. 1989. *The Religious Imagination in New Guinea.* New Brunswick, N.J.: Rutgers University Press.

Hess, D. J. 1991. *Spirits and Scientists.* University Park, Pa.: Pennsylvania State University Press.

Horkheimer, M. 1947. *Eclipse of Reason.* Oxford, England: Oxford University Press.

Hyde, L. 1983. *The Gift: Imagination and the Erotic Life of Property.* New York: Vintage.

Hyland, K. 1990a. "Cargo and Christianity in Kaliai." *Catalyst* 20 (1): 167–81.

Hyland, K. 1990b. "The New Tribes in Kaliai." *Catalyst* 20 (1): 261–66.

Irigaray, L. 1993. *Sexes and Genealogies.* New York: Columbia University Press.

Jackson, M. 1983. "Thinking Through the Body: An Essay on Understanding Metaphor." *Social Analysis* 14: 127–49.

Jackson, M. 1989. *Paths Toward a Clearing.* Bloomington: Indiana University Press.

Jackson, M. 1995. *At Home in the World.* Durham, N.C.: Duke University Press.

Janssen, H. 1970. "Notes on Recent Cargo Cult Movements in Kaliai, West New Britain." Mimeograph.

Janssen, H. 1974. "The Story Cult of Kaliai." *Point* 1: 4–28.

Jorgensen, D. 1985. "Fempsep's Last Garden: A Telefol Response to Mortality." In *Aging and Its Transformations,* ed. D. E. A. Counts and D. Counts. Washington, D.C.: University Press of America.

Kahn, M. 1986. *Always Hungry, Never Greedy.* Cambridge, England: Cambridge University Press

Kapferer, B. 1979. "Introduction: Ritual Process and the Transformation of Context." *Social Analysis* 1: 3–19.

Kapferer, B. 1983. *A Celebration of Demons.* Bloomington: Indiana University Press.

Kapferer, B. 1988. *Legends of People, Myths of the State.* Washington, D.C.: Smithsonian Institution Press.

Kaplan, M. 1995. *Neither Cargo nor Cult.* Durham, N.C.: Duke University Press.

Kolig, E. 1980. "Noah's Ark Revisited." *Oceania* 51: 118–32.

Lacan, J. 1977. *Ecrits: A Selection.* London: Tavistock.

Lacoue-Labarthe, P. 1989. *Typography.* Cambridge, Mass.: Harvard University Press.

Laing, R. D. 1960. *The Divided Self: A Study of Sanity and Madness.* London: Tavistock.

Laing, R. D. 1961. *The Self and Others: Further Studies in Sanity and Madness.* London: Tavistock.

Landtmann, G. 1927. *The Kiwai Papuans of British New Guinea.* London: Macmillan.

Langer, S. K. [1942] 1976. *Philosophy in a New Key.* Cambridge, Mass.: Harvard University Press.

Langer, S. K. [1953] 1963. *Feeling and Form.* London: Routledge and Kegan Paul.

Langness, L. L. 1967. "Sexual Antagonism in the New Guinea Highlands: A Bena Bena Example." *Oceania* 37: 161–77.

Langness, L. L. 1974. "Ritual Power and Male Dominance in the New Guinea Highlands." *Ethos* 2 (2): 189–212.

Lattas, A. 1989. "Trickery and Sacrifice: Tambarans and the Appropriation of Female Reproductive Powers in Male Initiation Ceremonies in West New Britain." *Man* 24: 451–69.

Lattas, A. 1990. "Poetics of Space and Sexual Economies of Power: Gender and the Politics of Male Identity in West New Britain." *Ethos* 18: 71–102.

Lattas, A. 1991. "Sexuality and Cargo Cults: The Politics of Gender and Procreation in West New Britain." *Cultural Anthropology* 6 (2): 230–56.

Lattas, A. 1992a. "Introduction: Hysteria, Anthropological Discourse, and the Concept of the Unconscious–Cargo Cults and the Scientization of Race and Colonial Power." *Oceania* 63 (1): 1–14.

Lattas, A. 1992b. "Skin, Personhood, and Redemption: The Double Self in West New Britain." *Oceania* 63 (1): 27–54.

Lattas, A. 1992c. "The Punishment of Masks: Ideologies of Representation in West New Britain Cargo Cults." *Canberra Anthropology* 15 (2): 69–88.

Lattas, A. 1993. "Sorcery and Colonialism: Illness, Dreams, and Death as Political Languages in West New Britain." *Man,* 28 (1): 51–77.

Lattas, A. 1996a. "Humanitarianism and Australian Nationalism in Colonial Papua: Hubert Murray and the Project of Caring for the Self of the Colonizer and Colonized. *TAJA* 7 (2): 141–65.

Lattas, A. 1996b. "Memory, Forgetting, and the New Tribes Mission in West New Britain." *Oceania* 66 (4): 286–304.

Lawrence, P. 1964. *Road Belong Cargo.* Melbourne: Melbourne University Press.

Le Goff, J. 1984. *The Birth of Purgatory.* Chicago: Chicago University Press.

Le Goff, J. 1988. *Your Money or Your Life: Economy and Religion in the Middle Ages.* New York: Zone Books.

LeRoy, J. 1985. *Fabricated Worlds.* Vancouver, Canada: University of British Columbia Press.

Levi-Strauss, C. 1963. *Totemism.* Boston: Beacon.

Levi-Strauss, C. 1966. *The Savage Mind.* Chicago: Chicago University Press

Levi-Strauss, C. 1972. *Structural Anthropology.* Harmondsworth, England: Penguin.

Levi-Strauss, C. 1979. *Myth and Meaning.* New York: Schocken.

Lindstrom, L. 1990. *Knowledge and Power in a South Pacific Society.* Washington, D.C.: Smithsonian Institution Press.

Lindstrom, L. 1993. *Cargo Cult: Strange Stories of Desire from Melanesia and Beyond.* Honolulu: University of Hawaii Press.

McCarthy, J. K. 1964. *Patrol into Yesterday.* Melbourne: Cheshire.

McDannell, C. and B. Lang. 1990. *Heaven: A History.* New York: Vintage.

Mcleod, M. 1975. "On the Spread of Antiwitchcraft Cults in Modern Asante." In *Changing Social Structure in Ghana,* ed. J. Goody. London: International African Institute.

Mair, L. P. 1948. *Australia in New Guinea.* London: Christophers.

Marcuse, H. 1955. *Eros and Civilization.* Boston: Beacon.

Marcuse, H. 1964. *One Dimensional Man.* London: Routledge and Kegan Paul.

Marwick, M., ed. 1975. *Witchcraft and Sorcery.* Harmondsworth, England: Penguin.

Maschio, T. 1994. *To Remember the Faces of the Dead: The Plentitude of Memory in Southwestern New Britain.* Madison: University of Wisconsin Press.

Mead, H. 1934. *Mind, Self, and Society.* Chicago: Chicago University Press.

Mead, M. 1966. *New Lives for Old.* New York: Apollo.

Meigs, A. S. 1984. *Food, Sex, and Pollution.* New Brunswick, N.J.: Rutgers University Press.

Merleau-Ponty, M. 1968. *The Visible and the Invisible.* Evanston, Ill.: Northwestern University Press.

Mimica, J. 1981. Omalyce: An Ethnography of the Ikwaye View of the Cosmos. PhD. diss. Australian National University, Canberra.

Mimica, J. 1988. *Intimations of Infinity.* Oxford, England: Berg.

Monter, E. W. 1976. *Witchcraft in France and Switzerland.* Ithaca, N.Y.: Cornell University Press.

Morrison, K. F. 1982. *The Mimetic Tradition of Reform in the West.* Princeton, N.J.: Princeton University Press.

Munn, N. D. 1971. "The Transformation of Subject into Objects in Walbiri and Pitjantjatjara Myth." In *Australian Aboriginal Anthropology,* ed. R. Berndt. Nedlands: University of Western Australia Press.

Munn, N. D. 1986. *The Fame of Gawa.* Cambridge, England: Cambridge University Press.

Murray, J. H. P. 1929. *Indirect Rule in Papua.* Port Moresby, PNG: Government Printer.

Myers, F. R. 1984. *Pintupi Country, Pintupi Self.* Washington, D.C.: Smithsonian Institute Press; and Canberra: Australian Institute of Aboriginal Studies.

Nietzsche, F. [1886] 1973. *Beyond Good and Evil.* Middlesex, England: Penguin.

Panoff, M. 1968. "The Notion of Doubled-Self Among the Maenge People of New Britain." *Journal Polynesian Society* 77: 275–96.

Patrol Reports. Gloucester Files, West New Britain, Papua New Guinea.

Pech, R. 1991. *Manub and Kilibob.* Point series no. 16. Goroka: Melanesian Institute.

Pelton, R. D. 1989. *The Trickster in West Africa.* Berkeley: University of California Press

Pomponio, A., D. R. Counts, and T. G. Harding, eds. 1994. Special Issue: Children of Kilibob. *Pacific Studies* 17 (4).

Radin, P. 1972. *The Trickster.* New York: Schocken. Rank, O. 1971. *The Double: A Psychoanalytic Study.* New York: Meridian.

Richards, A. [1935] 1975. "A Modern Movement of Witch Finders." In *Witchcraft and Sorcery,* ed. M. Marwick. Harmondsworth, England: Penguin.

Ricoeur, P. 1979. "The Function of Fiction in Shaping Reality." *Man and World* 12: 123–41.

Ricoeur, P. 1991. *From Text to Action,* Essays in Hermeneutics, vol. 2. Evanston, Ill.: Northwestern University Press.

Robbins, J. 1997. "666, or Why is the Millennium on the Skin? Morality, the State, and the Epistemology of Apocalypticism Among the Urapmin of Papua New Guinea." In *Millennial Markers,* ed. P. J. Stewart and A. Strathern. James Cook, Queensland, Australia: Center for Pacific Studies.

Rose, A. n.d. "Anthropological Fieldnotes and Tapes of Dr. Hermann Janssen, 1967–70, with Earlier Notes from Fr. Rose. 1959–64. Michael Somare Library, University of Papua New Guinea, AL341.

Rowley, C. D. 1958. *The Australians in German New Guinea, 1914–1921.* Melbourne: Melbourne University Press.

Russell, J. B. 1981. *Satan: The Early Christian Tradition.* Ithaca, N.Y.: Cornell University Press.

Russell, J. B. 1984. *Lucifer: The Devil in the Middle Ages.* Ithaca, N.Y.: Cornell University Press.

Russell, J. B. 1986. *Mephistopheles: The Devil in the Modern World.* Ithaca, N.Y.: Cornell University Press.

Sahlins, M. 1981. *Historical Metaphors and Mythical Realities.* Ann Arbor: University of Michigan Press.

Said, E. W. 1978. *Orientalism.* New York: Pantheon.

Sartre, J. P. 1948. *AntiSemite and Jew.* New York: Schocken.

Sartre, J. P. 1975. *Being and Nothingness.* New York: Washington Square Press.

Scharmach, L. 1960. *This Crowd Beats Us All.* Sydney: Catholic Press Newspaper Co.

Schieffelin, E. 1976. *The Sorrow of the Lonely and the Burning of the Dancers.* New York: St. Martin's Press.

Schilder, P. 1935. *The Image and Appearance of the Human Body.* New York: International Universities Press.

Schurmann, R. 1990. *Heidegger on Being and Acting.* Bloomington: Indiana University Press.

Serres, M. 1982a. *The Parasite.* Baltimore: John Hopkins University Press.

Serres, M. 1982b. *Hermes: Literature, Science, Philosophy.* Baltimore, Md.: Johns Hopkins University Press.

Serres, M. 1991. *Rome: The Book of Foundations.* Stanford, Calif.: Stanford University Press.

Serres, M. and B. Latour. 1995. *Conversations on Science, Culture, and Time.* Ann Arbor: University of Michigan Press.

Simmel, G. 1950. "The Sociology of Secrecy and of Secret Societies." In *The Sociology of George Simmel.* New York: Free Press.

Sisley, P. N. 1970. "Interim Report: Kaliai Cargo Cult." *Patrol Report,* Gloucester Files, West New Britain, Papua New Guinea.

Smith, J. Z. 1987. *To Take Place: Toward Theory in Ritual.* Chicago: Chicago University Press

Stanner, W. E. H. 1958. "On the Interpretation of Cargo Cults." *Oceania* 29 (1): 1–25.

Steinbauer, F. 1979. *Melanesian Cargo Cults.* St. Lucia, S.A.: University of Queensland Press.

Stephen, M. 1979. "Dreams of Change: the Innovative Role of Altered States of Consciousness in Traditional Melanesian Religion." *Oceania* 50 (1): 3–22.

Stephen, M. 1982. "'Dreaming Is Another Power': The Social Significance of Dreams Among the Mekeo of Papua New Guinea." *Oceania* 53: 106–22.

Stoler, A. L. 1995. *Race and the Education of Desire: Foucault's History of Sexuality and the Colonial Order of Things.* Durham, N.C.: Duke University Press.

Stoller, P. 1995. *Embodying Colonial Memories.* New York: Routledge.

Strathern, A. 1975. "Why Is Shame on the Skin?" *Ethnology* 14: 347–56.

Strathern, A. 1996. *Body Thoughts.* Ann Arbor: University of Michigan Press.

Strathern, M. 1988. *The Gender of the Gift.* Berkeley: University of California Press.

Swatridge, C. 1985. *Delivering the Goods.* Melbourne: Melbourne University Press.

Taussig, M. 1980. *The Devil and Commodity Fetishism in South America.* Chapel Hill: University of North Carolina Press.

Taussig, M. 1987. *Shamanism, Colonialism, and the Wild Man.* Chicago: Chicago University Press.

Taussig, M. 1993. *Mimesis and Alterity.* London: Routledge.

Taylor, M. C. 1984. *Erring: A Postmodern A/theology.* Chicago: University of Chicago Press.

Thurston, W. R. 1994. "The Legend of Titikolo: An Anem Genesis." *Pacific Studies* 17 (4): 183–204.

Todorov, T. 1992. *The Conquest of America.* New York: HarperPerennial.

Trevor-Roper, H. R. 1975. "The European Witch-Craze." In *Witchcraft and Sorcery,* ed. M. Marwick. Harmondsworth, England: Penguin Books.

Trompf, G. 1991. *Melanesian Religion.* Cambridge, England.: Cambridge University Press.

Tuan, Y. 1974. *Topophilia.* Englewood Cliffs, N.J.: Prentice-Hall.

Tuan, Y. 1976. *Space and Place.* Minneapolis: Minnesota University Press.

Turner, B. S. 1984. *The Body and Society: Explanations in Social Theory.* Oxford, England: Basil Blackwell.

Turner, T. 1980. "The Social Skin." In *Not Work Alone,* ed. J. Cherfas and R. Lewin. London: Temple Smith.

Turner, V. 1967. *The Forest of Symbols.* Ithaca, N.Y.: Cornell University Press.

Turner, V. 1969. *The Ritual Process: Structure and Antistructure.* Chicago: Aldine.

Valentine, C. A. 1955. "Cargo Beliefs and Cargo Cults Among the West Nakanai." Miscellaneous typescript reports, Pacific Manuscripts Bureau. National Library of Australia, Canberra. Microfilm.

Wagner, R. 1986. *Asiwinarong.* Princeton, N.J.: Princeton University Press.

Wagner, R. 1991. "New Ireland Is Shaped Like a Rifle and We Are at the Trigger: The Power of Digestion in Cultural Reproduction." In *Clio in Oceania,* ed. Aletta Biersack. Washington, D.C.: Smithsonian Institution Press.

Weber, M. [1930] 1976. *The Protestant Ethic and the Spirit of Capitalism.* London: Allen and Unwin.

Weiner, A. B. 1980. "Reproduction: A Replacement for Reciprocity." *American Ethnologist* 7: 71–85.

Weiner, J. F. 1984. "Sunsets and Flowers: The Sexual Dimension of Foi Spatial Organization." *Journal of Anthropological Research* 40 (4): 577–88.

Weiner, A. B. 1991. *The Empty Place.* Bloomington: Indiana University Press.

Weiss, A. S. 1989. *The Aesthetics of Excess.* Albany, N.Y.: State University of New York Press.

West, F., ed. 1970. *Selected Letters of Hubert Murray.* Melbourne, Australia: Oxford University Press.

Whitney, L. 1973. *Primitivism and the Idea of Progess.* New York: Octagon.

Williams, F. E. [1923] 1976. *F. E. Williams: "The Vailala Madness" and Other Essays.* London: C. Hurst.

Williams, R. H. 1990. *Notes on the Underground.* Cambridge, Mass.: MIT Press.

Wilson, B. 1975. *Magic and the Millennium.* London: Paladin.

Worsley, P. [1957] 1970. *The Trumpet Shall Sound.* London: Paladin.

Wyschogrod, E. 1985. *Spirit in Ashes.* New Haven, Conn.: Yale University Press.

Young, I. R. 1990. *Justice and the Politics of Difference.* Princeton, N.J.: Princeton University Press.

Young, M. 1982. "The Theme of the Resentful Hero: Stasis and Mobility in Goodenough Mythology." In *The Kula: New Perspectives on Massim Exchange,* ed. E. R. Leach and J. W. Leach. Cambridge, England: Cambridge University Press.

Young, M. 1983. *Magicians of Manumanua.* Berkeley: University of California Press.

Index

Administration: opposed to cargo cults, xii, xxv; its policies copied by cults, 6, 42–43, 59, 219, 286

Aikele, 57, 65–75, 89, 324 *n10*, 324 *n11*, 324 *n13*, 325 *n15*; Aikele's wife, 224

Akono (Akrit), 85–86, 88, 190, 264, 332 *n6*

Alienation, xxiii, xxx–xxxi, 45, 78–79, 103, 117, 141–42, 144–45, 174–75, 241–42, 298, 304, 314–15

Alphabet, 81, 83, 279, 280; painted on woman's vagina, 81, 158

Alterity, xxiv, xxxiv, xxxix, xl, 100, 101–2, 122, 146, 150, 166, 177, 206, 208, 312; using its traditional forms, 22–23, 36, 103, 117, 274, 290–91; and white bodies, 46–47, 241, 246, 248, 259; and women's bodies, 185, 188–89. *See also* Otherness

Ambiguity: its politics, xxiii, xxxviii, xliv, 44, 45, 47, 81–82, 83–84, 147–48, 163–64, 264, 269, 292, 308, 323 *n5*; and androgyny, 205–6, 219

America: land of the dead, xxxii–xxxiii, 83, 118, 265, 284, 298–301; land of God, xlii, 15, 50, 59–60, 75, 81, 118–19, 185–86, 324 *n13*; its romanticization, 32–33, 36–37, 62, 68, 82–83, 153–55, 159, 266, 272, 277, 279–80, 281–82, 288–89, 302–3, 322 *n1,* 333 *n13*, 338 *n5*

Anderson: on nationalism, xxix

Androgynous imagery: and the destabilization of differences, xli–xlii, 155, 205–8, 218–19, 225, 333 *n1*; and creation, xlii, 210–11

Appropriation: of meaning, xl, 105, 123, 268, 269, 273, 311–14; from women, xli. *See also* State power; Bible stories

Australia: as the land of the dead, xxxii–xxxiii, xxxiv, 70, 92, 249–50

Australians: killed God, xxxiv, 36–37; hiding the truth, xlii, 70–73; as the bad whites, 33, 62, 68, 266, 279, 296, 322 *n1*, 338 *n5*; monopolising the cargo, 49–50, 51, 164, 307; Independence from, 60–61, 62, 123, 140, 327 *n26*, 331 *n3*

Baptism: by Catholic Church, 17; in cults, 131, 133, 137, 144

Batari cult, 32–33, 37–49, 319 *n2*

Becoming white: reworking the process, xxii, 198, 222–24, 226–27, 233, 260–61, 267, 336 *n6*; mediated by the dead, xxv, 39–40, 44, 46–48, 243, 244, 246–47, 254–55; recaptured by New Tribes Mission, 289, 312

Bible stories: their re-interpretation, xxxii, xxxviii–xxxix, 17, 24, 74–75, 80, 82, 158–63, 196, 217, 228, 229, 284, 295, 296–98, 327 *n27*

Biblical sites: their localization, xiv, xl, 96, 99, 118–20; used to relocate identity, 100, 101, 114

Binary logic, 330 *n12,* 330 *n13*; its procreative potential, 15, 176–77; applied to race relations, 15, 322 *n1. See also* Moieties

New Directions in Anthropological Writing
History, Poetics, Cultural Criticism

GEORGE E. MARCUS
Rice University

JAMES CLIFFORD
University of California, Santa Cruz

GENERAL EDITORS

Nationalism and the Politics of Culture in Quebec
Richard Handler

The Pastoral Son and the Spirit of Patriarchy: Religion, Society, and Person among East African Stock Keepers
Michael E. Meeker

Belonging in America: Reading Between the Lines
Constance Perin

Wombs and Alien Spirits: Women, Men, and the Zar Cult in Northern Sudan
Janice Boddy

People as Subject, People as Object: Selfhood and Peoplehood in Contemporary Israel
Virginia R. Domınguez

Sharing the Dance: Contact Improvisation and American Culture
Cynthia J. Novack

Debating Muslims: Cultural Dialogues in Postmodernity and Tradition
Michael M. J. Fischer and Medhi Abedi

Power and Performance: Ethnographic Explorations through Proverbial Wisdom and Theater in Shaba, Zaire
Johannes Fabian